INTRODUCING LANGU.

Introducing Language in Use is a comprehensive coursebook for students new to the study of language and linguistics.

Written by a highly experienced team of teachers, this coursebook is lively and accessible, interactive and above all produced with students firmly in mind. Drawing on a vast range of data and examples of language in its many forms, the book provides students with the tools they need to analyse real language in diverse contexts. Designed to be highly adaptable for course use, the authors suggest a range of different routes through the book.

Introducing Language in Use:

- covers all the core areas and topics of language study: language, semiotics and communication, grammar, phonetics, words, semantics, variety in language, history of English, world Englishes, multilingualism, psycholinguistics, child language acquisition, conversation analysis, pragmatics, power and politeness, and language in education
- has units contributed by Sushie Dobbinson (Unit 8) and John Field (Unit 11), expanding the range of expertise
- adopts a 'how to' approach, encouraging students to apply their knowledge as they learn it
- presents many examples drawn from varied domains (including conversation, advertising and text messaging), always giving precedence to real language in use
- includes activities throughout the text with commentaries, summaries, suggestions for further reading and an extensive glossary of terms
- features a final unit which offers students further practice in analysing language in use
- is supported by a companion website, offering extra resources for students and lecturers.

This will be an an essential coursebook for all introductory courses in English language, and communication and linguistics.

Aileen Bloomer is a lecturer in linguistics at York St John College, having previously worked in Warwick, Germany, Vietnam and China.

Patrick Griffiths, now a professor of English at Beppu University, Japan, has previously taught at the Unversity of the South Pacific, The University of York (UK) and York St John College.

Andrew Merrison is currently a lecturer in linguistics at York St John College. He has taught at the Universities of Durham, Edinburgh, York, and at Queen Margaret College, Edinburgh.

Students' praise for

INTRODUCING LANGUAGE IN USE

In a nutshell, it encompasses all the richness of information found in similar textbooks and delivers it in a refreshingly student-friendly way. I wish I could have had it in my first year.'

The layout is impressive … the activities are useful and their respective commentaries are excellent. Very informative, lots of detail and, more importantly for first years, readable so therefore understandable.'

'The humour included in some of the chapters was very much appreciated – in fact I think it's a winning ingredient – it certainly made me want to carry on reading.'

'The writing style was excellent. I thought it was clear, conveying extremely accessible information and knowledge to the reader at all times, it ensured that the text could be easily understood and ideas could be communicated in a basic and "down to earth" way. The jargon was accessible, not daunting and the text itself felt as though it had been written with students and not professors in mind – it spoke the language of the "everyday" person.'

'In my opinion the book is perfect for 1st, 2nd and 3rd years as I believe everyone could take something from it.'

'I think this is a great reader for first years. It is easy to read because it is less formal – also it makes the material seem more accessible in the first instance.'

INTRODUCING
LANGUAGE IN USE

A COURSEBOOK

Aileen Bloomer,

Patrick Griffths

and

Andrew John Merrison

 Routledge
Taylor & Francis Group

LONDON AND NEW YORK

First published 2005
by Routledge
2 Park Square, Milton Park, Abingdon, Oxon OX14 4RN

Simultaneously published in the USA and Canada
by Routledge
270 Madison Ave, New York, NY 10016

Routledge is an imprint of the Taylor & Francis Group

© 2005 Aileen Bloomer, Patrick Griffiths and Andrew John Merrison

Typeset in Times and Optima by
HWA Text and Data Management Ltd, Tunbridge Wells
Printed and bound in Great Britain by
TJ International Ltd, Padstow, Cornwall

British Library Cataloguing in Publication Data
A catalogue record for this book is available from the British Library

Library of Congress Cataloging-in-Publication Data
A catalog record for this book has been requested

ISBN 0–415–29178–X (hbk)
ISBN 0–415–29179–8 (pbk)

For all our students and all those who have taught us.
May the two lists continue to coincide!

Contents

Figures

Tables

Texts

Acknowledgements

A lot happened while this book was being written: continents were crossed, career plans changed, weddings and graduations took place and babies arrived – to mention but some of the events. When the book was initially commissioned, five linguistics lecturers and an art student were all at York St John. Patrick moved to Japan but maintained a close interest and active participation in the book. Kate Trott and Sushie Dobbinson withdrew from major involvement when they switched to Speech and Language Therapy. Those left working on the book felt the loss, but understood their reasons. Rachel Johnston graduated and moved to Oxford but she too remained involved and her illustrations throughout the book add a welcome and much appreciated non-linguistic dimension to the text.

We are all very grateful to Kate Trott for generously sharing her drafts with those who took on her units and for sparing time to read and comment on them. We are delighted that Sushie Dobbinson decided to maintain her involvement by completing Unit 8. Whether Stuart knew when he and Sushie got together that part of the deal was illustrating that unit, we are not sure, but we do thank him for the phonetics illustrations. We also thank John Field very warmly for writing Unit 11.

We are grateful to all those who commented on individual chapters whether known to us or not. In all cases, their helpful suggestions led to changes being made to the text but of course they bear no responsibility for what has finally appeared.

We thank the linguistics students at York St John who commented on various drafts of different chapters and in particular we acknowledge the major contributions of Adele Bell, Andrea Beall, Annie Labunda, Ben Sutton, Dawn Hindby-Smith, Karen Whisker, Kate Whisker, Ollie Stewart and Rebekah Yore, who all read the complete text and made many useful and detailed comments from a student perspective – many of them working in a summer vacation period when they thought they were safe from being asked to do anything that resembled work.

We also thank all our students over the years for their inexhaustible and inspirational enthusiasm.

Colleagues at York St John, especially Ruth Ataçocuğu, Ralph Bateman, Nikki Clark, Chris Clay, Monty Feather, Angela Goddard, Ann Gregory, Jackie Mathers, Shirley Reay, Karen Rippon, Alex Swift and Dianne Willcocks were all very supportive of our effort and we thank them all. Without Karen's generous help on IT matters, some of the diagrams might never have seen any sensible light of day and without Nikki's advice on IPA fonts we might have missed yet another deadline!

We thank the following for providing us with rich sources of data: Adam Jaworski, Bob Redwood, Chris Clay, Dale Donley, Deidre Eliasson, DN, Felicity Breet, Gay Spiegel, Graham Turner, Henrik (Specs) Mikelson, Jim Miller, Josie Beszant, Kate Trott, Lucy Carey, Maria Phanou, Matthew Pepper, PK, Sally Merrison, Sandra Harris, Sheila Hawkins, Teah Bennett, and all the many 'unsuspecting unknowns' whose language in use we have, unashamedly, used.

As well as major change at York St John, there was also reorganisation at Routledge. Nevertheless, we felt encouraged in our endeavour by our editor, Louisa Semlyen, throughout the process – and not only through the provision of lunches. We are most grateful to her as well as to Christy Kirkpatrick and Kate Parker. In addition, we would like to thank John Hodgson at HWA Text and Data Management for all his support in the final stages of production.

Patrick Griffiths would like to set on record his gratitude to Beppu University and especially Professor Kenji Ueda for providing an environment conducive to authorship. As well as the several anonymous readers who contributed guiltlessly to modifications that have probably made Patrick's parts of this book clearer, he thanks the following known – but also blameless – people who kindly commented on particular sections: Professor Paul Nation, Dr Kate Trott, Dr Joanna Channell, Dr Han Yang, Professor Bencie Woll, Dr Rex G. Sharman and Ms Annie Labunda. None of them is responsible for the use made of their suggestions. Janet Griffiths didn't grumble too much about weeks that had no weekends. She is appreciated for that and much else.

And who does Andrew Merrison thank? Well certainly not the five pages of folks that he did last time he was writing one of these sections – having been holed up in our office all night (for over 15 hours), Aileen wants to get to the photocopiers (perhaps I shouldn't have spent quite so long looking for all those italic commas)! So to keep it short, I thank all of you who have made this period of writing so productive. You should know who you are. Some people, however, do deserve a special mention. Without John Local I would almost certainly never have entered the world of linguistics, and instead would have been doomed to a life as a chartered accountant. For that alone, as well as for his boundless enthusiasm and inspiration, I will be eternally grateful – long may we jump up and down in bright green jumpers. And without Graham Turner, I would never have serendipitously happened to meet John Local; Marjorie says 'Thank you, Joan – thank you very, very much'. And finally, there are two more people: they are to be found in many places throughout this book. They just happen to share my surname: Sally and Ben Merrison. You are the most important things in the world to me. I love you both – I love you more than any language could express.

Finally, and perhaps most importantly, mutual thanks from and to Patrick, Andrew and Aileen for suggestions, encouragement, patience and occasionally forbearing from speaking their minds. As well as the hard work, there has been a lot of fun in writing this book – thanks from each and to each for that! We hope that some of that sense of fun shows itself in the pages that follow and if you, dear reader, share but a fraction of our enthusiasm for linguistics, then you will be well blessed indeed!

FURTHER ACKNOWLEDGEMENTS

The International Phonetic Association (http://www.arts.gla.ac.uk/IPA/ipa.html) is the copyright owner of the International Phonetic Alphabet and the IPA charts. Reproduced with permission.

Figures from pages 63 and 64 of Charles Barber, *The English Language: A Historical Introduction*, 1993. Reproduced by permission of Cambridge University Press.

'A League of Our Own' by Jason Burt, from *The Independent* Sports online, 4 March 2003, © The Independent 2003. Reproduced with permission.

Figure from *Word Frequencies in Present Day British Speech and Writing* by Leech *et al.*, published by Pearson Education Limited, © Pearson Education Limited 2001. Reprinted by permission of Pearson Education.

Don't Sweat the Small Stuff by Richard Carlson. Copyright © 1997 Richard Carlson. Reprinted by permission of Hyperion (US) and Hodder and Stoughton Publishers (UK).

Poems Not on the Underground by Roger Tagholm, published by Windrush Press, © Roger Tagholm 1996. Reprinted by permission of Orion Publishing Group.

Language and Power by Prof Norman Fairclough, published by Pearson Education Limited © Longman Group UK Limited 1989. Reprinted by permission of Pearson Education.

Vaporesse advertisement 'The Gingham Press Heaven Scent', reproduced by kind permission of Lever Fabergé and Ogilvy & Mather.

Under Milk Wood by Dylan Thomas, first published 1954 by J. M. Dent & Sons Ltd. Copyright © 1954 in the United States of America by the Trustees for the

Copyrights of the late Dylan Thomas. Reproduced by permission of David Higham Associates (UK) and New Directions Publishing Corporation (US).

More! Magazine advertisement, 1997, reproduced by permission of Emap Elan.

'English as a Foreign Language' from G2, Shortcuts, *The Guardian*, 4 March 2003 © John Mullan.

Broca's and Wernicke's area from p. 40 of Bishop *Uncommon Understanding*, Psychology Press, 1997. Reproduced by permission of the publisher.

Figure from p.128 of Freeborn's *From Old English to Standard English: A Course Book in Language Variation Across Time*, © Dennis Freeborn 1992. Reprinted by permission of the University of Ottawa Press and Palgrave.

The Lord's Prayer in Old English from p. 62 of Baugh and Cable *A History of the English Language* (5th edition), Routledge, 2002. Reproduced by permission of the publisher.

The Language Instinct: The New Science of Language and Mind by Stephen Pinker (Allen Lane, The Penguin Press, 1994), copyright © Stephen Pinker, 1994. Reproduced by permission of HarperCollins Publishers (US), The Penguin Group (UK), and Abner Stein (UK).

English as a Global Language by David Crystal, 1997, © David Crystal, published by Cambridge University Press, reprinted with permission.

The White Man of God by Kenjo Jumbam. Reprinted by permission of Harcourt Education.

Petals of Blood by Ngugi Wa Thiong'o. Reprinted by permission of Harcourt Education.

'Uncle Ben's Choice' from *Girls at War and Other Stories* by Chinua Achebe, published by Doubleday. Reproduced by permission of David Higham Associates (UK) and Random House, Inc. (US).

'Reggae fi dada' by Linton Kwesi Johnson © Linton Kwesi Johnson, reproduced by kind permission of LKJ Music Publishers Ltd.

The Cambridge Encyclopedia of the English Language, 2nd edition, by David Crystal, 2003, published by Cambridge University Press, reprinted with permission.

Symbols and abbreviations

In general, we follow standard linguistic conventions:

Focus

Lx   indicates that the writer is referring to Line *x* in a chunk of language data

→   indicates that the particular nugget of language under discussion is to be found in the line against which the arrow occurs

Unacceptability

*   before an example indicates that the example is ungrammatical

!   before an example indicates that the example is seriously wrong semantically

?   before an example indicates that the example is odd semantically

Bracketing

[ ]   Phonetic symbols appear inside square brackets, e.g. [ɪ]

/ /   Phonemic symbols appear between slash brackets, e.g. /r/

{ }   Morphemes are enclosed in curly (also known as *brace*) brackets { }, e.g. {*-ing*}

< >   Letters appear inside angle brackets, e.g. <e>

Examples might make the bracketing clearer:

	In written language	*In spoken language*
What leaders do	<lead>	[lid]
A heavy metal	<lead>	[lɛd]
What leaders did	<led>	[lɛd]

In the word *leaders* there are three morphemes: {*lead*}, {*-er*} and {*-s*}

In syntactic analysis:

| | single vertical straight brackets indicate phrase boundaries
|| || double vertical straight lines indicate clause boundaries
||| ||| triple vertical straight lines indicate clause complex boundaries

In phonetic analysis:

|| || double vertical single lines indicate tone group boundaries

For all orthographic conventions for transcribing talk-in-interaction, see Unit 2

Using the book

➤➤   indicates a cross-reference to another unit in the book

o━   indicates that a commentary on the activity can be found at the end of the unit

PROLOGUE

We shall not cease from exploration
And the end of all our exploring
Will be to arrive where we first started
And know the place for the first time.

Eliot, *Four Quartets* (1944: 43)

USING THIS BOOK
Read me!

UNIT CONTENTS

- Introduction
- How do we think about language?
- Why is language worth studying?
- How to use this book
- Moving from one unit to another

INTRODUCTION

This book is an introduction to how **language** is used in infinitely intriguing ways and how even rigorous analysis of these areas can be fun and fascinating. We focus unashamedly on language. However, while it is a particularly important part of **communication**, we unreservedly accept that the **context** (linguistic and non-linguistic) within which language is used is crucial for understanding how language is being used and what meaning is being expressed. We recognize that language use is problematical – it is not as simple as many would like to believe. For instance, a recently produced *Alternative York Guide* is intended as a guidebook to the alternative scene in York (UK), but the title could be taken as meaning that it is simply another guide to the city, alternative to the ones that already exist. *Infamous antique shops* from the same publication is an interesting phrase. *Infamous* means the same as *notorious*. Is the writer using *infamous* with its conventional meaning of 'having a bad reputation' or using *infamous* with its newer meaning of 'famous'? This could be related perhaps to the way *wicked* is changing – at least for younger people – into a term of approval.

This is a book which describes language in use and shows how that language can be analysed. It is not a **prescriptive** book full of rules that you should obey nor a dictionary telling you what **words** mean. It will not tell you how you should pronounce words. It will not tell you how to talk to your boss or your friends. It will not tell you how many words your child must understand by the age of one year nor how your brain should process language. It will not tell you whether it is right that English is a (the?) world language nor whether any action should be taken in relation to this.

We adopt a functional approach to language and language analysis, an approach that starts with language in use rather than abstract theories. A function is a use to which something is put. Language is used for many purposes, which perhaps all have in common that meaning is conveyed. Meaning depends on context as in the following two conversations.

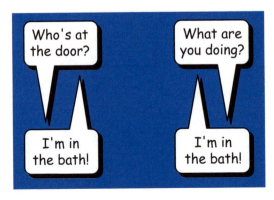

Exactly the same words are used to answer a question but one (which?) is simply providing information whilst the other is arguably explaining why s/he cannot go to the door to find out who is there. Speakers (and writers) make choices about what language to use (how to say and how to sequence the words they choose to use) in relation to their audience, their topic of conversation and the context of their **utterance**.

HOW DO WE THINK ABOUT LANGUAGE?

Many people think of language in terms of bricks (the sounds and words) and mortar (the grammar) in the creation of the building or wall (the linguistic **text**). We asked our linguistics students how they thought about language and language analysis and they produced some very creative responses. One said that 'language is like a new box of rubber bands – they are all messed up together and it is very hard to pull one single band out to use' and explained that there were so many aspects to language that, while recognizing the interconnectedness, you need to be clear about which aspect of language you were analysing at any one time.

Another said that 'analysing language was like climbing a mountain – just as you get to what you think is the summit, there is another peak on the horizon for you to consider … but that is what makes it fun' and so recognized that while it can seem hard-going at times to understand the basics, there is a clear pay-off later.

A third student said 'it's a bit like being in a very large swimming pool – everything is very easy on the surface but you know – or think you know – that there is a lot going on underneath'. This view recognizes very clearly the ability to use language to achieve our aims with the recognition that there are dangers in the deep waters and that using language sometimes goes wrong.

Another expanded this image to claim that 'it's more like bobbing around on the wide ocean where there are no landmarks to help you and you know that there are dangers lurking beneath the surface but somehow you make sense of it all'.

When we reported such comments to our colleagues, one of them replied that language analysis was all a bit like sex – infinitely creative and only any fun when you are doing it. We certainly believe that the best way to learn about language and about how to analyse it is to do it rather than simply be told how to do it and such an approach is at the heart of every unit in this book.

But how do we think about language? Do any of these images help?

Is language like a jigsaw such that all you have to do is get the right pieces in the right place and the picture is complete? Or does the image of cog wheels better allow for the dynamic nature of language and its ability to change constantly? Of course, cog wheels might suggest that language only moves in circles rather than in

any particular direction! Are humans the only animals capable of using language? In the same way that the scientists are looking to see if there has ever been life on Mars, is there a comparable language question of 'is there language out there?', never mind the already researched questions of the extent to which other animals use their own language or communication systems or the extent to which they are capable of acquiring human language?

Language may involve one or more people, for sure, but are they always happy when they use language and are they always revealing themselves? Is language sometimes used as a disguise?

What are the building blocks of language? An individual sound or an individual letter can be meaningless on its own but in combination with other symbols the meanings can be very significant. For any language, there are a limited number of words in a dictionary, a countable number of sounds and a restricted set of rules for combining sounds and words to create comprehensible utterances. If the resources of any language are finite, as it appears, how extraordinary that language in use appears to allow us to express novel and unique utterances to an apparently infinite extent.

How, then, is language to be analysed? In this book, we take the approach that the best starting point is to look at and listen to language in use and then analysis can begin to explain how the resources of the language are being exploited. There are clearly different approaches to analysis that are possible – the functional approach here considers the different forms of language, in use within given contexts, to express given meanings. Because of our emphasis on language in use, as far as possible the language extracts used for presentation or analysis are authentic pieces of language. Only where absolutely necessary have we created language samples to demonstrate a particular point.

WHY IS LANGUAGE WORTH STUDYING?

Some people want to argue that our ability to use language is actually the essence of what makes us human and that it marks us out from the other animals. For that reason alone, language in use is well worth studying but there are other reasons. We use language to convey information to each other, to ask about opinions or interpretations, to express our feelings to each other. Sometimes it is very easy to say what we mean and sometimes we find that we have said something that we did not intend. Sometimes we find that we are saying two things at the same time in the same way that artists can draw two things at once. Surely, the more the workings of language are understood, the more effective the desired communication is likely to be.

However, there are other, more instrumental, reasons for studying language and having a detailed knowledge of how the system works. There are many areas of work where a particularly detailed knowledge of how language works is very important.

- The caring professions of teaching and medicine use language to educate, to nurse, to explain and to reassure and specifically within this group:
  - foreign language teachers use the rules of language to help learners learn another language more effectively;
  - speech and language therapists use their insights into language to help people who find using language problematic in a variety of ways.
- Broadcast and print journalists use language to tell us what is going on in our world and many people choose which TV channel to watch or which newspaper to read by the way the language is used to present events. Other parts of the media in advertising and marketing use language in conjunction with visual images to persuade us that we really do want and need that stuff.
- A company's staff are its greatest asset, so there are financial reasons for having Human Resources managers who know how to use language in dealing with people.
- Some workers use language to talk about language: lexicographers (dictionary writers), editors, publishers, academics in universities.
- Actors use the insights of language analysis to achieve plausible renditions of accents for roles that they are playing; dramatists create dialogue that can be seen as realistic; novelists and poets craft their language with enormous care to enhance their readers' artistic experience.
- Legislative and criminal justice systems use language very precisely to frame and debate laws and decide innocence or guilt. Increasingly, forensic linguists are brought in as expert witnesses for the prosecution or for the defence.

Anyone who can justifiably claim that they have a detailed understanding of how language can be used to achieve specific aims has to be of interest to an employer. Writing this section led us to wonder yet again whether there are any human endeavours where a sound knowledge of how language works is not applicable – we still cannot think of many. Even a Trappist monk who has taken a vow of silence prays to his God – in silence, perhaps, but still using language.

HOW TO USE THIS BOOK
What is in each unit?

Each unit has been written so that it can be read fairly independently of the others, but frequent cross referencing (indicated by this symbol ➤➤) indicates how one area of language analysis might impinge on many others at the same time. The cross referencing also shows how the units link in sequences other than the order in which they are presented in the book – sequences which you will find explained later in this section where we suggest other routes through the material.

Each unit contains activities which you should carry out. Students very often learn better through an active approach to the material and we recommend very strongly that you should have a go at each of the activities. Do read the commentaries (indicated by the symbol ○┳) after you have tried to do the activity – they can include additional material on the topic that does not appear elsewhere in the unit.

Some units are likely to be easier to read than others. Some present the more technical concepts that you need for analysing language in use, making precise statements about it and understanding the work of professional linguists. Other units show you how to apply that core knowledge. This is clarified later in this unit where we show you different possible ways to access the material.

Many units suggest that you use a good dictionary. It is not our place to prescribe which dictionary you should use – though the Oxford English Dictionary or Webster's would certainly be good starting points. Whichever you choose to use, we would recommend that:

- the bigger the version of the dictionary, the better. Small dictionaries are unlikely to contain enough detail for the work you will be doing.
- the newer the dictionary, the better. It will then contain the most recent usages of different words.
- if you want to use a dictionary based on a corpus of English usage, Collins COBUILD is well worth considering.

All units follow conventional bracketing and notation systems which are listed on pages xix-xx.

The data that we use is mostly just language stuff that we happened to have. We did not sit down and invent the language samples to prove the point we wanted to make, nor did we rush round looking for particular examples to make our points – the language was there, all around us, and we simply adopted it as useful to our purposes. You can do the same, if you start looking and listening actively to what is going on around you. We have put some extra texts into Unit 16 to give you more samples on which to hone your analytical skills. We have also put data on the website associated with this book at www.routledge.com/textbooks/0415291798.

All units necessarily introduce some technical linguistic terms and by the end of the book you will have a large **metalinguistic** (language terms to talk about language) tool-bag. Many of these terms are in **bold type** to indicate that they are used in more than one unit and that they appear in the glossary. This is useful if you come across a term (for example in a unit where an explanation is not provided) and are uncertain of its meaning. The purpose of the glossary is to help your memory, not to teach you the item in the first place.

MOVING FROM ONE UNIT TO ANOTHER

As with any journey (and learning about something or simply reading a book can be seen as a metaphorical journey), there are different means of transport and different routes that can be taken. Imagine travelling from a country town to the capital city. How many routes are there? How many different modes of travel could you choose? In the same way, there are different routes through this book and we outline some of those here. You may come up with another route, though, that we have not thought of. If it is right for you then that is all that matters.

A straight line

This linear route will lead the reader from the wide issues of language and communication (Unit 1) to consideration of language in its most frequent manifestation of talk (Unit 2), hence starting from an aspect of language use with which all will be very familiar even if it is an unconventional place to start the analysis of language. When we talk, we are aiming to achieve our purposes in that talk (Unit 3) and we aim to achieve that purpose as effectively and as appropriately as possible (Unit 4). To achieve those purposes, we need to use words (Unit 5) with their associated meanings (Unit 6) and we combine those words according to the rules of **grammar** or **syntax** (Unit 7). To speak a language we need some knowledge of the **phonetic** system of that language (Unit 8) and there is a clear link from that topic to the topic of **accent** and **dialect** and other individual and group variation in use of language (Unit 9). All our current knowledge of language will have been acquired when we were young children (Unit 10) and we will have stored that acquired knowledge in our brains (Unit 11). Some children will have acquired more than one language from birth and others will have learnt another language later in life (Unit 12). What is certain is that patterns of language use change over time (Unit 13) and that the relatively recent phenomenon of English as a world language (Unit 14) has implications for everyone, not just for speakers of English. Some of those implications, especially within the field of education, are addressed in the penultimate unit (Unit 15).

We think that this is the most likely route through the book that students will choose to take.

However, tutors might wish to deal with the topics in a different order from the order that we might choose. There are other routes through the material and we suggest some here.

A topic-based route

For all their independence of each other and interdependence on each other, the units can be grouped in different ways. After this introduction, Unit 1 sets the scene for the whole book. Thereafter the units might be grouped in relation to content as follows:

- discourse is addressed in Units 2, 3 and 4
- core areas of linguistics are addressed in Units 5, 6, 7 and 8
- psycholinguistic and language acquisition issues are addressed in Units 10 and 11
- sociolinguistic **variety** is addressed in Units 9, 12, 13, 14 and 15.

These topics could, of course, be addressed in any order, not necessarily the order in which they are listed here.

A traditional route

A relatively traditional route through the material might initially consider the core areas of linguistics before moving on to the applications. The units might therefore be considered in the following order:

1 Unit 1 to contextualize language within the area of communication
2 core areas of linguistics in Units 5, 6, 7 and 8
3 discourse in Units 2, 3 and 4
4 sociolinguistic variety in Units 9, 12, 13, 14 and 15
5 psycholinguistic issues in Units 10 and 11.

A less conventional route

On this route, it is argued that for each peripheral area of linguistics, there is a related core area of study (or that each core area of study has a closely related application). The authors might prefer to move from language in use to the core areas but recognize that readers will have their own preferences in this matter.

Unit 1 sets the scene for all that follows (or provides a summarizing conclusion to what has been read) and then:

- Unit 9 deals with sociolinguistic variety with Units 5, 6 and 7 as supporting material
- Unit 2 discusses oral discourse with Unit 8 as supporting material
- Unit 4 addresses issues of linguistic politeness with Unit 3 as supporting material
- Unit 10 addresses issues of language acquisition with Unit 11 as supporting material
- Unit 14 addresses the role of English in the twenty-first century with Unit 12 as supporting material
- Unit 13 addresses how language use has changed over the centuries with Unit 15 as supporting material.

Arguably, this list of matched units could be read from top to bottom or from bottom to top. Another way of presenting this route might be as two concentric circles with the inner circle 'supporting' the outer circle. You could go either way round the circles.

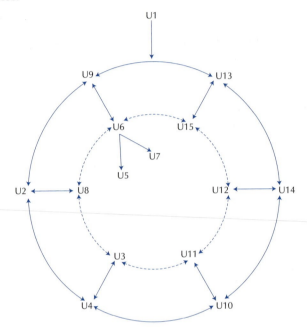

A serendipitous route

Of course, you could just stick a pin in to the table of contents and take that unit as the first one to read and then repeat the process until you have read all the units – or read as many as you want to read.

All we can hope now is that, wherever you start and whatever route you take, you continue reading, you enjoy learning about language and you become ever more fascinated by this amazingly complex phenomenon of language in use.

1 LANGUAGE, COMMUNICATION AND SEMIOTICS

UNIT CONTENTS

- Introduction
- Language and communication
- Linguistic communication and semiotics
- Language and art
- Human and animal communication
- Language families
- Summary
- Further reading
- Further activity
- Commentary on activities
- References

INTRODUCTION

Consider this situation and decide why you think the teacher is suspicious.

> A child in a school playground is asked by a teacher whether he kicked a ball against a window. He answers 'No', but simultaneously rubs his chin. His friends smile whilst the teacher looks on, suspiciously.

Your response will almost certainly have considered what the child said in relation to the whole situation: in other words you will have considered aspects of **language** use in **context**. That context includes what the child did as well as what other people did and you might have wondered whether rubbing the chin communicated anything. Many people feel reasonably comfortable in arguing that language and **communication** do not have the same meaning. However, many would be less confident if they were asked to specify the difference between the two. What do you think is the difference in meaning and use of the two terms? Activity 1.1 should help you clarify your thoughts.

 ## Activity 1.1 ⚬━┳

Do you think that all the participants in each of the scenarios below are using language? Why (not)? Discuss your opinions with others if possible.

1 A shop trader in India converses with a customer in English. He wobbles his head from side-to-side when agreeing to a sale price.

2 A woman notices an attractive man entering the room and simultaneously blushes.

3 A child of Asian background in a UK school is being reprimanded by a teacher. The child is looking at the floor and the teacher becomes increasingly annoyed, finally demanding, 'Look at me when I'm talking to you!'.

4 Gordon, aged 65, had a stroke and his ability to express himself through speech has been impaired. He vocalizes 'yes' and 'no' quite clearly and uses lots of exaggerated hand, arm and facial movements. However, his attempt to ask where a new helper at his support group comes from is met with the offer of a cup of coffee.

5 Annie, aged 87, speaks fluently. In fact, it is hard to get a word in edgeways. To see her, through her sitting room window, talking to her daughter, anyone would think they were having a real heart-to-heart. Inside the room, though, Annie's daughter has little

idea of what her mother is talking about. Annie's speech consists of largely unconnected phrases and clichés.

6   In a research centre, a chimpanzee uses American Sign Language (as used by people who are deaf) to sign 'food' to one of her human carers, and is given some.

7   A tout at a racetrack signs betting odds.

8   On receiving a call that some prospective buyers for their house are on their way, Alicia and James put on a pot of freshly ground coffee.

9   In Kenya, a vervet monkey spies a leopard nearby and vocalizes. Immediately, his group runs up trees onto the thinner branches, thus avoiding the danger as the leopard can't follow them there.

10   Ben and Emma correspond by e-mail and texting. They have never met and yet feel they know each other well, even though Ben lives in the USA and Emma in Australia.

Most people will probably accept that something is being communicated in each of these scenarios. However, the nature of the communication is different in each. It is equally clear that the extent to which language is being used varies from one scenario to another. Some people mistakenly think that communication is just another word for language, or vice versa. Some think that it is impossible to communicate without somehow involving language, whilst others argue that language involvement is not always necessary. In this book we argue that, although there are non-language based means of communication, language is rather special and that the context within which language is used can affect or even determine the way(s) in which it is used.

LANGUAGE AND COMMUNICATON

Crystal and Varley (1993: 4) state that 'Communication is the sending and receiving of messages. It refers to any message, not just the highly structured symbolic messages of language'. For them, communication is a broader concept than language, and language is included *within* what is meant by communication.

Jakobson's model of linguistic communication (Figure 1.1) is widely known and represents six major components of verbal communication. In his model, which is sometimes known as a '**code model**', a message giver (addresser) transmits a message to a receiver (addressee). The message must be such that it can be put into words (the **code**). There must be a point of contact linking the addresser and the addressee: there will be a psychological link between them as well as a physical

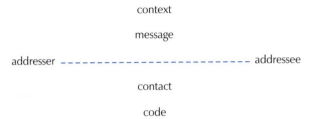

context

message

addresser ─ addressee

contact

code

Figure 1.1   Jakobson's communication model (Chandler 2002: 177)

contact whether that be face-to-face or at a distance. The importance of context in shaping or determining the form of the message has already been noted. Jakobson's model is helpful but it does not capture the circularity of much communication; during the same communication event the same individual is repeatedly both addresser and addressee.

Such circularity is more clearly shown in the model of communication (Figure 1.2) presented by Osgood and Schramm (in McQuail and Windahl 1993) which shows how the participants in the communication process, the interpreters, are both encoders and decoders of the different messages.

Whilst this model clearly shows the circularity of communication, such a circular model may not work quite so well as an illustration of the processes involved in reading a poem, for example, where the reader (as message decoder and interpreter) gives no immediate or direct feedback to the poet (as message encoder). Similarly, the diagram may not so usefully represent the communication involved in viewing a painting or sculpture or in listening to a symphony. While basically a multi-party phenomenon (at least two parties are involved), communication is, arguably, not always and not directly an immediately two-way process and such complexity cannot easily be captured in a two-dimensional model on paper.

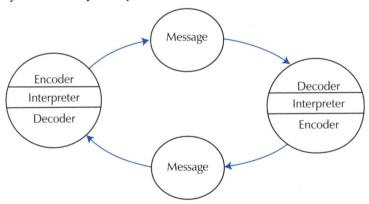

Figure 1.2 Osgood and Schramm's communication model (McQuail and Windahl 1993: 19)

Activity 1.2 ⚿

If possible, work in a group with two other people and be prepared to relax and lose your inhibitions! If you are working on your own, imagine carrying out the role plays and work out what you think the issues might be.

Photocopy the following list of role plays and then cut them up into slips of paper with one activity per slip. Divide the slips of paper between the members of the group, without reading them first. The person holding each slip of paper is responsible for following the instructions on the slip. Take turns 'acting out' the role play with a partner, in line with your instructions. Each role play requires two participants so, in each group, one person should take the role of observer and should make notes on what happens and how it happens. RP5a and RP5b must necessarily be done together.

Role Plays

RP1. Talk about how shy you are, but use very confident body language.

RP2. Talk about your family. When you talk, move your mouth *very* expressively but try to keep the rest of your body very still.

RP3. Talk about your favourite film to a specific partner. Maintain *intense* eye contact with them all the time.

RP4. Without saying a word, use *only* the *usual* everyday gestures, movements and facial expressions which you would normally employ alongside talking to convey the message to a partner that you have been upset by something they said yesterday.

RP5a. Your role is to explain to the selection panel the reasons why you think you are suitable for the job as a … (agree on the job with your partner who has RP5b).

RP5b. You are on a selection panel interviewing for a … (agree on the job with your partner who has RP5a). All you may say to the candidate is 'Yes, continue' or, in answer to a question, something on the lines of 'We will come back to that later'. Keep perfectly still and give no gestural feedback at all to the applicant as they are talking to you.

RP6. Talk about your most scary experience but keep your body and head *absolutely* still.

RP7. Without saying a word, use *only* the *usual* everyday gestures, movements and facial expressions which you would normally employ alongside talking to convey the message to a tutor that you haven't completed your coursework assignment on time.

If you are working in groups, listen to the observations from each observer and see what common features there are in the points they make. If you are working on your own, you will have your own ideas to compare with the commentary.

Activity 1.2 showed how people can use different types of communication and how hard it can be deliberately to present conflicting messages. Most of the time the systems work together to present a consistent message but it is sometimes possible that our body language can contradict what we are saying.

Many people consider language capable of expressing *any* message a human might wish to send but there is an opposing view that, however impressive language may be, it is not capable of expressing *every* message that a human might wish to convey. On the day after the bombings in March 2004 in Madrid, *The Guardian*, a UK daily newspaper, reported on the:

> biggest mass protest in Spanish history. At first, the worst thing was the silence. The loudest, most raucous city in Europe … was suddenly mute. 'There are no words to describe this' was the answer from the cleaners at the station, the Italian woman at the bus-stop. Language had failed everyone.

Maybe silence could better express people's feelings and if so there is a valid question about the communicative significance of silence (➻ Unit 2), whether that silence be during a conversation or during a concert.

LINGUISTIC COMMUNICATION AND SEMIOTICS

Simply put, semiotics or semiology is 'the study of signs' (Chandler 2002: 1) and almost anything can become a semiotic sign: what colour clothes you wear or how you speak, what food you eat or how fast you walk. Each of these behaviours can be interpreted as transmitting some message, whether intentionally or unintentionally. As you read the commentary on Activity 1.2, you will have noted comments about social norms and cultural understandings of particular behaviour as well as a recognition that different cultures might interpret the same behaviour in a different way. That the behaviours are interpreted means that they have some semiotic significance.

At the heart of semiotics lie notions of a sign and a symbolic system. In communication, signs are organized into systems within which each sign has a conventional meaning (➻ Unit 6). In other words, each sign has become associated with a meaning (a 'conventional meaning') which can be transferred or re-used from one context to another. Traffic lights represent a very simple symbolic system. Each light has an agreed meaning within the system; so much so that the traffic light system, or aspects of it, can be used as a metaphor in other contexts (for example, 'She gave me the green light on the company merger'). There are different relationships between the sign (sometimes called the *signifier*) and the **referent** (sometimes called the *signified*). Traffic lights are symbolic signs in that

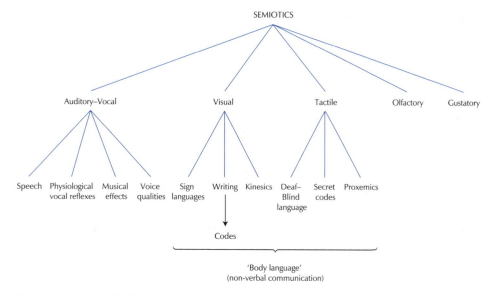

Figure 1.3   Semiotics (Crystal 1997: 403)

there is no intrinsic reason why the colour green should mean *go* and the colour red *stop*. It is a cultural consensus. Portraits and diagrams are iconic signs in that they represent more closely the referent to which they refer. Smoke is an indexical sign of fire in that it indicates its referent (rather than being symbolic or iconic) in the same way as egg-timers indicate time. You might like to consider the communicative value of different ring-tones on mobile phones or of different fonts (why is this book printed in Times and Optima and not in *Goteborg* or in **Postino**?). Recent work on semiotics stems from linguistics but a semiotic approach can be taken to any sign system, whether it be dance, food, clothes, music, soap operas or fairy tales.

Crystal (1997: 403) provides a very useful diagrammatic summary of semiotics and different forms of linguistic and non-linguistic communication which is reproduced in Figure 1.3.

The diagram first subdivides along the lines of the five senses which are used to send and receive messages: auditory-vocal (hearing/sound-based); visual (sight-based); tactile (touch-based); olfactory (smell-based); and gustatory (taste-based). These are often termed **modes** or channels of communication.

Each mode is then subdivided further into more specific manifestations, some of which are language-based (linguistic), others of which are not. The linguistic manifestations are listed here:

- *Speech* via the auditory-vocal channel. (Morse code – a system for conveying linguistic messages – can be transmitted by sound, though usually by machine rather than use of the vocal tract.)
- Visually-based *sign language*, where this 'replaces' speech. In other words, where the sign language has the capacity to express the same complex and highly structured messages as speech, as in Deaf sign language, semaphore (the use of flag positions to represent letters) and Morse code (when light transmitted).
- *Writing* (visually-based) and writing-related codes such as those produced by the World War II Enigma machines to send out secret messages about military movements.
- *Deaf–Blind language systems* (tactile mode): for example, the writing system Braille relies on touch for reading letters. Some deaf–blind systems make use of touch to spell out messages on the hand of the receiver.

One way of understanding why these systems are considered to be linguistic is to ask yourself whether a message on any topic could be conveyed using each of them. Language-based manifestations have special characteristics: they are capable of conveying highly complex and detailed messages, providing the language (or code) used is known by all communicating parties. It might take a long time to send a given message using some of the linguistic manifestations, such as semaphore or Morse code, but it is quite possible to communicate in detail about past and future as well as about here and not-here through these manifestations. The non-linguistic manifestations are not normally able to be used to send complex messages. The remaining manifestations within the diagram are not usually considered to be linguistic or language-based, though they do represent ways in which other types of message can be communicated. Activity 1.3 should help to clarify the distinction.

 Activity 1.3 ⚬━┳

Consider the following questions:

1   Could you communicate a simple message about meeting someone at 3 o'clock using only the olfactory (smell) or gustatory (taste) modes or channels?

2   Similarly, could you communicate that same message using only **voice quality**? All you actually say is 'ah' but you can produce that vowel in whatever way you like: you could try shouting, whispering or squeaking.

3   Could you signal that your guinea-pig died last Tuesday using only physiological-vocal reflexes (such as coughing or snoring)?

4   Could you discuss the price of tomatoes using facial expression and bodily gesture only?

5   Could you ask the bank manager for a loan using patterns of touch and physical distancing only?

6   Could a member of a Masonic Lodge inform another Mason of the state of his wife's health, simply through a Masonic handshake?

So it would seem that the term *body language*, so often used in everyday conversation, is a misnomer. Facial expression, bodily gesture, patterns of touch or embrace and the communicative use of body odour (e.g. perfume, aftershave) are not strictly language.

A term much preferred by communication specialists is **non-verbal communication** (NVC). It is used especially of kinesic (facial expression, bodily gesture) and proxemic (physical proximity) behaviour. Note that the term *verbal*, as used in this field, must mean 'language' or 'linguistic' and not 'spoken' or 'oral' as is often thought. So a 'verbal agreement' or a 'verbal warning' could be spoken or written.

Some gestures and facial expressions are designed to fill a role which could be occupied by speech (or language). For example, police directing traffic will use a combination of gesture, posture and bodily orientation, possibly combined with facial expression. This could be replaced by language, but the officer's gestures, being conveyed and received by the visual mode, are more efficient in communicating simple messages to drivers in enclosed vehicles in a noisy environment than sound-based verbal instructions might be. Other examples of NVC which are designed to substitute for language include the visual signalling which commonly takes place on the world's stock exchanges or racecourses, or the simple 'thumbs up' sign, now used in many parts of the world to mean something like *yes*, *OK*, *good* or *agreed*. However, even from these few examples, it can once again be noted that only relatively simple messages tend to be conveyed by such NVC.

Other NVC operates as part of an auxiliary system, to add emphasis or support to language. Examples of this include the unconscious hand gestures most of us make when speaking. Morris (1978) has attempted to classify such auxiliary NVC both within and across cultures. In terms of hand gestures used to accompany speech, he notes gestures such as:

- precision gesture – the hand appears to grip a small object between thumb and forefinger at the same time as a very specific point is made
- baton gesture – the hand appears to beat in time with the speech and to emphasize points being made

- hand chop – a decisive gesture, as though attempting to cut through an argument to the essential features
- palm down – a palliative gesture, though quite a dominant one, as though addressing inferiors.

Morris (1978) demonstrates how non-verbal behaviour can be very deeply embedded. In Japanese culture, how deeply one bows to one's interlocutor during face-to-face interaction is very significant and there are recordings of Japanese people bowing when speaking on the telephone, when there is usually no expectation of sending any visual message, though the development of videophones might make this behaviour less remarkable. Some non-verbal behaviour is intentionally communicative (e.g. nodding or winking) whilst other NVC (e.g. blinking or wheeziness) is unintentionally communicative or 'informative' in the way Lyons (1977: 33) uses the term when he says that 'a signal is informative if (regardless of the intentions of the sender) it makes the receiver aware of something of which he was not previously aware'. Did non-linguistic signals precede language? When acquiring a mother tongue (➻ Unit 10), children use gestures to express meanings before using language and in the evolution of communication and language, it appears that human beings could express meanings through the use of pictographs before writing was systematized.

In the light of this information, you might like to consider again the points made by the observers of each role play in Activity 1.2. To what extent can the information and the terminology that has just been introduced be used to describe what happened in the role plays?

Some people maintain that almost every conscious human activity involves language at some stage because language is inextricably bound to human thought processes. If it is true, then an artist will think through the process of painting using words and a musician will work out his/her composition using words. However, many would fiercely deny or play down the involvement of language in artistic expression; for them, artistic media such as dance, music, sculpture, fine art or photography express messages which sometimes can't be conveyed in words. Before reading any further, you might like to wonder whether you think that there are any human activities that do not involve language and to discuss your thoughts on this with somebody else.

LANGUAGE AND ART

One day in a linguistics class on **grammar**, Josie, a linguistics student and a professional painter, was struck both by the interconnectedness of the components of human communication systems and by their different qualities and capabilities

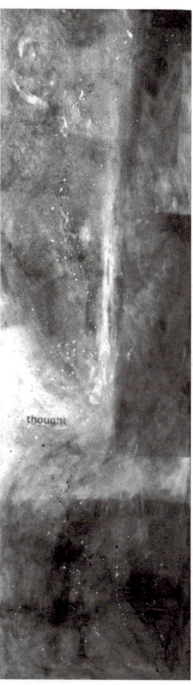

Figure 1.4 'safe' and 'thought'. We are grateful to Josie Beszant for allowing us to reproduce in black and white her paintings, 'safe' and 'thought'. You should be able to see the original colours on the website associated with this book at www.routledge.com/textbooks/0415291798

in conveying messages. Josie notes how the experience gave her 'inspiration for new paintings and quite a new way of working'.

 Activity 1.4a

Look at Josie's paintings, 'safe' and 'thought', in Figure 1.4. How do you interpret the images? Ask other people about their interpretations and compare their opinions with yours.

 Activity 1.4b

Read what Josie wrote when she was asked to reflect on what had happened and then consider the questions below.

> My paintings have previously fallen into the category of illustrations. They have been developed from a series of sketches and inspired by stories and the life around me. This new departure meant that I was painting instinctually, not starting with a sketch but with colour … After colour came textural layers and glazes and a feeling that I was painting a concept. The word or words on the painting came last in the process and I don't know how they were chosen, just that they were right for the image. One of the questions that kept recurring was 'Can a word say it all?' with the answer being a definite 'no'. The paintings are about what words can tell us, how each individual's perception of reality is unique and how we use words to try to bridge the gap between our realities. The paintings are also about the nuances, the word associations and the differences in meaning that can arise from simple words.

Were you surprised to hear that the words came last in the process of creating the images? What do you think are the implications of her last two sentences? In what way do you think a musician might make comments similar to Josie's comments about the process of composing?

HUMAN AND ANIMAL COMMUNICATION

Dr Dolittle is perhaps not the only person who has dreamt of talking to the animals or who has wondered what animals might be able to tell us if only we could talk to each other. Much of the research so far into animal communication has been based on trying to teach animals to use human language. Washoe, a chimpanzee, was raised by the psychologists, Beatrix and Allen Gardner, and was taught to use American Sign Language (ASL) to communicate with them. This choice of language was the result of earlier work with other chimpanzees, Viki and Gua, as a result of which it had become clear that chimpanzees, like other primates, are not able to produce the sounds of human language. Crystal (1997: 402) reports that Washoe 'had only 2 signs after 6 months of training' and that 'it took her just over four years to acquire 132 ASL signs, many of which bore striking similarities to the general word meanings observed in child language acquisition'.

Ann and David Premack chose to use coloured plastic shapes to encourage Sarah, another chimpanzee, to communicate with them. The different colours and shapes represented different actions or objects and Sarah manipulated these to express meanings. Some of these meanings could be in 'complex structures such as *If Sarah put red on green, Mary give Sarah chocolate*' (Yule 1996: 32).

The excitement from such projects about what chimps could do was tempered by the work of Herbert Terrace with the chimp, Nim Chimpsky, when Terrace demonstrated by using a freeze-frame video technique that Nim could be seen copying what his trainer had just done, thereby showing that he was imitating and apparently not using language in a creative way. Creativity is one of the essential design features of language devised by Charles Hockett, an American linguist whose work will be briefly summarized later in this unit.

Such research on the extent to which animals can communicate using some form of human language does begin to indicate what language is, by showing what the animals can't achieve in comparison to humans. From such research and from research into children's acquisition of language (➟ Unit 10), possible insights can be gained into the development of human language from its earliest beginnings. Pfeiffer (1978: 388) suggests that 'the first small steps toward language may have been under way at least 10 million years ago with the appearance of a few special gestures among creatures like *Ramapithecus*'. A Darwinian evolutionary perspective would argue that animal communication is in certain ways similar to early human communication and that, therefore, the more we can learn about animal communication, the greater our understanding of the development of human language from its earliest beginnings will be. However, Chomsky (2002: 148) claims that 'it seems to be absurd to regard it as an offshoot of non-human primate calls', a view which supports the argument that language is a unique characteristic of human beings. Pinker (1994: 18) argues that 'language is not a cultural artifact that we learn the way we learn to tell time' but that it is rather:

> a complex, specialized skill, which develops in the child spontaneously, without conscious effort or formal instruction, is deployed without awareness of its underlying logic, is qualitatively the same in every individual, and is distinct from more general abilities to process information or behave intelligently.

So he prefers to talk about the language 'instinct'.

Clearly, there are different opinions to consider: that human language has developed alongside animal communication systems (sometimes called the discontinuity theory) or that human language has developed out of animal communication systems (the continuity theory). Will we ever really know which is right?

Charles Hockett proposed certain features which differentiate language from animal communication and they are summarized here (see Yule 1996: 24 ff.). As was shown in the models of communication at the beginning of this unit, language is *reciprocal*: the sender of the message can also be the receiver of a message even within a single interaction. Some might want to argue that speech, or use of the auditory-vocal channel, is a defining feature of language but that cannot be right: sign languages used by Deaf communities demonstrate all the core features of language listed below. Language is *specialized* in that it is mostly used for a particular purpose and it is usually *non-directional* as you do not need to see the speaker in order to pick up an oral linguistic signal which fades rapidly. In addition:

- *Displacement* allows us to discuss the not-now and the not-here. This allows us to talk about events from our past and our future plans, and about places that we have never visited.
- *Arbitrariness* allows for the lack of any intrinsic link between the linguistic form (the linguistic sign) and its referent or meaning. Our four-footed best friend is called *dog* in English, *Hund* in German, *chien* in French and *gou* in Chinese – if there were a logical link between form and meaning, we would expect greater similarities between such labels. (➸ Other examples can be found in Unit 5.) Onomatopoeic terms perhaps show some link between form and meaning but even then one has to accept that cats say *miaow* in English, *meu meu* in Bengali, *niaou* in Greek and *(n)ya-ong* in Korean (Georgetown University 2004). Given this, if onomatopoeic terms do represent the sound, we must think that cats in different countries vocalize differently. What do you think? The Georgetown website has some fascinating information about animals and their sounds (you should visit it at www.georgetown.edu/ faculty/ballc/animals/cat.html).

- *Productivity* (or *creativity*) allows us to produce novel **utterances** whenever we need to. Of course, there are a lot of formulaic utterances that each individual repeats regularly, such as greetings, leave-takings and apologizing. Most individuals have their preferred forms (which greeting do you use most often – do you say *hello* or *hi*, for example?) though they are quite capable of using other forms in the repertoire. But such utterances as 'I love spinach – it's got a flexible decimal point, you know' or 'the kids were endearing in their bluntness as they threw a brick through my window' or 'I bet you're glad you've got hair' are clearly not formulaic and are most unlikely to be heard again other than as quotations of the original utterance. Each utterance was heard by at least one of the authors in everyday conversation.
- Without *cultural transmission*, language will not be passed from one generation to the next. A child in a linguistically impoverished environment will not acquire language to the same extent as a child towards whom language is constantly being directed (➡ Unit 10) and a child in a non-linguistic environment will not acquire language at all. The most frequently quoted example is that of Genie (Yule 1996: 171) who was discovered at the age of 13 with virtually no language as a result of the appalling conditions in which she had been raised with no linguistic input at all. She did later develop some ability in language and, indeed, went through many of the same early stages of language acquisition as have been observed in much younger children, but her tragic childhood experiences show how there has to be some language input for a child to acquire language.
- *Discreteness* relates to the fact that the individual sounds of a language may not appear to be so very distinct from each other and yet these differences are significant. Make a long *s* sound and then make a long *sh* sound. Now alternate these two sounds without any gap between them. They are very similar sounds (differing only in place of articulation ➡ Unit 8) but in English they are significantly different, as is shown by the English **minimal pairs** *lease* and *leash* or *so* and *show*. The sounds are not significantly different in Finnish: on the day that a Finnish friend of one of the authors became a British citizen, she announced 'Now I am Britiss'.
- *Duality* reflects the fact that in terms of speech production, there are two levels of patterning. Each language has its own discrete sounds (**phonemes**) but these phonemes do not individually carry any meaning. The sounds need to be combined in different ways to make meaningful **morphemes** and **words** as, for example, in the words *pot* and *top* which contain the same individual sounds but where the different orders have very different meanings.

LANGUAGE FAMILIES

It was noted in the characteristics of language summarized above that there is an arbitrary relationship between the linguistic sign and its referent. However, in some cases, there are clear similarities from one language to another and a speaker of English who is trying to learn German will have noted such similarities as German *Vater* and English *father*, German *Mutter* and English *mother*, just as a Spanish speaker learning French will notice the similarities between Spanish *padre* and French *père* and between Spanish *madre* and French *mère*. The examples can be replicated with other languages and with other lexical items, such as those listed by Barber (1993: 59) from which the examples in Table 1.1 are taken.

When they exist, similarities between languages such as those in Table 1.1 are interesting and can be helpful to language learners. However, unhelpfully, there are equally similar false friends between languages, such as English *sensible*, which is not translated by French *sensible*, as the latter means *sensitive* and the English meaning is translated by the French word *raisonnable*. The existence of similarities supports a claim that some languages are closely linked or related to one another (they have many similarities) and others are more distantly connected. From here it is but a short step to start talking metaphorically about language families. We have noted that there are similarities between modern languages. Philologists who study the history of language have also noted similarities between ancient languages and claim that these can be used to argue that many modern languages have a common ancestry.

Barber's (1993: 63) comparison of the numbers 1–10 in classical Latin, classical Greek, Sanskrit (an ancient language of northern India), Gothic (an extinct language spoken by the Goths and of which only one fourth century text, a translation of the Bible, remains) and Old English is revealing. His tabular format is reproduced in Table 1.2 which you need to study for Activity 1.5.

Table 1.1   Similarities in modern languages

English	German	Swedish
stone	Stein	sten
bone	Bein	ben
oak	Eiche	ek
goat	Geiss	get
one	ein	en

Table 1.2   Numbers in ancient languages

	Latin	Greek	Sanskrit	Gothic	Old English
1	unus	heis	eka	ains	ān
2	duo	duo	dvau	twai	twēgen, twā
3	trēs	treis	trayas	–	þrīe
4	quattuor	tettares	catvāras	fidwor	fēower
5	quīnque	pente	panca	fimf	fīf
6	sex	hex	sat	saihs	siex
7	septem	hepta	sapta	sibun	seofon
8	octō	oktō	astau	ahtau	eahta
9	novem	ennea	nava	niun	nigon
10	decem	deka	dasa	taihun	tīen

 Activity 1.5 o—┳

Look at Table 1.2 and identify any regularities or patterns that you can across the columns.

Barber (1993: 63–4) shows how there are other similarities across these ancient languages, reinforcing the claim that they are related. Greek and Sanskrit use <p> in the number *five* where Gothic and Old English use <f> and this similarity is maintained in words other than numbers. Table 1.3 reproduces some of his evidence (with slightly different formatting).

Table 1.3   Similarities in ancient languages

Modern English	Old English	Gothic	Latin	Greek	Sanskrit
father	fæder	fadar	pater	pater	pitar
nephew	nefa	–	nepos	–	napāt
far	feor	fairra	–	perā	paras
full	full	fulls	plēnus	plērēs	pūrna
feather	feþer	–	penna	pteron	patra
skin	fell	fill	pellis	pella	–

It is true that the correspondences between words might not be exact across the entire language systems but this evidence and similar evidence from syntax and **phonology** is sufficiently strong to allow Barber (1993: 64) to assert confidently that 'it is certain that these languages are related' and that they have a common ancestor. The name given to this ancestor language is Indo-European. Crystal (1997: 300) provides a family tree for Indo-European which is particularly useful in that it shows the surprisingly wide geographical distribution of the languages in that family. Trask (1995: 110ff.) takes the debate still further back in time to the ancestor of Indo-European, Proto-Indo-European (PIE), a language spoken 'around 6,000 years ago, probably somewhere in eastern Europe, possibly in southern Russia, by a group of people who rode horses and had wheeled vehicles, agriculture and domesticated animals' (Trask 1995: 116).

However, human language is likely to be much older than this. The difficulties of exploring such ancient languages are enormous, not least because of the lack of evidence. Proto-Nostratic is being postulated as 'a remote ancestor' (*ibid.*) of PIE and of other language families but the 'idea is still deeply controversial' (*ibid.*). Maybe we will never know exactly how old human language really is and where it really comes from, though that should not stop us from trying to explore a phenomenon that some would argue is central to what makes us human in the first place.

SUMMARY

This unit has addressed the relationship between language, communication and semiotics. It has shown how human language differs from animal communication systems and how attempts to teach animals to use language have been only partially successful. It has briefly addressed some of the links between different languages, both modern and ancient, as well as considering the possible origins of human language.

FURTHER READING

Semiotics: The Basics (Chandler 2002) and *The Routledge Companion to Semiotics and Linguistics* (Cobley 2001) both provide further detail on the relationships between language, linguistics and semiotics. *Discourses in Place* (Scollon and Scollon 2003) shows semiotic discourse in action and provides a wide range of data for further consideration. *Communicating* (Finnegan 2002 back cover) considers 'the amazing array of sounds, sights, smells, gestures, looks, movements, touches and material objects' of communication. *Gestures: The Do's and Taboos of Body Language Around the World* (Axtell 1998) provides an entertaining guide to gestures around the world – similar material but updated from *Manwatching: A Field Guide to Human Behaviour* (Morris 1978), which despite its age is still well worth looking at. Aitchison (1998) has a useful chapter on animal communication in *The Articulate Mammal*.

FURTHER ACTIVITY

 Activity 1.6

Identify as many modes of communication (linguistic or otherwise) as you can for, say, a fairy story such as *Snow White* or *Cinderella*. What are the advantages and disadvantages of each mode for the story telling?

 Activity 1.7

Think about the communication value of flowers, or of colour, or of music. Some concrete questions might help.

- How would you react if somebody gave you dandelions or roses, lilies or hyacinths – and does it matter whether you imagine that they give you a bouquet or a bunch?
- What colour(s) would you choose to paint your bedroom, your office or your living room and why? What is the effect or communicative value of different colours?
- What music do you think appropriate for different events? You might like to think about a graduation ceremony, a funeral, a wedding or a birthday party. For the latter event, might the age of the birthday person affect your decision and if so, how?

In each case, as you answer the question, explain your answer to yourself. If possible, ask other people the same questions and compare your response with theirs.

In the light of material presented in this unit, consider to what extent you think it makes sense to talk of the language of flowers, the language of colour and the language of music. You will be able to find further information on all of these areas on the internet.

COMMENTARY ON ACTIVITIES

Activity 1.1

1   The head nod as a sign of agreement is often thought to be universal. It is not and the Indian 'head wobble' as a sign of agreement is a good example of an exception. For others, see Morris (1978). This, and other examples, illustrate that there may be non-verbal communication (NVC) dialect boundaries, just as there are for speech.

2   This is an example of unconscious (and in this case reflex) NVC. It is potentially communication but certainly not language.

3   This provides an example of problems caused by non-matching cultural norms in NVC. In 'Anglo' cultures, it is often considered insolent or rude not to look at someone when they are reprimanding you (or simply talking to you). In some Asian cultures, it is disrespectful to make eye contact in such circumstances.

4   Gordon can't always send linguistic messages clearly in his present state but he can understand those sent to him; a highly frustrating situation indeed. His reliance on non-verbal communication to try to convey messages for which he needs language highlights the limitations of NVC, since his communication fails in this example. It is also interesting that, though Gordon can't express himself clearly in speech or writing, he can obviously still 'think'.

5   Annie is suffering from dementia and her language seems to have gone on to 'automatic pilot'. She demonstrates enough learnt behaviour from her long life to fool onlookers for a short time into thinking she is actually communicating. This underlines the fact that fluent speech, without understanding, relevance, creativity or coherence between utterances, does not fully constitute language, in the same way that a parrot merely reciting things is not demonstrating a language facility.

6   The chimp appears to be demonstrating 'semanticity' and 'arbitrariness' (which are discussed later in this unit) – the ability to name things using abstract labels. However, the chimp does not use **syntax** and the communication is driven by physical needs and thus cannot be said to be 'spontaneous' or 'creative' (also discussed later).

7   The tout may well be communicating successfully in this domain, using a visual code, but he could not use the limited 'tick tack talk' system to communicate on as diverse a range of topics in detail as he could with true language.

8   Alicia and James's choice of coffee for their prospective house purchasers signals a lifestyle message within their culture (in the UK, for example, successful, younger people are more likely to drink freshly ground coffee). They will be conveying a message via the olfactory channel; through the gustatory too, if the visitors actually drink some coffee. Alicia and James are probably conscious of the notion that certain types of aroma are said to encourage positive feelings about locations, though they may be in danger of crossing the line into cliché since the fresh-coffee-in-house-for-sale gambit is now so well-known.

9   The debate about whether vervet cries are evidence of them using signs like words has been ongoing for a number of years now. Are they just conditioned/acquired vocal

reflexes in response to different visual stimuli or are they really acting like words which are used to warn each other?

10   Ben and Emma do not require speech nor all the supporting NVC to forge a friendship. The written mode alone has been enough, in spite of the fact that it is relatively slow and unspontaneous. Communication by writing has avoided any potential communication problems which could have arisen because of different accents. The question is, can they sustain or develop their relationship using just the written mode or will they want and need more …?

Activity 1.2

RP1. This role play should, if well executed, clearly demonstrate how non-verbal communication can completely negate a simultaneous verbal message. There will, of course, be cultural differences in terms of how confidence is expressed non-verbally. In Western culture, it may involve establishing direct eye contact, smiling, and generally making wide use of facial expression, using expansive gestures with arms, moving freely when talking and leaning towards the addressee(s). What gestures and facial expressions were used by the 'falsely shy' speaker? Confidence may also be expressed through **intonation** features, especially through wide pitch movement, strong **stress** patterns and loud volume. Some linguists class these as paralinguistic features. Non-verbal ways of expressing confidence in Western culture would include style of hair and of dress (bright colours and flamboyant or revealing cut of the clothes; lots of heavy jewellery, for example).

RP2. You may have found watching this role play rather disconcerting, not perhaps so much as a result of the exaggerated mouth movements but because of the absence of other body movements. Most people make frequent conscious and/or unconscious body movements whilst talking. Some of these are as much of a personal trademark as our individual voice qualities and speech patterns. We often don't realize to what extent this is the case until we are forced to see ourselves as others do, for example on a wedding video or when rehearsing a part in a play where the director tells us our gestures are distracting.

RP3. Cultural norms on eye contact differ. A degree of eye contact is felt to be important to the smooth running of conversation in many cultures but, in most, the use of constant and intense eye contact is seen as threatening or unnerving. This is almost certainly linked to our evolutionary heritage: in the animal kingdom, staring eyes are a sign of fear and/or aggression. In many Mediterranean and Middle Eastern cultures, there is an enduring folk-belief in the 'evil eye', which claims that it is possible for some people to transmit harmful forces by a look or a stare. In many such areas, boats and other vehicles carry eye motifs, in an attempt to ward off the 'evil eye' and keep travellers safe. The Maori *haka* performed at rugby games by the New Zealand All Blacks team embodies the potent symbol of the staring eyes, designed to strike fear into opponents.

RP4. This role play should have illustrated how difficult it can be to put across even a fairly simple message using only non-verbal communication. You may have successfully conveyed the sense that you were upset; emotions are fairly easy to convey using facial expression, bodily gesture, specific types of eye contact and proxemic behaviour (e.g. withdrawing or turning away). However, did you manage to convey the sense that it was something they *said* which upset you, and that it happened yesterday? If you did, you may have resorted to a sort of mime or 'sign language' which, if you are honest, probably does not reflect the 'usual everyday gestures, movements and facial expressions which you would normally employ alongside talking' to which you were asked to limit yourself!

RP5a + b. Interviews are usually quite stressful events and both language and non-verbal behaviour can become both ritualized and also a tell-tale indicator of nervousness. You may not have felt the sort of genuine pressure in a mock situation which would produce such behaviour, though perhaps the observed role play itself was enough to achieve this. However, if your interviewer was doing his or her job well, you might have felt rather uncomfortable. Verbal and non-verbal feedback is what we rely on, to varying extents, to validate our role as current speaker in conversations. Again there are cultural differences; in Western cultures women are said to provide, on average, more minimal responses (such as 'Mmhm', 'Yes') and other **backchannel behaviour** (such as nods, smiles, eye contact, supportive proxemic behaviour ...) than men. What is clear, though, is that when this feedback is withheld, it can be very difficult to keep one's turn in a conversation going, and very easy to feel that the other person dislikes you, disagrees with you or at least isn't listening (➔ Unit 2). Manipulative people often use this device as a means of establishing or maintaining power in situations. If this happens on the telephone, one can feel tempted to ask 'Are you still there?'.

RP6. This role play should, as in RP2, illustrate how natural it is to accompany speech with non-verbal communication. When discussing a topic about which we might become very animated, such as a scary experience, we might expect non-verbal communication to be more pronounced. In fact, we might think there is something wrong, either medically or psychologically, with a person who stays completely still during such a situation. And, as usual, anything odd can soon start to seem unnerving or threatening. If you were the performer, you may have found it hard to keep your language animated given the restrictions placed on your other communicative channels.

RP7. This role play is obviously a variation on RP4 so many of the comments made there apply here too. However, the message to convey here is arguably more complex; it relies less on the simple expression of raw emotion. Moreover, the situation implies a far more formal relationship between tutor and student, on a serious issue related to regulations. In such situations in many Western contexts, it is considered desirable not to express emotions too fully. So what, if anything, did you manage to convey? Did you resort to mime (if so, you cheated)? This role play, perhaps more than any of the others, should underline the fact that non-verbal communication is a far cry from language in terms of the detail, clarity and overall complexity of the messages it can convey.

Activity 1.3

The answer to all of these questions is 'no'. These systems can communicate simple messages within specific domains but have nowhere near the complexity, versatility and clarity of true language-based systems.

Activity 1.5

Barber chooses Gothic and Old English to represent the Germanic family of languages as these are demonstrably ancestors of Modern English. As he (1993: 63) explains, 'where Latin and Sanskrit begin a word with *s*, Greek begins it with *h*; where Latin and Greek have *o*, Sanskrit has *a*'. Later on the same page, comparing the Germanic languages with the others, he points out that 'at the beginning of a word Germanic has *t* for their *d*' and 'it has *h* where they have *k* or *c*'. That there are such systematic similarities cannot be simply by chance – there has to be some reason for such phenomena and it can only be that there is some way in which current modern languages are derived from earlier forms of similar, and in that sense, related, languages.

REFERENCES

Aitchison, J. (1998) *The Articulate Mammal*, 4th edn, London: Routledge.

Axtell, R. (1998) *Gestures: The Do's and Taboos of Body Language around the World*, 2nd edn, New York: John Wiley & Sons.

Barber, C. (1993) *The English Language: A Historical Introduction*, Cambridge: Cambridge University Press.

Chandler, D. (2002) *Semiotics: The Basics*, London: Routledge.

Chomsky, N. (2002) *On Nature and Language*, Cambridge: Cambridge University Press.

Cobley, P. (ed.) (2001) *The Routledge Companion to Semiotics and Linguistics*, London: Routledge.

Crystal, D. (1997) *The Cambridge Encyclopedia of Language*, 2nd edn, Cambridge: Cambridge University Press.

Crystal, D. and Varley, R. (1993) *Introduction to Language Pathology*, 3rd edn, London: Whurr.

Finnegan, R. (2002) *Communicating: The Multiple Modes of Human Interconnection*, London: Routledge.

Georgetown University. Online. Available HTTP: <http://www.georgetown.edu/faculty/ballc/animals/cat.html> (accessed 23 October 2004).

Lyons, J. (1977) *Semantics, Volume 1*, Cambridge: Cambridge University Press.

McQuail, D. and Windahl, S. (1993) *Communication Models*, 2nd edn, London: Longman.

Morris, D. (1978) *Manwatching: A Field Guide to Human Behaviour*, London: Harper Collins.

Pfeiffer, J.E. (1978) *The Emergence of Man*, 3rd edn, New York: Harper & Row.

Pinker, S. (1994) *The Language Instinct: The New Science of Language and Mind*, London: Penguin Books.

Scollon, R. and Scollon, S.W. (2003) *Discourses in Place: Language in the Material World*, London: Routledge.

Trask, L. (1995) *Language: The Basics*, London: Routledge.

Yule, G. (1996) *The Study of Language*, 2nd edn, Cambridge: Cambridge University Press.

2 CONVERSATION ANALYSIS
Analysing talk-in-interaction

UNIT CONTENTS

- Introduction
- Analysing talk: conversation analysis or discourse analysis?
- Transcription
- Task-oriented data
- So how *is* talk organized?
- Summary
- Further reading
- Further activity
- Commentary on activities
- References

INTRODUCTION

Have you ever been in a situation in which one speaker effectively dominated a conversation? Even if you have not, do you recognize any of the following clichés in English which relate to this very scenario?

- He's a right chatterbox.
- She can talk for England.
- He can talk until the cows come home.
- She could talk the hind legs off a donkey.
- He never lets me get a word in edgeways.

Let us suppose that we heard someone make such a remark about someone. How might a linguist begin to verify the legitimacy, and study the implications of, say, 'He never lets me get a word in edgeways'? Among other things, the answer to such a question will involve an understanding of the organization of taking turns at talk, and that is what this unit is designed to provide: an understanding of the organization of turn taking in spontaneous talk-in-interaction.

Although there are exceptions, many syntacticians (linguists interested in **grammar**) would have you believe that the most important aspects of the theory of language are essentially aspects of the theory of sentences. Of course, sentence-sized chunks are an important part of language: they are discrete, very well organized and much fun to model theoretically (➤ Unit 7). But that doesn't mean that sentence-sized chunks are the *only* part of language which is discrete, very well organized and much fun to model theoretically. Let me dispel a myth: talk-in-interaction (henceforth 'talk') is *also* incredibly well structured, and while we are perhaps not able to publish 'grammars of talk', there are many regularities which Conversation Analysis (CA) has uncovered since its birth in the mid-1960s.

This unit therefore offers another view of the linguistic horizon by giving an introduction to some of the techniques and insights provided by CA with the aim of demonstrating 'how talk is organized'. What you should learn from this unit and its related activities is outlined below:

- some conventions for making detailed written records of talk
- talk is organized on a turn-by-turn basis whereby generally one speaker speaks at a time and overlaps (when they occur) are typically resolved quickly
- organization in sequences (sequential organization) is important; we need to give a careful detailed description/analysis of turns, their components and their sequential placement in the ongoing talk
- speakers design their talk for their recipient(s)
- each turn at talk provides the speaker with the opportunity to display to their **interlocutor** what they have made of their interlocutor's preceding turn (this provides a resource for analysts as well as for participants: we can make claims about what participants are doing with their talk by looking to see how it is treated by their interlocutor in next-turn position – i.e. our analysis is warranted by showing participant orientation to the talk/interactional task being analysed)
- everything gets into talk for a reason and conversation analysts ask 'what interactional task is this bit of talk addressed to/trying to accomplish?'
- CA's basic method is to look in detail at what people are doing at a particular point in interaction – what they are saying, what they are not saying, how they are saying something in a particular way, with particular sounds (**phonetics**), particular word order (**syntax**), particular choices of words (**lexical choice**) – in order to work out what this 'doing' might be a solution for (wording based on ten Have, 1999: 15)
- in other words, conversation analysts continually ask of their data: 'WHY THAT NOW?'.

ANALYSING TALK: CONVERSATION ANALYSIS OR DISCOURSE ANALYSIS?

This unit is concerned with the analysis of spoken interaction (talk). Because spoken interaction is often known as *discourse*, you will find a lot of literature under the heading of 'discourse analysis'. The main title of this unit, however, is 'conversation analysis'. So what's the difference between discourse analysis and conversation analysis? Very simply, discourse analysts tend to adopt a deductive methodology (reasoning from the general to the specific), focussing on rules for producing well-formed units of language larger than the sentence. Conversation analysts, on the other hand, tend to adopt an *inductive* methodology (reasoning from the particular to the general), being interested in the sequential organization of talk-in-interaction. Another potential difference stems from the ambiguity of the word *discourse*. Since 'discourse' can be used to refer to *any* continuous stretch of language use larger than a sentence, it can also be (and often is) used in relation to written language. Conversation analysis (CA), however, only ever applies to the study of spoken language. While the contributions to be made from discourse analysis are not to be denied, only techniques and insights provided by CA are addressed in this particular unit. (➤ For further discussion of discourse analysis, see Unit 7.)

Finally, the subtitle of this unit ('analysing talk-in-interaction') should be explained. While CA was originally concerned solely with *conversational* interaction, more recently non-conversational styles of talk have been analysed using CA principles: for example, courtroom interaction, interviews, medical consultations, political speeches, radio phone-in shows, speech and language therapy sessions, stand-up comedy, task-oriented interaction, and so on. For this reason, many writers and analysts prefer to speak of analysing 'talk-in-interaction', rather than the more specific (and restrictive) term 'conversation'.

Conversation analysis

CA is an academic discipline which was developed by Harvey Sacks, a sociologist working at the University of California, in the mid-1960s. The sociologists who followed Sacks (including Emanuel Schegloff and Gail Jefferson and many, many others since) are often called ethnomethodologists. They believe that the proper object of the study of language use is the set of techniques or methods that actual participants use in constructing and interpreting actual talk. Hence ethnomethodology: the study of 'ethnic' (participants' own) methods. Although 'pure' CA has its home in sociology, in this unit we will be looking at it through the eyes of a linguist.

Followers of CA are firm believers in data-driven theories. They believe that the analyst must not come to the data with pre-defined categories but rather must wait for the data to yield the real categories that the participants themselves orient to in talk. The focus of CA is on the (sometimes very mundane-looking) characteristics of spoken interaction. Just some of the many issues that have been investigated include: turn taking, repair mechanisms, agreements, disagreements, openings, closings, compliments and various issues relating to institutionalized talk. In this unit, however, we can concentrate on only a few aspects. So what should be covered and what left out? Following Sacks (1984: 27), the way that this dilemma will be dealt with will be to pick a bit of data that I just 'happen to have' and use it to demonstrate how talk is an organized phenomenon.

In order to conduct any rigorous study the analyst needs some body of evidence to observe. For the analyst of talk, that means finding instances of talk in order to make observations. But human ears and brains are not particularly efficient when it comes to accurately remembering all that goes on in the fast flow of speech. If you don't believe this, try Activity 2.1.

 Activity 2.1

Without warning, ask someone to repeat what you just said. If it was anything much more complicated than a minimally simple single **clause**, then it is doubtful that they will be able to give you a verbatim repetition. Sure, they may *paraphrase* what you said reasonably enough, but that won't do for analytic purposes. And even if they *are* able to give an accurate repetition of the words you used, they are certainly much less likely to be able to recreate your pauses and **intonation** pattern with much accuracy. (To fully check their (in)ability to do this, you may prefer to play them a bit of TV conversation that you have on video.)

TRANSCRIPTION

So how do linguists avoid relying on their less-than-perfect memories? They enlist the aid of audio (and often video) recordings of the interactions they are interested in. But even recordings have their problems, and at least in the first instance, it is sometimes easier to *see* what is going on in talk than hear it. Thus, in almost all cases, analysts also choose to work from a written record of what is on tape. It is called a **transcript** or transcription of the interaction.

Typically, transcriptions end up looking a bit like a script for a play, with abbreviated character names down the left hand margin and what they say to the right of the names – as in Extract 1, which is a transcript of a telephone conversation (now famous in the CA world) between Ilene (Ile) and Charlie (Cha). It was transcribed by Gail Jefferson. The extract is used here because of its fame: it is therefore just possible that your lecturer(s) may have access to a sound recording for you to listen to.

Extract 1: Trip to Syracuse

```
01   Ile:    Hullo:,
                     (0.3)
     Cha:    hHello is eh::m:: (0.2) .hh-.hh Ilene there?
     Ile:    Ya::h, this is Ile:[ne,
05   Cha:                       [.hh Oh hi this's Charlie about th'trip
             teh Syracuse?
```

```
        Ile:    Ye:a:h, Hi (k-ch)
        Cha:    Hi howuh you doin.
        Ile:    Goo::[d,
10      Cha:        [hhhe:h heh .hhhh I wuz uh:m: (.) .hh I wen' ah:- (0.3)
                I spoke teh the gi:r- I spoke tih Karen.
        (Cha):  (.hhhh)/(0.4)
        Cha:    And u:m:: (.) ih wz rea:lly ba:d because she decided of a:ll
                weekends fuh this one tih go awa:y
15                       (0.6)
        Ile:    Wha:t¿
                         (0.4)
        Cha:    She decidih tih go away this weekend.
        Ile:    Yea:h,
20      Cha:    .hhhh=
        (Ile):  =.kh[h
        Cha:        [So tha:[:t
        (Ile):              [k-khhh
        Cha:    Yihknow I really don't have a place tuh sta:y.
25      Ile:    .hh Oh:::::.hh
                         (0.2)
        Ile:    .hhh So yih not g'nna go up this weeken'?
        ( ):    (hhh)/(0.2)
        Cha:    Nu::h I don't think so.
30      Ile:    How about the following weekend.
                         (0.8)
        Cha:    .hh Dat's the vacation isn'it?
        Ile:    .hhhhh Oh:. .hh ALright so:- no ha:ssle,
                         (.)
35      Ile:    S[o-
        Cha:     [Ye:h,
        Ile:    Yihkno:w::
        ( ):    .hhh
        Ile:    So we'll make it fer another ti:me then.
40                       (0.5)
        Ile:    Yihknow jis let me know when yer g'nna go:.
        Cha:    .hh Sure .hh
        Ile:    yihknow that- that's awl, whenever you have intentions'v
                going .hh let me know.
45      Cha:    Ri:ght.
```

```
     Ile:    Oka::y?
     Cha:    Okay,=
     Ile:    =Thanks inneh- e- than:ks: anyway Charlie,
     Cha:    Ri:ght.
50   Ile:    Oka:y?
     Cha:    Oka[y,
     Ile:       [Ta:ke keyuh
     Cha:    Speak tih you [(   )
     Ile:                  [Bye: bye
55   Cha:    Bye,
```

Of course, this extract has a lot of 'stuff' in it that wouldn't be found in a play script. For example there are stray square brackets (as in lines 4 and 5, 9 and 10), odd punctuation (such as the commas at the ends of lines 1, 4, 9), line numbers in the left hand margin, numbers in parentheses and unconventional spellings. In the next section these conventions will be explained.

Transcription conventions

The transcription conventions used in CA are usually based on the system developed by Gail Jefferson (another good reason for picking the Syracuse data). It is very important to note, however, that not every researcher uses every convention, that some writers use some of the symbols differently, and that some even feel the need to invent their own notation symbols. However, whatever system an author chooses, they should always provide a listing of their conventions so that their readers can interpret the transcripts. Below we will see examples of many of these conventions with (where possible) examples from 'Syracuse'. (Don't worry if there are no examples in 'Syracuse' – there will be plenty in Activity 2.2.)

Overlapping turns

(1)   [When there is already someone speaking, a single left bracket [marks the start of overlapped talk. The transcripts are formatted so that when overlaps occur, the overlapping contribution is arranged on the page directly below the relevant part of the already on-going contribution. For example: lines 35–36 and 51–52.

(2)   ]   The offset (end) of all overlapped contributions is shown by a right bracket at the appropriate points in the turns of both participants.

Overlaps are very brief in 'Syracuse' and Jefferson has chosen not to mark the offsets. This highlights a very important point about transcription: while recognized guidelines exist, that is all they are – guidelines. That is why, as mentioned above, you will often find transcriptions using different symbols or possibly even using symbols differently. However, as long as any departures from the norm are explicitly noted, there should be few problems.

A useful convention for *multi*-party talk was developed by Karen Brown, one of our students. She distinguished the offsets of multiple overlaps in a turn by appending the closing brackets with a number in parentheses. For example, when](50) is used in a pair of **utterances** it indicates the 50th offset of simultaneous talk in the transcript. As](50) will appear twice, it clearly shows which utterances finish where.

Turns which start simultaneously

(3)   [[When there is no current speaker, onset of simultaneous contributions from both participants is marked using double left brackets.

Latched contributions

(4)   =   An utterance that immediately follows the preceding utterance without a gap is said to be a latched utterance. It is transcribed with a pair of = signs: one at the end of the preceding stretch of talk and one immediately prior to the onset of the latched utterance. For example: lines 47–48.

Pauses

(5)   (.)   A micro pause of less than 0.2 seconds. For example: lines 10 and 13.

(6)   (0.0)   Longer pauses are timed to the nearest tenth of a second and are put within parentheses. (3.1) therefore represents a silence of 3.1 seconds. For example: lines 2, 3 and 10.

Where silences cannot be attributed to a speaker, the pause is marked on its own line. For example: lines 2, 15, 17.

If you are transcribing but don't have access to a stopwatch, it might be useful to know that speaking at a normal speed produces approximately five syllables per second (hence 1 syllable = 0.2 seconds). Hence amateur photographers developing film, sky divers waiting to pull their rip cords and Ross Geller from the sitcom *Friends* (final series where he (mis)times his spray-on tan) often use 'Mississippi' as a counting tool: 'one Mississippi' = 5 syllables = 1 second.

(7) + Pauses may be transcribed with + signs if overlap needs marking (though the need for this is rare). Each + represents a pause of approximately 0.1 seconds in length.

(8) ((pause)) Long, untimed pauses are marked by ((pause)). These are rarely found because if a silence is long enough to be noticeable, it is long enough to be timed.

Characteristics of delivery

(9) > < Talk delivered at a faster rate than surrounding talk is transcribed within angled brackets pointing inwards (or >> << for *much faster* talk).

(10) < > Talk delivered at a slower rate than surrounding talk is transcribed within angled brackets pointing outwards (or << >> for *much slower* talk).

(11) - Indicates the utterance is cut off mid-flow. In terms of phonetics, this often involves **glottal** closure (⇢ Unit 8). It is a very powerful device for maintaining a turn. For example: lines 11, 43, 48.

(12) : Elongation of the preceding sound. The more colons, the longer the sound. For example: lines 1, 3, 4 and a really long stretch in L25.

(13) ? Gradual rising intonation. While a ? very often indicates a question (as in lines 3, 32, 46), it is important to note that it doesn't necessarily mean that. For example, the utterance in lines 5 and 6 is clearly a statement, and yet Jefferson has used a ? to indicate that the pitch gradually rises towards the end. This highlights the point that traditional punctuation marks are not used for punctuation, but rather intonation.

Because this non-question, high rising terminal (HRT) intonation is a feature of Australian speech, it is sometimes known as Australian Question Intonation (or AQI).

(14)   .   Gradual falling intonation. While a . very often indicates a statement (as in lines 11, 18, 24), it is important to note that it doesn't necessarily mean that. For example, the utterance in L8 is clearly a question (marked by the word *how*), and yet Jefferson has used a . to indicate that the pitch gradually falls towards the end. A similar example can be found in L30.

(15)   ,   Fall–rise intonation, often signalling an unfinished turn-in-progress.

For example in L4, the first comma after 'Ya::h' apparently indicates that Ilene has not finished her turn.

(16)   !   More animated intonation (often rise–fall).

(17)   …   Utterance 'trails off'.

Abnormal volume and pitch

(18)   ° °   Text surrounded by degree signs is quieter than the surrounding talk. I distinguish four levels of quietness: °quiet°, °°very quiet°°, °°°exceedingly quiet°°°, and °°°°virtually inaudible°°°°.

(19) CAPITALS   Louder than the normal surrounding talk. (This convention is often adopted in e-mails where capitalization can be interpreted as SHOUTING!) For example: L33 where the first syllable of 'alright' is transcribed as being louder. There are several other capital letters throughout 'Syracuse', but they are always isolated and don't represent loudness. For example, some transcribers use initial capital letters at the beginning of utterances – and some don't; some use them for proper names (like *Ilene, Charlie, Syracuse, Karen*) – and some don't; but nearly all transcribers (fickle as they are) tend to maintain a capital letter for the first person **pronoun**, 'I'.

(20)   ↑↑   Notably higher shift in pitch for the text between the upward pointing arrows.

(21)   ↓↓   Notably lower shift in pitch from the surrounding talk.

(22) underlining   Other emphasis/**stress** (sometimes indicated by *italics*). For example: lines 1, 3, 4, 5 – indeed, virtually <u>every</u> line seems to have some emphasis!

Non-verbal activity

(23)   (h)   Audible outbreath (number of hs corresponds to length of breath). Some authors don't put the hs in parentheses. For example: lines 3 (before 'Hello'), 23, 28.

(24)   (.h)   Audible inbreath (number of hs corresponds to length of breath). Again, some authors don't put the hs in parentheses. For example: lines 3, 5, 10. For obvious reasons audible inbreath occurs most often utterance-initially.

(25)   (ha)/(heh)   Syllable of laughter. (cha) is laughter involving some degree of friction. Again, some authors don't use parentheses. For example: L10 (twice).

(26)   ((cough))   Representations of non-verbal behaviour are transcribed within double parentheses.

(27)   ((LS))   'Lip Smack' represents the noise that lips make as they open at the beginning of an utterance (in fact there is often also a flavour of alveolar click ➻ Unit 8). I have never found anyone else who transcribes them like this, though. If you ever find them marked, they are usually noted (rather more ambiguously) as ((tut)).

Transcription doubt

(28)   ( )   Parentheses indicate talk that cannot be accurately transcribed. Any transcription within the parentheses indicates merely a *possible* hearing. (An X within the parentheses can be used to represent a syllable. Some authors may use Xs (or some other symbol) for syllables but without parentheses.) For example: in L12 there is doubt as to whether the speaker is Charlie (though he is the most likely) and also doubt as to whether it is an inbreath or a silence of 0.4 seconds. A similar example occurs on L28 with an outbreath (though here, the speaker is completely indeterminable). A final example occurs on L53 where Jefferson hears Charlie saying *something* while Ilene overlaps with 'Bye: bye' but she cannot offer even a best guess as to what.

Other conventions

(29) odd spelling   Non-conventional spelling is often used to more closely represent the actual pronunciation of words. Examples occur on most lines in 'Syracuse'.

(30)   anonymity   Where appropriate, personal details (such as names, addresses, telephone numbers, bank account details, etc.) are usually anonymized with alternative words of a similar syllable structure.

(31) line numbers   Transcript lines are numbered (not necessarily individually) in the left hand margin. For example: lines 1, 5, 10, 15 …

(32)   →   When analysing data, lines of particular interest can be indicated using an arrow in the left margin. We will see examples later in the unit.

TASK-ORIENTED DATA

Soon, Extract 2 will be used to illustrate what Sacks (1984: 27) calls 'a bunch of observations' about the orderedness of talk. However, because the content of this data might initially seem a little odd, some prior explanation will be useful.

The recording is of a pair of participants (PK and DN) engaged in a task that was designed to elicit natural, yet restricted dialogue. The task in question is known as the 'Map Task' (see Anderson *et al.* 1991). It has been widely used to support the study of spontaneous speech and **communication** of normally developing children, normal adults, sleep-deprived soldiers, dysphasic adults (➡ Unit 11) and children with speech and language disorders.

Two dialogue partners each have a schematic map drawn on a large sheet of paper (see Figure 2.1). The task involves one participant (designated the Information Giver (IG)) describing the pre-drawn route on his map to the other participant (the Information Follower (IF)), whose map has no route. The IG's ultimate aim is to get the IF to successfully draw the route. The participants sit opposite each other at a table constructed so that neither can see the other's map.

Although both IG and IF have copies of the basic map, differences exist between the two – specifically, the IG has three landmarks which are absent from the IF's map, which in turn has three landmarks that are not on the IG's. Thus, in total, there are six 'problem' points to be discovered *en route*. In the pair of maps in Figure 2.1, the three IG-specific landmarks are *cat, flower* and *kennel*; the IF-specific features are *flamingo, well* and *dog*. The reason for the existence of these landmark mismatches is to set up a genuine information gap between the participants.

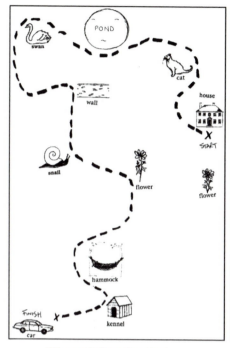
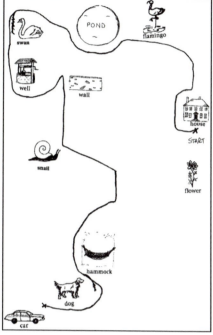

PK's map (information giver)   DN's map (information follower)

Figure 2.1   Maps for Extract 2

The participants are made aware that there may be discrepancies. They are also told that there is no time constraint. So while the data in Extract 2 is clearly not conversational, it is unscripted, natural and, most certainly, talk-in-interaction.

 Activity 2.2

Now you have seen examples of various transcription symbols, see how many of these conventions you can find in Extract 2.

All are present except: (7) +, (8) ((pause)) and (32) →.

Extract 2: Map task data (PK & DN)

You should be able to listen to this interaction at www.routledge.com/textbooks/0415291798

```
PK      ((LS)) First na[me?]

DN                  [Right.] Okay ((eyebrow flash))

PK      First name again?

DN      Dale.
```

05	PK	↓Dale.↓ (.) Right Dale. (1.0) To the right of your map roughly approximately,
	DN	°Aha°
	PK	say seven inches down or eight inches down,
	DN	[[>°Yeah°<]
10	PK	[[°°have you°°] have you got a ↑starting↑ mark.
	DN	Yeah I've got a- a starting mark and it's just below a house.
	PK	It's just <u>below</u> the house=
	DN	=°Aha°
15	PK	Okay. (1.3) ((cough)) °((LS))° If I was moving from (0.9) to the left o' the house and coming upwards, before you start drawing,
	DN	°Mm°
	PK	is there an obstruction above it?
20	DN	(1.2) Er (.) right at the top of the map there's a flamingo,
	PK	At the very top?=
	DN	=Yeah
	PK	Is there anything below that=
25	DN	=>There's nothing< directly below it °at all.°=
	PK	=°((LS))°=There's nothing below it.
	DN	[[°°No.°°]
	PK	[[Okay] So (.) imagine r:oughly about (.) <an inch and a half above the house.>
30	DN	°°°((LS))°°°=Yeah=
	PK	=You know the the the the the the left hand chimney
	DN	°°°((LS))°°°Aha.
	PK	And I want you take a (1.3) ((cough)) roughly (3.2) a route from the 'X' right?
35	DN	°°°((LS))°°°=°Yeah°
	PK	just past - just passing the lower edge of the house - left hand side o' the house,=
	DN	=°Yeah°
	PK	Bring it round in a circle,
40	DN	°°°((LS))°°°=°Yeah°
	PK	Okay? Until you stop roughly above the w- does it say ↑house above↑ your house.
	DN	(.) °↑Yeah↑°

	PK	Well okay bring it round in a circle and you stop just
45		about an inch which above the letter 'h' okay?
	DN	(0.8) >Oh d'you say there's another house.<
	PK	°Hmm?°
	DN	>Did you say there was another house<
	PK	>No no it's just the one hou- [no X] - =
50	DN	[°Right°]
	PK	=is< is er has it has it got the word 'house'
		on it?
	DN	°°((LS))°°=Yeah
	PK	↓°Well°↓ (.) just above the 'h' you should - come from
55		your start and draw your route,
	DN	Yeah
	PK	round in a circle. Come round i- out by about (.) an inch
		from the end of the ↑house↑
	DN	Yeah
60	PK	nice circle round (.) until you stop (.) roughly about-
		a- about an inch above (.) the letter 'house' - the
		letter 'h' (1.1) °where it says 'house'. Okay?°
	DN	Okay yeah.
	PK	Now [you stop there.]
65	DN	[Right >what by the left<] chimney (X)
	PK	Hmm?
	DN	Near the left chimney
	PK	°°((LS))°°=(.hh) No jus: above the left chimney
		[>but it's above<] the left chimney=
70	DN	[°°Yeah°°]
	PK	=you'd be stopping somewhere roughly about an inch and a
		half °°off. Okay?°°
	DN	°Okay°
	PK	°Okay?° So you stop there. (0.9) Now (.) bring your route
75		approximately up about another ↑inch↑ in a- er roughly an
		inch an' a half in from the edge o' yer map, going north.
	DN	°Yeah.° Straight up
	PK	°Straight ↑up↑ Ok[ay?°]
	DN	[Okay]
80	PK	Right. (0.8) Now (1.3) you should be approximately
		roughly (0.9) what say three and a half inches from the
		top o' your (.) map?

```
      DN        °Aha yeah° °°I'm [a bit more maybe°°]
      PK                        [°Okay?] That's good.° (1.2)
 85             Now °°°((LS))°°° before we start circling down- round to
                your left,
      DN        °°Mmm.°°
      PK        is there any other obstructions: say roughly about the
                middle of <your map(h)?> °°°((LS))°°°=Er near the head.
 90   DN        Er °°°((LS))°°° (1.9) on the left of the flamingo, (.) I've
                got a pond.=
      PK        =°That's it that's what we're looking for.°
      DN        °°Yeah°°
      PK        ((LS))=Okay? (.) Right. (0.9) Now where you've stopped (.)
 95             on your route,
      DN        °((LS))=Aha°
      PK        Right?
      DN        ((small nod))
      PK        I want you to circl:e up and round to your left, °(.h)°
100             until you c- is there a small mark (.) a- underneath
                where it says 'pond'.=
      DN        °°((LS))°° (.) Er no.
      PK        There's not.=
      DN        =°°Er no°°=
105   PK        =You know underneath - underneath the word 'pond' there's
                not a- a wee mark=
      DN        =>>Oh is like a<< wa:ve.
      PK        Like a wee wave.=
      DN        =°Yeah°=
110   PK        =↑°Yes°↑=
      DN        =>So there's thr[ee-<] there's THREE waves altogether.
      PK                        [Three]
      DN        [[<There's the one wave.°>]
      PK        [[There's three waves aye] it's it's like
115             (.) it's like the moon
                [you know two eye- two eyebrows and a … ((nod)) Okay!]
      DN        [°Yeah ((nod)) yeah. Got it. Yeah. (.) Aha° ((no]ds))
      PK        °(.h)° Right (1.0) now with you coming from >the< right
                hand side o' your map,
120   DN        °Yeah°=
```

```
      PK      =Okay? °(.h)° I want you to go up in your circle very
              gently and start moving to the left (.hhh) and the the
              head o' your circle should be equal w- with (.) that
              small wave which is approximately say (0.8) three eighths
125           (0.9) from the bottom o' the pond upwards?
      DN      ((LS))=Aha yeah.=
      PK      =Okay. So: (.) whe- where you left off (.) above the word
              house
      DN      Yeah
130   PK      (0.7) circle up, okay?
      DN      Yeah
      PK      And round [to your le]ft (.) very gently
      DN               [>°relative to°<]
      DN      °Yeah.°
135   PK      Okay? [[°And-°]
      DN            [[>Under the] flamingo<
      PK      (1.0) ((cough)) Well you're below the you'll be f-
              [below] the falingo [you're] er flamingo. Okay?
      DN      [>°Below it°<]        [°Yeah°]
140   PK      And head towards the word (.) towards 'pond' the the
              pond. Okay?=
      DN      =°Yeah°
      PK      °((LS))° And the the head o' your circle should be equal:
              (.) with the wave. Okay?
145   DN      °°°((LS))°°°=°Okay yeah°
      PK      °Okay?° °°°((LS))°°°=And start to dip down, (.) under the pond
              and pass it by quarter of an inch.
      DN      °Yeah°
      PK      (.) Okay? Come right round under the pond
150           [>until you're about<]=
      DN      [°°Yeah?°°]
      PK      =(.) quarter o' an inch (.) circling under the pond. Okay?
      DN      °↑Yeah↑°=
      PK      =°°°((LS))°°°=And when you get to the - as you start (.) to
155           the er the: to get parallel with the circle wi' the pond
              on the left hand side o' the pond,
      DN      °Yeah°=
      PK      =S'like to move up, (.) stop there. Okay?
      DN      °Okay.°
```

SO HOW *IS* TALK ORGANIZED?

Remember that the aim of this unit is to demonstrate *how talk is organized* and so the question is where to start. CA's rightful answer is always 'the data', and now that you have some appreciation of the tools for transcribing spoken interaction, we can begin to consider the dialogue between PK and DN. However, before starting to investigate the transcription of the data an all too obvious, but nonetheless importantly vital point must be made: Extract 2 is a transcription *of* the data – it is not the data itself. The data is the talk that was produced in the original interaction. The transcript is merely a *representation* (= re-presentation) of that data. While transcribers should always endeavour to represent the data as faithfully as possible (for readers may never have access to the original recordings – hence the level of detail put into transcriptions), it is important to recognize the limitations of translating one medium (talk) into another (the written record of that talk). Thus, while Extract 2 is often referred to as 'the data', that should always be read as shorthand for 'the transcript of the data'.

Turns

Even the very briefest glance at conversational data will uncover some basic observable facts and in their seminal paper on 'A simplest systematics for the organization of turn-taking for conversation', Sacks *et al.* (1974: 700f.) noted that the following observations seem to be worth trying to explain:

- speaker change occurs (people take turns)
- generally only one participant speaks at a time
- when overlap occurs it is usually brief
- the order and distribution of turns is not fixed in advance but varies within and between conversations
- the size or length of speaker turns varies from one turn to the next
- turns (or **turn constructional units**) can be composed of: a single lexical item (**word**); **phrases**; clauses; full sentences
- what participants say in their turns, or what actions they perform with their turns, is not restricted or specified in advance.

In order to account for these observable facts, Sacks *et al.* (1974) proposed a set of rules which operate on a *turn by turn basis*. It is assumed that a speaker initially gets just one unit of talk (turn-constructional unit or TCU). At the end of a TCU is what is called a **transition relevance place** or TRP and it is at these predictable (*projectable*) TRPs that speaker change can occur.

Sacks *et al.*'s rules operate at TRPs. In these rules (wording here is based on Levinson 1983: 298), C stands for 'current speaker' and N for 'next speaker':

Rule 1

(a)   If C selects N in current turn, then at the first TRP after N-selection, C must stop speaking, and N must speak next. C may select N by a number of means, for example by using N's name, by looking at N or by asking N a question.

(b)   If C does not select N, then any other party may self-select, with the first to speak gaining rights to the next turn (though *rights* are not the same as a *guarantee*).

(c)   If C has not selected N, and no other party self-selects (under option (b)), then C may (but need not) continue speaking (i.e. claim rights to a further TCU).

Rule 2 – applies at all subsequent TRPs

When Rule (1c) has been applied by C, at the next TRP Rules 1 (a)–(c) apply again until speaker change is achieved.

These rules predict that:

(1)   only one speaker will generally be speaking at any time (because each speaker will wait either until they are selected or until a legitimate opportunity arises where they may select themselves).

(2)   overlaps may occur where there are competing next speakers (as allowed by 1b).

(3)   overlaps may occur at misprojected TRPs. In other words N starts to speak where they (wrongly) anticipated a TRP but where C had not actually yet completed their current TCU.

 Activity 2.3 o—

Find examples of evidence for each of these three predictions in the data (Extract 2).

Overlap or interruption?

Thus far, **overlap** has simply been seen as a case of where more than one speaker speaks simultaneously. For some purposes, however (for example when analysing issues such as agreement, conflict, control, dominance or power), it can be useful to distinguish two specific types of simultaneous talk.

A very basic distinction can be made as follows: overlap does not violate the current speaker's turn – often because it occurs near a possible TRP; **interruption**, on the other hand, does violate the current speaker's turn – it is an attempt to take the floor from the current speaker while they are still producing their TCU. (For a finer distinction, see Hutchby and Wooffitt 1998: 54ff.)

 Activity 2.4 ○─┳

Find more examples of simultaneous talk in the data and decide whether they count as overlap or interruption.

The sounds of silence

Inter-turn silence

In addition to accounting for the brevity of simultaneous talk, Sacks *et al.*'s (1974) rules allow three different types of inter-turn silence (silence between turns) to be distinguished:

- lapses (due to the non-application of Rule 1)
- gaps (before the application of 1b or 1c)
- attributable silences (after the application of Rule 1a).

 Activity 2.5 ○─┳

Find examples of different types of silence in the data.

Intra-turn silence

Silence is not only found between turns. It also occurs *within* them.

 Activity 2.6 o—

Find examples of intra-turn (within-turn) silence in the data. When you have found an example, consider (a) why it is allowed to exist (in other words, why the other speaker doesn't start talking) and (b) what it might exist for (in other words, think about 'what interactional task it is trying to accomplish').

Sequences of turns

Having dealt briefly with how talk is organized into turn-sized chunks, in this section we turn our attention to larger chunks of organization – in other words, *sequences* of turns.

Adjacency pairs

When anyone says anything (so long as they are not the very first person to talk in the interaction), it will be assumed that their utterance is pertinent, relevant, fitted and somehow *related* to the immediately prior utterance. Or, as Sacks (1971) puts it:

> There is one generic place where you need not include information as to which utterance you're intending to relate an utterance to … and that is if you are in Next Position to an utterance. Which is to say that for adjacently placed utterances, where a next intends to relate to a first, no other means than positioning are necessary in order to locate which utterance you're intending to deal with.

(cited by Schiffrin 1988: 269)

This notion of immediate relevance (cf. Grice's third maxim ➛ Unit 3) leads onto the idea that utterances can be tied to one another in pairs by what Sacks (1995, vol. 1: 150) called 'tying rules'. Later these utterance pairs became known as **adjacency pairs**. Adjacency pairs are sequences of two communicative actions (usually, though not exclusively, performed by utterances) that are:

- (usually) produced by different speakers
- (usually) adjacent to one another

Table 2.1   Examples of possible adjacency pairs

	Part 1	Part 2
01	**Greeting** Hello!	**Greeting** Hi!
02	**Check** What's your name again?	**Clarification** John Doe
03	**Question** So why were you late today?	**Answer** I've already told you!
04	**Apology** I do apologize.	**Acceptance** Please – don't mention it.
05	**Compliment** That shirt really suits you!	**Thanks** Thank you.
06	**Opinion** Beethoven's fifth symphony is a masterpiece.	**Agreement** Yes – it's absolutely perfect!
07	**Accusation** It's all your fault we were late!	**Denial** No it isn't!
08	**Offer** Can I help you?	**Acceptance** Thank you very much!
09	**Assertion** I would like to do a linguistics degree here.	**Acknowledgement** Oh would you?
10	**Request** Can you lend me £5?	**Acceptance** Certainly – not a problem!
11	**Instruction** Say the password!	**Compliance** I only have postage stamps left.

- ordered as a first part and a second part
- categorized (or *typed*) so that any given first part requires a particular type of second (from a limited range).

In Table 2.1 there are some examples of paired utterance types.

While each time only one instance of a second part has been given, other types are, of course, quite possible and reasonable (e.g. we can ignore greetings, refuse to answer questions, disagree with opinions, decline offers and so on).

 Activity 2.7

1   With a friend, say the pairs in Table 2.1 out loud. How do they sound?
2   Now try them again starting from 1 but with your friend starting from 2. So the pairs go 1–2, 2–3, 3–4 etc. Stop when your friend has done number 11. How do they sound?
3   Now try once more but while you start at 1, your friend should start at 3 (so 1–3, 2–4, 3–5 …). Stop when your friend has done number 11. How do they sound?

Activity 2.8

Find examples of pairs in Extract 2 that are adjacent.

Insertion sequences

Of course, adjacency pairs need not be strictly adjacent as several sub-goals might first have to be initiated and resolved in order to get the top level task done.

 Activity 2.9 ⚬━

In Example 2 there are four question–response pairs. In the right hand margin, mark the questions (Q1–Q4) and their respective responses (R1–R4) to see which pairs are actually *adjacent*.

Example 2: Mair's Deli

Archie:	Can I have a sandwich to take away please?
Eric:	What would you like?
Archie:	What would you recommend?
Eric:	Are you a vegetarian?
Archie:	Yes.
Eric:	Well the pea and walnut pâté is good.
Archie:	Okay I'll have one of those then!
Eric:	Right, that'll be £2.20 please.

You should read the commentary on this activity at the end of the unit before continuing.

 Activity 2.10 ⚬━

Find examples of pairs which are not adjacent because of insertion sequences in Extract 2.

What is needed is a weakening of the criterion of strict adjacency to a notion known as conditional relevance: on the production of a first part, some second part becomes both relevant and expectable. Furthermore, if a second part is not produced it will be seen to be absent, and anything that is not a second part in next position will be seen to be some preliminary to doing the second part. In short, the first part of an adjacency pair sets up specific expectations which have to be attended to. This helps explain why the very first turns at talk in Extract 2 are neither a simple adjacency pair, nor a pair with an insertion sequence. For convenience those lines are repeated below:

Extract 2a

```
1    PK        ((LS)) First na[me?]

2    DN                        [Right.] Okay ((eyebrow flash))

3    PK        First name again?

4    DN        Dale.

5    PK        ↓Dale.↓ (.) Right Dale. (1.0)
```

In L1, PK begins the dialogue with the first part of a pair: he asks his partner his name. According to our story so far, what should then follow is a fitting second part to that query. Instead, DN does something which seems to function as a signal that he is ready to begin the task. But whatever L2 is, it is clearly possible to claim that it *isn't* a response to L1: 'Okay' is not Dale's first name! ('Right' has not been analysed as part of a possible response to L1 as it is quite unlikely that a reply could have been produced by DN *before* PK had finished his query). It seems, then, that DN has simply not heard PK's utterance (and hence, going back to the promise of commentary in Activity 2.3, it makes very little sense to class it as interruptive).

From this very small piece of analysis you should see that it is very important to consider not only the words spoken, but also their precise sequential placement with respect to other words spoken.

At the beginning of this unit it was noted that each turn at talk provides the speaker with the opportunity to display to their interlocutor what they have made of their interlocutor's preceding turn. Because of this, claims can be made about what participants are doing with their talk by looking to see how it is treated by their interlocutor in next-turn position – i.e. the analysis is warranted by showing participant orientation to the talk being analysed. It is therefore (initially) PK's third turn response to DN that justifies the analytic claim that L2 isn't a response to L1 *because that is the way PK treats it*. From L3 it is clear that PK takes DN's utterance as not offering his first name – because if it was, that would make asking for it again in L3 irrelevant and inappropriate. (Of course in L4 there is also the subsequent evidence from DN himself that his name is not 'Okay'.)

This is noteworthy, not because it is remarkable that PK recognizes that 'Okay' is not his partner's first name, but rather because he does not interpret it as *some preliminary to doing an appropriate second part*. In other words, PK treats L2 as in no way relevant to his first pair part query in L1: he apparently realizes that DN isn't shunning him – he just didn't hear the question!

What is yet more interesting in this sequence is that it provides us with evidence that the adjacency pair is indeed a strong organizing principle in talk-in-interaction. Because PK recognizes that an appropriate second part is truly and *totally* absent and because the organizational power of the adjacency pair is so strong, PK goes in pursuit of a fitting second pair part by redoing his query. (For further discussions of response pursuit see Pomerantz 1984.)

Chaining

Before this unit ends, another reason why it was important to mention adjacency pairs should be discussed – namely that adjacency pairs are linked into the system of turn taking by the following rule:

> **Adjacency pair rule**
> On the finished production of a first part of some pair, Current speaker must subsequently stop speaking to give Next an opportunity to produce some second part to the same pair.

Because of this rule, adjacency pairs are an extremely useful device for selecting potential next speakers. It is not just through the more obvious question–response pair type that Current speaker can select Next, but rather by using any first pair part of any type. And that – using one of Sacks' favourite words – is neat (in all senses of the word). What's even neater is that combined with this, the 'tying' strength of the adjacency pair (as we saw briefly in PK's pursuit of DN's name) can be responsible for preventing talk from grinding to a halt (even when in some cases we might like it to).

All utterances can potentially be analysed as belonging to some type of adjacency pair and so even the very first utterance in an interaction will demand some appropriate second part. If the second speaker on dutiful completion of their second part then appends a new first pair part, that will generate the need for further talk. If the first speaker responds in a similar way we no longer have just a pair of utterances, nor even just two pairs of utterances but rather the beginnings of a conversation.

This process is known as 'chaining' and a very simple example of this happened when Angelo (who lives at number 3) popped out to the shops to buy some milk. On the way, he noticed a neighbour (who lives at number 25) coming towards him. They know each other just sufficiently to say hello. Despite their lack of intimacy, however, politeness demanded a greeting, so Angelo tried to get away with a perfunctory 'Hi'. But his neighbour wasn't joining in doing perfunctory indifference – he was doing being friendly:

Example 4: Neighbours passing in the street

Angelo	Hi.	*Part 1: Greeting*
Neighbour	Hello, (.)	*Part 2: Greeting*
	How are you.=	*Part 1: Health enquiry*

Angelo	=I'm fine thanks,=	*Part 2: Response*
	=Are you?=	*Part 1: Health enquiry*
Neighbour	=Yes thank you!	*Part 2: Response*

Ironically, because of the neighbour's friendly appendage of 'How are you', Angelo was coerced (after an initial response of 'I'm fine thanks') into returning the friendly social enquiry. But by this time they had already passed each other, so although they were doing the business of organized talk-in-interaction, it was hardly very *social* interaction – each of them was delivering their final utterance into mid air rather than face-to-face!

 Activity 2.11 ⚬━

Find examples of chained utterances in the data. (Hint: you have already seen some.) You should note that separate first and second pair parts are not always needed. Sometimes a second pair part will simultaneously act as the first pair of a new sequence.

SUMMARY

This unit has done at least two things. It has introduced you to many of the conventions needed for detailed transcription and it has given you a flavour of some of the fundamental aspects relating to turn taking, namely: TCUs, TRPs, overlap, interruption, speaker selection, types of silence, adjacency pairs, insertion sequences and chaining. And this has been achieved by providing you with an extract of data in order for you to uncover for yourself part of the highly organized nature of talk-in-interaction.

FURTHER READING

For a brief but detailed introduction to CA see *Pragmatics* (Levinson 1983: Chapter 6). For fairly gentle introductions see *Analysing Talk: Investigating Verbal Interaction in English* (Langford 1994), *Everyday Conversation* (Nofsinger 1991), *The Language of Conversation* (Pridham 2001) or *Conversation Analysis: The Study of Talk-in-Interaction* (Psathas 1995). In class I use *Conversation Analysis: Principles, Practices and Applications* (Hutchby and Wooffitt 1998) which is very readable. I also use *Doing Conversation Analysis: A Practical Guide* (ten Have 1999) which, while slightly harder to read, does deliver exactly what it promises in its title. If you read only one journal article, it really should be Sacks *et al.*'s classic

(1974) paper on 'A simplest systematics for the organization of turn-taking for conversation' (a 1978 version of this paper can be found in Schenkein 1978).

Two really excellent websites must be mentioned. The first, maintained by Paul ten Have (2004), is accessible at <http://www2.fmg.uva.nl/emca/> (where 'nl' stands for 'Netherlands' so the l is an L not a one). The second which is accessible at <http://www.sscnet.ucla.edu/soc/faculty/schegloff/> is the home page of Schegloff (2004).

Finally, if the analysis of talk really excites you and you want to take things further still, then you should pick up a copy of Sacks' (1995) *Lectures on Conversation* – if only to feel the weight!

FURTHER ACTIVITY

 Activity 2.12

Return to the 'Syracuse' data. Rummage around in it and see what you can come up with. While you're rooting around in the data you might like to think about some of the following specific questions:

1 What displays of understanding are done (and *how* are they done)?
2 What's the difference between 'Hi' and 'Hello'?
3 What evidence is there of talk which is specifically designed with the recipient in mind?
4 What does 'Oh' do in lines 5, 25 and 33.
5 What does 'What¿' do in L16? (The ¿ represents a rise in intonation.)
6 How does Charlie treat (interpret) this 'What¿' in L16?
7 What are the consequences of Charlie's choice of interpretation?
8 What's the purpose (upshot) of the call?
9 Who formulates the upshot?
10 How does the upshot get formulated?
11 What other options were possible for formulating the upshot?
12 What differences are there between Charlie's positive responses and his negative responses?
13 What's going on in lines 34–38?
14 Why might Charlie change from 'girl' to 'Karen' in L11?
15 How is the call terminated?
16 What else is interesting?

Activity 2.13

Consider the following set of PK's silences in Extract 2. What interactional task (or tasks) are they designed to accomplish? In thinking about this, you might like to consider the close proximity of the words: 'right', 'okay' and 'now' and their placement within the overall task.

```
5    PK    (.) Right Dale. (1.0)

15   PK    Okay. (1.3)

74   PK    (0.9) Now (.)

80   PK    Right. (0.8) Now (1.3)

94   PK    (.) Right. (0.9)

118  PK    Right (1.0)
```

COMMENTARY ON ACTIVITIES

Activity 2.3
Prediction (1)
This happens most of the time, so almost any line will count as evidence.

Prediction (2)
Fragment 1

```
      24      PK      Is there anything below that=

              DN      =>There's nothing< directly below it °at all.°=

      26      PK      =°((LS))°=There's nothing below it.

→             DN      [[°°No.°°]

→     28      PK      [[Okay] So (.) imagine r:oughly about (.) <an inch and a
                      half above the house.>
```

In L26, with the falling intonation marked by the full stop, PK comes to the end of a TCU. DN can therefore legitimately self-select and he does so in L27. However, it appears that PK has also chosen to re-select himself and this therefore results in a very brief (if not fierce – cf. DN's quietness) period of competing speakership.

Fragment 2

```
      105     PK      =You know underneath - underneath the word 'pond' there's
                      not a- a wee mark=

              DN      =>>Oh is like a<< wa:ve.

              PK      Like a wee wave.=

              DN      =°Yeah°=

      110     PK      =↑°Yes°↑=
```

```
        DN     =>So there's thr[ee-<] there's THREE waves altogether.

        PK                     [Three]

→       DN     [[<°There's the one wave.°>]

→       PK     [[There's three waves aye] it's it's like

115            (.) it's like the moon
```

In L111, with the falling intonation marked by the full stop, DN comes to the end of a TCU. PK can therefore legitimately self-select and he does so in L114. However, it appears that DN has also chosen to re-select himself (L113) and this results in a very brief (again, if not fierce – cf. DN's quietness) period of competing speakership.

Prediction (3)
Fragment 3

```
149     PK     (.) Okay? Come right round under the pond

               [>until you're about<]=

→  151  DN     [°°Yeah?°°]

        PK     =(.) quarter o' an inch (.) circling under the pond. Okay?
```

In L149, 'Come right round under the pond' (because of its apparent syntactic, semantic and intonational completeness) represents a possible TRP. Projecting this possible TRP, DN therefore operates under Rule 1b and self-selects. However DN's projection of the end of the TCU was misguided as PK has yet more to add (PK clearly building the addition as a mere continuation of the ongoing TCU). Hence the brief overlap.

Activity 2.4
Here are some examples:

Fragment 4

```
05      PK     ↓Dale.↓ (.) Right Dale. (1.0) To the right of your map

               roughly approximately,

        DN     °Aha°

        PK     say seven inches down or eight inches down,

→       DN     [[>°Yeah°<]

→  10   PK     [[°°have you°°] have you got a ↑starting↑ mark.
```

Overlap? Yes. Because of Prediction (2) above? No.

Initially you may have assumed that because of the double brackets, this was just another case covered by Prediction (2) above. That would have been reasonable – if it had not been for the comma at the end of L8! Because this comma indicates continuing intonation, both parties know that PK has not finished his turn. Thus, because PK has not reached a TRP, this simultaneous talk is not covered by the turn taking rules. Sometimes complex TCUs are delivered in smaller non-TCU-sized instalments with continuing intonation inviting confirmation of the receipt of each instalment so that the speaker can continue – just think of getting telephone numbers from directory enquiries as in this example:

Example 1:

Switchboard:	What name please?
Caller:	York St John College fax number.
Switchboard:	That's zero one, (.)
Caller:	Aha?
Switchboard:	nine zero four, (.)
Caller:	Mhm?
Switchboard:	nine one two, (.)
Caller:	Yeah?
Switchboard:	<u>five</u> one two.
Caller:	Thanks.

Surely, this is what is going on in fragment 4: DN's '>°Yeah°<' in L9 confirms receipt of PK's instalment in the prior line. It is not an attempt to take the floor, but rather acts as a **backchannel** acknowledgement token (or continuer) – in essence, a 'please continue' signal. Although there is no TRP, there *is* an expectation (set up by the similar sequential organization of lines 5–7) that DN might select himself to speak. The simultaneous talk is therefore not interruptive, but rather overlap, and the choice of [[rather than [was an attempt to signal this complex case of expectation of DN self-selecting despite there being no apparent TRP in PK's turn.

Fragment 5

```
      60      PK    nice circle round (.) until you stop (.) roughly about-
                    a- about an inch above (.) the letter 'house' - the
      62            letter 'h' (1.1) °where it says 'house'. Okay?°
              DN    Okay yeah.
→     64      PK    Now [you stop there.]
→             DN         [Right >what by the left<] chimney (X)
      66      PK    Hmm?
              DN    Near the left chimney
      68      PK    °°((LS))°°=(.hh) No jus: above the left chimney
→                   [>but it's above<] the left chimney=
→     70      DN    [°°Yeah°°]
              PK    =you'd be stopping somewhere roughly about an inch and a
                    half °°off. Okay?°°
```

Lines 64–65: interruption. In L64, PK cannot have finished his turn after 'Now' – as Schiffrin (1987: 266) says, the function that *now* has is 'displaying attention to what is coming next … [focussing] on the speaker, and on upcoming talk'. Thus, DN's turn in L65 is an attempt to take the turn from his partner. Here he is successful: PK stops talking and DN gets a complete TCU.

Lines 69–70: overlap. The reasons are similar to those in fragment 4. In L70, DN is not attempting to take the floor. He is just saying 'please continue'. The reason that this fragment uses a single [is that here there is not such a strong expectation that DN might take a turn.

Fragment 6

	127	PK	=Okay. So: (.) whe- where you left off (.) above the word
			house
	129	DN	Yeah
		PK	(0.7) circle up, okay?
	131	DN	Yeah
→		PK	And round [to your le]ft (.) very gently
→	133	DN	[>relative to<]
		DN	°Yeah.°

Interruption. In L132, PK says 'And round', but that clearly doesn't constitute a complete TCU and so, as there is no TRP, DN's 'relative to' counts as an interruption even though it is not a particularly strong one (in that DN quickly drops out and apparently does not pursue his turn to completion).

You may have found a couple of cases where it is hard to determine whether the simultaneity counts as overlap or interruption:

Fragment 7

	80	PK	Right. (0.8) Now (1.3) you should be approximately
			roughly (0.9) what say three and a half inches from the
	82		top o' your (.) map?
→		DN	°Aha yeah° °°I'm [a bit more maybe°°]
→	84	PK	[°Okay?] That's good.° (1.2)
			Now °°°((LS))°°° before we start circling down- round to
	86		your left,
		DN	°°Mmm.°°

Interruption? Yes and no. PK is trying to take the floor while DN is in mid TCU – so yes, it appears to be interruption. That said, DN is uttering this TCU very quietly. It is therefore possible that PK hasn't heard it in which case as far as he is concerned it isn't even simultaneous talk. If this is the case, then we might prefer to analyse the simultaneity as a case not of violative interruption, but of innocent overlap.

An alternative analysis (which also yields an overlap conclusion) is that the simultaneous talk occurs very close to a TRP (the one after '°Aha yeah°'). It is therefore possible that PK believes he is entitled to self-select non-interruptively – it's just that he starts a little bit too slowly and in this way DN's extension to his turn has the effect of making PK *appear* to be in violation of the one speaker at a time convention when he probably had no such intention. In other words, this could just be a case of a slightly mistimed Prediction (2) overlap.

Fragment 8

```
→   01      PK      ((LS)) First na[me?]
→           DN                     [Right.] Okay ((eyebrow flash))
    03      PK      First name again?
```

This is an interesting one. Is DN trying to take the floor in L2? Yes. Is he interrupting PK? No. Justification for this claim will be provided in the section on insertion sequences.

Activity 2.5

Lapses

Lapses occur due to the non-application of Rule 1 – in other words when talk is suspended.

There are no lapses in this data.

A typical place to hear a lapse in Britain is in front of the fire after a large Christmas dinner. Often the effort to interact will seem just so overwhelming that everyone will temporarily suspend all talk. Elsewhere, Fasold (1990: 40f.) reports that lapses are common in a Lapp community (no pun intended) in northern Sweden as well as among some Native American groups.

Gaps

Gaps occur before the application of 1b – in other words before someone else self-selects:

Fragment 9

```
    146     PK      °Okay?° °°°((LS))°°°=And start to dip down, (.) under the pond
                    and pass it by quarter of an inch.
    148     DN      °Yeah°
→           PK      (.) Okay?
```

Gaps can also occur before the application of 1c – in other words before self-reselection:

Fragment 10

```
    3       PK      First name again?
            DN      Dale.
→   5       PK      ↓Dale.↓ (.) Right Dale. (1.0) To the right of your map
                    roughly approximately,
```

Attributable Silences

Attributable silences occur after the application of Rule 1a – in other words, it is the silence between the end of the turn where current speaker selects next speaker and the turn where Next speaker starts speaking.

Fragment 11

```
    19       PK    is there an obstruction above it?

→            DN    (1.2) Er (.) right at the top of the map there's a
                   flamingo,
```

Here, the (1.2) second silence in L20 is attributable to DN because PK has selected him to be the next speaker by asking him a question. The silences at the beginnings of lines 43 and 46 in Fragment 12 can be analysed in a similar way.

Fragment 12

```
    41       PK    Okay? Until you stop roughly above the w- does it say
                   ↑house above↑ your house.

→   43       DN    (.) °↑Yeah↑°

             PK    Well okay bring it round in a circle and you stop just
    45              about an inch which above the letter 'h' okay?

→            DN    (0.8) >Oh d'you say there's another house.<
```

Activity 2.6

There are many examples of silence within a turn. Here are just the first few of them:

Fragment Collection 13:

```
15  PK       ((cough)) °((LS))° If I was moving from (0.9)
             to the left o' the house and coming upwards, before you
             start drawing,


20  DN       Er (.) right at the top of the map there's a
             flamingo,


28  PK       [[Okay] So (.) imagine r:oughly about (.)  <an inch and a
             half above the house.>


33  PK       And I want you take a (1.3) ((cough)) roughly (3.2) a
             route from the 'X' right?
```

(a)   Why are these silences allowed to exist: why doesn't the other speaker start talking?
      In fragment collection 13, the silences occur at a point where the utterance is clearly

incomplete: syntactically, semantically and intonationally. If the TCU is still on-going, a TRP cannot have been reached and thus it is not a place where it is relevant for there to be a transition of speakers.

(b) What might these silences exist for: what interactional tasks are they trying to accomplish?

This is actually a much harder question to answer than at first it may appear, depending on which silences you have found. For example it is tempting to initially claim that silences occur to allow the speaker some thinking time. While that is likely to be one task silences can serve (as in lines 20 and 28 – take away just the silences in these turns and you are left with something that is perfectly well-formed), that might be only part of the answer.

Silences might also allow the speaker to somehow signal a 'repair' of their utterance (as in lines 15 and 33 where the ongoing TCU has been altered after the silence – take away the silences in these turns and you are left with something that is ungrammatical).

Other silences might indicate emphasis, or grammatical punctuation (for example in delivering lists, telephone numbers, or even larger chunks of talk). They might even perhaps indicate that the speaker has just been distracted mid-utterance. In short, silence can be multi-functional.

What is remarkable about the various functions of silence (including inter-turn silence) is that, as Levinson (1983: 329) notes:

> silence has no features of its own: all the different significances attributed to it must have their sources in the structural expectations engendered by the surrounding talk. So sequential expectations are not only capable of making something out of nothing, but also of constructing many different kinds of significance out of the sheer absence of talk. If conversational organization can map 'meaning' onto silence, it can also map situated significance onto utterances – and in fact it can be shown to regularly do so.

In other words, it is not just *what* happens (or, in the case of silence, *doesn't* happen) in talk that is important, but also *where* it happens in the wider sequential organization of talk.

Activity 2.7

1   1–1, 2–2, 3–3 … should all naturally 'fit' together quite happily.

2   With just some occasional tweaking, 1–2, 2–3, 3–4 … should also seem to 'fit'. This shows that first pair parts have possible alternative second pair parts.

In the first pair (1–2), your friend should offer a business-like formal handshake. If others don't seem to work you might need to experiment with different intonations: annoyed, condescending, excited, fearful, grateful, incredulous, imploring, mysterious, neutral, sarcastic, and so on.

NB: while the words from the second column 'fit', they don't necessarily belong to the same type as before. For example, while 10–11 fit together, 'I only have postage stamps left' is clearly not an example of compliance here.

3   1–3, 2–4, 3–5 … should all sound very odd.

This shows that while there are always possible alternative second pair parts, the possibilities are limited – it is *not* a case of 'anything goes'.

Activity 2.8

Adjacency pairs are such a common occurrence in spontaneous talk that they should be easy to find. Here are just a few. You may have uncovered more.

3	PK	First name again?	*Part 1: Question*
4	DN	Dale.	*Part 2: Response*
4	DN	Dale.	*Part 1: Response*
5	PK	↓Dale.↓	*Part 2: Acknowledgement*

10	PK	have you got a ↑starting↑ mark.	*Part 1: Question*
11	DN	Yeah I've got a- a starting mark	*Part 2: Response*
13	PK	It's just <u>below</u> the house=	*Part 1: Check*
14	DN	=°Aha°	*Part 2: Clarification*
14	DN	=°Aha°	*Part 1: Response*
15	PK	Okay.	*Part 2: Acknowledgement*

146	PK	And start to dip down, (.) under the pond	
147		and pass it by quarter of an inch.	*Part 1: Instruction*
148	DN	°Yeah°	*Part 2: Compliance*

Activity 2.9

Although there are four questions and four responses in Example 2, only the fourth pair (Q4–R4) displays strict adjacency, as can be seen in Example 3:

Example 3: Mair's Deli

Archie:	Can I have a sandwich to take away please?	Q1
Eric:	What would you like?	Q2
Archie:	What would you recommend?	Q3
Eric:	Are you a vegetarian?	Q4
Archie:	Yes.	R4
Eric:	Well the pea and walnut pâté is good.	R3
Archie:	Okay I'll have one of those then!	R2
Eric:	Right, that'll be £2.20 please.	R1

Each time a new pair is started before the previous first pair part has received its second pair part we say that the new pair is embedded or inserted within the first pair. This type of sequence is thus known as an insertion sequence. In the Mair's Deli example there are three insertion sequences inside the Q1–R1 pair, two insertion sequences within the Q2–R2 pair and one within Q3–R3.

Activity 2.10

While they are not as common as adjacent pairs, there are also insertion sequences in Extract 2. Here is one I found (with Pair B inside Pair A):

```
11   DN     I've got a- a starting mark
12          and it's just below a house.     A Part 1: Explanation
13   PK     It's just below the house=       B Part 1: Check
14   DN     =°Aha°                           B Part 2: Clarification
15   PK     Okay.                            A Part 2: Acknowledgement
```

And just to show that even within real talk there are insertion sequences within insertion sequences:

```
45   PK     okay?                            A Part 1: Question
46   DN     (0.8) >Oh d'you say
            there's another house.<          B Part 1: Question
47   PK     °Hmm?°                           C Part 1: Hearing Check
48   DN     >Did you say there was another house<   C Part 2: Clarification
49   PK     >No no it's just the one hou-    B Part 2: Response
            [no X]
50   DN     [°Right°]                        A Part 2: Response
```

There are other embedded sequences, but they are more complex than necessary for current purposes.

Activity 2.11

Here are a couple of examples of chaining which were first seen (in their component parts) in the commentary to Activity 2.8. Again, you may have uncovered more.

3	PK	First name again?	*A Part 1: Question*
4	DN	Dale.	*A Part 2: Response = B Part 1*
5	PK	↓Dale.↓	*B Part 2: Acknowledgement*

13	PK	It's just <u>below</u> the house=	*A Part 1: Check*
14	DN	=°Aha°	*A Part 2: Clarification = B Part 1*
15	PK	Okay.	*B Part 2: Acknowledgement*

Chaining and insertion sequences can work in conjunction to generate really quite tightly organized and often very complex sequences of talk. Below you can see the structures of a couple of examples:

10	PK	have you got a ↑starting↑ mark.	*A Part 1: Question*
11	DN	Yeah I've got a- a starting mark	*A Part 2: Response*
12		and it's just below a house.	*B Part 1: Explanation*
13	PK	It's just <u>below</u> the house=	*C Part 1: Check*
14	DN	=°Aha°	*C Part 2: Clarification =*
			D Part 1: Clarification
15	PK	Okay	*D Part 2:Acknowledgement =*
			B Part 2: Acknowledgement

This fragment is very interesting because it demonstrates that just as it is possible for a second pair part to simultaneously act as the first pair part of a new *inserted* sequence (as in L14, where C2=D1), it is also possible for a second pair part to simultaneously act as the second pair part to a *prior* previous first (as in L15, where D2=B2). A similar case can be seen in L79 in the fragment below:

74	PK	Now (.) bring your route	
75		approximately up about another	
		↑inch↑ in a- er roughly an	
76		inch an' a half in from the	
		edge o' yer map, going north.	*A Part 1: Instruction*
77	DN	°Yeah.°	*A Part 2: Acknowledgement*
		Straight up	*B Part 1: Check*
78	PK	°Straight ↑up↑	*B Part 2: Clarification*
		Ok[ay?°]	*C Part 1: Alignment*
79	DN	[Okay]	*C Part 2: Agreement =*
			A Part 2: Acknowledgement ctd.

REFERENCES

Anderson, A.H., Bader, M., Bard, E.G., Boyle, E., Doherty, G., Garrod, S., Isard, S., Kowtko, J., McAllister, J., Miller, J., Sotillo, C., Thompson, H. and Weinert, R. (1991) 'The HCRC map task corpus', *Language and Speech*, 34: 351–366.

Fasold, R.W. (1990) *Sociolinguistics of Language*, Oxford: Blackwell.

Have, P. ten (1999) *Doing Conversation Analysis: A Practical Guide*, London: Sage.

Have, P. ten (2004) Online. Available HTTP: <http://www2.fmg.uva.nl/emca/> (accessed 28 November 2004).

Hutchby, I. and Wooffitt, R. (1998) *Conversation Analysis: Principles, Practices and Applications*, Cambridge: Polity Press.

Langford, D. (1994) *Analysing Talk: Investigating Verbal Interaction in English*, Basingstoke: Macmillan.

Levinson, S.C. (1983) *Pragmatics*, Cambridge: Cambridge University Press.

Nofsinger, R.E. (1991) *Everyday Conversation*, Newbury Park, CA: Sage Publications.

Pomerantz, A. (1984) 'Pursuing a response', in J.M. Atkinson and J. Heritage (eds) *Structures of Social Action: Studies in Conversation Analysis*, Cambridge: Cambridge University Press.

Pridham, F. (2001) *The Language of Conversation*, London: Routledge.

Psathas, G. (1995) *Conversation Analysis*, London: Sage.

Sacks, H. (1984) 'Notes on methodology', in J.M. Atkinson and J. Heritage (eds) *Structures of Social Action: Studies in Conversation Analysis*, Cambridge: Cambridge University Press.

Sacks, H. (1995) *Lectures on Conversation, Volumes 1 and 2. Edited by Gail Jefferson*, Oxford: Basil Blackwell.

Sacks, H., Schegloff, E.A. and Jefferson, G. (1974) 'A simplest systematics for the organization of turn-taking for conversation', *Language*, 50: 696–735.

Schegloff, E.A. (2004) Online. Available HTTP: <http://www.sscnet.ucla.edu/soc/faculty/schegloff/> (accessed 28 November 2004).

Schenkein, J.N. (ed.) (1978) *Studies in the Organization of Conversational Interaction*, New York: Academic Press.

Schiffrin, D. (1987) *Discourse Markers*, Cambridge: Cambridge University Press.

Schiffrin, D. (1988) 'Conversation analysis', in F.J. Newmeyer (ed.) *Linguistics: The Cambridge Survey. Volume IV, Language: The Socio-Cultural Context*, Cambridge: Cambridge University Press.

3 PRAGMATICS

UNIT CONTENTS

INTRODUCTION

(1)   Specially made to meet their growing needs

What does (1) mean? All that can be claimed with any great certainty is that something (as yet unspecified) is made specially in order to fulfil someone(s)' (again unspecified) growing needs. Not very illuminating really! That is until we return this snippet of language to some of its original context as in (1'):

(1')   SMA PROGRESS follow-on milk for older babies and toddlers
       Specially made to meet their growing needs

With this additional contextual knowledge the meaning of (1) becomes more transparent: the something (previously unspecified) is SMA PROGRESS follow-on milk for older babies and toddlers and therefore it can now be assumed that this milk is made specially in order to fulfil the growing needs of older babies and toddlers.

But that isn't the whole story: what do *Specially made* and *growing needs* mean? Does 'Specially made' mean that SMA PROGRESS is 'bespoke' milk for this particular client group, or is it that the milk is made in an exceptional manner? Or both? And are the needs of the children expanding or is it rather that the milk is to suit the requirements of the children's growth? Or both? It is indeed possible that the writers intended all four meanings. Irrespective of the answers, these are questions for **pragmatics** which deals with analysing language in context.

If **semantics** is the study of meanings as stored in language, waiting to be put to use (⇒ Unit 6), then pragmatics focuses on how speakers and writers use their knowledge to convey meanings. In short, pragmatics studies how language is used in the interpretation of actual **utterances**. This means that people who study pragmatics are interested in *when* language is used, *where* it is used, *who* it is used by, *how* it is used, what it is used *for*, and, perhaps most importantly, *how it gets interpreted* as doing the things it is used for by the people who use it when they do so.

But how *do* speakers' intentions get interpreted by their audience? This unit provides the beginnings of an answer to that question, and in doing so covers such topics as: **entailment, ambiguity, context, deixis** and **reference, direct** and **indirect speech acts, inferences** and **implicatures** and Grice's maxims of conversation. All these issues are used to show that a **code model** of language (whereby a speaker 'simply says the **words**' and a hearer 'simply decodes them' to get the intended message) is too simplistic to explain a great deal of actual language use.

WHAT IS LANGUAGE USED *FOR*?

One reason (and some may say the *main* reason) for using language is obvious: language exists to say stuff about the world – *to convey messages*. And fortunately, for most of us at least, conveying messages with language is easy: we just have an idea, turn that thought into words (in the right order, of course), make various bits of our bodies move (lungs, **vocal cords**, tongue, lips ➤➤ Unit 8) and send the message out into the big wide world for someone to hear and (if they know the words and know about the **syntax** (or word order ➤➤ Unit 7)) consequently understand. In this way, then, a lot of the time, encoding and decoding (i.e. using) language *really is that simple* and such a model of how language works is called a code model (➤➤ Unit 1).

The code model

Let's look at some examples of the code model in action.

(2)   York is between Edinburgh and London.
(3)   London is between York and Edinburgh.
(4)   Edinburgh is between London and York.

If we understand the words *and*, *between*, *Edinburgh*, *is*, *London*, *York* and if we know the way English syntax works, then we will know that only one of (2), (3) and (4) can be true (and, as it happens, that one is (2)). That's because *between* means that, given three **entities** (entities are people, things, places, events, times, tunes, ideas – indeed, whatever we can think and talk about), the first entity is located on some line or scale with the other two entities towards opposite ends. The concept of entities links with those of participant and circumstance as outlined in ➤➤ Unit 7.

Frege's principle

What we have just discovered is that 'the interpretation of a sentence is a function of the interpretation of its parts and the syntactic relations holding between the parts' (Enç 1988: 240). This is known as Frege's principle. It is because of Frege's principle that we can understand that different processes are going on in (5) and (6) – because while the individual words are the same, the order is different and so the syntactic relations holding between those words are also different (in (5) Sally is the grammatical **Subject** and Ben the **Complement direct object** and in (6) it's the other way round ➤➤ Unit 7).

(5)   Sally changed Ben.
(6)   Ben changed Sally.

Entailment

So Frege's principle (*meaning = words + order*) does a lot of the work involved in understanding what people say. Another useful tool for getting at meaning is entailment. Entailments are the conclusions (inferences) which are *guaranteed* to be true given the truth of an initial **proposition**. (Entailment is also discussed in ⇥ Unit 6.) Thus, if we know that (7) is true, then we will *automatically* and *unquestioningly* know that (8)–(12) are also true:

(7)   Marjorie is a widow.
(8)   Marjorie is female.
(9)   Marjorie is alive.
(10)   Marjorie was at some time married.
(11)   The person who Marjorie was once married to is now dead.
(12)   Marjorie is at the current time not married.

We know that (8)–(12) *must* be true because if we try to cancel (deny) those inferences, something goes wrong (technically marked by the !) as shown in (8′)–(12′) – none of which can be *literally* true:

(8′)   ! Marjorie is a widow but she's not female.
(9′)   ! Marjorie is a widow but she's dead.
(10′)   ! Marjorie is a widow but she's never been married.
(11′)   ! Marjorie is a widow but her husband is still alive.
(12′)   ! Marjorie is a widow and she's married.

You may initially have doubts about (12) and (12′), but just think about Marjorie filling in an official document (say for a passport) and answering the marital status question. You should agree that if Marjorie ticks the 'widow' box then in all truth, she shouldn't be married, and if she ticks the 'married' box, then she is officially not a widow – she may have been a widow but she is certainly not one anymore!

Together, Frege's principle and entailments will generate a lot of the meanings in people's utterances and with them we can decode (13)–(15) as most likely having the meanings set out in (16)–(18):

(13)   We saw her duck.
(14)   He told Damien Hirst to paint the walls with fluffy white lambs.
(15)   The scientist spotted the monkey with the telescope.

(16)   The speaker and the people the speaker is speaking on behalf of viewed a water fowl belonging to a pre-specified female person.

(17)   'Hey – Damien! Paint fluffy white lambs on the walls!'

(18)   By using a tubular monocular magnification device, a pre-specified person who is professionally engaged in scientific activity caught sight of a pre-specified primate.

Ambiguity

 Activity 3.1 ⚬━

Look again at examples (13)–(15). Can you see any possible additional meanings other than (16)–(18) (in other words, can you spot how they could be ambiguous)?

There is a commentary at the end of the unit which you should read before continuing.

So given that many utterances are potentially ambiguous, if we used *only* the code model to work out what a message meant, then we would always have to allow *all* of the possible ambiguous interpretations for every single utterance and consequently we would never know which was the 'correct' version that the speaker had intended. But when we hear people talking we do not regularly find ourselves swamped by a baffling range of possible meanings, so clearly there must be some method for interpreters of messages to work out what the utterers of those messages must have intended and part of that method involves relying on the context of the utterance.

CONTEXT PART I: WHO? WHERE? WHEN?

In conveying messages about the world, we have to do two things: we have to refer to entities and we have to say something about those entities. In this section, let us concentrate on referring to an entity, which involves providing enough detail for the listener to successfully pick out whatever the speaker is referring to, as in (19):

(19)   Can I have one of the chocolate bars that are on the bottom shelf to the left of the Snickers and underneath the Mars bars?

As the typical linguistic act is speaking – where the speaker and listener(s) are usually face-to-face in the same place (at the same time) – generally, much can be understood just in relation to:

- the speaker and listener
- where they are in the location
- where other things in the location are relative to them
- the moment of speech/time of utterance.

Face-to-face, in a restricted location, speakers can use a minimal amount of description and yet still unambiguously pick out what's being spoken about by using expressions that make crucial use of the location of entities relative to speaker and hearer. Such expressions are called deictic and the act of using them is called deixis. Deixis (equivalent to verbal pointing) comes in three major types:

- person deixis
  (e.g. I, me, mine, my, you, your, yours, verb endings in some languages)
- time deixis
  (e.g. then, yesterday, now, in five minutes, verb tenses)
- place deixis
  (e.g. this, that, here, there, above, behind, left, right, come, go).

Consequently, a little boy was able to stand at the counter in a shop, point and say (20):

(20)   Can I have one of those?

and the shopkeeper knew (because she was there, could follow his pointing and implicitly knew about deixis) that what he wanted was a Milky Way chocolate bar (which just happened to be on the bottom shelf to the left of the Snickers and underneath the Mars bars)! Example (21) involves all three types of deictic expression:

(21)   I'll meet you here tomorrow at 3 o'clock and I'll give you one.

Without a good deal of contextual information, this utterance is extremely vague: who is *I*? who is *you*? where is *here*? when is *tomorrow*? *what* will be given? and is that 3*am* or 3*pm*?

Unless we know who the speaker and hearer(s) are (say Andrew and Aileen), where they are (say in Andrew's office in York), when the conversation is taking place (say 3 December 2004), and what the topic of conversation is (say Andrew's latest draft of this unit), then we will not be able to uncover the intended message which is made explicit in (22):

(22)   I, Andrew, will meet you, Aileen, in my office in York at 3 o'clock on 4 December 2004 and give you the latest draft of my pragmatics unit.

CONTEXT PART II: APPROPRIACY, LIKELIHOOD AND RELEVANCE

Assuming that the listener can work out which entities the speaker is referring to, how can context help disambiguate what is said about those entities? Above, we left unanswered how it is that we know whether the 3 o' clock in (21) is 3*am* or 3*pm*. What disambiguates this is knowledge of the way the world generally operates: because we don't expect academics to be in their offices in the wee small hours of the morning we are led to the *pm* interpretation and so we get (23) as the full explicit intended meaning behind (21):

(23)   I, Andrew, will meet you, Aileen, in my office in York at 3 o'clock *in the afternoon* on 4 December 2004 and give you the latest draft of my pragmatics unit.

In this way then, by drawing on general knowledge of appropriate and relevant ways the world can work, on seeing (24) on a leaflet advertising admission to a theme park, no-one will immediately worry about how they would cope as a parent, nor wonder which orphanage donated all the children to be given away!

(24)   Special Offer: free child with every full paying adult.

It is partly the context of knowing that the topic is about theme park admission that leads people to conclude that it is not a free *child*, but rather a free *child's admission* that is being offered. But perhaps equally important is their contextual knowledge of how the world works which helps to disambiguate the message – because they know that while it would clearly be 'special', giving away children is usually neither (a) legal, nor (b) much of an enticement to visit entertainment attractions!

By relying on knowledge of the way the world generally operates and on the context of the utterance – by taking into consideration who made the utterance, who they were speaking to, where and when they uttered it and what the topic of conversation was – a lot of the time all but one of the theoretically possible meanings become either inappropriate or irrelevant (which is why many of the answers to Activity 3.1 may have seemed very contrived). Thus, by taking into account the context, we are very often able to work out both uniquely and correctly what was intended by an utterance, and that (together with Frege's principle) is how information gets conveyed – but of course, not all utterances are simply concerned with conveying information, as we shall see in the next section.

SPEECH ACTS

When a speaker or writer produces a **declarative** sentence (see Table 3.1 later in this unit), they undertake a certain responsibility, or commitment, to the hearer that a particular state of affairs, or situation, exists in the world. When utterances work like this, they are called acts of assertion and this is what was happening in (24) – it was being asserted that if an adult were to pay full price, then (the admission for) a child would be free. Some more examples of assertions (statements which could be checked for their truthfulness) might include:

(25)   York beat Manchester Utd 4–3 on aggregate in the Coca Cola Cup.
(26)   Theeree's someething eextreemeely wrong with thee <EE> keey on my computeer keeyboard.
(27)   If you don't understand this unit you might find Grundy (2000) useful.
(28)   There's a wasp in your ear.
(29)   There's a piece of fish on the table.

However, many messages aren't just about making (asserting) descriptions about the way the world is in order to convey information. For example, while (24) did indeed *assert* the existence of a special offer (and so *informs* the readers of that special offer), it was simultaneously doing much more than that – it was also *advertising* the theme park, *offering* a free child's admission and, with that, *attempting to persuade* (*entice*) the reader to visit. And each of these doings (advertising, offering, enticing) was being done with words alone.

Now clearly we can perform actions by physically doing something. For example, it can be argued that we can:

- make a bid of £500 at an auction by nodding
- congratulate someone by giving them a pat on the back (or a hug or a kiss or a handshake)
- acknowledge a £12,000 loan by smiling and taking the cheque.

But we can also perform (*do*) the above acts by speaking/writing, as in (30)–(32):

(30)   I *bid* five hundred pounds.

(31)   I *congratulate* you.

(32)   We the undersigned, <FULL NAME> and <FULL NAME>, hereinafter referred to as 'the borrowers', both residing at <FULL ADDRESS> ... Edinburgh in the region of Lothian Scotland hereby *acknowledge* that we have received a loan of twelve thousand pounds sterling from Sheila Ena <SURNAME> of <FULL ADDRESS> ... Peterborough in the county of Cambridge England, hereinafter referred to as 'the lender'.

When our words perform some action – whether in speech, as in (30) and (31), or in writing, as in (32) – we say that they are performing a **speech act** and each of the three examples above both *describes* some speech act (*congratulating*, *bidding*, *acknowledging*) and simultaneously *performs* that act. These types of utterance are called performative.

Certain special **verbs** can make the utterance of a sentence performative; these are called performative verbs and many sentences use these performative verbs as an essential part of some act such that *without* them being uttered the act *cannot* be performed. This is very often the case in public ceremonies:

(33)   baptizing: I baptize you in the name of the Father, Son and Holy Spirit.

(34)   marrying: I now pronounce you man and wife.

(35)   sentencing: I sentence you to life imprisonment.

(36)   naming ships: I name this ship *Titanic*.

Felicity conditions

Of course, in order for these acts to be performed legitimately (or felicitously) certain conditions have to be met. Austin (1975: 14f.) called these conditions the felicity conditions of a performative and, as in Austin, they are categorized below using capitalized Greek letters:

(A.1) There must exist an accepted conventional procedure having a certain conventional effect: in the UK, a man simply saying to his wife 'I divorce you' any number of times won't count as a legal divorce, because simply saying 'I divorce you' is not, in the UK, the accepted conventional procedure.

(A.2)   Certain Acts can only be done by certain people in certain places with certain props. You can't name a ship if it already has a name; or if you are not the designated namer; nor without a bottle of champagne, a slipway and at least one witness.

(B.1)   The procedure must be done by all participants correctly. You have to say the right words. Thankfully, you can't marry someone by saying 'Please pass the mustard'.

(B.2)   The procedure must be done by all participants completely. If I say 'I bet you £5 you can't do a simultaneous voiced bilabial, alveolar uvular trill!' the bet is no good unless you say something to the effect of 'You're on!' – i.e. there must be satisfactory uptake.

(Γ.1)   Speakers should be sincere in their acts – they should have the appropriate thoughts or feelings (for example, someone who says *thank you* should in fact be grateful),

(Γ.2)   and their subsequent conduct should also be appropriate (for example, someone who makes a promise to do something – such as pay out on a bet – should subsequently fulfil that promise; and someone who advises should not subsequently chastise the person who acts on that advice).

If any one of these conditions is not met, then the act is said to be 'infelicitous' (or, as Austin also liked to call it, *unhappy*) – in other words, something can go wrong; exactly *what* might go wrong with the act depends on what type of condition is not met:

A.1–B.2 violations: misfires – the act is null and void

The first four conditions (sometimes called the 'necessary conditions' of a performative) state that:

- the act must be recognized by convention
- the person performing the act must have the authority to do so
- in certain cases, the occasion of the utterance must be right
- the act has to be executed correctly and completely.

If any one of these necessary conditions is not met, the act could 'misfire' and not count as the act that was intended.

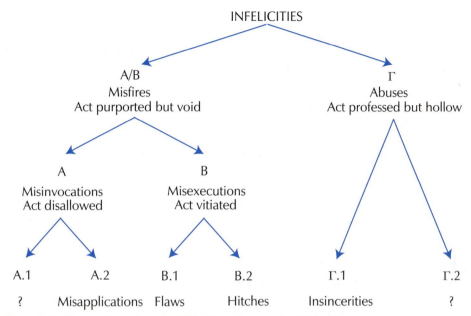

Figure 3.1   Types of speech act infelicity (based on Austin 1975: 18)

Γ.1–Γ.2 violations: abuses – the act is hollow

Γ.1 and Γ.2 are sometimes called the 'sincerity conditions' of a performative. These are the conditions of the situation (in which the utterance is made) that must be fulfilled if the act is to be carried out sincerely.

If the person performing the act does so insincerely (i.e. without the appropriate beliefs/feelings or by not carrying out certain actions) their act will *not* be null and void but they may be judged guilty of an 'abuse' (NB: sincerity may often be overridden by politeness, ➻ Unit 4).

The various infelicities are schematically summarized in Figure 3.1.

Explicit and implicit performatives

Performative utterances generally use sentences which have:

- first person subjects
- active simple present tensed verbs (➻ Unit 7)
- one of a special set of performative verbs (that allow the use of *hereby*).

In this way, then, you could perform (if somewhat awkwardly) the act of warning someone that a car is approaching by explicitly using the performative verb, *warn* in the simple present tense with a first person subject as in (37):

(37)   I (hereby) warn you that a car is approaching.

But you don't *necessarily* need the performative verb to be in the simple present tense with a first person subject to make an utterance do (perform) something. You could equally well warn someone that a car is approaching by uttering (38) in which there is a *second person* singular subject and a *non-active* (**passive** ➻ Unit 7) main **lexical verb**:

(38)   You are (hereby) warned that a car is approaching.

But you don't even *necessarily* need a performative verb. You can warn someone that a car is approaching by uttering (39) in which there is an implicit warning and a non-performative verb (hence the oddity/ungrammaticalness of *hereby* in (39′)):

(39)   There is a car approaching!
(39′)   * There hereby is a car approaching!

Furthermore, you can even completely do without either a subject or a verb. You can implicitly (and perhaps most appropriately) warn someone that a car is approaching by shouting (40):

(40)   Car!

It seems that simply by uttering words we can perform various actions (e.g. warnings) and furthermore these actions can be done either explicitly or implicitly. It seems some new definitions are needed:

- explicit performative: a performative utterance that uses a performative verb
- primary performative: a non-explicit performative (i.e. an utterance which tries to *do* something but without using a special performative verb)
- constative: a non-performative assertion (i.e. an utterance which is not trying to *do* anything other than make a simple statement).

A closer look at constatives

 Activity 3.2 ⚬⊸

Earlier we said that while (24) did indeed *assert* the existence of a special offer, it was simultaneously *advertising* the theme park and *offering* a free child's admission. Now reconsider examples (25)–(29) which were also used as examples of assertions (which we would now call *constatives*). Can you see any possible additional acts that these utterances might be performing over and above their obvious assertions? (Hint: try thinking of contexts in which they may be uttered.)

There is a commentary at the end of the unit which you should read before continuing.

By now, you should be getting the idea that given the right context, many utterances can perform many speech acts indeed (even those utterances which at first glance just look like declarative non-performative assertions). So it would seem that the original distinction we made between performatives and constatives is already becoming somewhat blurred. The performative–constative dichotomy was therefore eventually rejected in favour of a theory of speech acts in which just about all utterances can be thought of as actually *doing* something (see Austin 1975). For example, utterances can: *accuse, amuse, apologize, assert, boast, congratulate, console, demand, excuse, free, gloat, greet, hail, insult, jibe, kid, leer, mock, name, offer, persuade, please, promise, query, recommend, recriminate, scare, suggest, thank, urge, value, warn, yearn …*

Although there is not space here to go into any great detail, a flavour of the extended theory would be worthwhile. According to Austin, when we speak, we simultaneously perform several acts:

- phonic act: the act of making vocal sounds (➻ Unit 8)
- locutionary act: the communicative act of uttering a sentence (involving the acts of referring to certain objects in the world and saying stuff about them)
- illocutionary act: the act (defined by social convention) which is performed when making an utterance: e.g. accusing, apologizing, asserting, boasting, congratulating
- perlocutionary act: the (not necessarily intentional) act of causing a certain effect on the hearer (and possibly others) e.g. amusing, persuading, pleasing, scaring.

The type of speech act that we have mainly been dealing with up until now (accusing, apologizing etc.) is what Austin finally called the **illocutionary act** (or occasionally the illocutionary *force* of the act). But now what we also have is the notion of the *perlocutionary act* (which is often useful in discussions of miscommunication). It is important to recognize the existence of this type of act because **communication** is not a unilateral process – it always takes (at least) two! (➡ Unit 1.)

Consider a speaker apologizing for some wrong doing, or congratulating their colleague on the recent birth of their son, or warning someone of an impending car/wasp. People don't usually carry out these sorts of acts for the sake of it, but rather to produce certain perlocutionary effects: they apologize to receive forgiveness, they congratulate to make the hearer feel good, they warn to make the hearer take evasive action and so on. But before the hearer can do any of these things, they have to recognize that acts of apology, congratulation and warning have been done. In other words, there has to be what Austin calls illocutionary uptake, otherwise the initial act (no matter how well intentioned) will not be successful. Of course, simply recognizing and understanding the illocutionary force will not guarantee a successful perlocutionary effect – the hearer is always able to choose not to (re)act in the intended/anticipated manner: so non-compliance is not always about miscommunication (as many parents will affirm).

As an example, consider the perhaps universal children's playground activity of something like (41):

(41)   Child 1: Watch out – there's a wasp!   (PSEUDO-WARNING)
       Child 2: Where?!   (QUERY)
       Child 1: Made you look, made you stare,
                 made you lose your underwear!   (TEASE)

If Child 2 is too often subject to these sorts of playful teases, they may eventually come to not recognize the intention behind (40) *Car!* and instead interpret it as a joke (or a simple assertion) rather than as a warning. Sadly, not achieving appropriate illocutionary uptake in your addressees can have serious consequences (hence the fable about the boy who cried wolf).

Fortunately, however, most of the time we do correctly recognize the intended force behind utterances – even though that force can be conveyed either explicitly or implicitly (as seen above) and either directly or indirectly (as will be seen in the next sections).

Table 3.1 Sentence types and direct speech acts

Sentence Type (syntactic form)	*Typical Linguistic Act (pragmatic function)*
Declarative: Subject + Verb ...	Asserting
Interrogative: Verb + Subject ...	Questioning
Imperative: No overt Subject	Ordering/Requesting

Direct speech acts

English has three major sentence (or **mood**) types: **declarative**, **interrogative** and **imperative** (➣ cf. Unit 7). Each of these has associated with it a typical act, as in Table 3.1.

The **direct illocution** of an utterance is the illocution most directly indicated by the literal meaning of what is uttered. In other words, when syntactic form and pragmatic function match, the effect is called a **direct speech act**, as in (42)–(44):

(42) I like to play golf.
(*Declarative* form functioning as an *assertion*)

(43) Have you ever been lectured on pragmatics?
(*Interrogative* form functioning as a *question*)

(44) Promise me you won't laugh.
(*Imperative* form functioning as an *order*)

Indirect speech acts

In everyday conversations, however, the majority of illocutions are, in fact, *indirect*. The **indirect illocution** of an utterance is any further illocution an utterance might have. In other words, when form and function *do not* match, we call the effect an **indirect speech act**, as in (45)–(47):

(45) Context: At the ticket office of York railway station. Traveller to sales clerk.
Utterance: I'd like a saver return to Sheffield please.
Sentence Type: Declarative
Act: Ordering/Requesting: *Sell me a saver return train ticket to Sheffield.*

(46) Context: At a nightclub. One friend to another.
Utterance: Has he got a cute bum or what?
Sentence Type: Interrogative
Act: Assertion: *He's got a cute bum!*

(47)   Context: In a psychiatrist's office. Psychiatrist to client.
       Utterance: Tell me why you hate your father!
       Sentence Type: Imperative
       Act: Question: *Why do you hate your father?*

So because speech acts can be implicit and indirect, often what someone *means* is not actually what they *say*. Thus we must ask how it is that we seem to be able to work out the intended force of an illocution. The answer has a good deal to do with what background knowledge the hearer has – knowledge which helps determine what inferences (conclusions) and therefore what meanings it is reasonable to get from an utterance.

Useful knowledge

There are various types of knowledge that can be useful in interpreting what a speaker means with their utterance. These include knowledge of:

- the physical context of the situation
- the topic of conversation
- the participants in conversation
- the world (including culture, basic science, religion, current affairs …)
- how language works in principled ways.

Let us look at some examples:

Physical context

(48)   Can I have one of those?

Without being aware of the physical context of the situation, it would be impossible to tell both who *I* is, and also what *one of those* is.

Topic

(49)   Michael changed Ben.

Without knowing about the topic of conversation (and possibly also about the participants), it would be impossible to tell for sure whether Michael changed Ben's *character* or his *nappy*. Indeed, it might even be the case that Michael had a pet called Ben which he eventually got fed up with and so exchanged it for some other animal.

Participants

(50)   Dr Jones persuaded Mr Smythe that he should operate on him immediately.

Without knowledge of the participants it would be impossible tell for sure who does the operating and who gets operated on. For example, consider the following two possible alternatives for participant roles (where the subscript letters indicate which entities co-refer):

(50a)   Rob Jones is a doctor in a hospital; Tim Smythe is a patient of Dr Jones.
Dr Jones$_i$ persuaded Mr Smythe$_j$ that he$_i$ should operate on him$_j$ immediately.

(50b)   Rob Jones is a doctor in a hospital; Tim Smythe is a consultant surgeon.
Dr Jones$_i$ persuaded Mr Smythe$_j$ that he$_j$ should operate on him$_{k/i}$ immediately.
(The k subscript denotes that Smythe could sensibly operate on someone *other* than Jones.)

World

(51)   Marjorie: Would you like some chocolate?
Joan: Is the Pope Catholic?

Without knowledge of the world (specifically the religion of the Pope), it would be impossible to tell whether or not Joan wanted some chocolate.

HOW LANGUAGE WORKS

While knowledge of various aspects of the context can all clearly be involved in aiding the interpretation of utterances, what actually counts as *relevant* context is potentially vast. According to Sperber and Wilson (1995: 15f.), the context can be thought of as 'a subset of the hearer's assumptions about the world' and furthermore, it is 'these assumptions, ... rather than the actual state of the world, that affect the interpretation of an utterance'. This can have serious consequences for interpreting language in use. Let us use an example to illustrate.

Let us assume

Premise 1: $P \rightarrow Q$ (read as: 'if P, then Q')
which is logically equivalent to:
$\neg Q \rightarrow \neg P$ (read as: 'if not Q, then not P')

Now if we also *assume*

> Premise 2: $\neg Q$ (read as: 'not Q')
>   We are logically led to the conclusion: $\neg P$ (read as: 'not P')

Now let's use a worded example:

(52)   Marjorie: Will you have a piece of chocolate?
        Joan: If I eat chocolate I'll get fat.

        Let P = have (i.e. eat) a piece of chocolate
        Let Q = get fat

And, as before, let:

> Premise 1: $P \rightarrow Q$ (which is equivalent to: $\neg Q \rightarrow \neg P$)
> Premise 2: $\neg Q$
> _____
> Conclusion: $\neg P$

If we assume that, like a lot of body-conscious individuals, Joan wants not to get fat (i.e. if we assume Premise 2, not Q) then we will logically be led to conclude not P (i.e. Joan will not eat the chocolate), and hence that Joan is *implicitly* declining Marjorie's offer, which Marjorie should logically be able to work out. However, for Marjorie to reach this conclusion, *she* must also assume that Joan wants not to get fat (i.e. not Q). Any other assumption (i.e. Q) will not guarantee that she will understand Joan's response as a declination. While assuming that Joan *wants* to get fat (Q) is perhaps a little unusual, there is nothing absurd in the scenario where Joan is an actor who needs to put on weight for an up-coming role (or is a recovering anorexic, or is about to go on a polar expedition and needs to increase her fat reserves), and so it is of vital importance that both Joan and Marjorie share the same assumption – otherwise Marjorie will misinterpret Joan's response.

This has led Sperber and Wilson (1995: 18, emphasis added) to comment that 'the context in which an utterance is understood must be strictly limited to *mutual* knowledge; otherwise inference cannot function as an effective aspect of decoding'. Gazdar and Good put it a little more strongly, saying that 'comprehension can only be guaranteed by identical knowledge bases' but of course, if speakers and hearers shared exactly the same thoughts (had the same knowledge), that 'would render communication redundant' (1982: 100 footnote 7).

Clearly, none of us has exactly the same knowledge as anyone else, and consequently communication is indeed a necessary part of life. So the question we must ask now is, if we do not have identical knowledge bases, how do we ever manage to communicate anything which relies on inferences? H. Paul Grice proposed a solution.

GRICE'S THEORY OF CONVERSATIONAL ORGANIZATION

Grice was interested in how it is that we can imply something without actually saying it (as Joan implies a 'yes' in (51) and a 'no' in (52) despite not actually saying so). For him, the answer lay in the assumption that as rational communicators, we appear to take it for granted that an utterance should make sense in the given context (otherwise it would not be worth a speaker uttering it or a hearer processing it). He called this assumption the Cooperative Principle (CP):

> Make your conversational contribution such as is required, at the stage at which it occurs, by the accepted purpose or direction of the talk exchange in which you are engaged.

> (Grice 1975: 45)

To this overarching principle, he added four main maxims of conversation:

Maxim of quantity

1   Make your contribution as informative as is required (for the current purposes of the exchange).
2   Do not make your contribution more informative than is required.

Maxim of quality

1   Do not say what you believe to be false.
2   Do not say that for which you lack adequate evidence.

Maxim of relevance

1   Be relevant.[1]

Maxim of Manner (be perspicuous)

1   Avoid obscurity of expression.
2   Avoid ambiguity.
3   Be brief (avoid unnecessary prolixity).
4   Be orderly.

In other words, Grice suggested that when we talk, we *assume* that all participants orient towards successful communication as a goal and in so doing it is assumed that they are all appropriately *informative*, *truthful*, *relevant* and *clear*.

What can we do with these maxims?

We can ADHERE to them

(53)　Marjorie:　I need to speak to Tommy – is he in this morning, Joan?
　　　　Joan:　　Yes – he's in the kitchen.

Here we see Joan's response to Marjorie's question as being clear, relevant and (we assume) truthful. It is also adequately and appropriately informative (note that although Marjorie asked a yes–no question, a simple 'Yes' would have been an inadequate response because in order to speak to Tommy, Marjorie first needs to locate him). In short Joan is abiding by the CP and its attendant maxims. There are, however, occasions where speakers choose not to do so …

We can VIOLATE them because of a maxim clash

Some years ago when Alan was organizing a school reunion an ex-pupil (Bob) started talking about a fellow ex-pupil, Jay Walton. When it transpired that Jay wouldn't be attending, Bob said he would like to get in touch with him and so he asked where Jay lived:

(54)　Bob:　　Where does Jay live?
　　　　Alan:　　Somewhere in the South of France.[2]

Although Alan did not explicitly say so, if he was observing the CP (specifically trying to be as informative as appropriate for Bob's needs), he will have implied that he did not have any more specific information. The reasoning goes like this:

- There is no reason to suppose that Alan is deliberately shirking his conversational responsibilities and not observing the CP.
- Alan's answer is, as indeed he well knows, less informative than is required to meet Bob's needs – simply addressing a letter to 'Jay Walton, Somewhere in the South of France' is most unlikely to have been successful!
- This appears to be a violation of the maxim of quantity. (Make your contribution as informative as is required.)

■ An explanation for this apparent violation might be that had Alan been *more* informative, he would have violated the maxim of quality. (Don't say what you don't have evidence for.)

■ Therefore the implication is that Alan either does not know or can't remember which particular town in the South of France Jay lives in.

In British culture, it is considered more important not to tell untruths than to say what your interlocutor wants to hear. This is not necessarily the case for all cultures however.

We can FLOUT them (deliberately choose to not observe them)

On the whole, because we assume that participants in talk exchanges *do* adhere to these maxims, when a speaker appears to deliberately fail to observe any one of them (known as 'flouting' a maxim), a so-called conversational **implicature** obtains – since the hearer assumes that her interlocutor is observing the *overall* CP. In other words, in flouts, 'though some maxim is violated *at the level of what is said*, the hearer is entitled to assume that that maxim, or at least the overall Cooperative Principle, is observed *at the level of what is implicated*' (Grice 1975: 52, emphasis added).

Let's look at an example of how deliberately flouting the maxims leads to implied meanings.

(55)   Marjorie: Am I in need of a rather large gin and tonic after teaching pragmatics all afternoon!

        Joan: Well 'The Half Moon' is along the road ...

Considering only what Joan *says*, her response – even if truthful – seems to be rather obscure, bearing little relation to Marjorie's prior comment. It thus seems to be of little informative use to the thirsty pragmatics lecturer – Joan appears to be not adequately fulfilling her communicative role. However, if, rather than assuming she is being deliberately obtuse, it is assumed that Joan *is* following the CP and is *indeed* being informative, truthful, relevant and clear, then although she doesn't actually *say* so, Marjorie will be led to conclude that she is implying that 'The Half Moon' is a place which sells beverages (specifically, gin and tonic – in other words it isn't a coffee shop), that it will be open for the sale of such beverages and that the distance along the road which Marjorie would have to travel to get there is not unreasonable for the transport available. Since Joan will assume that Marjorie will assume that Joan is abiding by the CP and its maxims, Joan is able to imply all these things without actually saying them. And in this way, she is able to avoid an otherwise necessarily complex response such as in (55′):

(55′) Marjorie: Am I in need of a rather large gin and tonic after teaching pragmatics all afternoon!

       Joan: Well 'The Half Moon' is a place which sells beverages – specifically, gin and tonic – that will be open for the sale of such beverages and the distance along the road which you would have to travel to get there is not unreasonable for the transport available.

Implicature certainly has its uses and the following examples provide yet further evidence of this fact.

Flouting the maxim of quantity

(56) Interviewer: What do you think of Tony Blair as Prime Minister?
      Interviewee: He's always well dressed, he has a great smile and he likes jazz.

Here, by not providing sufficient information relating to Blair's qualities as a statesman, the interviewee has clearly flouted the maxim of quantity. However, rather than assume that they are being deliberately uncooperative, we instead assume that because the words themselves are apparently in violation of the maxim, the speaker must be *implying* something appropriately informative. Hence we are led to the inference that they do not rate him as prime minister. Very importantly, this type of implied inference is *not an entailment* – it is *not always necessarily true*, and as such, it is possible for it to be denied: should the interviewer explicitly confront the interviewee with this conclusion, the latter could always legitimately say that that was not what they had *said*!

If we are to be appropriately informative in our talk exchanges, we should always actually inform. That may seem too obvious to be worth mentioning – a tautology (necessary truth) in fact. And yet there are many expressions which when considered only at the level of the words uttered are indeed tautologous:

(57) Boys will be boys!

(58) What will be will be!

(59) It ain't over 'til it's over.

(60) When it's over it's over.

All these expressions have the underlying format of 'If P, then P', and, as can be seen, irrespective of what the proposition P is, the expression must necessarily always be true (hence they are all tautologies). As such, none of them should be able to *say* anything we don't already know. And indeed, they don't – but they do *imply* things.

The final pair of examples illustrate this point rather neatly: while on the surface they appear to be saying *exactly* the same thing (*if over, then over*), they *imply* different meanings – (59) implies that 'there is *still hope*' while (60) implies '*all hope is gone*'.

Flouting the maxim of quality

Alternatively, we can convey meaning implicitly by flouting the maxim of quality. Example (61) comes from a breakfast TV show where just before each advert break a celebrity did a small piece to camera. It was aired before 8am.

(61)   I'm Rufus and I'm asleep at the moment.

Clearly Rufus was literally not telling the truth. This utterance therefore contravenes the maxim of quality. And yet, rather than think that he was not following the CP, we assume that Rufus must have been trying to *imply* something. Thus we conclude that what he must have meant is that while obviously awake at the time of *recording*, at the projected time of *transmission* he would be asleep and in this way he is able to display some subtle (non-obvious) humour.

It is this assumption of implicit truthfulness which allows us to understand many non-literal expressions as idiomatic.

(62)   Marjorie: He got out of bed on the wrong side this morning.

Whenever someone says (62), it is nearly always the case that they can have no adequate supporting evidence: how could they possibly know which side of the bed he got out of, or indeed which side counts as the wrong one? And yet, rather than assume that the speaker is ignoring the second submaxim of quality by *saying* something for which they lack adequate evidence, we instead assume that they must be being cooperative in what they are *implying* (here, the idiomatic meaning that 'he' is in a grouchy mood). Again, note that this implicature is not an entailment as the idiom conclusion ('he is grouchy') could subsequently be reasonably denied (technically known as **cancelled**) as shown in Marjorie's third and final utterance in (63):

(63)   Marjorie: Have you seen your dad yet today?
       Timmy: No.
       Marjorie: He got out of bed on the wrong side this morning.
       Timmy: Oh! Is he grouchy?

Marjorie: No – the daft man got out of bed on my side and he's still wearing my slippers!

Flouting the maxim of relevance

(64)   Marjorie: Have you done your homework, Timmy?
        Timmy: What time's dinner?

Here, by changing the subject (by not being relevant), Timmy implies that he has not done his homework.

Flouting the maxim of manner

(65)   Marjorie: Has anyone taken the d-o-g for a w-a-l-k?

Although she is speaking in an obscure way, we wouldn't ordinarily assume that Marjorie is deliberately trying to be uncooperative. People often spell out (or otherwise avoid) words that should not, for some reason (often because they are taboo), be said out loud (such as the wizards in the Harry Potter books who cannot bring themselves to utter the name of the evil 'Lord Voldemort' and so instead use 'He Who Must Not Be Named' or 'You-Know-Who'). Thus we might infer that while the dog in (65) could perhaps understand the words *dog* and *walk*, it can't spell! Again, this is only an implicature, not an entailment – after all, Marjorie may often talk in this apparently odd way.

In case you are not convinced, consider the following examples where A, an **aphasic** individual (language impaired due to brain damage ➻ Unit 11), has problems with word retrieval, and yet is able to spell out words well enough to make himself understood. Indeed, this is apparently such a useful strategy that his non-aphasic interlocutor (B) also adopts it in (67) to ask about the elephant:

(66)   A   Is - is there anything in between the I-G-L-O-O and the
             house - and the dog?

        B   There's a noose.

(67)   A   And (2.2) I wonder (if) I've got that right 'cos we're no got
             a (1.4) hmm (1.9) and we're going to (2.0) a place that I (.)
             can't- can't say S-N-A-K-E?

        B   (1.0) Snake?=

        A   =Ye::s=

        B   =I don't have a snake. Where is the snake?

        A   Er (.) right north

```
B      (.hh) It's right north. Now do you have an elephant? (1.4)

       (.hh) Elephant (.) E-L-E->P-H-A-N-T?<=

A      =No

B      You don't have an elephant=

A      =No

B      OK. It's a bit confusing
```

SUMMARY

To interpret various speech acts we often need to go beyond literal meaning to get at speaker meaning. We often have to make inferences based on context. Not all these inferences will be entailments (and thus necessarily true in all circumstances). Some inferences will be implicatures that are generated because of a particular context.

When people use language, we assume they are being cooperative (in a Gricean sense) and are following Grice's maxims of conversation *viz.*: being informative, truthful, relevant and clear. We can adhere to these maxims; we can violate them because of a maxim clash; or we can flout (deliberately not observe) them to generate an implicature. Flouting a maxim will give rise to a conversational implicature since a speaker who might not appear to be observing the CP at the level of what is *said, can* be assumed to be observing the CP at the level of what is *implicated*. Importantly, while implicatures are inferences, they are not entailments, and can therefore be cancelled (denied).

What this unit has shown, then, is that in order to fully understand language in use – in order to be able to properly interpret utterances – we often need to consider issues such as *when* that language is used, *where* it is used, *who* it is used by, and what it is used *for* and *how*. Furthermore, very often we cannot rely solely on the literal meaning and syntactic ordering of the words in order to understand the intended meaning of an utterance. Much language is potentially ambiguous and for interpretation to be successful, various types of contextual knowledge as well as vital inferential processes and an assumption of cooperative linguistic behaviour are all required.

In short, a code model of language (whereby a speaker 'simply says the words' and a hearer 'simply decodes them' to get the intended message) is *too* simplistic to explain a great deal of actual language use and it is the discipline of pragmatics which is responsible for providing better explanations of how language is used in the interpretation of utterances.

FURTHER READING

There are many textbooks on pragmatics. *Pragmatics* (Peccei 1999) is an excellent entry level book full of good examples. *Pragmatics and Discourse* (Cutting 2002) is also a very accessible resource book for students, crammed with interesting examples and activities. Overall, I think *Doing Pragmatics* (Grundy 2000) offers perhaps the best all round introductory coverage: it is detailed, well exemplified, well written and, most of all, eminently understandable. That said, *Meaning in Interaction: An Introduction to Pragmatics* (Thomas 1995) covers some interesting ground and is especially good for aspects of indirectness. More comprehensive textbook coverage is offered in Mey's (2001) 392-page textbook, *Pragmatics*. Finally there is Levinson's (1983) 420-page *Pragmatics*. Despite (or maybe because of) its age, this is probably the widest referenced textbook on pragmatics – used both by lecturers and students. It is *very* thorough, but occasionally a little too technical for the novice. All serious linguists should own a copy eventually, though!

This unit has mainly covered speech acts and conversational implicature. Any serious investigators of these areas should really go to the original sources: *How To Do Things With Words* covers speech acts. Although it is written by Austin (1975), the father of speech act theory, it is really quite accessible and is certainly worth looking at. Grice's (1975) 'Logic and Conversation' is *the* canonical work on implicature (Grice 1999 is an edited version): every student of pragmatics should read it (at least once).

FURTHER ACTIVITY

 Activity 3.3

What implicatures might be generated by (68)–(70)? What (if any) special contexts are required?

(68) It's cold in here isn't it?!

(69) Have you had a fight with a lawnmower?

(70) Ben's crying!

COMMENTARY ON ACTIVITIES

Activity 3.1

You might have come up with interpretations such as these:

(16b)   We saw her bob down.
(e.g. to avoid hitting her head on a low doorway)

(16c)   We viewed her, and I'm your friend from Nottinghamshire/Derbyshire!
(*duck* is a term of endearment in some parts of the UK)

(16d)   We habitually cut up her waterfowl with a metal tool with jagged teeth.
(the additional meanings don't have to be pleasant!)

In English each of (16), (16b), (16c) and (16d) also has the added ambiguity of not being able to tell whether 'We' includes or excludes the hearer. This wouldn't be the case in Mandarin Chinese as it has two separate words for *we*: *za.men*, meaning 'us including the hearer(s)', and *wo.men*, meaning 'us excluding the hearer(s)'.

(17b)   'Hey – Damien! Paint only the walls which have the fluffy white lambs on!'

(17c)   'Hey – Damien! When you paint the walls, use fluffy white lambs instead of brushes!'
(the additional meanings are allowed to be bizarre)

(18b)   The scientist caught sight of the monkey which had run away with the telescope.

(18c)   The monkey with the telescope got painted with spots by the scientist.

(18d)   The scientist dipped the telescope in some paint and marked the monkey with spots.

(18e)   The scientist attended the monkey with the telescope while it was doing weight training.

(18f)   The scientist attended the monkey while it was doing weight training using the telescope.

Some of the above ambiguities are lexically ambiguous – they are caused by certain words having multiple meanings (➤ Unit 7 on **homophones**) and some are syntactically ambiguous – they are caused by the words having different functions within the sentence (➤ Unit 7 for how to analyse alternative syntactic structures). You might like to see if you can work out which of the ambiguities above are which.

Activity 3.2
Among many others, you may have thought of some of the following sorts of possible acts that each of the utterances might, in the right context, be *doing*:

(25)   York City beat Manchester Utd 4–3 on aggregate in the Coca Cola Cup.

Context 1:   Speaker = Manchester Utd fan; Hearer = Manchester Utd fan
Act 1:   complaining/doubting

Context 2:   Speaker = York City fan; Hearer = Manchester Utd fan
Act 2:   boasting/gloating/jibing/insulting

(26)   Theeree's someething eextreemeely wrong with thee <EE> keey on my computeer keeyboard.

Context 1:   Writing to a customer services department
Act 1:   complaining

Context 2:   Writing to your lecturer to explain why your assignment is poorly presented
Act 2:   explaining/excusing/apologizing

Context 3:   On a lecturer's OHP/Powerpoint lecture slide
Act 3:   explaining/excusing/apologizing/complaining

(27)   If you don't understand this unit you might find Grundy (2000) useful.

Context 1:   Speaker = Student; Hearer = Student
Act 1:   suggesting/advising/recommending

Context 2:   Speaker = Lecturer; Hearer = Student
Act 2:   suggesting/advising/recommending/demanding/ordering

Context 3:   Speaker = Student; Hearer = Lecturer
Act 3:   querying/mocking (doing the right **intonation** is important for mocking – as so often wonderfully illustrated by Eric Cartman in the cartoon series 'South Park')

(28)   There's a wasp in your ear.

Context 1:   There's a wasp in your ear
Act 1:   warning

Context 2:   Hearer didn't hear the Speaker's utterance the first time (presumably because there was a wasp in their ear)
Act 2:   clarifying

(29)   There's a piece of fish on the table.

Act 1:   complaining that the table hasn't been properly cleaned
Act 2:   warning someone not to let the cat into the kitchen
Act 3:   reassuring someone that dinner has not been forgotten
Act 4:   recriminating a child for raiding the refrigerator
Act 5:   offering of food
Act 6:   accusing someone of feeding the cat
Act 7:   mocking a whinging child (again, doing the right intonation)

Act 8:   consoling a friend who has just split up with his wife
            (some people are consoled by chocolate, some by alcohol, so there
            could be someone out there who might be ever so fond of fish!)
Act 9+:   and so on …

REFERENCES

Austin, J.L. (1975) *How to Do Things with Words*, 2nd edn, Oxford: Clarendon Press.

Cutting, J. (2002) *Pragmatics and Discourse: A Resource Book for Students*, London: Routledge.

Enç, M. (1988) 'The syntax–semantics interface', in F.J. Newmeyer (ed.) *Linguistics: The Cambridge Survey Volume I, Linguistic Theory: Foundations*, Cambridge: Cambridge University Press.

Gazdar, G. and Good, D. (1982) 'On a notion of relevance', in N. Smith (ed.) *Mutual Knowledge*, New York: Academic Press.

Grice, H.P. (1975) 'Logic and conversation', in P. Cole and J.L. Morgan (eds) *Syntax and Semantics 3: Speech Acts*, New York: Academic Press.

Grice, H.P. (1999) 'Logic and conversation', in A. Jaworski and N. Coupland (eds) *The Discourse Reader*, London: Routledge.

Grundy, P. (2000) *Doing Pragmatics*, 2nd edn, London: Edward Arnold.

Jaworski, A. and Coupland, N. (eds) (1999) *The Discourse Reader*, London: Routledge.

Levinson, S.C. (1983) *Pragmatics*, Cambridge: Cambridge University Press.

Mey, J. (2001) *Pragmatics: An Introduction*, 2nd edn, Oxford: Blackwell.

Peccei, J.S. (1999) *Pragmatics*, London: Routledge.

Sperber, D. and Wilson, D. (1995) *Relevance: Communication and Cognition*, 2nd edn, Oxford: Blackwell.

Thomas, J. (1995) *Meaning in Interaction: An Introduction to Pragmatics*, London: Longman.

NOTES

1 Sperber and Wilson (1995) have developed a theory of pragmatics (Relevance Theory) which claims that an assumption of relevance is really the only principle that is necessary.

2 Anyone who has read Grice's (1975) paper will see an uncanny resemblance to his example of 'Where does C live?'. It is indeed uncanny (and not plagiarism) as the exchange about Jay is 100 per cent true – as Andrew Merrison can testify!

4 POWER AND POLITENESS

UNIT CONTENTS

INTRODUCTION

This unit neatly links to ➤➤ Unit 3 because in many respects, power and politeness are both areas pertinent to applied pragmatics. Furthermore, power and politeness necessarily involve the analysis of interactional data which is most often talk (➤➤ Unit 2).

This unit provides a brief introduction to power, **face**, and face threatening acts (FTAs) to show that linguistic behaviour is linked to social **context**.

SOCIAL AND PRAGMATIC CONSEQUENCES OF LINGUISTIC CHOICE

In Unit 2 it is noted that conversation analysts should continually be asking of their data: WHY THAT NOW? In fact, in this book we would argue that any linguist interested in studying *language in use* should ask the same question. We always have a choice of what we say or write and one of the linguist's tasks is to uncover what *Choice X* does that *Choice Y* doesn't. Often the choices that we make differ in their social and pragmatic consequences. Consider something as relatively mundane as asking someone to get you a drink:

Example 4.1: Getting a Coke

The Scene

It's break time in a long linguistics seminar. Because you have been talking a lot, you're thirsty and want a drink. But you are also too exhausted to walk to the vending machine along the corridor and down two flights of stairs.

Below are seven choices for explicitly asking someone to get you a can of Coke. Rank them from least polite to most polite.

The Choices

(1)   Get me a Coke.
(2)   Get me a Coke, Andy!
(3)   You'll be a pal and get us a Coke won't you Andy?
(4)   Could you possibly get me a Coke from the machine please, Andy? I'll go next week.
(5)   If you're going to the machine, could you possibly get me a Coke while you're there please?
(6)   If you're going to the machine, would you possibly be so kind as to get me a Coke while you're there please?

(7)   I'm really sorry to ask, but if you're going to the machine, I'd be ever so grateful if you would possibly be so kind as to get me a Coke while you're there please.

A betting person might wager you had ranked these choices from (1)–(7), with (1) as the least polite and (7) as most polite. There are good reasons why you might have chosen this order and by the end of the unit you will be able to work out why.

But which of these choices would you *use* to ask someone to get you a can of Coke? The answer, hopefully, should be: 'It depends!'. More specifically, it would depend on who you are asking, how well you know them, how much power they have over you, how much effort it costs them to get the can of drink and perhaps even what benefits there might be for them if they get it. For example, you might use (1), (2) or (3) to your best friend, signalling the intimacy of your relationship (hence the friendliness of your request). On the other hand, you might choose (4) or (5) to a student in the class who you know less well. Finally, (6) and (7) are ways you just might ask your professor to get you the drink – (7) is almost certainly *not* a way to ask your best friend (they would think you were being sarcastic). Indeed, it is possibly so over the top that it verges on obsequiousness.

So in this unit we will investigate perhaps the most fundamental aspect of all language in use: linguistic choice – why do people choose to use language the way they do? Our answer covers issues of power and politeness (though in reality, these two concepts are intricately interlinked).

POWER

What, then, is power? This is actually a difficult question. Thornborrow (2002: 5) even likens it to a 'conceptual can of worms'. It is therefore not a question we can give a full answer to here (for further discussion, see Thornborrow 2002, Thomas *et al.* 2004 or Fairclough 2001). For now let's consider two definitions, both of which feature the term 'control'. For Fairclough, power 'is to do with powerful participants *controlling and constraining the contributions of non-powerful participants*' (2001: 38f., original emphasis). Brown and Levinson's (1987: 77) version is slightly more comprehensive:

> P[ower] … is the degree to which H[earer] can impose his own plans and his own self-evaluation … at the expense of S[peaker]'s plans and self-evaluation. In general there are two sources of P[ower] … material control (over economic distribution and physical force) and metaphysical control (over the actions of others …).

What both of these definitions allow for is the fact that power is not absolute and immutable but rather is contingent upon contextual factors. For example, when you are in a tutorial, your professor has power over you, but if they came to you for salsa lessons, you would have power over them. Activity 4.1 involves an example that happened recently.

 ### Activity 4.1 ⚬━

The scene
Abe (a linguist) telephones his sister. His 25 year old (ex-marine) police officer nephew (who normally lives away from home) answers. After some initial pleasantries, Abe gets to the purpose of his call.

The exchange[1]

		((telephone rings))
	Matt:	Hello?
	Abe:	Oh hi Matt. How're you doin'. How's that broken arm of yours.
05	Matt:	Oh it's okay thanks. (.) A bit itchy.
		((several turns omitted))
	Abe:	You've got *SKY*[2] haven't you.
	Matt:	At home, (.) yes.
	Abe:	Does that mean you can get *CBeebies*[3]?
10	Matt:	Hang on a minute mate, I'll just have a check.
		((long pause while Matt checks with his mum))
		Yes we can.
	Abe:	Can you do me a <u>hu:::ge</u> ↑fa↑vour.
	Matt:	Yeah?
15	Abe:	On *CBeebies* tonight,
	Matt:	Yeah?
	Abe:	At five to seven, *Newsround*[4] is on.
	Matt:	Yeah?
	Abe:	Could you possibly record it for me?=I'm interested in the
20		<u>exact</u> wording of the West Indian Cricket Board's apology for the West Indies' abysmal performance in the first test. They put up a quote of the apology and I keep missing it on terrestrial TV. Could you write it down for me and call me back with it?

25   Matt: Sure. No worries mate.
     Abe: Thanks ever so much. I'll talk to you later.
     Matt: Okay. Bye!
     Abe: Bye.

The questions
(a)   Who has what power in this interaction? Why?
(b)   What evidence of power is there? Is it linguistic or non-linguistic?
(c)   In what other possible scenarios (linguistic or otherwise) might there be a power differential between these participants? Why?

Activity 4.1 touched on some of the ways that social relations and situational contexts can determine who has what power to control the actions of less-powerful others – in short, who can expect to get their own way. The same sort of themes can be applied to all interactions where people want to achieve various goals. The basic point is this: to be successful in achieving your goal(s) you have to go about interacting in just the right way. To use an extreme example, it would be irrational and most churlish to attempt to get an extension for a linguistics essay from your professor by saying 'Give me an extension, bitch!'. To achieve our aims, we have to interact in a way that meets our addressee's expectations of how we should interact *in that particular context* and that often involves using linguistic politeness.

POLITENESS

For linguists, as Cutting notes (2002: 44, original emphasis), politeness does '*not* refer to the social rules of behaviour such as letting people go first through a door, or wiping your mouth on the serviette rather than on the back of your hand'. Nor is it simply a matter of saying *please* and *thank you* (think of the saying 'mind your Ps and Qs' – mind your *pleases* and *thank yous*), though that is indeed part of it. So what *is* politeness? There are many definitions depending who you read. Here is a collection ranging from the general to the more specific:

> 'Politeness' is the term we use to describe the extent to which actions, including the way things are said, match addressees' perceptions of how they should be performed.
>
> (Grundy 2000: 151)

> [Politeness refers] to whatever means are employed to display consideration for one's addressee's feelings (or face), regardless of the social distance between the speaker and the addressee.
>
> (Green 1996: 151)

> 'politeness' will be used to refer to behaviour which actively expresses positive concern for others, as well as non-imposing distancing behaviour.
>
> (Holmes 1995: 5)

Holmes' version comes closest to paraphrasing the highly influential ideas of Brown and Levinson (1987, 1999) who propose a theory of politeness phenomena heavily based on Goffman's (1967) notion of face (as in the phrases 'to lose face' and 'to save face') and the related face threatening acts (FTAs). Although their model has been incredibly influential, there are certainly criticisms to be levelled at, and also theoretical alternatives to, Brown and Levinson's ideas (for just some examples, see discussions in Watts *et al.* 1992; Eelen 2001 and Watts 2003). However, because it is so often necessary to have an understanding of Brown and Levinson's theory in order to be able to fully understand alternative models, it is an overview of Brown and Levinson's contribution which is the main concern of this unit.

Brown and Levinson (henceforth B&L) say that people have certain needs and that two of these are the need for freedom (autonomy) and the need to be valued (self-worth). And because these needs are fragile, they require careful tending by all participants involved.

While the following quotations are long, it is nevertheless useful to see how B&L (1987: 61) put it themselves:

> We make the following assumptions: that all competent adult members of a society[5] have (and know each other to have)
>
> (i)   'face', the public self-image that every member wants to claim for himself, consisting in two related aspects:
>
>   (a)   negative face: the basic claim to territories, personal preserves, rights to non-distraction – i.e. to freedom of action and freedom from imposition
>
>   (b)   positive face: the positive consistent self-image or 'personality' (crucially including the desire that this self-image be accepted and approved of) claimed by interactants
>
> (ii)   certain rational capacities, in particular consistent modes of reasoning from ends to the means that will achieve those ends.

A further assumption (1987: 61) which needs to be included is that:

In general, people cooperate (and assume each other's cooperation) in maintaining face in interaction, such cooperation being based on the mutual vulnerability of face. That is, normally everyone's face depends on everyone else's being maintained, and since people can be expected to defend their faces if threatened, and in defending their own to threaten others' faces, it is in general in every participant's best interest to maintain each others' face, that is to act in ways that assure the other participants that the agent is heedful of the assumptions concerning face given under (i) above.

Face threatening acts

So when people interact, they run the risk of threatening (and damaging) the face of those involved. As B&L say (1987: 65):

> certain kinds of acts intrinsically threaten face, namely those acts that by their nature run contrary to the face wants of the addressee and/or the speaker. By 'act' we have in mind what is intended to be done by a verbal or non-verbal communication, just as one or more 'speech acts' can be assigned to an utterance [➤ Unit 3].

Because it is possible to distinguish between positive face (self-worth) and negative face (autonomy), we can distinguish the sorts of acts that threaten each type of face.[6] This is done in the following sections which, while initially potentially tedious, will be crucial for applying B&L's ideas to data.

Threats to H's negative face

Closely following B&L (1987: 65f.), acts can threaten the hearer's (H's) negative face wants by indicating that the speaker (S) does not intend to avoid impeding H's freedom of action. For example:

(i)   acts that suggest that H will have to do some future act, A, and consequently put pressure on H to actually *do* (or refrain from doing) A:
    (a)   orders, requests
    (b)   suggestions, advice
    (c)   remindings
    (d)   threats, warnings, dares

(ii)   acts that suggest some positive future act on the part of S towards H which consequently put pressure on H to accept (or reject) and might therefore lead to H incurring a debt:

(a)   offers

(b)   promises

(iii)   acts that suggest some desire on the part of S towards H or H's goods which may put pressure on H either to protect the object of S's desire or to give it to S:

(a)   compliments, expressions of envy or admiration

(b)   expressions of strong negative emotions toward H (e.g. hatred, anger, lust).

Threats to H's positive face

When S indicates that they do not care about or are indifferent to H's feelings, H's positive face wants can be threatened. For example (still closely following B&L 1987: 66f.):

(i)   acts that suggest that S has a negative opinion of some aspect(s) of H's positive face:

(a)   expressions of disapproval, criticism, ridicule, complaints, reprimands, accusations, insults

(b)   contradictions, disagreements, challenges

(ii)   acts that suggest that S doesn't care about H's positive face:

(a)   expressions of violent emotions

(b)   irreverence, mention of taboo subjects

(c)   bringing bad news about H or good news about S

(d)   raising dangerously emotional or divisive topics

(e)   blatant non-cooperation

(f)   misuse of terms of address.

Just as acts can threaten the face of the Hearer, they can also threaten the face (negative and positive) of the Speaker. However, B&L treat these FTAs as less complicated by using a simple list (shown below) rather than a more complex system of categorization.

Threats to S's negative face

(a)   expressing thanks

(b)   accepting H's thanks or apology

(c)   excuses

(d)   accepting offers

(e)   ignoring H's *faux pas*

(f)   unwilling promises.

Threats to S's positive face

    (a)   apologizing

    (b)   accepting a compliment

    (c)   breakdown of physical control over body

    (d)   self-humiliation, self-contradiction, acting stupid

    (e)   confessing, admitting guilt or responsibility

    (f)   emotion leakage, non-control of laughter or tears.

Applying Brown and Levinson's ideas

If you have persevered this far through what must have seemed like an endless list, well done! Now comes the pay-off for your effort. Have a go at Activity 4.2.

 Activity 4.2 o—

The scene

A Friday night in 2003 in the UK. It was 9.30 pm and dark. Adam, a 38-year old white male, was walking along the street in a black suit, white shirt and black bow tie. He was carrying a briefcase. 50 metres ahead was a petrol station. 150 metres ahead was a newsagents and tobacconists. Two young teenage girls were walking a few paces in front of him wearing shell suits (casual sportswear).

The exchange[7]

01   Girl: Here mate c'n ya go to the shop for us please=

       Adam: =No.

03   Girl: Why?

       Adam: Because if you want *me* to go, it's for something illegal.

05   Girl: It's *only* for a packet of *FAGS*!![8]

The questions

Describe the face threatening acts going on in this exchange. You might find it useful to operate on a line-by-line basis asking yourself the following questions each time:

(a)   Whose face is threatened?

(b)   What type of face (positive/negative) is threatened?

(c)   What is it exactly that produces the threat?

(Hint: use the examples of face threatening acts given above.)

Calculating face threat

By now it should have become clear that engaging in normal interaction (either as Speaker or Hearer) runs the risk of losing face. Consequently, interactants have to jointly cooperate to maintain face, making sure to pay face whenever an FTA must be performed to meet the current goal. And that assumes we somehow know when an act is indeed a face threatening one and, more specifically, it assumes that we somehow know how *much* face paying is appropriate. How we gauge the seriousness of potential face loss is addressed in B&L's (1987: 76) formula expressed (in slightly modified form) as:

$$W_x = D(H,S) + P(H,S) + R_x$$

Where:
W_x = weightiness of FTA x
$D(H,S)$ = social distance between H and S
$P(H,S)$ = power H has over S
R_x = the degree to which FTA x is considered an imposition

This rather daunting-looking formula really isn't that scary. It's just a concise way of saying that the degree (or 'weightiness') of face threat caused by a speaker's act, x, depends on three main variables:

(*D*)   DISTANCE: how close (relatively speaking) the speaker is in social terms to their hearer (the less socially equivalent they are, the more threatening the speaker's act will seem – cf. asking a favour of friends vs. strangers); *and*

(*P*)   POWER: how much power (relatively speaking) the hearer can legitimately exert over the speaker (the more powerful the hearer, the more threatening the speaker's act will seem – cf. professors asking favours of their students vs. students asking favours of their professors); *and*

(*R*)   RANK: how imposing (relatively speaking) the act x is considered to be in the given culture (the more imposing, the more threatening the speaker's act will seem – cf. asking for the time vs. asking to borrow someone's brand new BMW).

B&L note that any numbers used in this formula represent only relative values (hence the 'relatively speaking' in each of the above). Furthermore, they suggest (1987: 287 footnote 18) that values between 1 and 7 ('or so') may be adequate for each variable. On this assumption then, an act which scores 21/21 can be thought of as extremely face threatening indeed, while one that scores just 3/21 will be hardly threatening at all. While on the subject of relativism, we should always remember that different interactants may differ in their estimates of D, P and R.

Two further very important points still need to be made about this weightiness formula. First, the degree of face threat depends upon the *combination* of *D*, *P* and *R*. In other words it doesn't matter whether a score of, say, 9 is made up of $D=2 + P=3 + R=4$, or $D=4 + P=3 + R=2$, or $D=1 + P=1 + R=7$, or … whatever. For B&L, a weightiness value of *N* is just a weightiness value of *N* and how *N* is actually made up is essentially irrelevant![9] Second (and more fundamental to B&L's theory) is the assumption that whenever an FTA must be performed to meet the current goal, the speaker should redress any face loss, paying compensatory face by using the most appropriate of five possible linguistic strategies.

Compensatory linguistic strategies

(1) Do the FTA on record (explicitly) without redressive action, baldly (i.e. directly, concisely, clearly, and unambiguously – cf. Grice's maxims ⇥ Unit 3).

(2) Do the FTA on record (explicitly) with positive politeness as redress (discussed below).

(3) Do the FTA on record (explicitly) with negative politeness as redress (discussed below).

(4) Do the FTA off record (implicitly ⇥ Unit 3).

(5) Don't do the FTA at all (it just ain't worth it!).

Which strategy is chosen depends on the estimation of the weightiness of the face threat (W_x): with a low estimation of risk of face loss, a speaker should choose a low numbered strategy; with a higher estimation of risk of face loss, a speaker should choose a higher numbered one. If the estimated risk is extremely high, then a speaker may consider it socially and pragmatically more sensible to entirely forego achieving their current goal and hence not attempt the act in any form whatsoever. These ranked options are set out in Figure 4.1 (based on B&L 1987: 69).

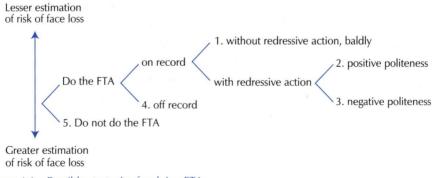

Figure 4.1 Possible strategies for doing FTAs

If we were to take B&L's values of '1 to 7 or so' to be 1–9 (for they do themselves (in their footnote 18) mention Miller's 'magical number 7 ± 2' ➤➤ Unit 11), we would reap the advantage of being able to neatly categorize each estimated relative value for D, P and R as being *low* (1–3), *mid* (4–6) or *high* (7–9). A range of 1–9 would also conveniently allow for W_x to have values from 3–27, which would then conveniently sub-divide into five equal sub-ranges: sub-range 1 = W_x values of 3–7; sub-range 2 = W_x values of 8–12; sub-range 3 = W_x values of 13–17; sub-range 4 = W_x values of 18–22; and sub-range 5 = W_x values of 23–27. From there we could make a working hypothesis that a W_x value in any sub-range would correspond to the equivalent-numbered linguistic strategy.

While such equally divided ranges are certainly a theoretical possibility, it is important to note that B&L do *not* make such a strong claim. Rather, their assumptions simply predict that rational people 'will choose a higher-numbered strategy as the threat increases' (B&L 1987: 83). Exactly how the W_x values co-vary with the linguistic strategy numbers will always be an empirical matter and, of course, it may well also be culture-specific.

Activity 4.3 looks more closely at these five possible strategies.

 ## Activity 4.3 ⚬━

The scene

Several weeks ago, Arthur's fairly new neighbours, James and Hannah, had a window put into the attic of their house. He can only guess that this was in the bedroom of Megan (the teenage daughter of the house), for on the evening of the window's installation a 'young gentleman caller' spent a considerable time 'conversing' with her as she draped herself out of the new aperture. Having recently breathed sighs of relief at the relocation of the previous occupants (who had a teenage daughter to whom many vulgar male teenage youths seemed to be inexorably and permanently attracted), he had visions of the tone of the neighbourhood plummeting. So here was his very real dilemma. Given that he would much rather live in a 'nice' neighbourhood than in a street awash with malingering sexually charged teenagers shouting at the top of their voices all night long, his goal was to get this type of undesirable pubescent behaviour to cease. His dilemma was how to do so. Fortunately, being a linguist, he had B&L to provide possible solutions – he obviously had a choice of five possible strategies. He also had other linguists to discuss this with later!

The choices

He could have chosen to:

(8)   do the FTA on record without redressive action, baldly
      'Tell your daughter to stop lowering the tone of the neighbourhood
      by hanging out of the attic window and shouting to her boyfriend
      down at street level.'

(9)   do the FTA on record with positive politeness redressive action
      'Hey Jim, I bet you had something to say last night about Megan's
      boyfriend's less than high standards of social considerateness didn't
      you?!'

(10) do the FTA on record with negative politeness redressive action
      'I'm sorry to ask, but could you possibly ask your daughter to be a
      tad quieter in the evenings in future please? Thanks.'

(11) do the FTA off record
      'Are you all enjoying the benefits of the new attic conversion?'

(12) not do the FTA at all

The questions

(a)   Which option do you think he chose?

(b)   Why? (Hint: think about possible values of D, P, R and hence, W_x.)

(c)   What possible consequences might his choice have had?

(d)   What possible consequences might each of the other four choices
      have had?

Politeness strategies

We have been discussing positive and negative politeness rather generally for some
time. Now it is time to put some flesh on the bones of these terms. In other words,
what *counts* as positive and negative politeness? In short, positive politeness is
linguistic behaviour signalling that the speaker wants/needs/appreciates (at least
some of) the same things as the hearer. Negative politeness is linguistic behaviour
which signals that the speaker recognizes the hearer's fundamental right to
unimpeded action. Using editorial brackets, we can now return to Holmes' (1995:
5) definition that we encountered earlier:

> 'politeness' will be used to refer to behaviour which actively expresses
> positive concern for others [positive politeness], as well as non-imposing
> distancing behaviour [negative politeness].

In the next two sections we provide more specific (though still general) examples of each of these types of behaviour.

Positive politeness strategies

The following list (taken from B&L 1987: 101–129) should begin to offer some ideas of ways of paying positive face. That B&L take 28 pages to do this while we use less than one should indicate that for anyone interested, there are plenty more details to be had than supplied here. While each example is numbered as in B&L, we have added a '+' to indicate these as positive politeness strategies. Note that the order of occurrence of these strategies does *not* reflect any degree of politeness.

Claim common ground

(+1)   Notice/attend to H's wants
(+2)   Exaggerate interest/approval/sympathy in/of/with H
(+3)   Intensify interest for H (use question tags; direct quotes; historic present)
(+4)   Use in-group identity markers (solidarity address forms; dialect; slang; contraction)
(+5)   Seek agreement (safe topics; repetition)
(+6)   Avoid disagreement (token agreement; pseudo-agreement; white lies)
(+7)   Presuppose/assert common ground (gossip; speak from H's point of view (use H's deictic centre); presuppose H's knowledge)
(+8)   Joke

Convey that S and H are cooperators

(+9)   Assert knowledge of H's wants
(+10)   Offer, promise
(+11)   Be optimistic (reduce degree of imposition)
(+12)   Include S and H in the activity
(+13)   Give (or ask for) reasons (why not …?)
(+14)   Assume/assert reciprocity (you scratch my back …)

Fulfil H's want for some X

(+15)   Give gifts to H (goods, sympathy, compliments …)

Negative politeness strategies

The following list (taken from B&L 1987: 129–211) illustrates ways of paying negative face. Again, we are forced into brevity, reducing B&L's 82 pages to half a page. Also again, each example is numbered as in B&L, but with a '–' to indicate these as negative politeness strategies. The order of occurrence of strategies does not reflect any degree of politeness.

Be direct

(–1)   Be conventionally indirect

Don't presume/assume

(–2)   Question, hedge

Don't coerce H

(–3)   Be pessimistic
(–4)   Minimize imposition
(–5)   Give deference (humble yourself; treat H as superior)

Communicate S's want to not impinge on H

(–6)   Apologize
(–7)   Impersonalize S and H (avoid pronouns *I* and *you*)
(–8)   State the FTA as a general rule
(–9)   Nominalize

Redress other wants of H's

(–10)   Go on record as incurring a debt

And so, at last, we are in a position to apply these strategies to our set of 'Coke utterances' from Example 4.1 at the beginning of this unit.

 Activity 4.4 ⚬━

(a)   Return to example 4.1 and work out which strategies are being used in each **utterance**.
      NB: you may well find more than one type of strategy in each.
(b)   Has this helped you understand why the utterances seem more polite as you go down the list?

There are three important points that still need making. First, although this account has mainly been concerned with various types of strategy for dealing with *on-record* FTAs, B&L also devote 16 pages to 15 ways of paying face off-record. Second, it must be made clear that being linguistically polite does not necessarily entail sincerity: there may actually be no common ground, no optimism, no intention of reciprocity, no deference, no regret at imposition and so on. All that matters, however, is the fact that someone *made the effort* to go through the motions of politeness and it is this effort that makes an act of linguistic politeness polite. And third, the examples in this unit have presented a somewhat Anglo-centric view of linguistic politeness – cross-cultural differences are not only possible, they are to be expected!

SUMMARY

This unit has investigated Brown and Levinson's theory of politeness in language use (incorporating a brief discussion of issues relating to power) and in doing so, has shown that linguistic behaviour is linked to social context. People always have a choice of what they say or write and it is the linguist's task to uncover how those choices differ in their social and pragmatic consequences – even in interactional tasks as socially diverse as asking someone to: (i) get a can of Coke, (ii) watch TV and write something down, (iii) buy cigarettes, or (iv) curb the behaviour of antisocial children.

In short, the take-home message of this unit is that by using redressive action in the form of appropriate linguistic politeness strategies, we are likely to be more successful in achieving the goals which our language use is employed to serve than if we paid no heed of our fellow humans' need for freedom (autonomy) and their need to be valued (self-worth).

FURTHER READING

For more encompassing discussions of power, see *Language, Society and Power* (Thomas *et al.* 2004) or *Power Talk* (Thornborrow 2002). For a quick and gentle coverage of politeness issues, see *Pragmatics* (Peccei 1999). For more general discussions see *Pragmatics and Discourse* (Cutting 2002), *Doing Pragmatics* (Grundy 2000) or *Meaning in Interaction: An Introduction to Pragmatics* (Thomas 1995). For details of B&L's theory see Brown and Levinson's *Politeness: Some Universals in Language Usage* (edited highlights are in their 1999 paper, while 1987 is the full version). For an alternative, maxim-based approach to politeness, see *Principles of Pragmatics* (Leech 1983). Finally, *Politeness in Language* (Watts *et al.* 1992), *A Critique of Politeness Theories* (Eelen 2001) and *Politeness* (Watts 2003) are all very good places to start any serious critical investigations (which should also include Goffman's classic 1967 or 1999 paper *On Face-Work*). Fruitful sources for journal articles include the *Journal of Pragmatics*, *Multilingua* and the newly founded *Journal of Politeness Research*.

FURTHER ACTIVITY

 Activity 4.5

Using the ideas discussed in this unit (with a particular emphasis on the social and pragmatic consequences of a speaker's various choices), provide analyses of the following data:

The scene
It's the beginning of a committee meeting. The chairperson has forgotten to bring paper.

The choices
(13) Give me some paper.
(14) Has anybody got a bit of paper I can have?
(15) Has anybody got a little bit of paper I can have?
(16) Has anybody got a little bit of paper I can borrow?

COMMENTARY ON ACTIVITIES

Activity 4.1
(a)   Who has what power in this interaction?
Both participants have power but for different reasons. Abe has power over Matt because Matt is his nephew and so Abe 'can impose his own plans' because of family seniority (respect your elders). Also, simply by calling, Abe has summoned Matt to the phone – if Abe had not called, Matt would still have been doing whatever he was doing. On the other hand, Matt has power over Abe because he can refuse to provide the service Abe wants. Because getting a service is the purpose of the call, Matt arguably has the most power overall.

(b)   What evidence of power is there? Is it linguistic or non-linguistic?
In order of appearance in the activity, power is evidenced as follows:

Exhibit A: Non-linguistic
Matt is 25. Abe is older. Abe has age on his side.

Exhibit B: Non-linguistic
Abe is Matt's uncle. Abe has family hierarchy on his side.

Exhibit C: Linguistic
Abe goes through the motions of initial pleasantries. In situations where power is more rigidly defined (say in the marines or the police force), requests (or orders) can (must?) be made more bluntly. Abe's power is therefore somewhat mitigated (cf. Exhibit D).

Exhibit D: Linguistic

Abe doesn't straightforwardly ask Matt to record the TV programme. Instead he builds his request with three **pre-requests** (lines 7, 9, 13), each of which offers Matt a possible reason to justify not doing the favour (they may not have satellite TV; they may not get the CBeebies channel; Matt might not want/be able to do Abe a favour). The request itself is also built in three instalments (lines 15, 17, 19–24) and the first two of these provide further opportunities for Matt to refuse (maybe Matt is busy tonight; maybe he is busy at five to seven).

Exhibit E: Linguistic

In L10, Matt forthrightly tells Abe to 'Hang on a minute' – in essence, here he is imposing his own plans on Abe.

Exhibit F: Linguistic

By L12, Matt would realize that Abe wasn't asking all this just for information, but rather was leading up to a request (that is after all the purpose of pre-requests). And yet in L12 he doesn't pre-empt Abe with something like 'Yes we can, do you want us to record something?'. Instead he waits for Abe to go on record as needing help.

Exhibit G: Linguistic

In lines 19–24, Abe makes the request (record *Newsround*) with an **indirect speech act** 'could you …' (➤ Unit 3) which deflects the force of the imposition. He then provides an account of why it is important for him ('I'm interested in the exact wording of …') and justifies why he can't do the task himself ('I keep missing it on terrestrial TV'). Finally Abe makes two more indirect requests ('Could you write it down for me and call me back with it?'). While you might intuitively think otherwise, the second of these ('Could you … call me back with it?') can actually signal subservience because if Abe were to offer to do the calling back, that might mean again imposing on Matt's free time. If Matt calls, he can decide to do so when it suits him.

Exhibit H: Linguistic

In L25, Matt chooses to say 'No worries'. This signals (even if only in a highly conventionalized form) that Matt recognizes that Abe's request may have been something that Abe was worried about. In other words, it signals that Abe is subservient to Matt.

Exhibit I: Linguistic

In L26, Abe says 'Thanks ever so much'. This serves three functions: (i) it fairly explicitly puts his debt on record; (ii) it signals the degree of gratitude is non-trivial ('ever so much') and hence (iii) it signals that Abe is subservient to Matt.

(c)   In what other possible scenarios might there be a power differential? Why?
Here are some suggestions.

Whenever Matt wants a favour from Abe the roles would be reversed.

If Abe ever delivered a course on **communication** skills to the Metropolitan Police force, Abe and Matt would be in a teacher–student relationship and Abe would hold power.

In a legal altercation, Matt would have power over Abe as Matt is an officer of the law.

In any type of physical contest Matt would have power over Abe: Matt used to be an anti-tank commando in the marines, Abe is an academic. Matt is 190cm tall and 87kg of mainly muscle, while Abe is 177cm and 115kg of mainly fat!

Activity 4.2

Line 1

Girl: Here mate c'n ya go to the shop for us please=

(a)   Whose face is threatened?
        Adam's (Hearer's).
(b)   What type of face is threatened?
        Negative face: Girl is imposing on Adam, putting pressure on him to do something for her.
(c)   What is it exactly that produces the threat?
        Negative face: (type i, sub-type a) request.

Line 2

Adam: =No.

(a)   Whose face is threatened?
        Girl's (Hearer's).
(b)   What type of face is threatened?
        Positive face: Adam suggests that he doesn't care about Girl's wants.
(c)   What is it exactly that produces the threat?
        Positive face: (type ii.e) blatant non-cooperation.

Line 3

Girl: Why?

(a)   Whose face is threatened?
        Adam's (Hearer's).
(b)   What type of face is threatened?
        Negative face: Girl is putting pressure on Adam to respond with an account for his non-cooperation (cf. the power of the first parts of **adjacency pairs** ➤ discussed in Unit 2).
        Positive face: Girl suggests that she has a negative opinion of Adam's action and that she doesn't care about his feelings.
(c)   What is it exactly that produces the threat?
        Negative face: (type i.a) request.
        Positive face:
            (type i.a) expression of disapproval, criticism, complaint
            (type i.b) challenge
            (type ii.d) raising dangerously divisive topic.

Line 4

Adam: Because if you want *me* to go, it's for something illegal.

(a)   Whose face is threatened?
         Girl's (Hearer's).

(b)   What type of face is threatened?
         Positive face: Adam suggests that he has a negative opinion of Girl.

(c)   What is it exactly that produces the threat?
         Positive face: (type i.a) expression of disapproval, criticism, reprimand, accusation.

Line 5

Girl: It's *only* for a packet of *FAGS*!!

(a)   Whose face is threatened?
         Adam's (Hearer's)
         Girl's (Speaker's).

(b)   What type of face is threatened?
         Adam's (H's) negative face: Girl's anger may put pressure on Adam to protect himself.
         Adam's (H's) positive face: Girl suggests that she has a negative opinion of Adam's action and that she doesn't care about his feelings.
         Girl's (S's) negative face.
         Girl's (S's) positive face.

(c)   What is it exactly that produces the threat?
         Adam's (H's) negative face: (type iii.b) expression of strong negative emotion (anger).
         Adam's (H's) positive face:
             (type i.a) expression of disapproval, criticism, ridicule, complaint
             (type i.b) challenge
             (type ii.a) expression of violent emotion (cf. emphasis and volume).
         Girl's (S's) negative face: (type c) excuse (Adam has just criticized Girl who has consequently been pressured into providing a good reason for her initial request).
         Girl's (S's) positive face: (type f) emotion leakage (anger – cf. Proverbs (a) ch 16, v. 32: 'He that is slow to anger is better than the mighty' and Proverbs (b) ch 29, v. 11: 'Stupid people express their anger openly, but sensible people are patient and hold it back').

Activity 4.3

(a)   Which option do you think Arthur chose?
         In fact, he chose the final option: he did not mention the event in any way whatsoever.

(b)   Why?
         Although James was a neighbour, he was a relatively new one. They were, therefore, essentially strangers. In other words, the social distance between them, *D*, was quite high (say 8 out of 9).

Similarly, James had potentially a lot of power over Arthur. He was certainly in a position to refuse Arthur's 'request'. He would also have been in a position to wreak some form of revenge (say by scratching Arthur's car, by making nuisance phone calls, or even by depositing undesirable material through his letterbox)! In other words, P was also high (say 8 out of 9).

Finally, telling anyone that their child's behaviour is undesirable is a double-edged (and thus doubly-dangerous) sword: not only is the child insulted, but also, indirectly, so is the parent for it is they, after all, who has been responsible for the upbringing of their offspring. Insulting someone's child risks getting verbal and possibly even physical abuse in return. In other words, R was very high (possibly even 9 out of 9).

Adding these values for D, P and R together yields a W_x score of 25/27 – clearly in the upper range of weightiness values. Consequently, it is perhaps not so surprising that FTA avoidance was the chosen option.

(c)   What possible consequences might Arthur's choice have had?

The best consequence of his (rationally chosen) option was continued neighbourly social relations (as James and his family were never actually offended). Hence there was no reason for a scratched car, verbal/physical abuse, or even nasty letterbox surprises. Indeed, avoiding the issue was so the right choice, as this type of anti-social teenage behaviour hasn't been repeated thus proving that sometimes it is indeed best to hold back (Proverbs (b) ch 29, v. 11).

(d)   What possible consequences might each of the other four choices have had?

Any of the first three options would almost certainly have led to some (though admittedly varying) degree of ill-feeling and possibly even concomitant revengeful acts.

The fourth option (of doing the FTA off-record) could have had two possible outcomes. On the one hand, the FTA might not have been recognized for what it was (request/complaint) which would thus have made it ineffective. This is always a possibility with implicit acts (➡ Unit 3). On the other hand, assuming the illocutionary force of the off-record act was recognized (as a request/complaint), if the response had been obviously hostile, Arthur could have legitimately denied the offending **implicature**. It is this deniability (**cancellation**) of implicatures that makes them so very useful in social interaction.

Activity 4.4

(a)   All these requests are explicit. All redressive actions are therefore 'on-record'. Below each utterance we pair linguistic items with corresponding politeness strategies (noted in parentheses).

(1)   Get me a Coke.

This is simply a bald on-record request (in the syntactic form of an **imperative** order).

Total number of strategies: 0 positive; 0 negative.

(2)   Get me a Coke, Andy!
Andy (+4).
Total number of strategies: 1 positive; 0 negative.

(3)   You'll be a pal and get us a Coke won't you Andy?
You'll be … won't you? (+11); a pal (+4); us (+4); won't you (+3)/(–2); Andy (+4).
Total number of strategies: 5 positive; 1 negative.

(4)   Could you possibly get me a Coke from the machine please, Andy? I'll go next week.
Could you (–1)/(–2); possibly (–3); please (–1)/(–10); Andy (+4); I'll go next week (+14).
Total number of strategies: 2 positive; 5 negative.

(5)   If you're going to the machine, could you possibly get me a Coke while you're there please?
If you're going to the machine (–4); could you (–1)/(–2); possibly (–3); while you're there (–4); please (–1)/(–10).
Total number of strategies: 0 positive; 7 negative.

(6)   If you're going to the machine, would you possibly be so kind as to get me a Coke while you're there please?
If you're going to the machine (–4); would you (–1)/(–2); possibly (–3); be so kind (+15)/(–5); while you're there (–4); please (–1)/(–10).
Total number of strategies: 1 positive; 8 negative.

(7)   I'm really sorry to ask, but if you're going to the machine, I'd be ever so grateful if you would possibly be so kind as to get me a Coke while you're there please.
I'm really sorry to ask (–6); if you're going to the machine (–4); I'd be ever so grateful (–10); if you would (–1)/(–2)/(–3); possibly (–3); be so kind (+15)/(–5); while you're there (–4); please (–1)/(–10).
Total number of strategies: 1 positive; 11 negative.

(b)   These results point to several basic observations about linguistic politeness in British culture:

  (i)   it is entirely possible to use both positive and negative strategies within the same utterance – even though B&L's broad categorization seems to imply a clear-cut, 'either/or' distinction

  (ii)   up to a point, the more polite utterances use more strategies (but too many may result in implied sarcasm)

  (iii) positive politeness tends to decrease in more polite utterances

  (iv)   negative politeness tends to increase in more polite utterances

(v)   where utterances have equal amounts of linguistic politeness (as in (4) and (5) with seven strategies in each), it is the one with more negative strategies which is likely to be considered more polite overall

(vi) at a more simplistic level, it is often longer utterances which appear more polite.

These observations are represented in Figures 4.2 and 4.3:

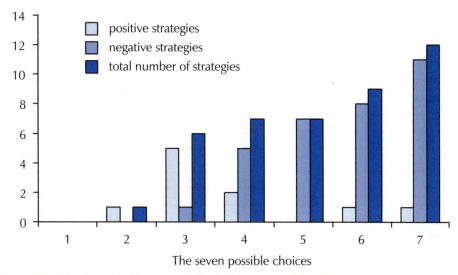

Figure 4.2   Number of politeness strategies in the seven possible Coke utterances

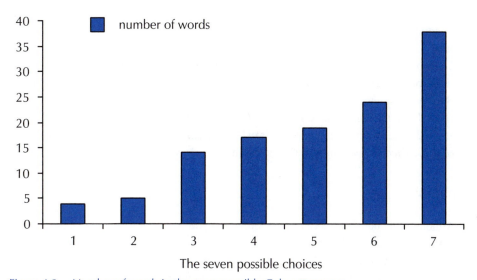

Figure 4.3   Number of words in the seven possible Coke utterances

REFERENCES

Brown, P. and Levinson, S.C. (1987) *Politeness: Some Universals in Language Usage*, Cambridge: Cambridge University Press.

Brown, P. and Levinson, S.C. (1999) 'Politeness: some universals in language usage', in A. Jaworski and N. Coupland (eds) *The Discourse Reader*, London: Routledge.

Clark, H.H. (1996) *Using Language*, Cambridge: Cambridge University Press.

Cutting, J. (2002) *Pragmatics and Discourse: A Resource Book for Students*, London: Routledge.

Eelen, G. (2001) *A Critique of Politeness Theories*, Manchester: St Jerome Publishing.

Fairclough, N. (2001) *Language and Power*, 2nd edn, Harlow: Longman.

Goffman, E. (1967) 'On Face-Work: an analysis of ritual elements in social interaction', in E. Goffman *Interaction Ritual: Essays on Face-To-Face Behavior*, New York: Pantheon Books.

Goffman, E. (1999) 'On Face-Work: an analysis of ritual elements in social interaction', in A. Jaworski and N. Coupland (eds) *The Discourse Reader*, London: Routledge.

Green, G.M. (1996) *Pragmatics and Natural Language Understanding*, 2nd edn, Hillsdale, NJ: Lawrence Erlbaum Associates.

Grundy, P. (2000) *Doing Pragmatics*, 2nd edn, London: Edward Arnold.

Holmes, J. (1995) *Women, Men and Politeness*, Harlow: Longman.

Jaworski, A. and Coupland, N. (eds) (1999) *The Discourse Reader*, London: Routledge.

Leech, G. (1983) *Principles of Pragmatics*, Harlow: Longman.

Levinson, S.C. (1983) *Pragmatics*, Cambridge: Cambridge University Press.

Peccei, J.S. (1999) *Pragmatics*, London: Routledge.

Proverbs (a), in *The Holy Bible*, King James Version.

Proverbs (b), in *Good News Bible*, (1976) London: Collins.

Thomas, J. (1995) *Meaning in Interaction: An Introduction to Pragmatics*, Harlow: Longman.

Thomas, L., Wareing, S., Singh, I., Peccei, J.S., Thornborrow, J. and Jones, J. (2004) *Language, Society and Power: An Introduction*, 2nd edn, London: Routledge.

Thornborrow, J. (2002) *Power Talk: Language and Interaction in Institutional Discourse*, Harlow: Longman.

Watts, R.J. (2003) *Politeness*, Cambridge: Cambridge University Press.

Watts, R.J., Ide, S. and Ehlich, K. (eds) (1992) *Politeness in Language: Studies in its History, Theory and Practice*, Berlin: Mouton de Gruyter.

NOTES

1 Although this data was not audio recorded, CA transcription conventions are used to represent the interaction as best as possible. Although details are certainly not fully accurate, the transcript is sufficient to serve current purposes.

2 'SKY' is the trade name of a satellite television provider.

3 'CBeebies' is a UK TV channel for young children.

4 'Newsround' is a news and current affairs programme for children.

5 Here, Brown and Levinson add this footnote: 'Juvenile, mad, incapacitated persons partially excepted'.

6 Although the terms 'positive face' and 'negative face' are used in this unit (in line with B&L's usage), these are actually potentially dangerous labels – it is often mistakenly assumed that 'positive' face is inherently *good*, and 'negative' face inherently *bad*. We therefore prefer Clark's (1996) terms: *self-worth* and *autonomy* which avoid this possible confusion.

7 Although this data was not audio recorded, CA transcription conventions are used to represent the interaction as best as possible. Although details are certainly not fully accurate, the transcript is sufficient to serve current purposes.

8 In the UK 'fags' is a slang term for cigarettes.

9 Whether the supposed irrelevance of the make up of W_x should be accepted entirely without question is a matter well worth considering – though sadly not one we can take up here.

5 WORDS

INTRODUCTION

A section of a newspaper article that is going to be analysed in this unit was headed 'The noughties'. What does *noughties* mean? If you don't know, how about looking it up in a dictionary?

It was the last in a series of headings: *The fifties*, *The sixties*, …, *The nineties*, *The noughties*. If you didn't already know, you can presumably now see that *noughties* is used to refer to the years 2000–2009. It is a newish word, as shown by the fact that it did not turn up, even once, in a very large representative sample of late twentieth-century British English writing and speech (see the biggest table on the website associated with Leech *et al*. 2001).

What do people know when they know a **language**? Rules of **grammar** (➻ Unit 7), conventions for use (➻ Units 3 and 9), a pronunciation system (➻ Unit 8) and – as everyone is aware – lots of **words**: the vocabulary of the language.

A word is a like a knot joining some threads. Each word joins a meaning (➻ Unit 6) to a pronunciation (➻ Unit 8; a spelling too for people who can read and write) and a syntactic word class (e.g. **noun**, **adjective**, **conjunction**; ➻ Unit 7). For instance, learning the word that is spelt <annoy> involves getting to know that the meaning 'make mildly angry' goes with the pronunciation [əˈnɔɪ] and fits into sentences as a **verb**. Vocabulary learning requires storage of many items in memory (➻ Unit 11), and the main aim of the present unit is to look at how many words a language user needs. The quantity and the different kinds of words needed can be gauged from the occurrence of words in **texts**. Don't worry: if you can count and work out percentages, the unit should be intelligible to you.

Quantifying word usage requires decisions about what will be counted. If we want to know how long a chapter of a book is we could count pages. Newspaper articles were traditionally measured in column inches. The length of a speech could be given in minutes. But pages come in many sizes, columns in various widths and some people talk faster than others; and what if we want to compare the length of a written chapter with the length of a speech? The number of words in a speech or chapter is one reasonable way of indicating length. Every occurrence of a word has to be counted; repetitions of words that have appeared earlier add to the total.

But that is not how words are counted when talking about **vocabulary** size. For example a claim that a young child has a vocabulary of about 100 words soon after age one and a half years (➻ Unit 10) is based on counting different words that the child knows; repetitions do not add to the total. Thus a repetition counts for just as much as a different word when measuring the length of a text, but repetitions count for nothing when we are estimating how varied a person's vocabulary or the usage of words in a text is. These distinct notions of what counts as a word will be explained in more detail later.

When words are counted, questions soon arise regarding the sorts of difference that can be ignored when lumping items together as different forms of 'the same word'. *Chalk* and *cheese* are obviously different, but is *cheesy* a different word from *cheese*, or just a different form of the same word, and what about *cheesed* in *cheesed off*, or the fact that *chalk* can be either a noun (as in *a piece of chalk*) or a verb (as in *chalk it up*)?

Vocabulary involves more than just the remembering of items. When words are built up out of meaningful parts, there are recurring patterns (consider, for example, *football* or *handball*, made from *foot* or *hand* plus *ball*; or the making of the nouns *manager* and *teacher* by putting the **suffix** {*-er*} on to the verbs *manage* and *teach*). A short account of word-building is the final topic in this unit, because it is needed as part of a framework for understanding what is being done when occurrences are either grouped together or treated as different.

Here is an example of how memorized items are distinct from assembly according to patterns. Assuming you agree that 5,280 is a bigger number than 4,840, how do you know that? You are not likely to have learnt it as a specific item: '5,280 is bigger than 4,840'. Presumably you learnt principles about numbers, and those principles can be used to compare any two numbers for size.

How about the label for one's head: the English word *head*? If you know the word, then it is surely something you learnt as a specific item. People who know French have learnt, as an item, that that body part is called *tête*; and German speakers store in their memories the word *Kopf* for the same thing. That different languages can have different words for 'head' indicates that the connection between a word and its meaning can be a matter of arbitrary convention (➤ Unit 1). Neither *head* nor *Kopf* nor *tête* can be split into smaller parts that contribute separately to the meaning. Memorization is the only way to handle arbitrary conventions. A word like *fire-fighter*, on the other hand, has meaningful parts (*fire*, *fight* and {*-er*}) that give hints about the meaning of the whole word.

 Activity 5.1 ⚿

An *undertaker* is not a person who carries things into a cellar, nor someone who conducts tours to Australia. An undertaker (in the USA, a *mortician*) has the job of seeing to the arrangements for funerals.

Suggest what the following words *might* have meant on account of the meanings of their parts and say what they generally do mean in English.

a *cooker*   a *password*
a *windbreak*   an *egghead*
to *overtake*

It might seem that the words in Activity 5.1 are a selection of weird ones that happen to have somewhat unpredictable meanings. Perhaps we would see principles at work in a more normal set of words – *hairbrush*, *makeover* and *downsize*, for example. However, even with these three (chosen pretty well at random) there are details that just have to be memorized:

- hairbrushes could have been made from hair, but aren't; they are brushes *for* hair
- a makeover involves appearance and styling; not just any remaking
- downsizing usually includes a reduction in the number of employees.

Very many words, like *head* – ones that are not put together out of more than one **morpheme** (= meaningful part that cannot be split into smaller meaningful parts) – do not offer any basis for predicting the meaning; so all of them just have to be learnt too.

This unit does not aim to solve all the puzzles connected with counting words, but going through a real text will illustrate the issues. One of the practical applications of this kind of work is found in estimating the vocabulary needs of language learners, as will be seen.

WORDS IN A TEXT

Activity 5.2 presents a text that will be used quite a lot in this unit to illustrate features of the distribution of words.

 Activity 5.2 ○━┳

Part of a newspaper article on racism in football is reprinted below. Find all the words in it that are closely linked to racism or football; also count how many times each of these topic-specific words occurs.

Here is a start: *racism* (2), *football* (1), *midfield* (1). The words *launched*, *his* and *currently* could be used in relation to many other topics besides racism and football, so they are not reasonable answers here.

The noughties
The Londoner Joel 'Jobi' McAnuff, 21, has recently launched his professional football career. He currently plays in midfield for Wimbledon.

'To be honest, there is not a lot of racism now on the terraces and any abuse you get from the fans does not tend to be about your colour. I have been subjected to racist abuse only once, five years ago when I was in the youth team. It was an FA Youth Cup game with a club notorious for its attitude. The spectators were shouting "black this and that", and directing abuse at the parents and away fans as well as the players. It even carried on after the game, which we won, which made them even more angry. We told the manager, who had witnessed it himself. But there wasn't an awful lot we could do.

The situation has undoubtedly improved enormously. An older black player at Wimbledon, Michael Thomas, told us what it was like in the 1980s with bananas being thrown and abuse. Back then it was definitely much harder to make it as a black player. If the racists had had their way then there would not have been any black players at all.

Despite my experiences, I still believe that not enough is being done to counter racism, especially by the authorities. Organisations such as Uefa and Fifa should be taking a stronger stance, especially in European games. Clubs who have a problem with racists should be penalised. It is as simple as that.'

(Source: Jason Burt, *The Independent*, 4 March 2003)

Including the two words in the heading, this text is 254 words long. (Near the end of the second paragraph, *wasn't* was counted as two words: *was* and *n't*.) Only a rather small proportion of the words in the text are ones with a close connection to racism or football. If the list given in the commentary is accepted, then only 39 are closely related to its topics. (The figure 39 comes from 4 instances of *abuse* added to 4 instances of *black*, and so on through the rest of the list in the commentary, ending with one each of *won*, *manager*, *Uefa* and *Fifa*.) Thirty-nine words out of 254 is just over 15 per cent. The remaining nearly 85 per cent of the 254 printed words are not closely linked with the text's two main topics.

Tokens, types, families and headwords

Before looking at the nature of the other 85 per cent of the words, some distinctions need to be explained. These are commonly used by corpus linguists[1] and others investigating the distribution of words in texts.

Every occurrence of a word in a text is called a (word) *token. The noughties* text is 254 tokens long. The technical term (word) *type* means 'word as a distinct item in a list'. *The noughties* has 254 tokens, but there are fewer word types because some words are recycled: for instance the type *Wimbledon* is represented in the text by two tokens (one in the first paragraph and one in the third paragraph), the type *with* is represented in the text by three tokens.

Types that are related can be grouped together into a *word family*. The text includes the following tokens: *The The the the the The the the the the The the the the*. One way of summarizing them is to say that there are 14 tokens of the family *The/the*, which groups together the types *The* and *the*. Although a capital letter can distinguish words (e.g. *turkey* is a bird, but *Turkey* is a country), an initial capital does not change *the* into a different word. Four tokens in the text have the spelling *not* and one token is spelt *n't*. When the word *not* is tacked on to the end of a verb it takes the form *n't*; so it is reasonable to group *not* and *n't* together and say that there are five tokens in the text of the family *not/n't*.

When types are grouped together as a family, one of the types is usually chosen to stand for the group. This chosen item is called the *headword*. The type selected as the headword is generally:

- the type that is the most basic form in the family, for example one that lacks an **affix** (= **prefix** or **suffix**) in preference to one that has the affix, e.g. *launch* would be the natural headword for *launch/relaunch/launching/launched/...*
- the type that has the largest number of tokens, e.g. five of the eight tokens of *a/an/An* in the text are *a*, so *a* is a sensible choice for headword of this family
- the form that dictionary-makers usually choose to list alphabetically.

 Activity 5.3 ⚬━╍

Here are lists of tokens in *The noughties* text representing some families of words. Choose an appropriate headword for each family, count the tokens and write out summaries like: 'The word family *game/games* under the headword *game* is represented by three tokens'.

racist racists racists
has have had has had had have have
be is be been was was were was was being was been is being be be is
does do done
and and and and and and

Racist and its plural *racists* are clearly variants of the same word, but should they perhaps have been put into the same word family as *racism*, a word type with two tokens in the text? The meanings are different: a *racist* is a person, but *racism* is a condition of societies. *Racist* and *racism* are related, but the issue is whether the meaning relationship ('a __*ist* is someone who upholds __*ism*') is obvious enough to make one meaning predictable from the other. Separate storage in memory is not required for information that can be predicted from knowledge of patterns. Proficient speakers of English would generally make the connection, and for them *racist* and *racism* are members of the same family. For an intermediate-level learner of English who does not know the relevant word-making patterns, *racist* and *racism* might be treated as belonging to different families, i.e. separately-stored memory items.

Content words and grammatical words

Words that carry the content of our communications are called **content words**. These are the words that connect language to the world outside of language: to the people, creatures, things, ideas, places, times, events, qualities, actions and relationships that we talk and write about. Content words are nouns, verbs, adjectives and **adverbs**.[2] Many words in the sample text are content words: for instance the nouns *authorities* and *problem*, the verbs *shouting* and *penalised*, the adjectives *professional* and *notorious*, the adverbs *currently* and *enormously*. These are not as closely associated with the topics of *The noughties* as the words picked out in Activity 5.2, but they make important connections to the world that is being written about. Of course, words like *racists*, *racism* and *football*, which are closely connected to the text's topics, are also content words.

Grammatical words, such as *the*, *it* and *with*, do not have links – close or distant – to topics; they are used in texts about anything and everything. Grammatical words carry some very general meanings and they link words into sentence structures. When content words and grammatical words are counted we find differences.

Of the 254 word tokens in the text of Activity 5.2, there are 146 tokens of grammatical words (57 per cent) and the remaining 108 tokens (43 per cent) are content words. Other texts might well have different proportions. However, when headwords are considered, there are usually more content words represented in a text than grammatical words: the tokens of content words in this text are from 87 different content headwords, but the tokens of grammatical words come from only 55 different families. Think about it: lots of grammatical word tokens (146) come under relatively few headwords (55). On average there should be more tokens for a given grammatical word than for a given content word. The following figures fit this expectation. They are for headwords that have at least three tokens each in *The noughties*.

Grammatical words (with number of tokens of each shown in brackets):

be (17), *the* (14), *have* (8), *a* (8), *it* (7), *and* (6), *as* (6), *not* (5), *in* (4), *to* (4),[3] *we* (4), *there* (3), *do* (3), *I* (3), *with* (3), *at* (3).

Content words (numbers of tokens in brackets):

abuse (4), *black* (4), *player* (4), *racist* (3), *game* (3).

Grammatical words tend to be recycled a lot. This is because there are fewer of them (a few hundred headwords only; see Nation 2001: 430–1) and they are needed regardless of what people are writing or talking about. How often tokens of a word appear in large, balanced samples of text is the *frequency (of use)* of the word. Frequency of use is commonly stated as number of tokens per million words of text.

An up-to-date reference book on the frequency of use of words in written and spoken English (Leech *et al.* 2001) was based on a very large collection of texts, totalling 100 million words. Its figures show very high frequencies for some grammatical words: for instance tokens representing the word family *be* averaged out at more than 40,000 times per million words of text and tokens of *the* more than 60,000 times per million. By contrast, the same book shows much lower frequencies for content words, e.g. the noun *abuse* had 37 tokens/million, the adjective *black* 226/million, and there were 138/million for *player*. There are thousands of content headwords to choose from; so, on average, individual ones do not get used as frequently as a typical grammatical word.

A rank table – a sort of 'league table' of popularity of words – in the Leech *et al.* word frequency book (2001: 120) shows that all of the top 50 word types in English are grammatical words and a large majority of the 50 next most frequently used types are also grammatical words. The most frequently used content word types are the verb form *said* (53rd in the ranking, with 2,087 tokens per million words of text) and the nouns *time* (1,542/million) and *people* (1,241/million).

Table 5.1 shows that there is a wide range of frequencies for both grammatical words and content words, from rarely used words (with one token or fewer per million words of text) to ones with tens of, hundreds of, or more than a thousand tokens per million words of text. However, it is only among grammatical words that we find families represented by tens of thousands of tokens per million words.

The frequencies in Table 5.1 are for word families, e.g. 25,056 next to the headword *a* is the sum of 21,626 for the type *a* and 3,430 for *an*, and the total number of tokens of *prowl*, *prowls*, *prowling* and *prowled* gives a rounded average of 2 tokens per million words of text. Some of the families shown have only one type, e.g. *about* and *real* are 'one-member families'.

The distribution of labour amongst words is highly skewed. Relatively small numbers of words are used again and again, while others rest for a long time

Table 5.1 Frequency of use (in tokens per million words) of selected grammatical words and content words (figures from Leech *et al.* 2001 and the associated website)

Grammatical words									
of	29,391	*so*	1,893	*every*	401	*albeit*	14	*outwith*	1
a	25,056	*about*	1,524	*someone*	187	*ours*	17	*ere*	1
Content words									
		see	1,920	*bring*	439	*spare*	19	*prowl*	2
		year	1,639	*real*	227	*forever*	18	*bigot*	1

between appearances. There are plenty of types that are in some sense words of English but which get used so rarely as to be unknown to many users of the language. In their computer analysis of 100 million words of text, Leech *et al.* (2001: 8) found three-quarters of a million different types (757,087 to be precise) and 52 per cent of these were represented by only one token each.

Three-quarters of a million is far more than the number of words that a speaker of English needs to store in memory. Many of the items included in this total were big numbers, e.g. *1,040,325* (yes, it's a word) and other words constructed for an occasion (e.g. *turquoise-striped*). Language users typically make up such words by rule rather than taking them from memory as 'prefabricated' wholes. There were plenty of names too, including *John-go-to-bed-at-noon* (which seems to have occurred at least twice among the 100 million tokens analysed), technical words (e.g. *acetylsalicylic*), verbal mimes (such as *aaaaargh*) and many spelling variants.

HOW MANY WORDS DO INDIVIDUALS HAVE?

This is a hard question to answer. The usual approach is to test people on a selection of the large number of words that it is assumed they could potentially know. Then the percentage of words they know out of the selection is used to estimate the size of their vocabulary. Higher figures are obtained with recognition tests than in tests requiring recall. Tricky decisions have to be made, such as which types to group under headwords and whether to exclude proper nouns (names of people, etc.) from consideration. Paul Nation – an applied linguist – and his colleagues have undertaken detailed studies that offer some well-founded estimates.

Nation (2001: 9, 365) gives 20,000 word families as an approximate figure for the vocabulary size of a young university graduate whose first language is English. Because of the very large numbers of people, world-wide, who learn English as a foreign language (➤➤ Unit 14), it is of practical interest to get some idea of the minimum number of words needed to use English for particular purposes. One focus of research has been the vocabulary needs of people who have English as a foreign language and wish to study for a university degree through the medium of English. If a native English-speaking student ends up with knowledge of the words grouped under something like 20,000 headwords, is that what a student with English as a foreign language has to aim for, or will fewer words suffice in English for Academic Purposes (EAP)?

The question can be approached by examining the distribution of words in the materials that undergraduates in an English-language university have to handle, starting with the books they are expected to read. Written texts usually have a richer selection of words than speech; so what the students meet in lectures and seminars is likely to be a subset of what is found in their books.

Nation (2001: 17) reports some quite surprising results. Knowledge of only the types grouped under the 1,000 most frequently used headwords of English will allow EAP students to read nearly 74 per cent of the tokens they are likely to meet in academic texts, which is to say that they should, on average, be able to cope with eight of the words in a typical 11-word line in an academic textbook. Knowledge of the next 1,000 most frequently used word families would give them access to another 4.5 per cent of the word tokens in academic writing. Two thousand is far fewer than the 20,000 word families that native-speaking university students probably know.

With a vocabulary only one-tenth that of a native-speaker undergraduate, it is astonishing that nearly 80 per cent of the word tokens in an academic text become accessible. The diminishing return is striking too: the EAP learner gets a lot more access for learning the hardest-working 1,000 words than for learning the next 1,000 most frequent words. The first 1,000 includes almost all of the grammatical words, which – as noted in the previous subsection – are re-used a lot, as well as the most popular content words, e.g. *say*, *see*, *sell* and *people*. With the second 1,000, the learner has started into the great mass of content words, with each one generally having a relatively small chance of occurrence in a given text.

Remember that a headword is the head of a family of word types (though some families have only one member, like the conjunction *whether*). In the research done for the word frequency book of Leech *et al*. (2001) the verb *believe* headed a group of four verb types *believe, believes, believing, believed*; a different headword, the noun *belief*, headed the pair *belief* and *beliefs*; and *disbelief* was a separate headword. However, in the first of the 1,000-word lists used by Nation (2001) the family headed by *believe* encompasses all seven of these word types. The justification for grouping all of them together is that a grasp of relevant systematic relationships between words (e.g. the effect of the suffix {-*ing*} on a verb, or the effect of the prefix {*dis*-}) should enable someone who has learnt one of these words to work out the likely meanings of the others when they are encountered in text. These different groupings under headwords opted for by different teams of researchers are both justifiable. The important thing is to know how types were grouped for a given tabulation.

In the research of Nation and his collaborators, the first 1,000 word families of English include 4,119 types, and 3,708 types are grouped under the second 1,000 headwords. Thus the 20,000 headwords thought to be known by a first-language English-speaking graduate might subsume up to 80,000 word types.

Figure 5.1 is a version of *The noughties* from Activity 5.2 showing tokens representing only the 1,000 most frequent headwords of English. The number of tokens is 195, which is 77 per cent of the original 254. (This version of the text was produced using Paul Nation's vocabulary program *Range*, downloaded on 16 July 2003 from http://www.vuw.ac.nz/lals/software.htm.)

Most readers of this stripped-down text are likely to recognize that race features in it, but it would take a lucky guess to tell that it is about football.

The _____

The _____ _____ '_____' _____ , 21, has recently _____ his _____ _____ _____ . He currently plays in _____ for _____ .

'To be _____ , there is not a _____ of _____ now on the _____ and any _____ you get from the _____ does not _____ to be about your colour. I have been subjected to _____ _____ only once, five years ago when I was in the youth _____ . It was an _____ Youth _____ game with a _____ _____ for its _____ . The _____ were _____ "black this and that", and directing _____ at the _____ and away _____ as well as the players. It even carried on after the game, which we won, which made them even more _____ . We told the ____, who had _____ it himself. But there wasn't an _____ _____ we could do.

The situation has undoubtedly _____ _____ . An older black player at _____ , _____ _____ , told us what it was like in the 1980s with _____ being thrown and _____ . Back then it was _____ much harder to make it as a black player. If the _____ had had their way then there would not have been any black players at all.

_____ my experiences, I still believe that not enough is being done to _____ _____ , _____ by the _____ . Organisations such as _____ and _____ should be taking a stronger _____ , _____ in _____ games. _____ who have a problem with _____ should be _____ . It is as simple as that.'

Figure 5.1 Newspaper text (Jason Burt, *Independent* 4 March 2003) preserving word tokens representing only the 1,000 most frequent word families of English (_____ represents a missing word) © 2005, Bloomer, Griffiths and Merrison.

The next version of *The noughties* (Figure 5.2) – again prepared with the aid of Nation's *Range* program – shows the tokens that should be recognizable to a person who knows the top-ranked 2,000 word families of English. The 18 tokens (another 7 per cent of 254) representing headwords from the second thousand have been underlined.

Eighty-four per cent (77 + 7) is more than the 78 per cent coverage reported by Nation (2001: 17). However, his figure was for academic texts, which this is not. Even with 84 per cent of the words readable, however, the text still does not make full sense. If the names *Londoner*, *Joel 'Jobi' McAnuff*, *Wimbledon* and *Michael Thomas* had been left in, then it might help a reader to at least identify these as names, by their initial capital letters. Proper nouns were intentionally excluded from Nation's lists of the first and second thousand headwords of English, though both *Michael* and *Thomas* (not any of the others) occur often enough to be in the top 2,000.

The _____

The _____ _____ '_____' _____ , 21, has recently _____ his _____ <u>football</u> _____ . He currently plays in _____ for _____ .

'To be <u>honest</u>, there is not a <u>lot</u> of _____ now on the _____ and any _____ you get from the <u>fans</u> does not <u>tend</u> to be about your colour. I have been subjected to _____ _____ only once, five years ago when I was in the youth _____ . It was an _____ Youth <u>Cup</u> game with a <u>club</u> _____ for its _____ . The _____ were <u>shouting</u> "black this and that", and directing _____ at the <u>parents</u> and away <u>fans</u> as well as the players. It even carried on after the game, which we won, which made them even more <u>angry</u>. We told the <u>manager</u>, who had <u>witnessed</u> it himself. But there wasn't an _____ <u>lot</u> we could do.

The situation has undoubtedly <u>improved</u> _____ . An older black player at _____ , _____ _____ , told us what it was like in the 1980s with _____ being thrown and _____. Back then it was _____ much harder to make it as a black player. If the _____ had had their way then there would not have been any black players at all.

_____ my experiences, I still believe that not enough is being done to _____ _____ , <u>especially</u> by the _____. Organisations such as _____ and _____ should be taking a stronger _____ , <u>especially</u> in _____ games. <u>Clubs</u> who have a problem with _____ should be _____ . It is as simple as that.'

Figure 5.2   Newspaper text (Jason Burt, *Independent* 4 March 2003) preserving word tokens representing only the 2,000 most frequently used English headwords (_____ represents a missing word) © 2005, Bloomer, Griffiths and Merrison.

In books and talks on specialized subjects – bird-watching, mountain bikes, dance, chemistry, medicine, antiques – we find **technical words**, ones that tend to be used with relatively high frequency in texts in the particular topic area and which often have special meanings in the subject. Chung and Nation (2003) found that about 31 per cent of the tokens in an anatomy textbook were technical words (e.g. *organ* and *thorax*). In an applied linguistics textbook about 21 per cent of tokens were technical words such as *instruct* and *lexicon*. People tend to learn technical words as part of becoming acquainted with a particular subject.

Some technical words are used fairly frequently in texts of all kinds (e.g. *organ* and *instruct*, from among the four examples just given), but they tend to be used with even higher frequency when they have a special role in a technical text. They are also likely to have restricted meanings when used technically; for instance *instruct* in an applied linguistics context usually has reference to what happens in language classes. Technical words like *thorax* and *lexicon* tend to appear in a limited range of texts, mainly in discourse from the technical field in question. The very fact of their occurrence sometimes signals 'this is technical talk/writing' (➤ Unit 9). *The noughties* is not a piece of technical writing, but Activity 5.2 was something like an assessment of a text's technical words.

How many technical terms have to be learnt in mastering a subject? Chung and Nation (2003) report the technical vocabulary for the anatomy book as 4,270 word types and that of the applied linguistics book as 835 word types.

Knowledge of the top 2,000 word families of English can give an EAP learner access to well over 70 per cent of the word tokens in quite difficult material (84 per cent for the *noughties* text). This is why up-to-date learner dictionaries like the *Collins Cobuild New Student's Dictionary* (Sinclair *et al.* 2002) mark the highest frequency words distinctively. Language learners will often have knowledge of technical words from their subject training and this can increase access to nearly 90 per cent of the tokens in a text. So a reader could handle almost 9 out of 10 word tokens in a technical text in a given subject by knowing the most common 2,000 general words of general English and somewhere between about 1,000 and 4,500 technical words. What about the 10 per cent or so of text tokens still not accounted for? Some of these will be names, some will be numbers. Having to look into a bilingual dictionary for one word out of every ten is perhaps not an intolerable burden. Furthermore, **context** alone might enable a reader to guess the meanings of some of these remaining words (➤ Unit 3).

The last part of this unit is about how words are constructed and the extent to which the meanings of some words can be correctly guessed from recognizing the components and the way they have been put together. The point is that what can be worked out does not have to be stored in memory.

MAKING WORDS

In commentary on a televised cricket match in August 2002, Simon Hughes spoke about *Hoggard's close-to-the-stumps-ness*. Hoggard is a fast bowler. The expression *close-to-the-stumps-ness* is a word, of a kind called a *phrasal word*, because it has a whole **phrase** *close to the stumps* packed inside it. We know it is a word because the morpheme {-*ness*} is a suffix that appears only on words, where it has the effect of making adjectives into abstract nouns, e.g. *good* + {-*ness*} → *goodness*, *contradictory* + {-*ness*} → *contradictoriness*. *Close*, the head of the phrase, is an adjective, which is why {-*ness*} can be put on the end.

Another phrasal word is *A4-and-a-bit-on-the-side*. This is in the full internet listing of data for Table 1.1 of Leech *et al*. (2001). It occurred less often than once per million words. Will it or *close-to-the-stumps-ness* or *noughties* appear in dictionaries in the future? That depends on whether they catch on or not. Coining a word (making it up) is a different matter from the word passing into general use and becoming an item that users of the language store as part of their knowledge of the language. *Acronymy* is a widely-used strategy for coining a word from a phrase: a spelling is made from the initial letters of the phrase, which can then be pronounced, e.g. *SARS* for the illness 'severe acute respiratory syndrome'. In the *noughties* article, *Uefa* and *Fifa* are acronyms.

People cannot usually be expected to guess the meaning of a new acronym, so when newsreaders began using the word *SARS*, in 2003, they generally explained its meaning. Languages also have processes that transform existing words more directly to produce ones with different meanings, as when *unsalaried* 'not receiving a salary' was formed from *salaried*, itself derived from the word *salary*. In such cases there is some basis for guessing at the meaning (although it is possible to be mistaken). Rules that derive a word with a predictable new meaning from an existing word are called *derivational rules*.

Derivational rules may change the syntactic class of a word, e.g. *salaried*, an adjective, is derived from a noun *salary*. But derivational rules do not always affect syntactic class; for instance *unsalaried* is an adjective derived from an adjective. *Inflectional rules* (⇥ Unit 7) are different. They never change syntactic class. Instead of being used to make words with new meanings, inflectional rules produce the appropriate type of a word to suit different positions in sentences, e.g. the plural is the type of noun required to fit with plural determiners such as *these*, *those* or *both*.

Inflectional rules relate the different members of a word family, e.g. the family headed by the verb *throw* includes the inflected types *throws*, *threw*, *throwing* and *thrown*. The meaning differences that come from inflecting words are usually highly predictable; for instance changing any verb to past tense adds the meaning 'before now' and pluralizing a noun adds 'more than one' to the meaning. However, the meaning changes introduced by derivational rules can be quirky; for instance although *salaried* means 'receiving a salary' and the adjective *waged* means 'receiving a wage', *moneyed* (also spelt *monied*) means 'having a lot of money', rather than 'receiving money'.

Because of unpredictabilities in the meaning changes introduced by derivation, some researchers (e.g. Leech *et al.* 2001) choose not to accept them as uniting types under a headword, while others (e.g. Nation 2001) feel that there is often sufficient predictability in familiar derivational processes to use them for grouping types into families. This difference was pointed out earlier, when discussing the number of word types in a native English-speaking university graduate's vocabulary.

Two kinds of derivational process will be looked at here: a process called conversion and, briefly, the use of suffixes and prefixes. Also to be discussed is compounding, the making of a word by putting together a pair of existing words (e.g. *youth team*, in the text of Activity 5.2).

Growing up as speakers of English, children as young as two and a half years old are able to make new words according to patterns (Clark and Hecht 1982). The earliest is the simplest: no change at all, just press a new duty on to an existing word, as when a child uses the word *broom* to mean 'sweep'. This is called *conversion*: one word is converted into another. Using the noun *broom* as a verb is not conventional in adult English, but the process of conversion is widespread in the language, e.g. *to brush* means to 'clean or tidy with a brush'. The fact that English has two different headwords *broom* and *sweep* is an argument for regarding the noun *brush* and the verb *brush* as different types.

At around the same age as the first instances of conversion, young children begin making **compound words** (Clark 2003: 285). In a compound, two (or more) words are put together to make another word, as with the child word *blow-machine* meaning a 'machine that blows' (a *blower* or *fan* in adult English). The child was using a pattern common in English, for example a *blow hole* (in rocks or on a whale) is 'a hole that blows'.

There is more to compounding than just putting words together. They have to be put into the correct sequence. If there was an English compound word *paper journal*, it would be some kind of journal, but the French expression *papier journal* does not denote a kind of journal or newspaper; it means 'newsprint', a kind of paper, the kind that newspapers are printed on.

English compound words have two features that justify thinking of them as words in their own right. First, they often have idiosyncratic meanings. The words *windbreak, overtake, password* and *egghead* in Activity 5.1 were compounds and the point was made that their meanings are not entirely predictable. There are aspects of each that simply have to be learnt. This implies that compounds have to be stored as items in memory.

Second, English words tend to be pronounced with strong **stress** somewhere near the beginning, e.g. *consequence* is pronounced with the stress on the first syllable, as if it were written CONsequence; *terrible* is pronounced TERrible. The same is true of many compounds, particularly those that are nouns: UNdertaker, NEWSprint, BLOW hole, LETterbox, STEAM-roller. In passing, it should be noted that English written usage is rather inconsistent on whether compounds appear as single words <steamroller>, or with hyphens <steam-roller> or with internal spaces <steam roller>. The presence of a space in writing is no assurance that you are not dealing with a single compound word (see Bauer 1998: 68–9).

Compounding makes words that can, in turn, be put into compounds. For instance, the text in Activity 5.2 contained the compound *FA Youth Cup game*. *Youth Cup* is a compound word, meaning 'trophy for young players'. The FA (the Football Association) is responsible for this particular Youth Cup; so, making a compound out of the words *FA* and *Youth Cup*, we can refer to it as the *FA Youth Cup*. To talk about a game played for the FA Youth Cup, we can make a more elaborate compound, by putting the compound word *FA Youth Cup* with the word *game*: *FA Youth Cup game*.

English has prefix morphemes (e.g. {*un-*}, {*re-*}) and suffix morphemes (e.g. {*-er*}, {*-ly*}) that are used to make words from existing words by adding meanings such as 'not' (as in <u>un</u>*happy*), 'again' (e.g. <u>re</u>*run*), 'one who does it' (e.g. *teach<u>er</u>*), 'in a … way' (e.g. *wild<u>ly</u>*).

SUMMARY

Many words have unpredictable meanings and just have to be remembered. In the sentence 'If the racists had had their way then there would not have been any black players at all' there are two tokens of the word type *had* and one token of the type *have*. The types *have* and *had* (as well as *has* and *having*) can be grouped into a word family under the headword *have*. Grammatical words, like *have*, are used in communications about anything. There is a limited number of them and some are used very often. Content words, e.g. *black* and *players*, link to what is spoken or written about. There are many of them, some having very low frequency of use. Knowledge of 2,000 high frequency word families and a couple of thousand relevant technical words can give access to nearly 90 per cent of the tokens in difficult written texts. New words are made by imaginative invention, but also systematically through compounding and by the derivational processes of conversion, prefixing and suffixing.

FURTHER READING

Aronoff and Anshen's (1998) handbook article on 'Morphology and the lexicon' is short, clear and interesting, with good discussion of how words relate to the rest of a language system. In Clark's book *First Language Acquisition* (2003), her chapter on young children's word-building is an accessible general introduction. *Word Frequencies in Spoken and Written English* (Leech *et al.* 2001) is a fascinating – and fairly affordable – reference book. It is worth reading the introduction to this one (even if you do not usually look at the stuff at the beginning of dictionaries). Carstairs-McCarthy's *An Introduction to English Morphology* (2002) is a small book and easy to understand, but very informative about words.

FURTHER ACTIVITY

 ## Activity 5.4

Photocopy the version of the *noughties* text that retains tokens of only the most frequent 2,000 word families of English (Figure 5.2). Write *Londoner, Joel 'Jobi' McAnuff, Wimbledon, Michael Thomas, FA, Fifa* and *Uefa* into the appropriate gaps. Then ask a friend to read it and 'think aloud' while guessing what words should go into the remaining gaps. You should note down your friend's thoughts. The least frequent ones amongst the missing words, according to Leech *et al.* (2001), are *notorious* (9/million), *enormously* (8/million), *penalised* (4/million including the version spelt with < z >) and *racist/s* (2/million). Are tokens of these four harder to guess than the others? Anyone who correctly identifies *noughties* as the word missing from the heading should be congratulated on having uncanny insight!

COMMENTARY ON ACTIVITIES

Activity 5.1

The point is that even words made from meaningful parts (like *under* + *take* + {*-er*}) have conventional meanings that can be different from what might seem to be justified by the meanings of their parts.

A *cooker* is not someone who cooks. Such a person is a *cook* or *chef*. A *cooker* is a cooking-stove (or, for some speakers of English, an apple suitable for cooking).

Unlike a *coffee break*, a *windbreak* is not time out for wind; nor is it a belch (as might be suggested by the meaning of *to break wind*). A *windbreak* is a line of trees or some other barrier that gives shelter from the prevailing wind.

To *overtake* is not to take control of an organization – that's a *takeover*. Overtaking is done by catching up with others and then going beyond them.

A *password* is not the word *pass* said when you don't want to participate. It is a secret word or phrase or string of symbols that has to be given before you can pass a barrier.

An *egghead* is not the head of an egg (whatever that might be), but a brainy person with an intellectual focus.

Activity 5.2

There could be disagreement over the list below (e.g. should *attitude* have been included, as a word connected with racism, *professional* as one related to football; should *penalised* have been added, as a word of relevance to both racism and football; is *manager* too general to be claimed as football-related?). Nonetheless, the following appear to have close connections with the themes of racism and football. (The number of occurrences in the text are shown in brackets. Words that occur most often are listed first.)

> *abuse* (4), *black* (4), *player(s)* (4), *racist(s)* (3), *game(s)* (3), *racism* (2), *fans* (2), *club(s)* (2), *Wimbledon* (2; OK, this name is associated with tennis, but it was also the name of a famous football club), *football* (1), *plays* (1), *midfield* (1), *terraces* (1), *colour* (1), *team* (1), *spectators* (1), *FA* (1), *Cup* (1), *won* (1), *manager* (1), *Uefa* (1), *Fifa* (1).

Activity 5.3

The word family *racist/racists* under the headword *racist* is represented by three tokens. (The plural form is made by adding a suffix {-s} to the singular form *racist*; so the singular form is more basic. In counts based on large collections of text data, tokens of singular types substantially outnumber tokens of plural types; see Biber *et al.* 1999: 291.)

The word family *has/have/had* under the headword *have* is represented by eight tokens. Perhaps you chose *had* as the headword. Almost no linguists would do that. They would argue that *had* is a past tense or past participle form and such forms normally involve a suffix, so *have*, which has no suffix, is a more basic form. Try looking up *has*, *have* and *had* in an English dictionary. *Have* will be in there, probably with quite a lot said about it. If *has* and *had* are separately listed, their entries will be brief, probably just indicating that *have* is the form to consult for details. A more refined analysis might split this family between two headwords, the **auxiliary verb** *have* and the main verb *have*; and the same could be done for *be*, below, but that would be unnecessarily sophisticated for present purposes.

For the word family *be/been/was/were/is/being* under the headword *be* there are 17 tokens. (Long tradition in English grammar makes *be* the headword here, even though *is* and *was* are used more often overall in English – see Leech *et al.* 2001: 33. Note that both *been* and *being* are made by adding a suffix to *be*; so *be* is more basic than *been* and *being*.)

The word family *does/do/done* – headword *do* – is represented by three tokens.

The word family *and* is represented by six tokens. (This is a one-member family.)

REFERENCES

Aronoff, M. and Anshen, F. (1998) 'Morphology and the lexicon: lexicalization and productivity', in A. Spencer and A.M. Zwicky (eds) *The Handbook of Morphology*, Oxford: Blackwell.

Bauer, L. (1998) 'When is a sequence of noun + noun a compound in English?', *English Language and Linguistics*, 2: 65–86.

Biber, D., Johansson, S., Leech, G., Conrad, S. and Finegan, E. (1999) *Longman Grammar of Spoken and Written English*, Harlow: Pearson.

Carstairs-McCarthy, A. (2002) *An Introduction to English Morphology*, Edinburgh: Edinburgh University Press.

Chung, T.M. and Nation, P. (2003) 'Technical vocabulary in specialised texts', *Reading in a Foreign Language*, 15: 103–16. Online. Available HTTP: <http://nflrc.hawaii.edu/rfl/October2003/chung/chung.pdf> (accessed 14 October 2003).

Clark, E.V. (2003) *First Language Acquisition*, Cambridge: Cambridge University Press.

Clark, E.V. and Hecht, B.F. (1982) 'Learning to coin agent and instrument nouns', *Cognition*, 12: 1–24.

Leech, G., Rayson, P. and Wilson, A. (2001) *Word Frequencies in Written and Spoken English*, Harlow: Pearson. Additional tabulations online. Available HTTP: <http://www.comp.lancs.ac.uk/ucrel/bncfreq/flists.html> (accessed 14 July 2003).

McEnery, T. and Wilson, A. (2001) *Corpus Linguistics*, Edinburgh: Edinburgh University Press.

Nation, P. (2001) *Learning Vocabulary in another Language*, Cambridge University Press. Related software available online. Available HTTP: <http://www.vuw.ac.nz/lals/software.htm> (accessed 16 July 2003).

Sinclair, J. *et al.* (eds) (2002) *Collins Cobuild New Student's Dictionary*, 2nd edn, Glasgow: HarperCollins.

NOTES

1 A corpus (plural corpora) is a representative sample of texts (written or spoken or both). The sample is usually millions of words in length and in computer-readable form. A corpus linguist is one whose work is focused on corpora. See McEnery and Wilson (2001).

2 Though *be* and *do* are verbs, they are grammatical words (see the next paragraph in the body of the unit) rather than content words. Furthermore, some members of other syntactic classes – especially **prepositions** – carry content, e.g. *above* and *below* are used to express different relations among things. Thus the distinction between content words and grammatical words is not as straightforward as suggested in the present unit.

3 If you have been checking the figures, then perhaps you counted five tokens of *to*, rather than four. However, there are two different types with the same spelling in the text and grouping them together is not justified. They do different work in sentences. In 'subjected to racist abuse' *to* is a preposition. The other four tokens represent a *to* that goes in front of verbs (➻ Unit 7).

6 SEMANTICS

INTRODUCTION

Unit 3 introduces **pragmatics**, one part of the study of meaning. Unit 6 is about **semantics**, the other essential component. When people know a **language** they have a powerful system – **grammar** plus **vocabulary** – for communicating meanings. Semantics is the study of meanings as stored in language, waiting to be put to use. Pragmatics focuses on how speakers and writers actually use their language knowledge to convey meanings.

The story of how a young man from an alcohol-free family found himself paying for other people's drinks in a British pub illustrates the difference between semantics and pragmatics. Alan was not a linguist. He was training as a social worker. He knew English, so he knew the following items of semantic information implicitly (even if he wasn't all that sure about the terms **verb**, **noun phrase**, **pronoun** and **suffix**):

- the meaning of the verb *drink*
- that there are *drinks* called *beer*, *whisky*, *wine*, *lemonade,* etc.
- that the pronoun *you* is used to refer to the person(s) being spoken to
- that putting the suffix {*-ing*} on to an action verb and at the same time putting *are/is/am* in front of the verb indicates that the action is currently happening (➺ progressive aspect in Unit 7)
- that *what*-questions ask for specific information, usually in the form of a noun phrase.

Alan had been brought up in a strictly teetotal household. He had never been in a pub, but felt that if he was going to be a social worker he had better learn something about pubs. He stepped into one, desperately hoping for inspiration on what to do next. To his relief, he recognized one of two men chatting at the bar. He decided to go and say hello, casually ask what they were drinking and then order the same for himself. Maybe they would even offer to buy him a drink and that way he could discover the routine involved in placing an order.

Alan walked across, smiled, greeted his acquaintance and, with a momentary look at the men's glasses, asked: 'What are you drinking?'. They were pleasantly surprised, waved over the barman and said 'Our friend is getting us another round'. Alan asked for a lemonade for himself and paid for all three drinks!

Alan had the semantic knowledge needed to frame the question 'What are you drinking?' but in a British pub someone who says this is usually understood as offering to buy the next lot of drinks. The offer meaning arises from social knowledge and conventions about what is done in pubs, taken together with thoughts about why a speaker might pose that question in a pub. Semantically, 'What are you drinking?' is just a question, with the word *what* marking the object of the verb as missing information. The offer meaning is a **context**-dependent elaboration. Our pragmatic skill enables us to construct contextual meanings on top of semantic foundations.

In different contexts there are other sentences that can be used to offer to buy drinks and there are different uses that can be made of the sentence 'What are you drinking?' (e.g. when an anxious parent sees a four-year-old drinking something that looks dubious). A full account of meaning in language requires both semantics and pragmatics. The present unit is about semantics, the study of meaning in the abstract system of a language – important because the central characteristic of language is that it encodes meanings (➻ Unit 1).

Unit 5 mentions the obvious fact that words have meanings. Unit 6 focuses on the nature of word meanings and how they can be described. It should be noted, however, that grammar (➻ Unit 7) also has a bearing on meaning, because arranging the same words differently can change meaning, e.g. *The boat is in the water* means something different from *The water is in the boat*, and a *flower garden* is not the same kind of thing as a *garden flower* (➻ Unit 5 on compound words).

Most approaches to semantics begin with this question: what meaning equivalences are there among the words and sentences of a language? Thinking about English, answers to that question would include the information that the verb *drink* means the same as *consume liquid*; and that a long-winded equivalent of *I'd like a drink* could be *I'd like some water or lemonade or beer or whisky or …*

Understanding what counts as a normal answer to 'What are you drinking?' depends on knowing the labels for different beverages that belong under the general noun *drink* (Grandy 1987: 261). Thus the semantic knowledge that 'lemonade is a drink', 'beer is a drink', '… is a drink' are first steps in explaining what goes on when people ask and answer questions such as 'What are you drinking?'.

There are several theories of semantics, with many substantial differences between them. This unit does not go into semantic theory, but the concepts explained here figure in most theories. Linguists look for generalizations that can be made across different languages, usually aiming to be methodical, accurate and concise.

Linguists doing semantics attempt to account for meaning as stored in language systems. An important part of this is word meaning. It turns out that word meaning cannot adequately be studied by thinking of words in isolation. For instance, it could be irrelevant to answer the question 'What does bear mean?' by talking about 'giving birth to'. See Figure 6.1 (and also think about the ambiguity of words pronounced in isolation, like [naɪt] – knight or night). Semanticists find that they need to consider words in terms of how the words contribute to the meanings of sentences.

Figure 6.1   'Knight/night on bear/bare mountain' (apologies to Mussorgsky)

WORD MEANING IS FOUND IN SENTENCES

 Activity 6.1

Here are three questions as preparation for what comes next in the unit, so please answer them before reading on. First-reaction answers will do.

- Are snakes animals?
- Are birds animals?
- Do the words *thief* and *robber* have exactly the same meaning?

There is no commentary on this activity. The purpose of the questions should become clear fairly soon.

Example (1) is a news story to illustrate some important starting points.

(1) **Snakes stolen from zoo**

BORDEAUX, France, AFP –

Slick thieves stole two boa constrictors and a python from a zoo in southwest France, officials said.

The robbers also stole five parrots, a cockatoo and four turtles in an overnight raid at the zoo in Pessac near Bordeaux.

Police are questioning animal specialists in the region on the trail of the missing animals.

(*Fiji Times*, 15 July 1995)

Think about learners of English who are unsure about the meanings of some of the words in the report. Partial knowledge of word meanings can lead to confusion. The headline mentions *snakes*, and diligent learners who look up words in bilingual dictionaries would find that both *python* and *boa constrictor* – the first two creatures listed – are snakes; so why not guess that all the stolen creatures were snakes? It's not very likely, but it is just imaginable that someone with an insecure grasp on English could think that parrots, cockatoos and turtles are kinds of snakes, because that seems to fit the headline! Readers with a good knowledge of English do not even begin to make that sort of mistake because they have much more of an idea of which species labels come under the general term *snakes* and which don't. And the word *also*, before *stole* in the second paragraph, indicates that other things were stolen besides snakes.

SEMANTIC KNOWLEDGE VERSUS ENCYCLOPAEDIC KNOWLEDGE

Those aspects of meaning that are part of the vocabulary (➤ Unit 5) and grammar (➤ Unit 7) of a language are termed *semantic knowledge*. Semantics is not an attempt to catalogue all human knowledge. The difference between the knowledge of meaning that comes from knowing a language – English for example – and knowledge that is beyond semantics can be illustrated with the snake theft report (Example 1).

Biologists say that pythons are different from boa constrictors, but many competent speakers of English who aren't snake specialists probably couldn't distinguish between the two. Some might even think that the two words label the same kind of snake. Ordinary speakers of English can learn some zoology by asking snake experts about the classification of snakes, but it can't seriously be claimed that this improves their knowledge of the English language. From a semantic point of view, people know the meanings of this part of the vocabulary of English so long as they know that a *python* is a kind of *snake* and a *boa constrictor* is a kind of *snake*. They might or might not also know that a *python* is not a *boa constrictor* (and a *boa constrictor* is not a *python*).

Encyclopaedic knowledge of how to connect words to the world is shared out among the members of a speech community. Different people have different specialisms: embroidery, hydrology, biology, stamp collecting, electronics, cooking, metallurgy, knitting, bicycle maintenance and so on. English semantic knowledge of the meanings of *boa constrictor* and *python* is not enough to identify and distinguish specimens of these snakes with certainty. Not being able to tell snakes apart could be an embarrassment for someone who works in a zoo, but it is not a sign of an imperfect grasp of English!

Note that different words do not always have different meanings. Languages have **synonyms**, words with the same meaning. For example *wildebeest* and *gnu* are synonymous. In the newspaper story (Example 1) it is *and* in the phrase 'stole two boa constrictors and a python' that indicates absence of synonymy; in a different story the journalist could not sensibly write 'stole two wildebeest and a gnu …'.

As a rough and ready test, the distinction between semantic knowledge and encyclopaedic knowledge can be made by considering who could best help if you lack a particular piece of information. If the obvious best person to go and see would be a language teacher, then you are probably dealing with semantic knowledge. If some other specialist – an embroiderer, biologist, chemist or cook, for example – is the obvious best person to ask, then it is probably encyclopaedic knowledge.

🖉 Activity 6.2 ⚗

State some items of semantic knowledge about the following words and some items of encyclopaedic knowledge about them: *shoes, footwear, clothing, boots, sandals, soles, heels.*

The semantics of five of the words in Activity 6.2 are sketched in (2).

(2)
$$
\begin{array}{c}
clothing \\
| \\
footwear \\
|
\end{array}
$$

heels → are parts of *soles* → are parts of *shoes*

Diagrams like (2) will become familiar in the course of this unit.

How to discover word meanings

Activity 6.1, near the beginning of this unit, asked whether birds and snakes are animals and whether *thief* and *robber* have the same meaning. People might be inclined to answer 'Well, maybe' or 'It depends' or 'I'm not sure'. Some would feel that the way to handle that sort of question, if you are unsure, is to look up the words in a dictionary. That is a reasonable thing to do, but you should wonder how the dictionary makers know what answers to give.

The meaning of a word is discovered by observing how it is used in sentences. Looking at the newspaper report on Pessac Zoo's losses, it is clear that the reporter treated *robbers* and *thieves* as synonymous. *The* in front of *robbers* is a pragmatic signal: 'at this point in the article you already know something about these individuals' (➤ Unit 7). Please look back at Example (1). At the start of the second paragraph, how could the reader already know about the robbers? It must be that the journalist is referring to the same individuals as the ones called *thieves* in the first paragraph; so, in this particular report, *robbers* and *thieves* have the same meaning. (The writer might well have a more formal style in which *robber* and *thief* differ in meaning, e.g. a *robber* might be a thief who uses violence.)

The final paragraph of the newspaper report sums up in terms of 'missing animals'; so, in this report, the word *animals* is used as a general term covering *snakes, boa constrictors, pythons, parrots, cockatoos* and *turtles*.

The point of this section has been that knowledge of a language gives us good intuitions about the meanings of sentences, but our intuitions about the meanings of isolated words are less confident. Word meanings contribute to sentence meanings and we have ways of working out word meanings from seeing how they are used in sentences. This is often clear when one person asks another about the meaning of a word, for example when a child who is reading a book asks 'What does *portend* mean?' most adults would want to know the whole sentence before answering.

Chicken first or egg first?

 Activity 6.3 o—

Which seems better to you: attempting to explain the meaning of *thief* as 'one who steals', or explaining the meaning of *steal* as 'doing what a thief does'?

Explaining the meanings of words in terms of other words is a natural way to proceed. And when linguists are engaged in semantics they do it too. (*What means the same as what else?* is the fundamental question in semantics.)

Dictionary makers, whose job includes semantics, prefer to write their definitions using words that are more familiar than the word being defined. *Thief* should then be defined via *steal*, because *steal* (used, on average, 48 times per million words) is more common than the word *thief* (17 times per million words) (figures for frequency of use from Leech *et al.* 2001).

The next section introduces a way of understanding how the meanings of words tie in with what we can be sure of when a given sentence is true. For instance, if it is hot news that some turtles have been stolen then they must now be missing; and this follows from a connection in meaning between the words *steal* and *missing*.

ENTAILMENT

Whatever is a collie must be a dog. If (3a) is true then (3b) must be true too – as long as we are talking about the same animal.

(3a)   That animal is a collie.

(3b)   That animal is a dog.

(3c)   ! That animal is a collie, but it is not a dog.

Sentence (3c) is a contradiction: we know that all collies are dogs, but the **clause** *but it is not a dog* attempts to **cancel** that idea. An exclamation point (!) at the beginning of an example, like (3c), marks the sentence as one that is seriously wrong semantically.

The **inference** that (3b) must be true whenever (3a) is true – provided the animal referred to is the same one – is an example of **entailment** (➤ Unit 3). A test for it is that, as in (3c), you get a contradiction from any attempt to cancel an entailment.

The sentences in (4) are another illustration of entailment. Sentence (4a) entails all three of (4b–d). Each of them must be true whenever (4a) is true.

(4a)   *It's a sandal*
        entails

(4b)   *It's an item of footwear.*

(4c)   *It's got a sole.*

(4d)   *Its upper part is ventilated.*

Look at it the other way round too. Unless something is footwear with a sole and a ventilated upper, it can't be a sandal; when any of (4b–d) aren't true, (4a) can't be true. The entailments (4b–d) are among the set of sentences that would normally be used to explain the meaning of *sandal*. Thus entailments highlight essential aspects of the meanings of words in an entailing sentence, (4a) here, which is why the concept of entailment is useful for doing semantics.

If one sentence entails another, then both of the following conditions are met:

- when the first sentence is true the other sentence is also true
- when the *second* sentence – the entailed one – is false, the first sentence is false.

Informally, when one sentence entails another, we say that 'the second sentence follows from the first one'.

Take (4a) as the first sentence in the definition and (4b) as the second sentence. Anything that is a *sandal* has to be *footwear*; there is no way of dodging that. And – second bullet point, with (4b) as the second sentence – if something isn't footwear it is not going to stand a chance of counting as a *sandal*.

 Activity 6.4 o––ᴛ

Try working through the definition again, but this time think of (4c) as the second sentence, while keeping (4a) as the first sentence.

Entailed sentences are necessary conditions for the truth of sentences that entail them: unless they are true the entailing sentence cannot be true. Entailment is associated with sentence meanings, but words make important contributions to the meanings of sentences, and that is going to be explored next.

Why use words in sentences?

When people tell you something, you generally do not just memorize what they say. Instead you draw inferences (conclusions like 'if that is so, then this, that and the other are going on'). Entailments are a semantic kind of inference. A pragmatic sort of inference called **implicature** is introduced in Unit 3 (➡ Unit 3).

The point of using words in sentences and of making choices about which words to use is that different words can give a sentence different entailments, i.e. changing a word in a sentence can change the entailments of the sentence. And with different entailments, the sentence can lead listeners or readers to different inferences.

When (5a) is true then (5b) must be true.

(5a)   Marc has found Jo's shirt.
(5b)   Marc knows the whereabouts of Jo's shirt.

The fact that (5b) is not an entailment of *Marc has lost Jo's shirt* highlights the role of *found* in making (5b) available as an entailment for (5a). With *lost* in place of *found*, the sentence would entail, amongst other things, that *Marc does not know the whereabouts of Jo's shirt*. And some other sentences that can be made by replacing *found* or *lost* with another word would not give any firm information about Marc's knowledge of where the shirt is. For example neither *Marc has seen Jo's shirt* nor *Marc has washed Jo's shirt* guarantees the truth of either *Marc knows the whereabouts of Jo's shirt* or *Marc does not know the whereabouts of Jo's shirt*.

A semantic description of a word's meaning is an account of the entailments that become available when the word is used in sentences. The data come from intuitive judgements about which sentences follow from which other sentences, which do not, and about what contradicts what. Some examples of judgements about data are presented in (6). Sentences judged to be unproblematic are presented without any special marks. Exclamation marks at the beginning indicate sentences that are seriously problematic semantically, and question marks are put in front of ones that are semantically odd but not as peculiar as the ones with exclamations. (The words *so* and *but* have been deliberately capitalized to draw attention to them. They are useful words to use in testing intuitions about entailments.)

(6)   It's a sandal SO its upper is ventilated.
         She is a head teacher SO she is in charge of a school.
         It's a knife SO it has a blade.
      ? She is a head teacher SO she knows a foreign language.
      ! Henry is a dog SO Henry is a vegetable. (contradiction)
         Henry is a dog SO Henry is not a mouse.
      ? Henry is a dog BUT Henry can bark.
      ! Henry is a dog BUT Henry is a vegetable. (contradiction)
         Henry is a dog SO Henry is an animal.
      ! Martha has lost Henry SO she knows precisely where he is.
         (contradiction)

The difference between semantic knowledge and encyclopaedic knowledge has already been explained informally. Entailment makes it possible to firm up the distinction. The semantic knowledge associated with a word is no more and no less than the entailment possibilities that come from using the word in sentences. The entailments are necessary conditions for the entailing sentence to be true. And features of word meanings that influence necessary conditions for the truth of sentences must be regarded as important.

Activity 6.5 🔑

This activity is a double-check on some basic knowledge needed for understanding most of the rest of the unit.

(i)   She is swimming across the bay.
(ii) She is in the water.

1   Assuming that 'she' is the same person in both cases, then, talking about the same moment in time, we can be sure that sentence (ii) is true if sentence (i) is true. What is the technical term for this inference from (i) to (ii)?

2   Assuming that 'she' is the same person in both cases and that we are talking about the same moment in time, what could we conclude about the truth of sentence (i) when sentence (ii) is *false*?

3   Under the same assumptions, what could we conclude about (i) when sentence (ii) is *true*?

SEMANTIC RELATIONSHIPS

The rest of this unit is about meaning relationships between words. These semantic relationships indicate the entailments that words will permit when used in sentences, and they are an important part of a full description of the meaning system of a language. Seven different semantic relationships between words are going to be described and illustrated in the rest of the unit.

Hyponymy

This relationship can be thought of as meaning 'kind of' or 'type of'. It holds between, for example, *footwear* and *clothing* (*footwear* is one kind of *clothing*), or between *clothing* and *stuff* (*clothing* is one kind of *stuff*), as depicted in (7).

(7)   *stuff*   (a **superordinate** for the words below it in the hierarchy)
          |
        clothing   (a **hyponym** of *stuff*, but a superordinate for *footwear*)
          |
       footwear   (a hyponym of *clothing* and also, via *clothing*, a hyponym of stuff)

A superordinate is a word with more general meaning than the specific terms 'under' it. Words under a superordinate that have more specific meanings are hyponyms of the superordinate. Hyponymy is the relationship that holds between a hyponym and its superordinate(s).

The semantic relationship between *sprint* and *run* is hyponymy: *sprinting* is a particular kind of *running*, namely 'fast running'. This fact relates to entailment as follows: putting these two words, in turn, into a given slot in a sentence, like the slot represented by the underlining in *I saw you _____ to the library yesterday*, gives two sentences and one of them entails the other, but the entailment does not go back from the second sentence to the first. See (8a, b).

(8a)   *I saw you sprint to the library yesterday*
        entails *I saw you run to the library yesterday*.

But

(8b)   *I saw you run to the library yesterday*
        does not entail *I saw you sprint to the library yesterday*.

Proof that (8a) is an entailment is seen in the contradictoriness of (9a): people can't sprint without running. If it is true that the speaker saw the addressee sprinting then it must be true that the speaker saw the addressee running.

(9a)   ! I saw you sprint to the library yesterday, but you weren't running.
(9b)   I saw you run to the library yesterday, but you weren't sprinting.

Example (9b) is not contradictory, because, although someone who ran to the library might have sprinted, the person could, alternatively, just have jogged there. Because (9b) is not contradictory, 'does not entail' has been written between the two sentences in (8b). (Of course, 'does not entail' means something different from 'entails … not'.) The entailment goes from a sentence containing *sprint* to a sentence with *run* in it, as noted in (8a), while (8b) records that there isn't an entailment in the reverse direction.

To summarize: hyponymy licenses one-way entailments between sentences that are identical except for substitution in one slot. There is a rule that is generally true:[1] the sentence that – like *I saw you sprint* …, in (8a) – gives the entailment is the one that contains the hyponym, and the entailed sentence – in (8a), *I saw you run* … – contains the superordinate.

Hyponymy is a relationship that passes up through superordinates: if X is a hyponym of Y and Y is a hyponym of Z, then X is a hyponym of Z. This was illustrated in (7), which showed *footwear* as a hyponym of *clothing* and, via *clothing*, of the superordinate *stuff*. Another example is: *sprint* is a hyponym of *run*; and *run*, in turn, is a hyponym of *move*; so *sprint* is a hyponym of *move*. Evidence for this is that (10a) makes good sense but (10b) is contradictory.

(10a)   I saw you sprinting, so you were moving.

(10b) ! Carl sprinted, but he did not move at all.

Figures 6.2 and 6.3 show sets of words linked by hyponymy. (The branches with *etc.* on them indicate that the diagrams are incomplete. For instance, *do (something)* has other hyponyms, such as *make* and *hit*.)

The meanings given in single quotation marks for some of the words in Figures 6.2 and 6.3 demonstrate that the meaning of a superordinate is part of the meaning of its hyponyms. The meaning of a hyponym is that of the superordinate altered by a modifier. For example, the word *jog*, a hyponym of *run*, is equivalent in meaning to 'run slowly': the meaning of *run* – the superordinate term – plus a modifier, 'slowly'. Take *lawyer* as another example. It is a hyponym of *professional* and means 'professional who gives advice on the law' (*who gives advice on the law* is a modifier called a **relative clause** ➻ Unit 7). Thus the words of a language can be seen as 'shorthand' expressions for more roundabout ways of saying things.

Hyponyms of a given superordinate are **co-hyponyms** of each other, e.g. *amble*, *stride* and *march* are co-hyponyms under the superordinate *walk* (see Figure 6.2 and Activity 6.6).

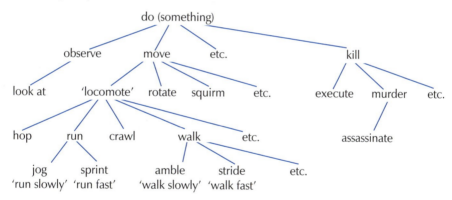

Figure 6.2   Some hyponyms of *do (something)*

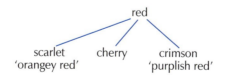

Figure 6.3   Some hyponyms of *red*

Activity 6.6 o—▼

If the following verbs were added to those in Figure 6.2, where should they be positioned?

fly, march, massacre, watch

Writing a brief meaning for each of the verbs, in the form of a superordinate word with an appropriate modifier, should make it clear where the words belong in the diagram.

Synonymy

Amble and *stroll* have the same meaning. Technically, they are synonyms; the relationship between them is **synonymy**. This ensures that the two-way pattern of entailment shown in (11) holds for this pair of words. (Compare (11) with (8), where the entailment went in one direction only.)

(11)   *They ambled round the square*   entails   *They strolled round the square.*
And
They strolled round the square   entails   *They ambled round the square.*

If there are two-way entailments between a pair of sentences, as in (11), and those sentences differ only by the replacement of one word, then the substituted words are synonyms.

Scarlet and *vermilion* are also synonymous, which allows (and can be diagnosed by) the same pattern of entailment, as shown in (12).

(12)   *I painted my wheels vermilion*   entails   *I painted my wheels scarlet.*
And
I painted my wheels scarlet   entails   *I painted my wheels vermilion.*

A technical term for two-way entailment between sentences, as in (11) and (12), is *paraphrase*. (Paraphrase is a relationship of sameness of meaning between sentences; synonymy is the corresponding relationship between words.)

Some more synonym pairs are listed in (13).

(13)   leave/depart
famous/renowned
bucket/pail
spotless/immaculate
view/prospect (the nouns, not the verbs)

lorry/truck
begin/commence

Entailment is based purely on truth conditions. **Sociolinguistic** differences of **dialect** and style (➻ Unit 9) are irrelevant to synonymy defined in terms of entailment. *Trash, rubbish* and *garbage* are synonymous even though their use correlates with various social and geographical factors.

Synonymy gives a language user the potential to construct paraphrases by mere substitution of one word for another. Converseness, the semantic relationship to be discussed next, requires substitution plus reordering of noun phrases before it will yield sentences equivalent in meaning.

Converseness

North (of) and *south (of)* are a converse pair. See (14).

(14)   *Europe is north of Africa* entails *Africa is south of Europe.*
       And
       Africa is south of Europe entails *Europe is north of Africa.*

As with synonymy, illustrated in (11) and (12), there is two-way entailment in (14): one sentence entails another and is itself entailed by the sentence that it entails (i.e. the two sentences are paraphrases of each other). And, as with synonymy, words have been substituted: one sentence has *north* where the other has *south*. Unlike synonymy, the entailment pattern for converses involves an additional change: noun phrases are swapped around: one sentence starts with *Europe* and ends with *Africa*, but the other sentence has them in reverse order.

Pairs of adjective 'comparative forms' (such as *wider~narrower, more careful~ less careful*) are also converses, as shown in (15).

(15)   *The Amazon is wider than the Thames*
       entails *The Thames is narrower than the Amazon.*
       And
       The Thames is narrower than the Amazon
       entails *The Amazon is wider than the Thames.*

Incompatibility among co-hyponyms

The relationship called *incompatibility* holds among all the hyponyms of a given superordinate, except if they happen to be synonyms. Synonymy is sameness in meaning. Incompatibility is one kind of difference in meaning. (Other sorts of meaning difference are antonymy and complementarity, to be described later.) In

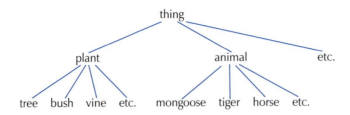

Figure 6.4 Some hyponyms of *thing*

Figure 6.4, *tree*, *bush* and *vine* are co-hyponyms. Calling them co-hyponyms signifies that they come under the same superordinate, *plant* in this case. Saying that the co-hyponyms are incompatible draws attention to their being different kinds of plant.

Other sets of incompatible co-hyponyms in Figure 6.4 are: *mongoose*, *tiger* and *horse* (under the superordinate *animal*); *mongoose*, *tiger*, *horse* and *plant* (under the superordinate *thing*); *plant* and *animal* (under *thing*); and so on.

The relationship of incompatibility gives entailments from affirmative sentences to negative sentences, as shown in (16). As well as being negative, the negative sentences differ from the affirmative sentences by inter-substitution of members of a set of incompatible terms. (Look at Figure 6.4 if necessary.)

(16) *That's a horse*   entails *That's not a tiger.*
      That's a horse   entails *That's not a mongoose.*
      That's a horse   entails *That's not a plant.*
      That's a horse   entails *That's not a tree.*
      That plant is a tree entails *That plant is not a bush.*
                                       etc.

However, it is not possible to switch sentences between the left-hand and right-hand columns in (16). Incompatibility does not license entailment from a negative sentence to a corresponding sentence with one of the other co-hyponyms. For instance, *That's not a tiger* does not entail *That's a horse*. The animal being spoken about could be a mongoose, or perhaps not even an animal (*That's not a tiger, it's my stripy beach towel*).

It might seem that everything is incompatible with everything else, but that is not so. While *run*, *walk* and *hop* are incompatible with each other, *run* is not incompatible with *sing*, nor with *think*, nor with *whistle*, nor with many other actions and states of affairs. See (17).

(17) *Marcia was running at the moment when I saw her*
      entails *Marcia was not walking at the moment when I saw her.*
      And

Marcia was running at the moment when I saw her
entails *Marcia was not hopping at the moment when I saw her.*
But
Marcia was running at the moment when I saw her
does *not* entail *Marcia was not whistling at the moment when I saw her.*
Similarly
Marcia was running at the moment when I saw her
does *not* entail *Marcia was not tall at the moment when I saw her.*

The point is that incompatibility is not just any old difference in meaning. It is difference against a background of similarity (the similarity being given by the contribution to the meanings of the words from their shared superordinate).

Antonymy

The term **antonymy** is often used as a general purpose label for 'oppositeness' in meaning, but here (following Lyons 1977) it is going to be restricted to oppositeness with the pattern of entailments shown in (18). All four lines of the pattern are required to establish that *hot* and *cold* are antonyms.

(18)			
	The water is hot	entails	*The water is not cold.*
	The water is cold	entails	*The water is not hot.*
	The water is not hot	does not entail	*The water is cold.*
	The water is not cold	does not entail	*The water is hot.*

When looking at the last two lines of (18), bear in mind that water that is *not hot* (or *not cold*) could be tepid, or lukewarm.

Antonymy holds between pairs of words which, when substituted for each other in a sentence frame, produce entailments only from affirmative to negative sentences (the first two lines of (18)), not in the reverse direction (the third and fourth lines in (18)). This makes antonymy a special case of incompatibility, namely incompatibility holding between pairs of terms rather than within larger sets, something that can be confirmed by comparing (16) and the associated discussion with (18).

In practice, members of antonym pairs usually have another characteristic too: they are gradable **adjectives** or **adverbs**. In English, gradability can be tested for by the possibility of modification with *very* and *more* or {*-er*} (➤ Unit 7, on comparative forms). Such modification is acceptable in (19a, b), but not in (19c–e). The conclusions about gradability are shown in brackets.

(19a)   very tight (*Tight* is gradable.)
(19b)   This light is very bright, but that one is brighter (*Bright* is gradable.)

(19c) ? The lid is very shut (*Shut* is not gradable.)

(19d) ! This light is onner than that one ('Electrical' *on* is not gradable.)

(19e) ! The street lamp is even more on ('Electrical' *on* is not gradable.)

Complementarity

This relationship (also called *binary antonymy*) is a non-gradable type of oppositeness. For **complementarity**, there are entailments both from affirmative sentences to the corresponding negative sentences (which is what ordinary antonymy allows) and from negative sentences to the corresponding affirmative sentences, which is where complementarity goes beyond the antonymy pattern shown in (18). See (20) for the entailment pattern that establishes complementarity as the relationship between *on* and *off* (when talking about electrical appliances).

(20) *That light is on*   entails *That light is not off.*

That light is off   entails *That light is not on.*

That light is not on   entails *That light is off.*

That light is not off   entails *That light is on.*

Between them, a pair of complementaries occupies the whole of a dimension. The English language does not recognize middle ground between 'electrical' *on* and *off*, or – another complementary pair – between *pass* and *fail*; you either *pass* a test or you *fail* it. In (19d, e) it was shown that electrical *on* is not gradable, and it is generally the case that complementary adjectives are not gradable. This comes from the absence of hazy middle ground between the members of a complementary pair.

Examples of complementaries are hard to find. It seems that they have a tendency to give up some of the middle ground, and drift off into being gradable antonyms.

 Activity 6.7

Compare the patterns in (18) and (20). Make sure you can see the differences between the entailments that arise from a pair of antonyms and those that come from using a pair of complementaries in sentences.

Activity 6.8 ⚬━

Giving reasons to support your decisions, say whether the relationship within each of the following pairs is converseness, incompatibility, antonymy, or complementarity: faster/slower, light/heavy, sparrow/wren, precede/follow, right/wrong, rise/fall, cheap/expensive, be stopping/be starting.

MERONYMY

Meronymy relates 'parts of' to wholes. Figure 6.5 gives examples, using arrows to distinguish this relationship from hyponymy (shown in Figures 6.2–4).

A word X is a meronym of another word Y if sentences of *both* of the patterns in (21) are well-formed (Cruse 2000: 153).

(21a) *An X (or Xes) is (/are) part of a Y.*
(21b) *A Y has an X.* (Or: *A Y has Xs.*)

Examples are given in (22a, b). Because the first sentence in (22c) is semantically problematic, we can tell that *driver* is not a meronym of *truck*.

(22a) A toe is part of a foot.
A foot has toes.
(22b) A cab is part of a truck.
A truck has a cab.
(22c) ! A driver is part of a truck.
A truck has a driver.

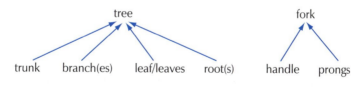

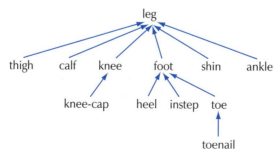

Figure 6.5 Some meronyms of *tree, fork* and *leg*

Unlike the other semantic relationships, meronymy has not been defined in this unit in terms of an entailment pattern. However, meronymy does connect with entailment possibilities, as suggested in (23); so a proper definition in terms of entailment patterns should be feasible.

(23)   *The prongs are broken*   entails   *The fork is broken*
       (with reference to the same fork at the same point in time).
       My toe is injured   entails   *My foot is injured.*
       But
       The driver is ill   does not entail !*The truck is ill.*
       (Therefore *driver* is *not* a meronym of *truck*.)

Note that meronymy is different from hyponymy: a *thigh* is part of a *leg*, not a kind of *leg*; a *handle* is part of a *fork*, not a kind of *fork*. And, in contrast: a *leg* is a kind of *limb*; a *fork* is a kind of *utensil*; etc.

SUMMARY

Semantics is the study of equivalences in the meaning systems of languages and this is what underlies the way we ordinarily explain the meanings of words using other words. Semantics does not include all our knowledge of the world. We have clear intuitions about the meanings of sentences and the meaning of a word is seen in the contributions it makes to sentence meaning. Substituting one word for another in a sentence can affect what the sentence entails. (Entailments are what must be true if a given sentence is true.) Semantic relationships, such as synonymy, converseness and antonymy hold between words, but they summarize patterns of entailment between sentences containing those words.

FURTHER READING

Kearns's book *Semantics* (2000) is a reader-friendly way to considerably extend your theoretical understanding of semantics. Kearns's examples also cover a lot of interesting features of the meaning systems of English. Saeed's *Semantics* (2002) is a bigger book that includes more topics than Kearns's. Cruse (2000), *Meaning in Language*, is a big book too. It might not be all that easy to read, but it offers many fascinatingly subtle semantic distinctions. Kreidler (1998), in *Introducing English Semantics*, deals with the meanings of large numbers of English words, worth looking through if you are worried that semantics might just be about a few well-chosen examples.

FURTHER ACTIVITY

Activity 6.9

!*The child shouted softly when she saw what had happened* is contradictory, because *shout* licenses an entailment to the effect that the **utterance** in question was loud, whereas *softly* yields an entailment that it was not loud. The contradictoriness of the example indicates that 'loudly' is part of the meaning of *shout*.

Test whether or not each of the following verbs, when used in sentences, causes the sentences to entail what is shown in brackets on the right.

yell	(The utterance is loud.)
blare	(The sound is loud.)
bark	(The sound is loud.)
whisper	(The utterance is relatively quiet.)
amble	(The motion is slow.)
run	(The motion is fast.)

You need to make up sentences and then judge whether they are okay or problematic, e.g. *The dog barked softly*; *I was embarrassed when he whispered so loudly*; *They ambled rapidly to the other side of the park*.

Activity 6.10

Try to find a way of expressing the meaning of each of the following in terms of an expression which includes the word *have*.

take, own, get, keep, borrow, give

Here is a start: *X takes Y (from Z)* means 'X causes X to have Y (and Z not to have Y)'.

COMMENTARY ON ACTIVITIES

Activity 6.2

A semantic description of English needs to include the information that *shoes*, *boots* and *sandals* are kinds of *footwear*; *footwear* is a type of *clothing*; *boots* are not *sandals*; *shoes* have *soles*; and part of the *sole* of a shoe is the *heel*. Encyclopaedic knowledge in this area is the business of shoemakers, cobblers, shopping fanatics and sales assistants. It covers shoe sizes and prices, materials commonly used for making soles, the height of different kinds of boot, how shoes can be decorated and so on.

Activity 6.3

Intuitively, it seems more promising to define *thief* as 'one who steals'. *Steal* can then be explained in terms of 'illegal taking', and *take* seems a basic sort of word. By contrast, starting by saying that *steal* means 'doing what a thief does' leads to the problem of explaining the meaning of *thief* without making use of the word *steal*. (It would be unsatisfyingly circular to claim that *stealing* is 'doing what a thief does' while at the same time offering 'one who steals' as an explanation for the meaning of *thief*.)

Activity 6.4

First sentence (4a): *It's a sandal*. Second sentence (4c): *It's got a sole*. Sentence (4a) entails (4c): a thing that is a *sandal* must have a sole; and if it hasn't got a sole it can't qualify to be called a *sandal*.

Activity 6.5

1   The inference that she must be in the water when she is swimming across the bay is an entailment. Being in fluid is a necessary condition for swimming. The entailment cannot be cancelled without contradiction, and that is a test for entailment: !*She is swimming across the bay but she is not in the water*. (Remember that ! at the beginning of a sentence signifies that the sentence has a serious meaning problem.)

2   When (ii) is false, then sentence (i) must be false. If she is not even in the water then she cannot be swimming across the bay. Confirm that this fits the definition of entailment given earlier.

3   If (ii) is true, then she might – or might not – be swimming across the bay, we cannot tell; for example she might be in the bath. Again, have a look at how this fits the definition given for entailment.

Activity 6.6

Fly 'move through the air' is a hyponym immediately under the superordinate *move*; *march* 'walk in formation' belongs under *walk*; *massacre* 'violently murder many people' under *murder*; *watch* 'look at attentively' under *look at*.

Activity 6.8

Converses – see Examples (14) and (15): *faster/slower* and *precede/follow*. Incompatibles – see Example (16): *sparrow/wren*, *rise/fall* and *be stopping / be starting*. Antonyms – see Example (18): *light/heavy* and *cheap/expensive*. Complementaries – see Example (20):

right/wrong. Here is the pattern of entailment that establishes *rise/fall* as members of a set of incompatible co-hyponyms:

The temperature rose	entails	*The temperature did not fall (in that period)*.
The temperature fell	entails	*The temperature did not rise (in that period)*.

But

The temperature did not rise does not entail *The temperature fell (in that period)*.
The temperature did not fall does not entail *The temperature rose (in that period)*.

The temperature might have remained constant, which is why we do not get entailments from the negative sentences here.

Maybe you listed *faster* and *slower* as antonyms. That is correct, because *faster* and *slower* have the entailment pattern of Example (18):

This jetfoil is faster than that hovercraft	entails	*This jetfoil is not slower than …*
That hovercraft is slower than this jetfoil	entails	*That hovercraft is not faster…*

But, because the two kinds of vessel could be equally fast:

The jetfoil is not slower than the hovercraft does not entail *The jetfoil is faster …*
The hovercraft is not faster than the jetfoil does not entail *The hovercraft is slower…*

It is important that, even though *faster* and *slower* are antonyms, you should see that they are also converses. Note too that, because *faster* and *slower* already have the suffix {*-er*}, they do not pass the tests for gradability: !*fasterer*, !*more faster*, !*very faster* etc.

REFERENCES

Cruse, A. (2000) *Meaning in Language*, Oxford: Oxford University Press.
Grandy, R.E. (1987) 'In defense of semantic fields', in E. LePore (ed.) *New Directions in Semantics*, London: Academic Press.
Kearns, K. (2000) *Semantics*, Basingstoke: Macmillan.
Kreidler, C.W. (1998) *Introducing English Semantics*, London: Routledge.
Leech, G., Rayson, P. and Wilson, A. (2001) *Word Frequencies in Written and Spoken English*, Harlow: Pearson. Additional tabulations online. Available HTTP: <http://www.comp.lancs.ac.uk/ucrel/bncfreq/flists.html> (accessed 14 July 2003).
Lyons, J. (1977) *Semantics*, 2 vols, Cambridge: Cambridge University Press.
Saeed, J. (2002) *Semantics*, 2nd edn, Oxford: Blackwell.

NOTE

1 The rule does have exceptions, for instance entailment goes the other way round if the sentences are negative, but the matter is not discussed further in this book.

7 GRAMMAR
Syntax to text

Text 7.1   Fresh strawberries and cream

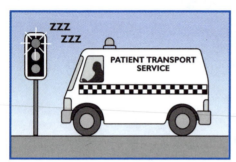

Text 7.2   Patient transport service

Text 7.3   Good children's jokes

INTRODUCTION

The phrases *fresh strawberries and cream*, *patient transport service* and *good children's jokes* are **ambiguous** because each can be understood in more than one way. The pictures demonstrate possible meanings of each phrase. If you understand the ambiguity, then you have a clear understanding (implicit if not explicit) of **syntax** or **grammar** as the ambiguity in each of them is, in some way, based on grammar rather than on lexical features (➵ Unit 5). Many people use syntax and grammar as virtual **synonyms**. Grammar traditionally has been used quite broadly to cover any aspect of the structure of the language including **semantics** and **phonetics**. Syntax is more narrowly defined as the structure of sentences, clauses and phrases (see Figure 7.1).

Everybody can appreciate a beautiful garden whether they can name the flowers or not. Those who can name the shrubs and the flowers can have more detailed and more technical discussions, even more interesting discussions, perhaps, as they can say things more quickly and more precisely. They can explain why plantings or arrangements of flowers work well together while other groupings are not so successful. Similarly, chemists who know the names of the chemicals and of the chemical processes with which they are working can talk more efficiently about the experiments they are carrying out. Each of us knows the technical language of subjects in which we are particularly interested and before you read any further, you should think of your own areas of interest and the specialist language that you know as a result.

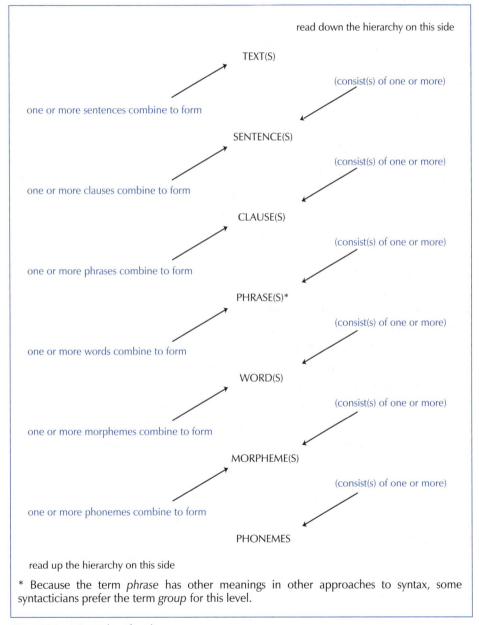

Figure 7.1   Hierarchy of rank

That you use English to communicate means that you understand how to use the structures of the language. That you understood and maybe smiled at Texts 7.1–7.3 means that you understand some of the complexities of the syntax of English. It does not necessarily mean that you have a vocabulary or a language to talk about the grammatical structure of English – or a **metalanguage**. By the end of this unit, you should have.

Words (➻ Unit 5) are fundamental to language use and a language user knows that each word in a language can only be used in certain ways within the rules of that language. The **hierarchy of rank** (Figure 7.1) shows how words relate to other parts of grammar. They allow the message giver (the encoder ➻ Unit 1) of a language to create oral or written texts which are meaningful to the addressee of the message (the receiver ➻ Unit 1), though in some cases, as in Texts 7.1–7.3, the message is not always as clear as the message giver might wish. In diagram form, the hierarchy of rank can be seen in Figure 7.1 and the brackets indicate how to read the hierarchy. So we can read from top to bottom of the hierarchy and say that a **text** (whether written or spoken) consist of sentences, each sentence consists of **clauses**, each clause consists of **phrases**, each phrase consists of **words**, each word consists of **morphemes** and each morpheme consists of **phonemes**. Alternatively we can read from the bottom to the top of the hierarchy and say that one or more phonemes combine to form a morpheme, one or more morphemes combine to form a word, one or more words combine to form a phrase, one or more phrases combine to form a clause, one or more clauses combine to form a sentence and one or more sentences combine to form a text. A text could consist of a single sentence which consists of a single clause which consists of a single phrase which consists of a single word which consists of a single morpheme, such as a warning sign saying simply *Stop*.

There are various approaches to the study of syntax. Because of our focus on language in use, we adopt a functional approach, which analyses language use in relation to what people want to say about the world all around them. In introducing such a model of language analysis, Halliday (1994: 106) asserts that language 'enables human beings to build a mental picture of reality, to make sense of what goes on around and inside them' and continues that 'the clause plays a central role, because it embodies a general principle for modelling experience – namely, the principle that reality is made up of processes'. In Halliday's view, humans experience reality as a sequence of 'goings-on' and he uses the term 'processes' to talk about these experiences. He argues that people recognize that things happen, that they think and feel, and that they generalize from their experiences to make statements or to ask questions, to exclaim or to give instructions in relation to the world around them. He recognizes three major types of process:

1 material processes – events which occur in the external world around us
2 mental processes – events which occur in the inner world of our minds
3 relational processes – states which exist in the world around us.

He claims that all languages are structured to allow people to discuss and report their experience of the world and that there is a link between people's understanding of their world and their language use. In other words, the meanings that people want to express affect the linguistic choices that people make in expressing those meanings. In this unit, we focus on the structure of English.

Before moving into the main part of this unit, though, you might like to reflect on the following questions which arise from the points just made. Each language has its own grammatical system and any learner of a second language has to learn not just the words and sounds of that second language, but also its structure. However, if the structure of a language is so closely related to language users' experience of the world, there is a question about how far use of a language influences (or to put it more strongly, determines) our perception of the world around us. When learning another language, does the second language learner have to learn to understand the world in a different way? In other words, can you learn a second language without learning how that language is used to represent the world? Do different languages, therefore, because they have different linguistic systems, represent different world views? These apparently simple questions will provide much food for background thought as you develop your skills in linguistic analysis.

Issues of meaning are directly addressed in other units (➤➤ Units 3, 5 and 6) and so the focus in this unit is on syntax, on the ordering of words within phrases and clauses and how those clauses then combine to form sentences and larger chunks of text. Though we would not wish to deny the value of other approaches to syntax or the insights that other approaches can offer, our preference for a functional approach to language relates to our focus of analysing language in use rather than as a purely symbolic system.

Syntactic analysis can be approached from a bird's eye view or from a worm's eye view. The bird's eye view of grammar would start with a large chunk of text and pull it apart to see how it is constructed. It would start at the top of the hierarchy of rank and work down through the layers. The worm's eye view of grammar would start at the bottom of the hierarchy and gradually build up to the text. This unit will begin by looking at word classes (for information about morphemes ➤➤ Unit 5) and gradually build up to the larger structures which form text.

Creative Deception

When the world was still very new, the sun and the moon were equals and shone with
2   the same brightness. They were good friends and often went round together. But one
day everything changed.
4
They had decided to take their families bathing in the river. The sun took his family
6   out of sight, round a bend, so that they could get ready for their swim in private. (In
those days everybody was very polite.)
8
'I'll jump first,' said the sun as he went off. 'You'll know I'm in the water when it
10   starts to boil.'

12   But as soon as the sun was out of sight he ordered his children to cut down branches
from the trees. 'Set fire to them,' he said, 'and throw them into the river.' So they did.
14
The minute the moon saw the water bubbling and boiling, he jumped in. As he swam
16   about, clouds of steam swirled around his head. It was very hot indeed.

18   When he climbed out again the moon discovered he had turned very pale. He was
frosty and cold and his brilliance was only a shadow of what it had been before.
20
The sun mocked him. 'Now I will always be brighter than you,' he jeered. 'We didn't
22   go swimming at all!' It was a very cruel trick and the moon decided there and then
that he would have his revenge.
24
Time passed and a great famine came upon the earth. Every day people were dying.
26   The moon saw his chance to get his own back on the sun. But he hid his anger and
paid the sun a visit.
28
'We must kill our children,' he said, 'if we are to survive. There are too many people
30   to feed. Some must be sacrificed. I shall take my family upstream where you once
bathed in the river, and I shall kill them all. When you see the water running with
32   blood you will know that they are dead. Then you must start killing yours.'

34   The sun agreed and when he saw that the river had turned red he killed every member
of his family and threw their bodies into the water. But the moon had done something
36   very cruel. He had not killed his family at all. He had merely told his children to
throw handfuls of red clay into the river, to make it look like blood.
38
The sun, who had had so many wives and children, was now alone. And he is still
40   alone, shining up there in the sky in great majesty. The moon is much less bright, but
he still has a family. These are the crowds of stars that shine with him, night after
42   night.

Text 7.4   Creative Deception (CD for quick reference) (Source: Pilling 2001)

WORD CLASSES

Syntacticians (specialists in the study of syntax) use the traditional word class labels of **noun**, **verb**, **adjective**, **adverb**, **pronoun**, **preposition** and **conjunction** but add newer terms like **determiner** to complete the list. The older notional definitions on the lines of *a noun is a naming word*, *a verb is a doing word* and *an adjective is a describing word* are not particularly helpful as the basis of a rigorous and detailed linguistic analysis. Does the verb *swing* not 'name' an action and do all verbs do something? What about verbs like *seem* and *be*? What are they 'doing'? In the phrase *a gravel path*, does 'gravel' not describe the path even though the word *gravel* is a noun not an adjective?

There are four open classes of words – open in that we often create new words in these categories and these classes are noun, verb, adjective and adverb. The other word categories – pronoun, preposition, determiner and conjunction – are closed categories. There have been no newly coined words in these closed categories over the centuries though there have been attempts recently to find a gender neutral pronoun to indicate he+she. Political correctness challenges the use of *he* to include females and hence apparently new pronoun forms such as *s/he* or *he/she* have appeared but it is noticeable that whilst these may appear in written text, there are few examples occurring easily in speech.

In the following explanation of the word classes, most of the examples are taken from *Creative Deception* (Text 7.4) which you should read before you go any further. Line references for examples from the text are indicated as L#. If no line reference is provided, this indicates that the item appears in many places in the text.

Open classes

The noun class is probably one of the largest in English. There are three subsets. Nouns can be sub-classified as count nouns, non-count nouns and proper nouns. Count nouns can be singular (e.g. *world* L1, *day* L3, *bend* L6) or plural (e.g. *friends* L2, *families* L5) and the regular plural inflection in English is to add {-s} to the end of the word. Not all plurals are regular. What is the plural of words like *man*, *goose*, *foot*, and *mouse*? Some words do not mark the plural but we know we can count sheep or fish so they must have a plural form even if there is no plural morpheme added to the word stem. Non-count nouns (e.g. *brightness* L2, *brilliance* L19) cannot be counted so the noun cannot be made plural. The final subset within this word class is that of proper noun of which there are no examples in *Creative Deception*. Proper nouns name, for example, an individual person or a people, a place or a river: e.g. *Chris*, *the Spanish*, *York*, *the White House*, *India*, *the Thames*. In English, a proper noun (but not the other kinds of nouns) is written with a capital letter wherever it appears in a sentence. In German, all nouns are always written with a capital letter.

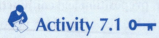

Activity 7.1

Identify as many nouns as you can from *Creative Deception* L34–37. Classify each noun as precisely as you can.

A similarly large word class is that of verb. Verbs are inflected for tense (to give an indication of the time of an action) and as the usual (unmarked) tense of narrative is the simple past, that is the form of many of the verbs in *Creative Deception* (e.g. *shone* L1, *were* L2, *went* L2). For each example, a present tense form can be created but so can other forms as Table 7.1 shows. The present tense forms can be used to narrate a story, especially in oral language. When used in that way, it is often referred to as the *historic present*. The form that appears in *Creative Deception* has been *italicized* in Table 7.1. Not all the verbs from *Creative Deception* appear in the table.

Table 7.1   Verb forms

	A	B	C	D	E
Line	finite if used as present tense, otherwise non-finite form	finite forms (indicate tense)		non-finite forms (do not indicate tense)	
		present tense (he/she/it)	past tense	the {-ing} form (called the present participle* in many grammars)	the {-en} form (called the past participle* in many grammars)
1	be	is	*was were*	being	been
2	go	goes	*went*	going	gone
3	change	changes	*changed*	changing	changed
5	*take*	takes	*took*	taking	taken
12	*cut*	cuts	cut	cutting	cut
15	see	sees	*saw*	seeing	seen
16	swirl	swirls	*swirled*	swirling	swirled
22	swim	swims	swam	*swimming*	swum

*These traditional labels are potentially confusing as the {-ing} form does not only appear in present tense but can appear in past tense (e.g. Michael was chang<u>ing</u> Ben's nappy) and the {-en} form can appear in the present tense (e.g. On arrest, the individual is tak<u>en</u> to the police station) and, indeed, the two forms can appear in the same verb group (e.g. The words were be<u>ing</u> spok<u>en</u> quietly).

In Table 7.1 we can see that, in standard English, all main or **lexical verbs** (auxiliary verbs will be considered later in this unit) have five forms. A **finite** form of the verb shows past or present tense. A **non-finite** form does not indicate tense. Past tense forms (Column C) all refer to completed actions in the past. The present tense forms in Column B must have the third person singular (he/she/it) as grammatical subject as in *He swims, the steam swirls* or *she sees*. With first or second person subject (see Table 7.2 overleaf), the present tense form looks like the base form as in Column A. The use of the non-finite forms (as in Column D and Column E) will be explained later in this unit.

Verbs can be transitive or intransitive in English. For current purposes, we can say that intransitive verbs relate to processes with only one obligatory participant (e.g. *He sleeps, The sheep died* or *Robert sneezed*) whereas transitive verbs relate to processes with two (or more) obligatory participants (e.g. *Liz cleaned the cooker, Jonathan likes steak, Giles gave his children a treat* or *Vernon put the dinner in the oven*).

In English, adjectives appear before nouns in noun phrases (see next section) and from *Creative Deception* there are examples like the *same* brightness (L2), *good friends* (L2) and a *very cruel* trick (L22). Adjectives also appear in position Y in structures like 'X is/was Y' as in *Creative Deception* where the reader is told that 'The world was still very new' (L1), that 'everybody was very polite' (L7) and that 'it was very hot' (L16). Many adjectives also admit comparison and then **suffixes** can be added as in *new, newer, newest*. Some adjectives form the comparative and superlative forms by using the intensifying adverbs *more* and *most* as in *more beautiful* and *most exciting*. Some adjectives have irregular forms as, for example, the adjective *good* has the comparative form *better* and the superlative form *best*. Not all adjectives can be graded or compared – something is either unique or it is not and you cannot be more or less alive (➔ Unit 6).

Adverbs describe actions or modify verbs rather than things and tend to give information about time, place and manner. Like adjectives, adverbs can also be compared but adverbs appear in different structures in English. This will become clearer as we move up the hierarchy of rank. The comparative and superlative forms of adverbs are formed in the same way as they are formed in adjectives. In *Creative Deception* (L9), the word *first* gives information about the timing of the jump and so is an adverb. Similarly in L16, the word *about* tells the reader where the moon swam and so the word *about* is an adverb in this sentence.

Closed classes

It would be logical to think that pronouns should stand in place of nouns. True, but they also stand in place of noun phrases. In *Creative Deception*, the pronoun *They*

Table 7.2   Pronouns: number and case

Number	Singular			Plural		
Person	subject case	object case	possessive case	subject case	object case	possessive case
1st person (refers to speaker)	I	me	mine	we	us	ours
2nd person (refers to hearer)	you	you	yours	you	you	yours
3rd person (neither speaker nor hearer)	he she it	him her it	his hers its	they	them	theirs

(L2) refers to 'the sun and the moon' (L1) but in L6 what appears to be the same pronoun, *they*, refers to *the sun and his family* (L5). When the sun says (L9) *I'll jump*, the reader knows that *I* refers to the sun and generally *I* refers to whoever is speaking. In the same line, *you* refers to the moon (the hearer) but in other examples *you* refers to whoever is the addressee or receiver of the message. Pronouns differ according to number and relation to speaker (see Table 7.2) and are inflected for case which means that there are different forms of the pronoun depending on the syntactic function of the pronoun in the sentence. In other languages all noun phrases, not just pronouns, are inflected for case. These inflections, or inflectional morphemes, are added to the word for syntactic reasons. They do not change the word class of the word to which they are added as derivational morphemes do (➟ Unit 5).

Determiners indicate the range of **reference** of a noun and examples can be found in *Creative Deception*. The words *their*, *his* (L5) and *every* (L25) as well as *the* and *a* (which appear throughout the text) are all examples of determiners as are words like *each*, *this*, *that*, *those*, *some* and *any*. Using the definite article *the* tells the addressee/receiver that there is a specific **referent** whereas using the indefinite article *a/an* means the speaker could be referring to any example. How does the speaker decide whether to use *a* or *an*?

 ## Activity 7.2

Think about the difference in meaning between these two examples:
  (a) Can I have a pen, please?
  (b) Can I have the pen, please?
     What is the difference in meanings? What assumptions is the speaker making in each question?

Each preposition has only one form. Examples of prepositions from *Creative Deception* include *with* (L1), *round*, *for* and *in* (L6), *out of* (L6) – the two words together form one preposition (➤➤ phrasal words in Unit 5). Other examples would include *next to*, *under*, *by*, *at*, *before*, *after*, *between* to name but a few.

 Activity 7.3

Find 12 prepositions from *Creative Deception* or you could use the 12 prepositions listed in the last paragraph. What do these prepositions mean? If you are unsure, then use a good dictionary to look up the meaning of each.

Conjunctions are words which join or link two words, phrases or clauses and there are two main groups. The coordinating conjunctions in English are *and*, *but* and *or* and the same structure normally appears on either side of the coordinating conjunction. Examples from *Creative Deception* are (*the sun*) *and* (*the moon*) on L1 where the two noun phrases being conjoined have each been bracketed. Other examples show coordinated clauses (*They were good friends*) *and* (*often went round together*) on L2, adjectives (*frosty*) *and* (*cold*) on L19 and adverbs (*there*) *and* (*then*) on L22. Subordinating conjunctions normally link a subordinate clause into a main clause: in the example 'let's have lunch <u>when class is over</u>', the underlined subordinate clause indicates the time when the main action of meeting for lunch should happen and could be seen as similar to saying 'let's have lunch tomorrow' (where an adverb indicates the time of the main action of having lunch). Examples of subordinating conjunctions from *Creative Deception* would include *when* (L1), *so that* (L6), *as* (L9) and *as soon as* (L12).

 Activity 7.4 ○━┳

You have already (Activity 7.1) identified all the nouns in lines 34–37 of *Creative Deception*. Now identify the word class of all the other words from those same lines. Try to do this from your understanding of the material covered in this unit but if you get stuck, remember that this information is provided in all good dictionaries.

For extra practice, any other paragraph from *Creative Deception* or, indeed, any other text could be used. When in doubt, a dictionary will help you but remember that there might be some variations on this classification (particularly in relation to determiners).

PHRASES

According to the hierarchy of rank (see Figure 7.1), words combine to form phrases – a term which in linguistics has a clear definition, unlike the more general use of the word. There are five types of phrase in English, three of which have a very similar basic structure. These three are the **noun phrase** (NP), the **adjective phrase** (AdjP) and the adverb phrase (AdvP). A noun is the headword of an NP, an adjective the headword of an AdjP and an adverb the headword of an AdvP and they are similar in that in each phrase, there is a headword whose word class determines the label of the phrase. The prepositional phrase (PP) is easily recognized, as its structure is defined as preposition + noun phrase: *the café* would be analysed as an NP but *at the café* as a PP. We use the term **verb group** (VG) not the term **verb phrase**. You should be aware that the term *verb phrase* might have different definitions in different approaches to grammar.

Noun phrases, adjective phrases and adverb phrases

The headword of a phrase is the only obligatory element in the phrase. Modification is optional. From the hierarchy of rank, it is clear that an NP can consist of one word only (and that must be a noun or a pronoun) or it can consist of more than one word. The following examples have the same headword *snow* but the modification varies and includes premodification before the headword (<u>underlined</u> in the examples below) and postmodification after it (<u><u>double underlined</u></u> in the examples below).

(1)   Examples of NP

(a)		snow	
(b)	<u>crisp white</u>	snow	
(c)	<u>snowball</u>	snow	
(d)	<u>that beautiful</u>	snow	<u>on the branches of the trees</u>
(e)	<u>some slushy melting</u>	snow	<u>on city pavements</u>
(f)	<u>the</u>	snow	<u>which covers the fields</u>

The NP structure is clear from these examples. Example (a) shows a single word NP. If there is a determiner (e.g. *that*, *some*) then the determiner will be the first word in the phrase. Adjectives (e.g. *crisp*, *beautiful*, *slushy*) and nouns (e.g. *snowball*) can be used to premodify the head noun. In the postmodification slot, there is often a PP (e.g. *on the branches of the trees*, *on city pavements*) or there can be a **relative clause** (e.g. *which covers the fields*) – a structure that will be addressed later in this unit. The noun phrase structure found in *Creative Deception* is not particularly complex.

Get Comfortable Not Knowing

There once was a village that had among its people a very wise old man. The villagers
2 trusted this man to provide them with answers to their questions and concerns.

4 One day a farmer from the village went to the wise man and said in a frantic tone,
'Wise man, help me. A horrible thing has happened. My ox has died and I have no
6 animal to help me plow my field! Isn't this the worst thing that could have possibly
happened?' The wise old man replied 'Maybe so, maybe not.' The man hurried back
8 to the village and reported to his neighbors that the wise man had gone mad. Surely
this *was* the worst thing that could have happened. Why couldn't he see this?
10
The very next day, however, a strong, young horse was seen near the man's farm.
12 Because the man had no ox to rely on, he had the idea to catch the horse to replace his
ox – and he did. How joyful the farmer was. Plowing the field had never been easier.
14 He went back to the wise man to apologize. 'You were right, wise man. Losing my ox
wasn't the worst thing that could have happened. It was a blessing in disguise! I never
16 would have captured my new horse had that not happened. You must agree that this is
the *best* thing that could have happened.' The wise man replied once again, 'Maybe so,
18 maybe not.' Not again, thought the farmer. Surely the wise man had gone mad now.

20 But, once again, the farmer did not know what was to happen. A few days later the
farmer's son was riding the horse and was thrown off. He broke his leg and would not
22 be able to help with the crop. Oh no, thought the man. Now we will starve to death.
Once again, the farmer went to the wise man. This time he said, 'How did you know
24 that capturing my horse was not a good thing? You were right again. My son is
injured and won't be able to help with the crop. This time I'm sure that this is the
26 *worst* thing that could possibly have happened. You must agree this time.' But, just as
he had done before, the wise man calmly looked at the farmer and in a compassionate
28 tone replied once again, 'Maybe so, maybe not.' Enraged that the wise man could be
so ignorant, the farmer stormed back to the village.
30
The next day troops arrived to take every able-bodied man to the war that had just
32 broken out. The farmer's son was the only young man in the village who didn't have
to go. He would live, while others would surely die.
34
The moral of this story provides a powerful lesson. The truth is, we *don't* know
36 what's going to happen – we just think we do. Often we make a big deal out of
something. We blow up scenarios in our minds about all the terrible things that are
38 going to happen. Most of the time we are wrong. If we keep our cool and stay open to
possibilities, we can be reasonably certain that, eventually, all will be well. Remember,
40 maybe so, maybe not.

Text 7.5   Get Comfortable Not Knowing (GC for quick reference) (Source: Carlsson 1998)

The noun phrases in (2) come from another text, *Get Comfortable Not Knowing*. In this table which certainly does not contain all the NPs in Text 7.5, two NPs contain a relative clause in the postmodification slot (the examples in L1 and L6–7). Such clauses can be finite or non-finite, terms which will be further explained in the next section on the verb group. In the following table, the relative clauses are finite.

(2)   Noun phrases

Line no	premodifier		HEAD	postmodifier
1	a		village	that had among its people a very wise old man
1	the		villagers	
4	a		farmer	from the village
4	the	wise	man	
4	a	frantic	tone	
5		wise	man	
5	my		ox	
6–7	the	worst	thing	that could possibly have happened
7	the	wise old	man	
8	his		neighbors	
11	a	strong young	horse	
11	the man's		farm	

NP structure can be ambiguous. Look again at Texts 7.1–7.3 and consider the following questions. Is the cream fresh as well as the strawberries? Is the service patient or is the service for the transport of patients? Are the children's jokes good or does the book contain jokes only for good children? These questions can be answered and the ambiguity explained if you think about the scope of the premodification in each NP.

In order to show the structure of a noun phrase, one of two types of diagrams is conventionally drawn. Box diagrams have already been demonstrated in (2). Tree diagrams showing the two possible meanings with the relevant structure for each meaning of *good children's jokes* would look like those in (3). In these tree diagrams, *mod* is an abbreviation for modifier and *poss* an abbreviation for possessive.

(3) Good children's jokes

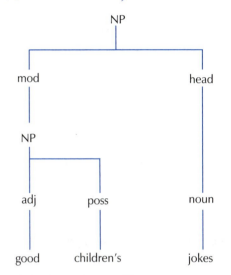

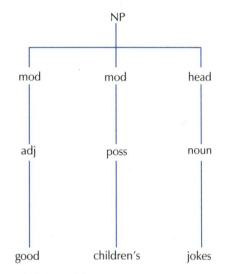

This is the structure for the meaning
that the jokes are only for good children

This is the structure for the meaning that
the jokes are good and for all children

 Activity 7.5 0━┱

Draw out either two box diagrams or two tree diagrams to show the
structure of each of the two meanings of *fresh strawberries and cream* and
of *patient transport service*.

A noun phrase can be replaced by a pronoun. If we were to replace each NP in L4
from *Get Comfortable* it would read 'One day he went to him and said in it'.
Speakers and writers choose when to use nouns and when to use pronouns
depending on how much information they think the addressee/receiver already
knows and how much needs to be made explicit. This will be discussed later in this
unit.

Adjective phrases (AdjPs) and adverb phrases (AdvPs) operate on a similar
principle of modifier + head, where the word class of the obligatory headword in
the phrase will determine the phrase type. So in *Creative Deception* (L1) the
intensifier *very* modifies the adjective *new* and so the phrase *very new* is an AdjP.
By similar reasoning, *very polite* (L7), *very hot* (L16), *very cruel* (L22) and *so
ignorant* (GC L29) are also adjective phrases. Though neither text has an example,

we can create adverb phrases such as *extremely fast* and *quite carefully* in a comment such as 'She drives extremely fast but quite carefully'.

There are examples of a prepositional phrase (PP) in *Creative Deception* at L5 (*in the river*), L6 (*round a bend*) and L13 (*from the trees*). In *Get Comfortable Not Knowing* there are examples at L1 (*among its people*), L11 (*near the man's farm*) and L15 (*in disguise*).

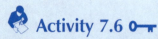

Activity 7.6 o━━

Identify the NPs, AdjPs, and PPs in L4–9 of *Get Comfortable*.

Verb group (VG)

The verb group is the most complex of all the group structures in English and has the greatest effect on clause structure which is discussed later in this unit.

The VG can consist of a single verb (e.g. *Creative Deception* L15: *swam*, L34: *agreed*) or there can be more than one word in which case there will be **auxiliary verbs** before the lexical verb (*Creative Deception* L5: *had decided*, L23: *would have*). These verb groups (whether one word or more than one word) are finite because they show tense. In a finite verb group in English, the first word in the group always carries tense.

Auxiliaries

There are two types of auxiliary verbs in English and there can be more than one auxiliary in a VG.

Primary auxiliary verbs

The auxiliary *do* can be used to make the negative form of the verb as in *Get Comfortable* where 'the farmer did not know what was to happen' (L20) or 'who didn't have to go' (L32–33). *Do* can also be used for the **interrogative** (or question) form. In L6–7 the man from the village could well have asked the wise old man 'Do you agree with me?'. *Do* is only used for the negative and the interrogative where there is no other auxiliary verb.

The auxiliary verb *have* (in either present or past tense) is used to create the perfective **aspect** of the verb when it is combined with {-*en*} (or the past participle) form. Trask (1997: 21) defines aspect as being 'the way in which an action or a situation is distributed in time'. This can be exemplified in the two texts being used in this unit. If you read the first four sentences of *Creative Deception* (L1–5) and list the events in chronological order, then the list would look something like this:

1 the world was new
2 the sun and the moon were equals
3 they shone with the same brightness
4 they were good friends
5 they went round together
6 they decided to go bathing
7 everything changed.

The decision to go bathing has to precede in time the fact that everything changed because that decision sparks off the whole series of subsequent events. Use of perfective aspect ('they <u>had</u> decid<u>ed</u>' L5) shows the reader clearly what the chronological order of events is. Of course, narrators, or story-tellers, do not always choose to narrate the events in the order in which they occur.

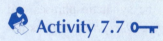 **Activity 7.7 ⚬━**

Read *Creative Deception* L34–37. Work out the chronology of events and relate that to the use of perfective aspect.

The auxiliary verb *be* and the {*-ing*} form of the main verb together create the progressive aspect in English. Read L21 in *Get Comfortable Not Knowing*. The son had not finished riding the horse when he was thrown off. If he had, the text would have read 'the farmer's son rode/had ridden the horse and was thrown off'. Surely the meaning is that while he was riding the horse, he was thrown off and this means that the action of riding was incomplete. The progressive aspect is used to indicate this.

The other major use of the auxiliary verb *be* is in combination with the {*-en*} form (or the past participle) to create the **passive voice**. In grammar, the voice system allows the possibility of talking about the same event in different ways. In L11 of *Get Comfortable Not Knowing* the writer chooses not to tell us who saw the horse but to focus on the fact that the horse 'was seen' – which in structural terms is the auxiliary verb *be* + {*-en*} / past participle of the verb *see*. If the author had written in the **active voice** then he would have to have told us who saw the horse.

Modal auxiliary verbs

Modal auxiliaries allow for a range of meanings to be expressed. Obligation can be expressed through the use of the modals *must*, *should* or *ought to*; permission can be sought and granted through the use of *can, could* or *may*; and possibility or prediction through the use the modal auxiliaries *will, may, might, could* (think of the language of horoscopes or the weather forecast). In conditional sentences, such as 'I would do that if I were you' the modal *would* appears and *shall* is still used in offers, such as 'Shall I open the door for you?'.

Activity 7.8 o──

From Text 7.4 and Text 7.5, identify the verb groups which contain modal auxiliary verbs and decide what meaning each modal verb is expressing.

Activity 7.9 o──

As a conclusion to this section, identify all the syntactic phrases and groups in the first paragraph (L1–3) of *Creative Deception*. It does not matter if you do not account for every word in the paragraph.

SIMPLE CLAUSES

Working up the hierarchy of rank (Figure 7.1), the next level is that of the clause. The structure of a clause can be very complex but we will address simple structures first. It is very clear to see that the first paragraph of *Creative Deception* consists of three sentences. The third sentence contains one clause, the second contains two clauses and the first contains three clauses as shown in (4).

(4) Clauses in Creative Deception L1–3

Sentence number	Clause identified by letter with sentence number	Conjunctions linking clauses	Clauses
S1	1a	When	the world was still very new
	1b		the sun and the moon were equals
	1c	and	shone with the same brightness
S2	2a		They were good friends
	2b	and	often went round together
S3	3a	But	one day everything changed

Each clause contains a finite verb: the verbs are all in the past tense. Clauses 1a, 1b and 2a all describe something. Clauses 1c, 2b and 3a all say something happened. It is worth noting at this point that clauses 1b and 1c are coordinated clauses, as are clauses 2a and 2b, because they are linked with a coordinating conjunction (ccj). Clause 1a is linked to 1b with *when*, a subordinating conjunction (scj) and Clause 1a is therefore a subordinate clause. Clause 3a starts with a coordinating conjunction but stands alone in the sentence. It could have been linked into sentence two but the author chose to write it as a separate sentence.

The elements of clause structure are the **Subject** (S), the **Verb Group** (VG), the **Complement** (C) (of which there are three types: **direct object** (do), **indirect object** (io) and **intensive** (int)) and the **Adjunct** (A). The VG is divided into the **Finite** (F) and the **Predicator** (P) (the rest of the verb group), terms that will be clarified in later analyses in this unit. The Subject and the Complement usually refer to one of the obligatory participants in the process being expressed in the clause. The Adjunct usually refers to any circumstances which surround the process and the obligatory participants. Adjuncts express meanings – such as time, place, manner, reason, result – which the message giver chooses to provide and which, unlike the (obligatory) participants, can usually be seen as optional. A simple example might clarify this. In (5), *I will have finished this unit by the end of the week*, the obligatory participants are *I* and *this unit* and it is quite grammatical to say simply 'I will finish this unit'. The circumstance of time is additional and optional information and would be labelled as Adjunct (time).

(5)   *Simple clause analysis.*

This row shows the clause being analysed.	I	will	have finished	this unit	by the end of this week
This row shows the elements of clause structure.	S	F	P	Cdo	A-time
This row shows which type of phrase is used in each element of clause structure.	NP	VG		NP	PP
		aux	lex		

Declarative clauses declare things – or make statements. **Imperative** clauses issue a command or an instruction. Interrogative clauses ask a question. Declarative clauses usually have a Subject and a verb group, and the subject usually precedes the verb group. In an interrogative clause, the auxiliary verb and the subject are inverted (the order in which they appear in the clause changes). Imperatives do not normally have a subject explicitly stated in the clause (➻ Unit 3).

There are many ways or tests to identify the subject of a clause. We discuss only two.

Test 1: Find the verb group of the clause and ask the question 'who/what <u>verbs</u>?'. The answer to this question will always be the subject of the clause. For example, in *the world was very new*, the verb group is *was*. The question, therefore, is 'who/what was very new?'. The answer is 'the world' and therefore the NP *the world* is the grammatical subject of the clause.

Test 2: Add a tag question to a declarative clause and the pronoun in the tag question always refers back to the subject of that declarative clause. Adding a tag question to the sentence *the sun and the moon were equals* yields *the sun and moon were equals, weren't they?* and the pronoun *they* refers back to *the sun and the moon* therefore the NP complex *the sun and the moon* constitutes the grammatical subject of the clause. An NP complex occurs where two or more NPs are coordinated (and together have the same syntactic function in the clause).

 Activity 7.10 o—┱

Use whichever test you prefer (or both) to determine the grammatical subject of the remaining clauses in (4).

The verb determines what type of complementation is needed in the clause. The examples in (6) are taken from *Creative Deception* and all the verbs are intransitive. Though the clauses express different meanings (describing somebody/something or saying that something happened), each clause is only talking about one **entity** or participant and each clause has a Subject and a Verb. You should note that within the verb group, the first auxiliary is labelled as F (for Finite). All other parts of the verb group are labelled P (for Predicator). The label F/P indicates that there is a single finite lexical verb in the verb group. You should also note that these verbs, expressing these meanings, do not need anything to follow them in the clause and such types of verbs are called intransitive verbs.

(6)   Clause analysis SV

L25			Time	passed	
			S	F/P	
L25	and	a great famine	came	upon the earth	
	ccj	S	F/P	A-place	
L25	Every day		people	were	dying
	A-time		S	F	P
L34			The sun	agreed	
			S	F/P	

Transitive verbs must be complemented (or completed) to make sense: there must be something that comes after them in the clause. Transitive verbs usually express processes with two or more obligatory participants. Therefore, the complement is obligatory with transitive verbs as the examples in (7) show. There are three different types of complement and which type is used depends on the verb and the meaning being expressed.

(7)   Clause analysis SVCdo

L21	The sun		mocked		him
	S		F/P		Cdo
L29	We		must	kill	our children
	S		F	P	Cdo
L30	Some		must	be sacrificed	
	S		F	P	
L34–35	he		killed		every member of his family
	S		F/P		Cdo
L35–36	the moon		had	done	something very cruel
	S		F	P	Cdo
L41	he	still	has		a family
	S	A-time	F		Cdo

The examples in (7) are taken from *Creative Deception*. The verbs are all transitive and take a complement direct object (Cdo). In terms of meaning, there are two distinct participants in each event or process and in a declarative active clause, the doer of the action will appear in the subject slot of the clause. If you talk about mocking or killing somebody, you must name the target of your mockery or your killing, you cannot simply say *he mocked* or *he killed*. If, in relation to L21, you ask the question 'Who did the sun (=Subject) mock?', the answer is 'him' and that answer fills the Cdo slot in the clause. A rather odd-looking question is 'who/what did <u>Subject</u> <u>verb</u>?' but the NP in any clause that answers that question will always fit into the Cdo slot for that clause. Such odd-looking questions can be very useful in syntactic analysis.

There are always two distinct participants in the process of *sacrifice* (somebody must sacrifice something) but in this clause (L30) only one is named. This is because the verb is in the passive voice and therefore the subject slot will not name the doer but another participant. Any optional circumstances, such as when, where or why something happened, are realized in the Adjunct slot (e.g. L41).

The second type of complement, complement indirect object (Cio), appears in *Creative Deception* on L27 where the reader is told that the moon 'paid the sun a visit'. There is apparently no Subject in this declarative clause (the Subject is in fact carried over from the first clause in the sentence) but there do appear to be two object complements. The process of 'paying a visit' necessarily involves three obligatory participants: somebody who goes to visit, somebody who receives the visit and the visit itself. Similarly, the processes of showing, giving, demonstrating and offering, amongst others, all involve three obligatory participants. Therefore, necessarily, the syntax of the clause must allow for this meaning to be expressed. The indirect object always carries the meaning of the recipient – the one who benefits from the process. Another question can be added to those used earlier in this unit to identify clause elements. Remember that 'who/what <u>verbs</u>?' identifies the Subject and that 'who/what does <u>Subject</u> <u>verb</u>?' identifies the Complement direct object. The question to identify the Complement indirect object is 'to/for whom does <u>Subject</u> <u>verb</u>?'. In L27, therefore, *a visit* will be analysed as Cdo and the recipient *the sun*, is labelled complement indirect object (Cio) as shown in (8):

(8)   Clause analysis SVCio

L26	But	he	hid		his anger
		S	F/P		Cdo
L26–27	and		paid	the sun	a visit
	ccj		F/P	Cio	Cdo

The third and final type of complement is called an intensive complement (Cint). In terms of meaning, this structure realizes single participant processes where an attribute or quality of the participant is being provided. The examples in (9) are taken from *Creative Deception* but you should note that this is not an exhaustive list of all the examples from that text.

(9)   Clause analysis: SVCint

L1	When	the world	was	still	very new
		S	F	A-time	Cint
L1		the sun and the moon	were		equals
		S	F		Cint
L2		They	were		good friends
		S	F		Cint
L6–7	In those days	everybody	was		very polite
	A-time	S	F		Cint
L40		The moon	is		much less bright
		S	F		Cint

 Activity 7.11

From *Get Comfortable*, analyse these selected clauses in terms of SFPCA (Subject, Finite, Predicate, Complement, Adjunct). As a strategy, find the verb group in the clause first, then find the subject and then decide what kind of complement (if any) appears. Finally, decide if there are any Adjuncts.

(a)   A horrible thing has happened (L5)
(b)   The man hurried back to the village (L7–8)
(c)   The very next day, however, a strong, young horse was seen near the man's farm (L11)
(d)   Once again, the farmer went to the wise man (L23)
(e)   You were right again (L24)
(f)   The moral of this story provides a powerful lesson (L35)
(g)   Often we make a big deal out of something (L36–37)
(h)   Most of the time we are wrong (L38)

COMPLEX CLAUSES

In the hierarchy of rank (Figure 7.1), it is clear that clauses can be combined to form sentences and this is evident in the two, relatively uncomplicated, texts that have been used in this unit. In the first paragraph of *Creative Deception*, some of the clauses are linked with the coordinating conjunctions to form compound clauses – sentences which contain coordinated clauses. Other examples can be found in *Creative Deception* on L18–19, L25, L26–27, L40–41, the latter example showing the clauses coordinated with *but*. The coordinated clauses can simply be numbered in the order in which they appear in the sentence, as shown in (10).

(10)   Coordinated clauses in compound sentences

They	were	good friends	and	often	went	round together
S	F	Cint	ccj	A-time	F/P	A-circ
1			2			

The combination of clauses within a written sentence or within a spoken **utterance** can become very complex, and speakers of English do not always realize the complexity of the structures they are using. In *Creative Deception* L9–10, the sun says, 'You'll know I'm in the water when it starts to boil'. There are four distinct verb groups, so there are four clauses. The first two clauses can be dealt with first. In the process of *knowing*, there are two participants: the knower and the known or in other words, the knower knows something. That something, which in SFPCA would be analysed as Cdo and normally realized by an NP, is in this example still Cdo in clause structure (remember the question to ask: what will subject (=you) verb (=know)?) but it is realized by a clause and so it is enclosed in double square brackets to make clear that it is a **rankshifted** clause (a clause found in another clause where you would normally expect to find a noun phrase). A similar phenomenon occurs later in the sentence: *to boil* must be the obligatory Cdo for the previous verb *start* and it must be obligatory because the VG *to boil* cannot simply be omitted from the sentence. If it were omitted, the sentence would sound incomplete or unfinished. This analysis of the sentence is shown with each rankshifted clause enclosed in double square brackets as shown here:

You'll know [[that I'm in the water]] when it starts [[to boil]].

The final clause in this sentence tells the moon when he will know that the sun is in the water (*when it starts to boil*), and therefore it is functioning in the same way as any other Adjunct, giving, in this example, information about time. It is a subordinate clause because it cannot stand on its own as a sentence. Subordinate clauses are enclosed in double vertical lines. Triple vertical lines are used to indicate the boundaries of the entire clause complex. In written text, the clause complex boundary is co-terminous with the sentence boundary but when spoken language is being analysed there are no full stops to help us recognize the boundaries (➥ Unit 2). The full analysis of this sentence, therefore, would look like this:

||| You'll know [[that I'm in the water]] || when it starts [[to boil]] |||

or in the now familiar box diagram format it looks like this:

(11)   Complex clause analysis Creative Deception

||| You	'll	know	[[that	I	'm	in the water]]	|| when	it	starts	[[to boil]] |||
			[[	S	F	A-place]]	scj	S	F/P	[[Cdo]]
S	F	P	[[Cdo]]				|| A-time			

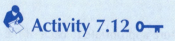

Activity 7.12

Analyse in terms of SFPCA the sentences in *Creative Deception* L25–27.

Text 7.6   Flying pigs can be exciting

 Activity 7.13 🔑

Look at the 'Flying Pigs' cartoons which are based on the same structural
ambiguity as the classic example from many linguistic textbooks 'Flying
planes can be dangerous'. The ambiguity is located in the Subject slot of
the main clause and is explained thus:

either   the {-*ing*} form of the verb is premodifying the noun so the clause
         is talking about pigs which fly
or   the Subject is realized by a rankshifted clause and it is the action
         of flying pigs which is exciting.

    Draw out the diagrams to show the structure appropriate to each of the
two meanings.

TEXT

Moving up the hierarchy of rank, clauses combine to form sentences and text. Text grammar is not as tightly constrained as sentence or clause grammar and a writer has more choices available but the sentences which form a text are going to be linked together in some way. It is hard to argue that the sentences in Text 7.7, each quite grammatical and meaningful on its own, form a coherent and cohesive text.

We went to the furniture shop and looked at chairs. You sentenced the criminal to four years in prison. Zoë liked the dolls very much.

Text 7.7   Is his a text?

There are ways of linking sentences to create texts and to make clear to the reader the meaning of the whole discourse as well as the meaning of the individual sentences. Before you read any further, look again at Texts 7.4 and 7.5. It is quite clear that the individual sentences in these texts are somehow linked together in a way that those in Text 7.7 are not. In terms of a functional approach to grammar, the textual function of language is being exploited, a function which Bloor and Bloor (2004: 11) characterize as 'the use of language to organize the text itself'.

There is no doubt that Text 7.4 and Text 7.5 are structured as narratives: they each tell a story. Labov (1999: 227, 234) presents an overall structure of narrative that is more detailed than the simplistic 'beginning', 'middle' and 'end'. He suggests that the following stages can be found in most narratives (➻ also Unit 9) and provides indicative or 'underlying questions' for each stage:

Abstract	–	what is this about?
Orientation	–	who? when? where? what?
Complicating Action	–	then what happened?
Evaluation	–	so what?
Result or Resolution	–	what finally happened?
Coda	–	closure of the narrative.

In *Get Comfortable Not Knowing*, the title forms the abstract. The orientation occurs in the first paragraph and then the action starts: the ox dies, the horse throws the son, and the troops arrive. The resolution to the narrative is the war, and the evaluation and coda appear in the final paragraph which begins quite explicitly with 'the moral of this story', a feature which frequently indicates narrative closure in texts.

This organization and sequencing of events in narrative is one way in which a text becomes a text. Another way this can be seen is through the grammar of the text and how sentences in a text are linked to each other using the structural resources of the language.

The use of pronouns in the linguistic system of reference is a clear way of relating a later sentence to an earlier one. In *Get Comfortable*, after he has been introduced, the farmer is later referred to using the pronoun *he* (L12). However, it should be noted that in direct speech the farmer refers to himself as *I* (L5) and *me* (L6). Other characters are referred to using the pronoun *he*: on L9 *he* is the wise man and on L21 *he* is the farmer's son. On L9, the pronoun *this* can only be understood if the reader looks back to a previous event in the narrative. Part of the skill of reading is working out the referent for each pronoun. Alternatively, part of the skill of writing is referring in an unambiguous way.

Activity 7.14

Identify all the pronouns in *Get Comfortable* and the referent for each pronoun. As you do this task, you will be exploring **deixis** which Trask (1997: 65) defines as 'linguistic pointing'. (➟ Deixis is also discussed in Unit 3.)

Determiners in NPs can be part of the reference system. In *Get Comfortable* the existence of the village is asserted in L1 and here the village is non-specified and the determiner used within the NP structure is the indefinite article *a*. The village does not have a name and the reader cannot refer to a map to identify it. On L4, the definite article *the* is used to specify that it is the same village that has been referred to earlier in the text. The reader can still not locate the village on a real-world map but can locate it as the one that was mentioned earlier in the text. Now look at L4 and L7 to see how the farmer is referred to. The choice of determiners helps to create a text.

The last part of the reference system involves comparison and in this text it is clearest in the use of superlative adjectives. As soon as the farmer says (L16–17) to the wise man 'You must agree that this is the *best* thing that could have happened', there is an implicit comparison with everything that could possibly have happened in the village, if not in the world. Similarly, with the comparative form there must always be a point of comparison.

Ellipsis, the omission of linguistic elements within a clause, is evident in *Get Comfortable Not Knowing* when the Subject element of the second clause in L4 appears to have been omitted. There is no syntactic reason for its omission but a writer/speaker can omit the grammatical Subject (and/or other elements) in a second or later coordinated clause, where that Subject (or those other elements) is/are the same as in the first clause. This process clearly links clauses together but there are important considerations of meaning. Consider the following two sentences:

(a)   A man came into the pub and bought a pint of beer.
(b)   A man came into the pub and a man bought a pint of shandy.

How many men are involved in the actions in (a) and in (b)?

Rather than omitting words, a speaker/writer often substitutes one word for a previously used word or phrase. **Substitution** can be of three types, as demonstrated in these examples:

Clausal substitution:

A   Can I help you?
B   I hope so.

where *so* substitutes for *that you can help me*.

Verbal substitution:

A   We need to feed the cat.
B   I have done.

where *done* substitutes for *fed the cat*.

Nominal substitution:

A   Which flowers would you like?
B   I'd like those blue ones.

where *ones* substitutes for *flowers*.

Conjunction is clearly a way by which clauses and sentences in a text can be held together. Clauses can be coordinated with *and* (*GC* L5–6, L21–22) and they can also be bound together by subordinate conjunctions such as *while* (L33). Temporal conjunction occurs with phrases that indicate the sequence of events. The events of the narrative begin *one day* (L4) and continue *the very next day* (L11). *Once again* (L20) the farmer cannot predict the future but *a few days later* (L20) the next disaster hits him. You will find other examples throughout the text.

Lexical cohesion is a powerful way of holding a text together. Some of the lexical cohesive devices in *Get Comfortable* are:

■ repetition: e.g. *the wise man, the farmer*.
■ different ways of referring to the main protagonists: e.g. *the farmer, the man*.

- different ways of referring to the main place and its inhabitants: *the village, the villagers, his neighbors*.
- the terms relating to agricultural activities and animals such as *animal, plow, field, ox, horse* and *crop*.
- different verbs to indicate how the man went to see the wise man: *went, hurried back, stormed back, arrived, didn't have to go*. Whilst these last two examples refer to the actions of the troops, they are still part of the lexical field of verbs of movement (➥ Unit 6).
- indicators of time: *once, one day, the very next day, once again, a few days later, this time*.

Such patterning through the text is one way of making sure the text coheres together and the lack of any such patterns in Text 7.7 is one of the clearest reasons why those sentences do not form a text.

 Activity 7.15 o—

Show how *Creative Deception* is a coherent and cohesive text. You should consider:

(a)   the narrative structure of the text
(b)   the reference system
(c)   ellipsis and substitution
(d)   conjunction
(e)   lexical patterning.

WHO AND WHAT ARE TEXTS FOR?

Who are texts created for? When students produce a coherent text (oral or written) on a given topic, it takes far more effort on their part than the effort needed when they are informally sitting with friends talking about the same topic. Why is that? Is it simply that this coherent version will be judged by tutors and that grades will be dependent on this specific text? If that is the case, then it is worth thinking about other written texts. It takes more effort to write a postcard or a letter (where grades are irrelevant – but perhaps we still care about what the reader thinks) than to make a phone call to transmit the same information. Many would say that it takes more effort to write a postcard or a letter than to send an e-mail or to text a message. If that is true, then arguably the sheer physical effort of writing needs to be considered as well as the mental effort of organizing and creating the text.

Some will argue that modern technology might well make the physical process of writing easier for a writer. Others will argue that the relative ease of writing with the assistance of modern technology (word processing, texting) means that there is less control over the writing process and that writers now use more words to make the same point than earlier writers did. It is certainly true that it is easier to edit a text with modern word processing facilities than it was in the past. There still remains the problem of deciding at what point the text is ready for public consideration – whether that text is commercially published or simply shared among friends or colleagues. There are many texts on the worldwide web and the author of each has decided that the text is in a state where it can be released to the world – quite a big decision.

Discourse analysts who adopt a critical linguistic approach to text argue that no text (written or oral) is constructed in isolation. Fairclough (2001: 21) proposes a model (Figure 7.2) which shows clearly how the text is central to the process of production of writer/speaker (or the addresser) and interpretation of reader/hearer (or addressee) and how that interaction is influenced by the social conditions of production and interpretation. Of course, the addresser may well be the creator of the text as s/he writes/speaks it. The addressee, however, interprets the text and therefore is arguably creating his/her own understanding of the text which may be different from another person's understanding of the same text and from the meaning intended by the addresser. Both addresser and addressee operate as individuals but each works within more widely-accepted constraints of what constitutes a particular type of text.

Fairclough's view (2001: 21) of 'language as discourse and as social practice' necessitates an analysis of 'the relationship between texts, processes and their

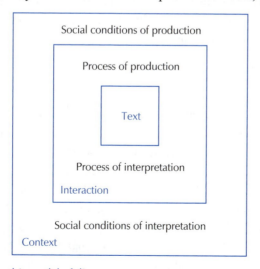

Figure 7.2   Fairclough's model of discourse

social conditions, both the immediate conditions of the situational context and the more remote conditions of institutional and social structures'. This approach, which links the text with its social **context** (⇢ cf. Jakobson's model in Unit 1), becomes particularly relevant when looking at news reports, whether oral or written. The reporter chooses what words and syntactic structures to use. What are the implications of those choices? Despite claims to unbiased reporting, something as simple as the choice of words to refer to participants in the narrative (a classic example is to consider the different implications of describing somebody as a freedom fighter as opposed to a terrorist) or to name participants (President Bush as opposed to George W.) can give an indication of the reporter's own views. The reporter has to choose whether to use active or passive voice: if the reporter states that X did Y (active voice) then responsibility for the action is stated but if the claim is that Y was done (passive voice), the reader might be left wondering who is responsible for the action and the writer cannot then be held responsible for the reader's interpretation of the report. An added bonus of using the passive is that the reporter cannot be sued for libel because they have not explicitly stated that a particular person is responsible for the action being reported. (Cf. the deniability of implicatures ⇢ Units 3 and 4.)

Modifying the poet John Donne's comment that 'No man is an Island, entire of it self [*sic*]', it can be argued that no text is created in isolation but always with reference to other texts. So when someone starts to write a letter to their bank manager to ask for a loan or to their closest friend to share some good news, there are wider influences on the writing than just the individual's own linguistic choices. Newer **communication** media such as e-mail or writing on the web are developing their own conventions. Texting is a particularly clear example of how the linguistic conventions are changing.

 Activity 7.16

Consider how you write e-mails. Do you begin with 'Dear X', 'Hi!', just the name of the person you are writing to or do you go straight into the message? How do you sign off at the end? Does your e-mail language represent spoken language more than written? Does your e-mail have only complete sentences in it? Do you use capital letters? Draft an imaginary postcard to your parents or to close friends to tell them about your current holiday. Then draft an e-mail to them to tell the same audience about the same holiday. To what extent has your use of language changed because of the different transmission media?

Some texts are written for the author only and are not intended for a more public reading – diaries written to record the diarist's reflections on previous events are a very clear example. Whether the events were public or private, the reflections are often private and intended for the author's eyes only. Is a diary, therefore, no more than an aide-mémoire? Instructions are sometimes left in a writer's last will and testament that when s/he dies, their diaries, unread by anyone, are to be destroyed by their executors. Not all diaries are private documents, however. Politicians write diaries which are clearly intended to provide at a later date a public account of the private reasons behind the individual's political activities and such diaries often indicate the writer's private opinions of their colleagues.

If the target audience affects the construction of any written text in whatever written medium, what is the effect on the style of the text of the purpose for which the text has been constructed? Why do you think that the author of *Get Comfortable* chose to write a piece of self-help advice in the form of a narrative?

Instruction manuals are easily recognizable in a wide range of contexts. Texts instructing the reader how to set up a video, how to cook a favourite dish or meal (in this case called a recipe), how to construct a piece of furniture bought as flat-pack (sometimes called assembly instructions) or how to write an essay (often called study guides) all have basically the same structure. The writer is shown what tools and/or ingredients are needed to carry out the task (either by diagrams or in a list). The directions are provided in chronological order for the process that is to be carried out and are often numbered to make that quite explicit for the reader. The directions will, most probably, be in imperative mood, with the minimum number of words possible. There may be a lot of images to help the reader see what has to be done. There will be no use of figurative language as the writer wants to ensure as far as possible that the reader has no scope for understanding the message in any other way than that intended by the writer. Figurative language incorporates the use of metaphor and simile and other non-literal uses of language, used every day in normal conversation as well as in literary works. In an instruction text, literal language use will be adopted to ensure clarity as far as possible.

 Activity 7.17

Find two examples of instructive texts from different arenas of life. In the light of what you have just read and these guide questions, identify the common features that are demonstrated in the texts you have chosen.

1   Is there any visual support for the instructions? If so, are iconic or symbolic visuals used to represent various processes (➻ Unit 1)?

2   Identify the specialized lexis which relates to the area of instruction.
3   Are the sentences in imperative mood? If not, how is it made clear to the reader what s/he must do?
4   How is the order in which the instructions are to be carried out made clear? Are they numbered or is the sequence made clear in some other way?

Advertisements follow different conventions from instruction manuals. Whilst an advertiser is not allowed actually to lie about the product, there is scope for figurative and creative use of language to persuade the potential purchaser actually to buy the product. Quite simply, that is the purpose of the advertisement.

The text advertising Comfort Vaporesse (Text 7.8) appeared in *Good Housekeeping* magazine in the UK in July 2002. The advertisement is for a fabric conditioner and the language works deliberately on two levels – talking about fabric and fabric care in the context of a newspaper article about the possible breakdown of a marriage. The newspaper reader is clearly made out of fabric (her ring has a button where normally there would be a precious stone) as are the two main participants in the saved-marriage story. Lexical items which relate to the field of fabric and fabric care include the names of the main participants, Gary and Veronica Paisley, the reporters John Tweedy and Quentin Quilter and the county where the tanker spillage occurred (Hempshire, a play on the name of a real UK county, Hampshire). The headline and one of the picture captions revolve around a pun based on the **homophones**, *scent* and *sent* (both phonetically [sɛnt]) where the two meanings are clearly relevant to the tale being told. The other caption reports that Mr and Mrs Paisley can 'iron out' their problems – a caption that is clearly based on the literal meaning of ironing creased clothes (as in the picture) as well as the metaphorical use of the same **lexical item** in relation to abstract problem solving. The headline in the second article is also based on homophones, in this case *dye* and *die* (phonetically [daɪ]), and is reminiscent of the all too frequent newspaper headlines which proclaim that large numbers of people die in accidents daily (an example of intertextuality where one text is read with another text in mind). Figurative language use abounds in the text: 'spell the end of marriage guidance', 'heading straight for the divorce courts' and 'Our marriage has really lost its spark' are just some of the examples. Such language use entices the reader to read further. Modal verbs are widely used in advertisements and so the claims about the success of the product are acceptable (if unlikely in this case – will a fabric conditioner really spell the end of marriage guidance?) and within the UK guidelines that advertisements have to be legal, decent, honest and truthful. To claim that something is possible cannot be challenged in the same way as one can challenge a fact.

Text 7.8   Heaven Scent

In this advertisement, there has been great play made on the newspaper industry. In the original, the name of the newspaper is printed on a red background, reminiscent of the UK tabloid newspapers which have a solid red band as masthead at the top of the front page but the check-pattern is reminiscent of gingham fabric, the name given to the 'newspaper'. The text is printed in columns. The language used to report the tanker spillage could almost read as a genuine accident: lorries do overturn, they do spill chemicals, experts do work overnight and emergency centres are set up for immediate victims. Such tabloid papers regularly have offers for the reader to 'win a luxury …' – which in this text introduces the element of humour through bathos (or anti-climax) by the juxtaposition in the reader's mind (so another example of intertextuality) of the luxury night for two at a top hotel with the 'night for two at a dry-cleaners!'.

There is linguistic humour in the advertisement in:

- the pun on 'stained for life' which could be compared with the oft-used 'scarred for life' in genuine reports
- the unlikely presence at an accident of 'stain removal experts' though experts are regularly present at genuine incidents
- the emergency centres are for 'bleaching'.

This text is read with a typical accident report in mind – a form of intertextuality and linguistic humour reminiscent of that found in parody. Humour is often used within advertisements to encourage the consumer to purchase but it is important to note that advertisements, like literary texts, can borrow language from any and all registers for their particular purpose as can be seen in the advertisement for 'more!' magazine (Text 7.9) which looks more like an invitation to a party than an advert for a magazine.

Advertisements also use sound patterning to make the slogan memorable and this is simply an extension of the way poetry uses sound patterning to particular effect. Think of the slogans for some of the products currently being advertised. Whether in print or on the broadcast media, there will be sound patterning to help the hearer/reader remember the advertisement, and therefore, hopefully, the product.

 Activity 7.18

Find some advertisements and examine how they exploit the resources of the language. If you look at cosmetics advertisements, you might want to consider how often they exploit the **register** of science to support their claims about the product. Consider the language used to persuade the consumer to buy yet another computer, phone or car. How do banks advertise?

Text 7.9   more!

 Activity 7.19

Find advertisements which focus on the sound patterning of the language.
What phonological features in particular are being exploited?

Written text appears in all shapes, sizes and forms. Some texts are created simply for the pleasure of using language in an innovative, creative and entertaining way such as Text 7.10.

Tube, or not Tube: that is the question:
2   Whether 'tis nobler in the mind to suffer
    The stinks and elbows of obnoxious passengers,
4   Or to take refuge in your Walkman,
    And by ignoring end them? To die: to nod off:
6   No more; and, by nodding off to say we end
    The bone-ache, the delays, the thousand disturbances
8   The Underground is heir to, 'tis an escape
    Devoutly to be wish'd. To die, to have a kip;
10 To sleep; perchance to miss our stop: ay, there's the rub.

Text 7.10   Tube or not Tube (Source: Tagholm 1996: 16)

 Activity 7.20 o—

Does Text 7.10 *Tube or not Tube* sound familiar at all? What does it sound like?

The original text is well known and indeed is often quoted out of context in normal everyday conversation, if not in its entirety, then certainly the first few words. The source of a parody may well never have been seen before by the reader. Nevertheless, the reader recognizes that in some ways (but not in others) the text which they are reading is closely linked to some other text.

 Activity 7.21 o—

Identify in *Tube or not Tube* where Tagholm has altered the lexical items from the original. Identify where the syntactic structures have been maintained and assess how far this helps to maintain the reference to the original. How does this help to create the humour of the parody?

Whether the speaker knows the source text is immaterial, texts find their way from the literary canons to which they originally belong and appear in many and much wider contexts. Not only literary texts are widely quoted: so too are religious texts such as the Bible (in surprising places, sometimes, even in linguistic textbooks ➛ Units 4 and 14) or catchphrases from current television programmes such as soap operas or quiz shows. Can you think of any?

Parody is one very clear example of intertextuality in that one text is read in the context or with the knowledge of another text. The reader cannot fully appreciate the parody without recognizing the original text which is being parodied. Another example of intertextuality would be where an author quotes directly from another text. Some texts, such as novels and advertisements, borrow from all registers and styles of text. Other texts, such as legal texts or academic essays, are more constrained by their conventions.

HOW TO ANALYSE A TEXT

A text can be analysed in a variety of ways but a linguistic analysis will aim to show primarily how the finite resources of a language are used creatively to produce an individual text that serves the author's purposes. An analysis should be systematic so that results can be compared and thus contrasts between different types of text become more apparent. Consideration of the following questions will provide a clear and systematic approach to text analysis – the responses will vary in length and detail depending on the particular text under scrutiny. Whilst the points can be addressed in any order, the following sequence does provide a practical approach to the analysis of text but you should note that questions in each section are indicative rather than definitive.

(a)   What is the purpose of the text? Why has it been written? Is the reader simply to enjoy the text (as with a novel or a poem) or to carry out instructions, to consider taking the advice presented or to read the legal document very carefully before signing?

(b)   How is the text constructed? Is it a narrative, a descriptive or an instructive text? Or does it contain elements of all three? Is it simply a list or is it a carefully constructed argument putting thesis and antithesis before coming to a synthesis or conclusion?

(c)   Is there any deliberate manipulation of the phonological systems of the language? Are there aspects of rhyme (where the final vowel and consonant sequences of syllables are patterned as in *seemed* which rhymes with *teemed*) *or* alliteration (where the initial consonants of syllables like *summer* and *sun* are the same) which is often a feature of verse or poetic prose? Is the language metrically patterned such that the rhythm of the language becomes marked or is the text written with the normal stress patterns that occur in every day language use?

(d)   What **lexical choices** have been made? Does the text have examples of formal or informal lexis? From what lexical sets are the **lexical items** taken? Is there a preponderance of polysemic words (with more than one unrelated meaning, e.g. *fair*) or is the meaning of each word clear and unambiguous? Has modern lexis been used or, from the reader's perspective, are the lexical items ones that have fallen into disuse in the modern world? Is the language used figuratively (as in sports reports where defeat is described as tragedy, or where an untidy bedroom is described as looking like 'a bomb site') or literally?

(e)   What syntactic choices have been made? Do noun phrases contain much modification or very little? Are the sentences markedly long or short? Do they contain simple or complex clause structures? Does one syntactic mood predominate over others or is there a roughly equal mix? In which tense is the text written? Which syntactic voice has been chosen? What patterning or foregrounding of syntactic elements has been chosen?

SUMMARY

In this unit, you have seen how a text can be constructed by choosing which words to use in which grammatical pattern. Each individual text is constructed by its creator to suit the intended audience and to achieve the intended purpose. Texts can range from the completely literal (to prevent any possible misunderstanding) to the highly figurative where deliberate plays on language might allow for a multiplicity of meanings to be expressed and retrieved. Despite the deliberate uniqueness of each text, there are similarities across different individual texts where they are constructed for a similar purpose and systematic analysis of the linguistic features of any text(s) allows for generic comments to be made as well as specific.

FURTHER READING

Introductions to functional grammar abound. Bloor and Bloor (2004) provide a readable and very useful entry to the area of functional grammar based on *An Introduction to Functional Grammar* (Halliday 1994, Halliday and Matthiesen, 2004) which despite its name is a complex account of the topic. *Working With Texts* (Carter *et al.* 2001) provides a wide range of texts for practical analysis, most with a commentary so that the student is supported through their learning. A more discursive but similarly text-based approach to style can be found in Carter and Nash (1990) *Seeing Through Language*. In *Style*, Freeborn (1997) analyses texts ranging from the literary classics to newspaper articles in a book which demonstrates clearly the insights to be gained from a linguistic analysis of text.

FURTHER ACTIVITY

 Activity 7.22

Text 7.11 was published in *The Guardian*, one of the national broadsheet newspapers in the UK, after a public examination candidate had written their answers in text-language rather than in Standard British English. How does the language of this text vary from standard language as you know it? Consider the relationship between sound, spelling and punctuation. What is the journalist's view of the use of this **variety** of English in the context of examinations? How can you tell?

Dnt u sumX rekn eng lang v lngwindd? 2mny wds & ltrs? ?nt we b usng lss time & papr? ?nt we b 4wd tnking + txt? 13yr grl frm w scot 2ndry schl sd ok. Sh rote GCSE eng sa (abt hr smmr hols in NY) in txt spk. (NO!) Sh sd sh 4t txt spk was "easr thn standrd eng". Sh 4t hr tcher wd b :) Hr tcher 4t it was nt so gr8! Sh was :(& talkd 2 newspprs (but askd 2 b anon). "I cdnt bleve wot I was cing! :o" -!-!-! OW2TE. Sh hd NI@A wot grl was on abt. Sh 4t her pupl was ritng in "hieroglyphics".

Edu xperts r c:-&. Thy r wrrd tht mobile fone spk has gn 2 far. SQA (Scot Qual Auth) has sd txt spk oftn apprs "inappropriately" in xms. Dr Cynthia McVey (Glasgw Cal Univ Psychol lect) sez "Yng pepl dnt rite ltrs so sitng dwn 2 rite is diff ... txting is more aTractve". (Sh is COl). But Judith Gillespie spokeswmn 4 Scot parent/tcher assoc sez we mst stmp out use of txting 4 eng SAs (Y not hstry, geog, econ, etc? she dnt say). no1 can rite. no1 can spel. "u wd b :-o @ nos of 2ndry pupls wh cant distngsh btwEn 'ther' & ther'". R tchrs a prob? 2 mny tchrs (she sez) thnk pupls 3dom of xpreSn shd nt b inhibtd.

B frank. Do u care? Wot if all eng bcame txt spk? AAMOF eng lits gd in txt spk. "2BON2BTITQ." "2moro & 2moro & 2moro." C? Shakesprs gr8 in txt! 2dA he wd txt all hs wk. May b. Nethng is psble in txt spk.

2 tru. 13yr grl noes wots wot. I say 2 hr URA*! KUTGW! 1OTD yr tcher wll b tching txt. I say 2 edu xperts, 4COL! Gt rl! Eng lang must b COl 2 b xitng. Eat y <3 out! @TEOTD ths is 24/7 wrld! IIN! 01CnStpTxtng. Hax shd tke hEd. I no 10TD Gdn wll b in ext.

Text 7.11 'English as a Foreign Language'

COMMENTARY ON ACTIVITIES

Activity 7.1

Count nouns in the singular: sun, river, member, family, moon

Count nouns in the plural: bodies, children, handfuls

Non-count nouns: water, clay, blood

Are there any contexts where somebody might want to make the non-count nouns countable? Think about a potter or a haematologist, for example.

Activity 7.4

Verbs: agreed, saw, had, turned, killed, threw, done, had, told, throw, make, look

Adjectives: red, cruel

Adverbs: very, at all[*], not[†], merely

Pronouns: he, it, something

Determiners: the, every, his, their

Prepositions: of, into, like

Conjunctions: and, when, but

[*] *at all* needs to be treated as a single lexical item, even though it is written as two words. It therefore only really fits into the adverb group.

[†] not is often labelled as a negative particle.

You might have thought that *to* is a preposition. This is only the case when it comes before a noun phrase. Before a verb it is often labelled with the following verb as a *to-infinitive*.

Activity 7.5

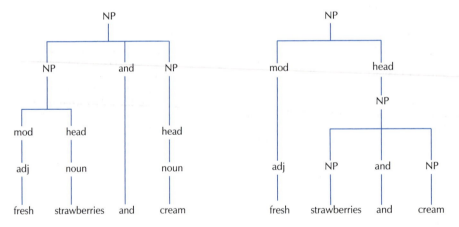

This structure means that only the strawberries are fresh

This structure means that both the strawberries and the cream are fresh

The same meaning in box diagrams would look like this:

NP				NP			
NP		and	NP	modifier	head		
mod	head		head		NP	and	NP
adj	noun			adj	noun		noun
fresh	strawberries	and	cream	fresh	strawberries	and	cream

For the NP *patient transport service*, the different structures are shown here:

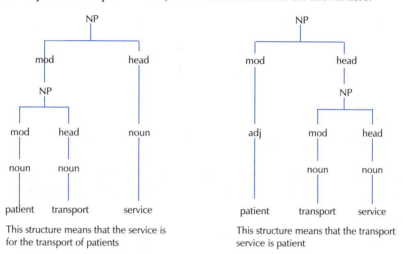

This structure means that the service is for the transport of patients

This structure means that the transport service is patient

The same meaning in box diagrams would look like this:

NP			NP		
NP		NP	mod	head	
mod	head		adj	NP	
noun	noun			mod	head
patient	transport	service	patient	transport	service

Activity 7.6

Noun Phrases	NP realized by pronouns
one day	me, I, me, he, this, this, he, this
a farmer from the village	
Wise man	Adjective Phrases
A horrible thing	mad
My ox	
no animal	Prepositional Phrases*
my field	from the village
the worst thing that could have possibly happened	to the wise man
The wise old man	in a frantic tone
The man	to the village
the wise man	to his neighbors
the worst thing that could have happened	

* Remember that PPs contain NPs so in each of the PPs that you have found there must also be an NP.

For more practice, try other paragraphs in these texts or in any other text but remember that not every text will have examples of every structure that you might be looking for.

Activity 7.7

CD34–37 The chronological order of events looks like this:

1 the sun agreed (L34)
2 the moon did something very cruel (L35–36)
3 the moon told his children to throw handfuls of red clay into the river (L36–37)
4 the river turned red (L34)
5 the sun saw the new colour of the river (L34)
6 the sun killed his family (L34–35)
7 the sun threw their bodies into the river (L35)

It is the use of the perfective aspect on the VG *had done* (L35) that indicates the sequence of events shown here and that the reader understands as they read the narrative. Arguably, *the moon did not kill his family* (L36) is not part of the sequence of events as nothing happened despite the fact that the clause appears in the narration of the events. But non-events (like silence ➤ Unit 2) can be very significant, as in this narrative. Now think about *had turned red* (L34) and *had merely told* (L36).

Activity 7.8

In *Creative Deception* there are modal verbs expressing physical ability (*could* in L6), possibility/probability (*'ll* in L9, *will* in L21, *would* in L23, *shall* in L30) and obligation (*must* in L29, L30 and L32).

In *Get Comfortable Not Knowing* there are examples of the modal verbs *can* and *could* expressing possibility and ability (L6, L9 with positive and negative forms, L17, L26, L28, L39), of the modal verbs *will*, *won't*, *shall* and *would* expressing possibility/probability (L21, L22, L25, L33, L39) and of the modal verb *must* expressing obligation (L16, L26).

As an extension to this activity, choose another text from this book or from another source. Identify all the modal verbs and decide what meanings are being expressed.

Activity 7.9

The important thing is that the groups have been recognized, not that your list looks exactly like this one.

	NPs	AdjP	AdvP	PP	VG
S1	the world	very new	still	with the same brightness	was
	the sun and the moon				were
	equals				shone
S2	They		often		were
	good friends		round		went
			together		
S3	one day				changed
	everything				

Activity 7.10

In 1c, the subject is the same as in 1b and because of the coordination it does not need to be repeated. The subject in 2a and 2b is *they* (though not repeated in 2b for the same reason of coordination as in sentence 1). In 3a, the subject is *everything*.

Activity 7.11

(a)

A horrible thing	has	happened
S	F	P

(b)

The man	hurried	back	to the village
S	F/P	A-place	A-place

(c)

The next day	however	a strong young horse	was		seen	near the man's farm
A-time	A-con*	S	F		P	A-place

* A-con = conjunctive adjunct. These adjuncts link pieces of text together in a similar way to conjunctions. It is an Adjunct because it is movable and could appear in different places in the clause, at the beginning or at the end, for example. In this sentence, *however* shows that this sentence is intended to contrast in some way with what has gone before.

(d)

Once again	the farmer	went	to the wise man
A-time	S	F/P	A-place

(e)

You	were	right	again
S	F	Cint	A-time

(f)

The moral of this story	provides	a powerful lesson
S	F/P	Cdo

(g)

Often	we	make	a big deal	out of something
A-time	S	F/P	Cdo	A-place*

* This clause could be analysed as having a Cdo (*a big deal out of something*) and no Adjunct. Or it could be analysed as here by arguing that *out of something* (from somewhere and hence an Adjunct of place) we make *a big deal*. Which do you think is the better interpretation?

(h)

Most of the time	we	are	wrong
A-time	S	F	Cint

Activity 7.12
L25

||| Time	passed	|| and	a great famine	came	upon the earth |||
S	F/P	ccj	S	F/P	A-place

L25

Every day	people	were	dying
A-time	S	F	P

L26

the moon	saw	his chance [[to get his own back on the sun]]		
		[[P	Cdo	]]
S	F/P	Cdo		

L26–27

||| But	he	hid	his anger	|| and	paid	the sun	a visit |||
ccj*	S	F/P	Cdo	ccj	F/P	Cio	Cdo

* This is a coordinating conjunction. It has a linking function in the text similar to that of *however* in Activity 7.11(c). On those grounds it could be analysed as A-con. Unlike *however* in (c), it cannot be moved to a different place in the clause and therefore is not an Adjunct.

Activity 7.13

The structural ambiguity is shown in the familiar format.

Meaning 1

Flying	pigs	can	be	exciting
premodifier	head			
NP				
S		F	P	Cint

Meaning 2

[[Flying pigs]]	can	be	exciting
[[P Cdo]]			
[[S]] F		P	Cint

Tree diagrams would look something like this.

Meaning 1

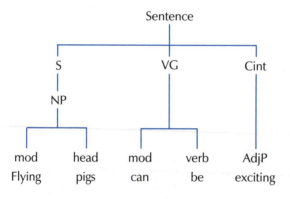

Meaning 2

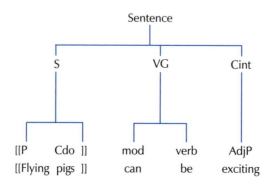

Activity 7.15

You may have considered other points as well as these.

(a) the narrative structure of the text

The abstract of this text is less explicit as it is not clear to the reader at the start of the text what the deception is, nor what the outcomes might be. The orientation appears in the first paragraph and the actions then start (bathing in the river, deception, famine, sacrifice of the families). Evaluation occurs throughout the text with comment on the actions of the sun and the moon and the final result is in the final paragraph which brings the reader to the present time and the current state of the sun, alone in the sky and the moon, surrounded by stars.

(b) the reference system

Pronouns are used to refer to the moon and the sun, once they have been introduced into the narrative. On L1, *the world, the sun and the moon* are introduced with the definite article. There is only one world, one sun and one moon and thus exophoric (referring to something uniquely locatable outside the text) direct reference is appropriate. Only in science fiction texts might an author want to refer to other worlds and so need the indefinite article. On L21 there is an example of comparative reference where both parts of the comparison are named.

(c) ellipsis and substitution

Subjects are omitted in coordinated clauses (e.g. L1–2).

There is an example of verbal substitution in 'So they did' (L13).

(d) conjunction

There are examples of coordination with *and* and *but* throughout the text but there are also examples of subordination such as *when* (L1), *as* (L9), *as soon as* (L12), *if* (L29).

(e) lexical patterning

Examples of repetition include the frequent naming of the sun and the moon. There are many words that relate to brilliance and splendour: *brightness* (L2), *frosty* (L19), *brilliance* (L19), *shadow* (L19), *brighter* (L21), *shining* (L40), *majesty* (L40), *less bright* (L40). A range of lexically related terms introduce the speech: *said* (L9), *ordered* (L12), *mocked* (L21), *jeered* (L21), and *agreed* (L34). There are also chains of words related to family and kinship as well as to temperature and to time.

Activity 7.20

This text is, in fact, a parody and the original of this comes from Shakespeare's *Hamlet* (III.1 L56–65). Here is the original version from Shakespeare:

	Hamlet:
56	To be, or not to be – that is the question;
	Whether 'tis nobler in the mind to suffer
58	The slings and arrows of outrageous fortune
	Or to take arms against a sea of trouble
60	And by opposing end them? To die, to sleep –

No more – and by a sleep to say we end

62   The heart-ache and the thousand natural shocks

That flesh is heir to. 'Tis a consummation

64   Devoutly to be wished. To die, to sleep:

To sleep – perchance to dream. Ay there's the rub.

Activity 7.21

Hamlet's soliloquy contemplates one of the great philosophical questions – that of how to confront evil. The parody maintains the lexis of the original (L2, L9), the syntax of the original (L4–5), the syllable structure and other aspects of phonetic patterning (L3). The parody does not slavishly follow the iambic pentameter of the original but each line has 9–11 syllables divided roughly into 5 feet, each foot having 2 beats in a x/ pattern (where x represents a weak beat and / a strong beat). The sleep to which Hamlet compares death is replaced by the highly colloquial terms *to nod off* and *to have a kip*, both of which relate more to the kind of sleep experienced by travellers on the London Underground railway together with the most worrying consequence of that kip, namely sleeping past one's tube stop which contrasts with the greatly to be feared dreams that might come in the sleep of death.

The triviality of travelling on the tube is compared implicitly with the greatness of topic to be found in the original and therein lies the humour. In a parody, enough of the original text is maintained for the original to be read 'with' the parody or for the parody to be read with the original in the reader's mind and hence the contrast and the humour is reinforced.

REFERENCES

Bloor, T. and Bloor, M. (2004) *The Functional Analysis of English: A Hallidayan Approach*, 2nd edn, London: Arnold.

Carlson, R. (1998) *Don't Sweat the Small Stuff … and It's All Small Stuff*, London: Hodder Headline.

Carter, R. and Nash, W. (1990) *Seeing Through Language: A Guide to Styles of English Writing*, Oxford: Blackwell.

Carter, R., Goddard. A., Reah, D., Sanger, K. and Bowring, M. (2001) *Working with Texts: A Core Introduction to Language Analysis*, 2nd edn, London: Routledge.

Donne, J. (1996) 'Devotions upon Emergent Occasions (1624) Meditation XVII', in A. Partington (ed.) *The Concise Oxford Dictionary of Quotations*, revised 4th edn, Oxford: Oxford University Press.

Fairclough, N. (2001) *Language and Power*, 2nd edn, Harlow: Longman.

Freeborn, D. (1997) *Style: Text Analysis and Linguistic Criticism*, Basingstoke: Macmillan.

Halliday, M.A.K. (1994) *An Introduction to Functional Grammar*, 2nd edn, London: Arnold.

Halliday, M.A.K. and Matthiesen, C.M.I.M. (2004) *An Introduction to Functional Grammar*, 3rd edn, London: Arnold.

Labov, W. (1999) 'The transformation of experience in narrative', in A. Jaworski and N. Coupland (eds) *The Discourse Reader*, London: Routledge.

Pilling, A. (2001) 'A Story from Cameroon', *New Internationalist Calendar*, Market Harborough: New Internationalist.

Shakespeare, W. (1996) *Hamlet*, London: Penguin.

Tagholm, R. (1996) *Poems Not on the Underground: A Parody*, Moreton-in-Marsh: Windsurf Press.

Trask, R.L. (1997) *A Student's Dictionary of Language and Linguistics*, London: Arnold.

8 PHONETICS

UNIT CONTENTS

INTRODUCTION

Why study **phonetics**? Some knowledge of speech sounds is essential for any linguist. In the hierarchy of linguistic units (Figure 7.1) speech sounds are at the base. Sounds make up **morphemes**, which make up **words** which make up **phrases** which make up **clauses** which make up **sentences** which make up **text** (➳ Unit 7).

Phonetics is important in analysing spoken linguistic material. Foreign language teachers, as well as students of foreign languages, need to be able to pick out the relevant speech sounds in a language which make it distinct from other varieties. The letter symbol <p> in Spanish, for example, is pronounced differently to English <p>: Spanish /p/ is unaspirated meaning it sounds closer to English /b/ than English /p/. A knowledge of phonetics will enable a conscientious tutor to train their native English speaking students to pronounce more accurately the sound that Spanish speakers would make in the same **context**.

Conversely, the Teacher of English as a Foreign Language will do well to understand the problems that students are likely to encounter when learning spoken English. For example, some Southern Chinese speakers have difficulty making a distinction between the sounds at the beginning of the two words *rift* and *lift*. While these sounds are distinct in English, they sound the same to many Southern Chinese speakers. When speech sounds from a person's native language influence how they pronounce (or even understand) words in a foreign language in this way it is known as *interference*. Interference accounts for much of the difficulty people have in making themselves sound like authentic native speakers of the language they are learning. Interference can be viewed positively (for example, English speakers often remark on the attractiveness of English when it is spoken with a foreign accent), but for the foreign language learner it can be a major source of frustration.

Teachers in both primary and secondary schools will also find a knowledge of phonetics useful. Children's spelling and reading errors are often a result of a mismatch between the spelling system and the actual sounds that are used to pronounce a word. When you consider that there are 44 different speech sounds (**phonemes**) in the **Received Pronunciation** (or **RP**, also known as BBC English) **variety** of English but only 26 letters, then it seems obvious that at some point most young readers will get confused trying to map speech onto writing and vice versa. For example, notice the different pronunciation of <o> in the words below.

hot comb done lose one more crowd women

Activity 8.1

Find as many different pronunciations of the letters <i>, <u> and <e> as you can in English words. Why do you think English has so many different pronunciations for letters, when in some other languages, there is a much more regular relationship between letters and their pronunciation?

There is not, then, a neat, one-to-one correspondence between sounds and letters in English: the same letter is used to reflect many possible sounds. This might be expected, when one considers there are many more speech sounds than letters available. However, the opposite situation also occurs in English where the same speech sound may be represented by different letters. Consider the examples below.

fear   enough   phoenix   cuff

Here the speech sound [f] is represented by the letter <f> and also by the letter pairs (digraphs) <gh>, <ph> and <ff>.

Activity 8.2

Find some other examples where the same speech sound is represented by different letters, digraphs or letter combinations. Two words which might help get you started are 'ceiling' and 'knock'.

Because of the complex way in which spoken English has evolved, particularly since the time when printing effectively 'froze' the English spelling system to reflect the variety of the time, the task of learning to read and write can be fraught with difficulty. Teachers who have an awareness of phonetics can address their pupils' needs in a systematic way since they will be able to spot the lack of correspondence between spelling and speech.

Perhaps out of all of the professions, phonetics is of the most importance to Speech and Language Therapists (SLTs) or, as they are also called, Speech and Language Pathologists. SLTs will often be involved in enabling a client to produce speech sounds in a way that makes them more easily understood. This may be a child who, while she seems to understand those around her and who has recourse to a variety of ingenious strategies including pointing and showing to make her message clear, has speech that is extremely difficult to understand. Or it may be an adult whose speech has become slow and laborious since suffering a stroke

(⇥ Unit 11). While it should be remembered that SLTs do not work on just speech but also language, the range of speech impairments is so diverse and prevalent that it is likely to form an important cornerstone of their professional activities.

The other category of professionals that make use of a knowledge of phonetics are those who may be grouped under the heading of 'wordsmiths': writers, actors and journalists for example. To take just one of these, actors, it is often the case that they have to take on roles where they must reproduce the speech characteristics of a different region from that of their own **accent** (⇥ Unit 9). Often this means producing sounds in a way that is impossible to capture with ordinary writing. Think about how difficult it is to write dialogue for a character speaking with an accent in such a way that the intended pronunciation is clear and unambiguous. Speakers of West Yorkshire English, for example, often produce the final sound of words like *holly* with a vowel that is closer to the middle sound in *pet* than the middle sound in *feet*. Closely reproducing such characteristic and distinctive pronunciations will help enormously in making an actor sound authentic.

 ## Activity 8.3 ⊶

The following extract is from *The Poor Mouth* by Flann O'Brien. What effect is obtained by the unconventional spellings used? How effective is the technique?

At last he spoke:
– How many?
– Twalf, sor! Said the Old-Grey-Fellow courteously.
– Twalf?
The other man threw another quick glance at the back of the house while he considered and attempted to find some explanation for the speech he heard.
– All spik Inglish?
– All spik, sor, said the Old-Fellow.
Then the gentleman noticed me standing behind the Old-Grey-Fellow and he spoke gruffly to me:
– Phwat is yer nam? said he.
– Jams O'Donnell, sor!

THE ORGANS OF SPEECH

Before we look at the various speech sounds and their classification it is important to become familiar with the organs of speech and the architecture of the vocal tract.

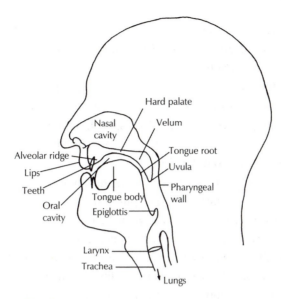

Figure 8.1   The vocal tract

Phonetics is often best understood when one engages practically with the material. Performing some of the exercises below may make you feel silly (and this means you should think carefully before picking up your phonetics text books in the library!) but it is the best way to understand and learn about speech sound taxonomy. The variety of English used in most of the examples is RP. This is not because RP is considered to be in any way superior or 'better' than other varieties of English (➤ Unit 9), but simply because it is important to have an indexical accent to which other varieties may be compared.

By vocal tract we mean those parts of the body that are normally involved in the production of speech. This involves everything from the lungs to the mouth. While humans are unique amongst animals in their use of spoken language it is perhaps surprising to realize that all of the organs used for speech have a primary function which is something other than speech. The tongue is used to form food into a bolus for swallowing; the lips are used to make a tight seal of the oral tract to keep food in and undesirable substances out (just try swallowing with your mouth open and see how useful this seal is!); the **vocal folds** (often also called vocal cords) are used to shut off the airway and stabilize the chest to enable muscular effort, as when lifting heavy objects for example.

AIRSTREAM MECHANISMS

There are really two important components to speech: initiation and articulation. Speech sounds are created by manipulating or shaping an airflow. Initiation produces the airstream on which the sounds are carried, while articulation shapes the airstream to create different sounds. Most initiation is pulmonic: that is, it is a product of the lungs. The direction of airflow is usually outwards, that is, egressive. It is possible to produce sounds using non-pulmonic airstreams (see below), as well as to reverse the direction of airflow so that the air moves from outside the body down towards the lungs (ingressive). Most speech sounds, however, are made using a pulmonic egressive airstream mechanism. The airflow is initiated by the lungs and moves outwards from the body.

There are three possible sites of initiation: the lungs (pulmonic), the glottis (glottalic) and the velum (velaric). During pulmonic speech, breathing is slowed right down. Normally a breath is taken between 12 and 15 times a minute (children take more and older adults take fewer breaths per minute), and the time taken to breathe in and breathe out is about equal. During speech, breathing loses this rhythmical quality. In-breaths are deeper and faster and breathing out can take anything up to 30 seconds. People who talk all day such as teachers, often complain that their work makes them tired; this fatigue is very real and in fact a large part of it is likely to be caused by the reduced volume of oxygen they are taking in over a day due to the modification of their breathing for speech. Most people can feel the effects of fatigue after talking continuously for only an hour or so.

When speech sounds are made with a glottalic or velaric airstream mechanism, there is a closure made at the glottis or velum. The column of air above the closure point is forced out of the body by muscular action and the speech sounds are made by modifying its shape. It is clear that the non-pulmonic airstreams will give a speaker less air with which to speak than a pulmonic airstream, or, in other words, a speaker will run out of breath relatively quickly. This is why pulmonic airstreams are used in far more languages and for far more speech sounds than any other airstream.

The vocal tract

Vocal folds: phonation

Air coming from the lungs passes up through the bronchi and into the trachea (see Figure 8.1). At the top of the trachea in the upper respiratory tract is the larynx. The vocal folds are contained in the larynx and are a critical component of the speech mechanism. The larynx is made of three paired cartilage structures and three unpaired cartilage structures and sits at the front of the neck. In males, the most prominent part of the cartilage structure is clearly visible as the Adam's apple. This is the thyroid cartilage. Just below this, and shaped like a signet ring with the widest

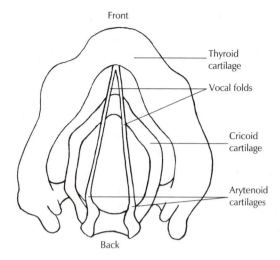

Figure 8.2   The cartilages of the larynx and vocal folds as seen from above (conus elasticus omitted for clarity)

part facing backwards, is the cricoid cartilage. The paired arytenoid cartilages are attached to the back of the cricoid and articulate with it (see Figure 8.2). The thyroid, cricoid and arytenoid cartilages are the most important of the laryngeal cartilages for speech. The vocal folds are strung between the thyroid and arytenoid cartilages where most advantage can be taken of the wide range of movement allowed by the cartilage arrangement. The laryngeal cartilages are connected to each other by muscles, ligaments, membranes and two pairs of synovial joints. These joints allow rotational and gliding movements enabling a wide degree of movement and fine control during speech. The structure is therefore flexible whilst being strong enough to protect the vocal folds.

Just above the vocal folds is a second set of folds, called the *false* or *vestibular folds*. Their function is to keep the true vocal folds lubricated. This lubrication is essential if the vocal folds are to vibrate as the vocal folds themselves have no intrinsic lubrication and cannot vibrate dry. If the vocal folds become extremely dry, the larynx will become inflamed, resulting in laryngitis. Frequent bouts of laryngitis caused in this way can result in long term damage to the vocal folds in the form of vocal nodules. Like most components of our bodies, if used excessively with no opportunity for rest and recovery, the vocal folds will cease to function effectively. Singers and other professional voice users have to learn to look after their vocal folds by resting them and adopting voice techniques that cause less damage.

The vocal folds lie horizontally across the path of the air stream. They are attached together at the front to the thyroid cartilage and at the back to the arytenoid cartilages in a V shape with the apex at the thyroid and the feet at the arytenoids (see Figure 8.2). The folds themselves are mainly muscle. Because of the flexible design of the laryngeal skeleton and the nature of the muscle itself, very fine control of the vocal folds is possible. The default position of the vocal folds is open to facilitate breathing. They can also be firmly closed. If airflow continues while the vocal folds are closed, pressure builds up beneath them. If the vocal folds are then opened suddenly, the release of this pressure is audible. This is what happens when we cough. In fact, coughing has the specific function of dislodging any foreign bodies, mucus or crumbs of food that may have fallen onto the vocal folds during eating. The vocal folds are very sensitive to touch and automatically shut to protect the airway below. Foreign bodies entering the lungs can be extremely dangerous, resulting in choking or, if the material is allowed to remain in the lungs, infection and possibly pneumonia.

The vocal folds may also be held lightly closed in the air stream. Just as a blade of grass held between the thumbs can be made to produce a rasping sound when air is blown past it, so the vocal folds can produce what we know as *phonation* or **voice** by the action of air pressure from beneath them. At the larynx, the channel for the air is effectively narrowed since the larynx is narrower than the trachea. Therefore the air travelling up from the lungs has to fit into a smaller space. This can only happen if the air molecules squash closer together, or, in other words, by increasing air pressure. If the vocal folds are held close together with just the right amount of tension, then this pressure forces them apart. Once the vocal folds are apart, the air pressure is reduced and the vocal folds fall back into their lightly closed state again. The cycle then repeats over and over again. The sound that can be heard appears continuous because of the fast rate at which it takes place. The speed at which this happens determines the pitch of the sound that is heard. The faster it is, the higher the pitch. The habitual rate of vocal fold vibration (that is, the pitch of a normal speaking voice) for men is around 120 cycles a second and for women around 220 cycles.

Sounds made with the vocal folds in this state are known as **voiced**. Some English consonants and all English vowels are voiced. All of the sounds in each of the words *bomb, vole, zoom, gender,* gaze, and *dune* are voiced. Figure 8.3 shows the state of the vocal folds during voiced sounds.

If you produce an 'aaah' sound and then try to reduce the pitch as low as you can, you may be able to produce what is known as *creaky voice*. This is the sound that children sometimes make when imitating a creaky door or a monster's voice. During creaky voice, vocal fold vibration is very slow (around 20 to 60 cycles a second). The staccato quality of the sound you hear is a product of this very slow vibration. Creaky voice may be heard in older males as their habitual speaking

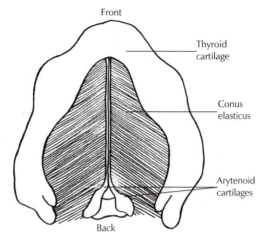

Figure 8.3   Glottis lightly closed for voiced sounds

voice. The position of the vocal folds during creaky voice production is shown in Figure 8.4.

The gap between the vocal folds is called the glottis. As the position of the vocal folds changes, so does the shape of the glottis. The air moving up from the lungs is thus forced through different types of channel depending on the state of the glottis. For example, if the vocal folds are held open, then air moving up from the lungs will pass through the glottis easily with minimal resistance. However, since the trachea is wider than the glottis there is bound to be some turbulence as the air reaches this point, even if the glottis is in its most maximally open position. A

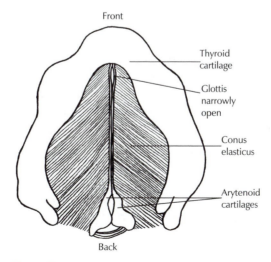

Figure 8.4   Glottis set for creaky voice

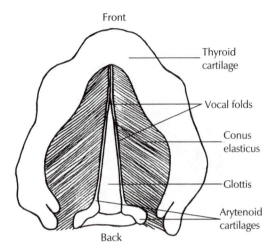

Figure 8.5   Glottis set for voiceless sounds

similar effect can be achieved if you blow gently through the channel in a loosely made fist. Speech sounds which are made with an open glottis are known as **voiceless** (see Figure 8.5). The first sounds in these words are all made with this type of phonation: *pound*, *foal*, *sip*, *throw*, *chest*, *shame*, *cap*, *tuck*. Notice that the first sounds in *foal*, *sip*, *throw*, *shame* can be produced continuously.

 Activity 8.4

Produce the sounds at the beginning of the words *foal*, *sip*, *throw*, *shame* on their own and continuously. Now move between the sounds in a continuous sequence (sounding something like ffffssssthththththshshshsh). The turbulent rushing noise you can hear is partly due to the air passing through an open glottis and partly due to the type of stricture through which the air passes higher in the vocal tract. Notice how the oral strictures change the sound but the quality of 'rushing hushiness' remains. This is the quality of voicelessness. If you open your mouth keeping your tongue relaxed and low and make a controlled exhalation as if breathing on a mirror, you will be able to hear air passing through the glottis without any significant stricture above it. Notice how quickly you run out of air in comparison with when making the earlier sounds. This is because the narrow channel made for the earlier voiceless articulations slows down the air expulsion rather effectively.

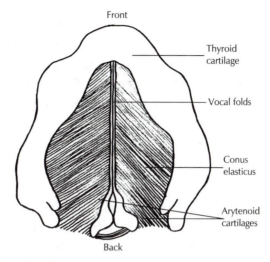

Figure 8.6   Firmly closed glottis

The vocal folds may also be closed completely so that no air at all can get through (Figure 8.6).

If there is airflow from the lungs and the vocal folds are held in a tightly closed position, nothing will be heard until the folds are opened. When this happens the air escapes suddenly and almost explosively and a sound known as a **glottal stop** is produced. This sound is heard in many accents of English and is particularly associated with London varieties where, for example, it may replace the middle sound in *letter* or the final sound in *what*. People sometimes refer to this as 'dropping the t'. In fact, the [t] sound has not been missed out of the word, but replaced by a glottal sound.

 Activity 8.5

To make a glottal stop you should practise by producing a series of quiet coughs. The slight constriction you feel in your throat just before you cough is the sensation of closing your glottis. You will be aware that you are effectively holding your breath as you have shut off the path from your lungs. In order to make the coughing sound there has to be a pulmonic airstream mechanism and the glottis has to be closed. Air then builds up behind the closed glottis until it is suddenly released. The only audible part of this process (that is, the cough itself) is the release stage of the glottal closure. While you are making the coughs, concentrate on the closure phase and try to hold your vocal folds in the closed position as if you were about to cough but stopped yourself immediately before producing the sound. If you flick your neck above the larynx whilst holding the glottis in this position you will notice the sound is quite clear and its pitch can be altered by changing the shape of your mouth. While in a relaxed state, this sort of flicking will only produce a dull type of thud.

 ## Activity 8.6

English has many voiced/voiceless sound pairs: that is, sounds that are produced with exactly the same type of articulation but with the glottis in different states: lightly closed for the voiced sound; open for the voiceless sound. The sounds at the beginning of the words *zip* and *sip* are just such a voiced/voiceless pair. In order to make yourself familiar with the difference between the voiced and voiceless sounds, take a deep breath and produce a continuous ssss sound. Half way through the sound, switch to making a zzzz sound. Continue switching between the two without pausing between the sounds. The sound you are making could be written sssszzzzssssszzzzsssszzzz. As you make the sound put your thumb and forefinger on either side of your larynx (at the location of the Adam's apple). As you make the switch from the voiceless to the voiced sound you should feel vibration during the zzzz phase which stops when you change to the ssss phase. What you are feeling is the rapid vibration of your vocal folds moving in the way described above. If you read this section of text aloud while keeping thumb and forefinger on your larynx you will notice how voicing is switched on and off during speech. Amazingly, this fine control is subconscious and rarely goes wrong for adult speakers. Children learning to speak, however, take some time to get their vocal folds under control and to begin with voice all speech sounds.

Above the larynx: places of articulation

The area above the larynx is called the *supralaryngeal area*. The supralaryngeal area can be thought of as comprising three chambers: the pharynx, the oral cavity and the nasal cavity (see Figure 8.7). The cavities can be closed off from each other by the velum and the tongue. The vocal folds and the mouth can close the three cavities at either end. By making a glottal stop and holding your lips together at the same time you will have effectively isolated your supralaryngeal system from the rest of the respiratory tract. While the larynx is usually associated with phonation in

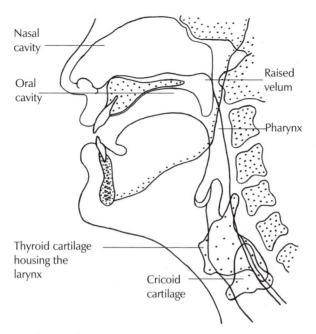

Figure 8.7   The supralaryngeal area

speech, the supralaryngeal area is most commonly associated with the places of articulation. You should note, however, that the glottis can itself be used to make three speech sounds: glottal stop and two glottal fricatives. Glottal stop is discussed in Activity 8.5; glottal fricatives are discussed further later in this unit.

The pharynx extends from the top of the larynx to the rear of the mouth (or oral cavity). The nasal cavity begins at the velum which can be lowered or raised thereby shutting the nasal cavity off from the oral and pharyngeal cavities. In normal breathing the velum is lowered so that air can pass down the nose and unimpeded into the trachea and thence the lungs.

The pharynx shape can be constricted by pulling together the faucal pillars, by raising the larynx or by retracting the root of the tongue back into the pharynx. The faucal pillars are the first set of arches that are visible from the front when you look into an open mouth (the space immediately behind the faucal arches is where the tonsils are located). The pharynx is not a particularly effective **articulator** but languages such as Arabic do make use of pharyngeal consonants and a pharyngeal quality can be introduced into sounds in many other languages as well.

Moving into the oral cavity, we discover the most important articulators in the vocal tract: the tongue, lips, teeth, alveolar ridge, hard palate and, forming the valve link into the nasal cavity, the velum, or soft palate (see Figure 8.1). Within the oral cavity, the tongue and lips can be thought of as active articulators while the alveolar

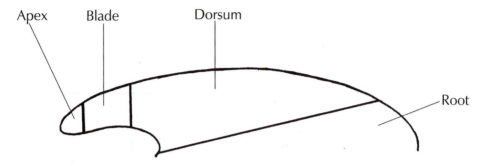

Figure 8.8   Areas of the tongue

ridge and hard palate are passive. By this it is meant the passive articulators do not move but are moved against by an active articulator.

The lips can be closed or open, brought together or used to articulate with the teeth. As well as this they can adopt a fairly relaxed or spread position, or a rounded position. The lips are involved in the articulation of the sounds at the start of the words *fox*, *boom*, *motor*, *picket*, and *vague*. For the middle sound of the word *freak* the lips are spread, while for the middle sound in *loop* they are rounded. Sounds involving the lips as major articulators are called *labial*.

The tongue can be divided into the tip (apex), blade (lamina), underblade, back (dorsum) and root (see Figure 8.8). The remarkable flexibility of the tongue makes it the most useful articulator of all. Not only is the tongue connected by muscles to the various structures which surround it, but it also contains muscles running along its length, across it from side to side and vertically from the underside to the upper surface. So complex is the muscular control of the tongue that no one is quite sure which muscles or combinations of muscles produce precisely which movements. The tip can articulate against the teeth, as in the first sound in the word *thistle* or the middle sound in *feather*, or the alveolar ridge as in the first sounds in the words *dumb* or *tickle*, or it can curl over to touch the alveolar ridge or the front part of the hard palate with its underside as it does in Dravidian languages, such as Tamil or Malayalam (the word 'Malayalam' has the added linguistic curiosity of being a palindrome – a word spelt the same backwards as forwards). The sides may curl up, as during the first sound in the word *soup*, or down as in the first sound in the word *leech*. The back of the tongue can articulate against the hard palate as in the first sound in the word *yodel*, or against the soft palate as in the final sound in the word *flog*.

> **Activity 8.7** 🔊
>
> Try to work out where and how the tongue moves for the sounds underlined in the words listed below.
>
> | | | |
> |---|---|---|
> | <u>ch</u>ew | <u>s</u>ugar | <u>t</u>una |
> | boo<u>z</u>e | <u>c</u>istern | a<u>qu</u>a |
> | <u>sh</u>aft | jun<u>c</u>tion | bu<u>ck</u>et |
> | ti<u>ss</u>ue | <u>tr</u>aitor | ha<u>gg</u>le |
> | <u>thr</u>ow | <u>g</u>aiter | mi<u>cr</u>ophone |
> | fro<u>ck</u> | <u>l</u>oiter | <u>l</u>isp |
> | <u>g</u>oogle | bub<u>bl</u>e | <u>y</u>esterday |
> | <u>d</u>oodle | mi<u>ss</u>ion | <u>y</u>outh |
> | <u>n</u>ifty | <u>j</u>uice | |

The teeth can be used as a surface for the tongue to articulate against. The back of the upper teeth or their lower edge can be used as a passive articulator for the tip of the tongue in words such as *thinker*. Speakers differ as to where they make their dental articulations. Compared to the teeth of monkeys which are uneven, the level surface of a human's teeth makes this type of delicate articulation possible. Had they the ability to speak, monkeys would find the pronunciation of the first sound in the word *think* impossible. Sounds which are made with the teeth as a major articulator are known as *dental*. In English we also use the upper teeth as an articulator with the bottom lip to produce the first sound in the word *fix* or the first sound in the word *vixen*. The side teeth are also used in a more peripheral way for sounds such as the first sound in the word *lexical*.

The alveolar ridge, sometimes also called the teeth ridge (see Figure 8.1), is directly behind the upper set of teeth on the hard palate. It can be found by running the tongue tip up the back of the front teeth and up into the region of the hard palate. In some speakers the ridge is very small in size or even apparently non-existent. These speakers use the region where the alveolar ridge would have been for alveolar articulations. The alveolar ridge is used in articulation of the first sound in the words *seedy, zephyr, torture, devoted, noodle.*

The hard palate is often referred to by non-linguists as 'the roof of the mouth'. It is a bony structure with a single ridge running lengthways down it. If the tongue tip is allowed to continue running backwards from the alveolar ridge it will encounter the highest part of the hard palate. Sounds with the label palatal are made in this region. The only palatal sound in English is the first sound in words such as *yacht* and *yoghurt*. Most English speakers also have a palatal sound immediately preceding the first vowel in words such as *music* and *beautiful*. Norfolk English speakers are usually an exception to this however (➻ Unit 9).

If the tongue tip's travel continues backwards, the hard, bony surface of the hard palate will give way to a softer region at the back of the mouth. This is the velum or soft palate. The velum is important in speech for two reasons:

1 the back of the tongue can articulate against it to create velar sounds, such as those that occur finally in the words *hack*, *hag* and *hang*;
2 the velum can be lowered and a complete obstruction made in the oral cavity, for example at the lips or alveolar ridge, so that air flows out of the nose rather than the mouth to make nasal sounds.

The nasal sounds in English are those made at the end of words such as *boom*, *span* and *gong*.

In normal breathing the velum is lowered so that air can pass through the nose, down into the lungs and out again. In normal speech however, when nasal sounds are not being made, the velum is raised to prevent air escaping through the nasal cavity. Sounds made with the velum raised are known as *oral*. When speakers have a blocked nose due to a cold, air will not be able to escape via the nasal cavity and they may be unable to make nasal sounds. Word pairs such as *boo* and *moo* and *dock* and *knock* will in this case sound identical.

If speech is produced with the velum lowered and no obstruction (or an incomplete obstruction) in the oral cavity, then it will have a particular quality caused by the air resonating in the nasal cavity and oral cavity at the same time. Sounds that are made like this are called **nasalized**. Some speakers, for example of some varieties of American English, habitually lower their velums during speech, making their speech characteristically nasalized in quality. Speakers who are unable to raise their velums to close off the nasal cavity during speech, for example because of a cleft palate, may also produce speech which is characteristically nasalized in quality.

Finally, speech sounds can be made by articulating with the back of the tongue against the uvula. The uvula is the drop shaped piece of tissue suspended at the back of the throat. While there are no uvular speech sounds in English, they do occur in some Western European languages such as German, French and some varieties of Italian, Russian and Swedish.

MANNER OF ARTICULATION

In order to produce speech sounds, articulators must move together in some way. Just as sounds differ according to their airstream mechanism (pulmonic, glottalic or velaric), phonation (voiced or voiceless), place of articulation (glottal, pharyngeal, uvular, velar, palatal, alveolar, dental or labial), and nasality (oral or nasal), so they differ according to how the articulators move in relation to one another. Simply put, manner of articulation can be thought of as variation in the degree of closure (or stricture) between articulators. The degree of stricture ranges from maximally close (articulators are clamped together preventing air from flowing past them) to maximally open (articulators are wide apart so that air flows through them unimpeded). Effectively, the way in which articulators move together shapes the air flow from the lungs (or other place of articulation), changing the sound by changing the shape of the channel through which the air moves. Just as a tall narrow bottle makes a different sound when tapped to the sound made by a short squat bottle of the same volume, so the nature of the constriction in the vocal tract can alter the nature of the speech sounds made in it.

Stops: plosives and nasals

Articulators held together tightly so that the airflow is completely stopped, as the lips are in pronunciation of the first sound in *bumble*, *pixie* and *malice* for example, are called *stops*. There is an important difference between these three sounds. While the first sounds in *bumble* and *pixie* are brief and, if made in isolation, have an explosive quality, the first sound in *malice* can be drawn out for as long as the air flow continues. In fact, English speakers sometimes use this long drawn out *mmmm* sound to express the desirability of something, particularly food. Sounds which can be drawn out in this way are known as *continuants*.

The sounds at the start of *bumble* and *pixie* belong to a subset of the stop family called *plosives*. Plosive sounds involve three stages: approach, hold and release. During the approach stage, the articulators (upper and lower lips for the initial sounds in *bumble* and *pixie*) move closer together. During the hold stage, the articulators are sealed shut. Meanwhile air flow continues, building up behind the closure, increasing pressure as it does so. Finally, the closure is opened and the air released, making a 'puff' sound which is characteristic of the release stage of plosive consonants. This puff sound can be heard more clearly in the voiceless plosives than in their voiced counterparts. This is because generally a more energetic airflow is used to produce voiceless sounds to overcome their lower audibility (remember that the vocal folds do not vibrate during voiceless sounds). The English plosives are represented by the initial sounds in the words *bumble*, *pixie*, *delicate*, *tuxedo*, *galley* and *cavern*. Glottal stop is also a plosive but is not usually regarded as a speech sound in English. Readers who are interested in the reason behind this should refer to Ladefoged's book in the further reading section at the end of this unit.

Activity 8.8

Identify the places of articulation for the initial plosive sounds in the words *bumble, pixie, delicate, tuxedo, galley* and *cavern*. In addition, try to identify which of the sounds are voiced and which are voiceless. What do you notice about the set of English plosives with regard to voicing?

The initial sounds in the words *malice, nebula* and the final sound in *ring* represent the set of English stops that are not plosives. As well as being stops these sounds also represent the set of English nasals. Nasals are sounds which are made by directing the air flow through the nose by lowering the velum. Air is prevented from escaping through the mouth during a nasal sound by a complete closure somewhere in the oral cavity. The particular sound quality associated with nasals derives from the air from the lungs resonating in the nasal and, to a lesser extent, oral cavities.

Fricatives

Articulators held close together with sufficient tension so that air forced between them produces audible vibration are known as *fricatives*. Fricatives produced with vocal fold vibration have a 'buzzing' quality. Those produced without vocal fold vibration have a much softer quality, suggestive of rushing air. The sounds at the beginning of *Viking, those, zone* and between the vowels in *treasure* are all voiced fricatives. The sounds at the beginning of the words *faint, thorn, sash, shifty* and *hockey* are all voiceless fricatives.

Activity 8.9

Identify the places of articulation for the fricatives at the beginning of the words *Viking, those, zone, faint, thorn, sash, shifty* and in the middle of the word *treasure*. What do you notice about this set of fricatives with regard to voicing and place of articulation? You may find it helpful to refer back to Activity 8.8.

The sounds here represent the set of English fricatives. The initial sound in *hockey* is also included in the set of English fricatives. This sound is known as a *voiceless glottal fricative*. It may strike you as unusual in that its vocal tract configuration seems to vary according to the context in which it is used.

 Activity 8.10 ○━

Produce the words *house, hoof, heart, heat, hug, horse* in front of a mirror. Focus on the position of your lips and the degree of opening of your jaw during production of the initial sound (extend the sound if you like to make the observation easier). What do you notice?

The voiceless glottal fricative is made by holding the vocal folds in such a position that the air can be heard rushing between them. The apparently different vocal tract configurations for its production in different contexts (as explored in Activity 8.10) are not in fact features of the voiceless glottal fricative itself, but rather demonstrate the way in which articulators prepare for upcoming sounds. For example, the spread lip position and fairly closed jaw position for the initial sound in *heat* is a result of the articulators preparing for the spread lip position and fairly closed jaw position associated with the vowel sound which follows. In other words, the voiceless glottal fricative tends to take on the articulatory postures of the sounds which succeed it. This behaviour is not unique. All speech sounds do this to some extent. Speech is produced so quickly that sounds must by necessity run into one another and, in doing so, take on one another's characteristics. This phenomenon is known as *co-articulation* and is a topic to which we will return later when we discuss assimilation.

Approximants

Approximants have a wider degree of opening than fricatives. No friction is audible, instead approximants mainly rely on shaping of the vocal tract to make them distinctive from other sounds. The English approximants are represented by the first sounds in the words *wriggle*, *linguist*, *whisk* and *yawn*.

Trills

Trills are made by a rapid and intermittent contact between two articulators. Airflow and tension of articulators is controlled so that the articulators touch and almost immediately burst apart. The air pressure behind the contact is not sufficiently strong to create the explosive burst associated with plosives but is strong enough to force apart the weakly held contact for a brief moment. In a similar way to the vocal folds during voiced articulations, once the pressure behind the closure is released, the articulators fall back together, the pressure builds up again to force them apart, and so the cycle continues. The resulting sound has a rhythmic, vibratory quality. There are no trills in RP English as such but readers may recognize the bilabial trill from the noise typically made by people to demonstrate how cold they are feeling, often written as 'Brrrr!'. To make this sound, the lips are pursed together in a slightly pouting position and air is forced between them. The alveolar trill is made by holding the tongue tip against the alveolar ridge and forcing air between them. English speakers sometimes refer to this sound as *rolled r*. When used as a speech sound, there are usually two or three periods of vibration during a trill although this may be extended, particularly if the sound is used emphatically. Russian, Finnish, Spanish, Swedish, Italian and some varieties of Scots English have alveolar trills as distinctive speech sounds (phonemes). The term 'apical' is often used for these sounds because they are made with the apex of the tongue. Uvular trills are also possible.

Taps and flaps

Taps and flaps are made by the active articulator making a brief contact with the passive, either as the active articulator passes the passive articulator during its arc of movement (flap), or by moving the active articulator from its resting position to make a rapid, momentary contact before returning to its resting position (tap). The active articulator is generally controlled with a degree of tension such that its contact has an elastic quality. Briefer than a plosive articulation, for English speakers the sound is best exemplified by the alveolar tap heard in American English varieties as the middle sound in the words *ladder* and *butter*. Taps can also be heard in some varieties of Spanish.

Affricates

Affricates are made by moving from a plosive to a fricative sound at the same place of articulation. Affricates occur in many of the world's languages. In British English there are two: the first and final sound in *church* and the first and final sound in *judge*.

Table 8.1   The components of speech sounds

Airstream mechanisms	Pulmonic (lungs) Glottalic (glottis) Velaric (velum)
Phonation	Voiced (vocal fold vibration; lightly closed glottis) Voiceless (no vocal fold vibration; wide open glottis)
Place of Articulation	Glottis Pharynx Uvula Velum Palate Postalveolar Alveolar Dental Labiodental Bilabial
Manner of Articulation	Plosive Nasal Fricative Approximant Trill Tap Flap Affricate

SPEECH SOUNDS: PUTTING IT ALL TOGETHER

The preceding sections describe the ways in which speech sounds are made. To begin with, we looked at the various types of initiation that can give rise to the air flow on which speech sounds are imposed. The various types are pulmonic, glottalic and velaric. By far the most common air stream mechanism used in the world's spoken languages is pulmonic.

Next we looked at phonation, or vocal fold vibration. While many types of phonation are possible, for English speech sounds the most important distinction is between lightly closed and vibrating vocal folds and an open glottis; that is, respectively, voiced and voiceless sounds.

Next we looked at the places of articulation that are important for making speech sounds. We identified the glottis, pharynx, lips, teeth, alveolar ridge, palate, velum and uvula as important in speech. The tongue is critically involved in the majority of speech sounds, either as an active articulator or in shaping the vocal tract. We made a further distinction between oral and nasal sounds. For oral sounds the velum is raised and the air is released through the mouth. For nasal sounds the velum is lowered, an obstruction is made at some point in the mouth to prevent air escaping orally and air is released through the nose. Sounds in which air is released both orally and nasally are called nasalized.

Finally, we looked at manners of articulation identifying stops, plosives, nasals, fricatives, approximants, trills, taps, flaps and affricates.

The information so far is summarized in Table 8.1.

VOWELS

Alert readers will have noticed that our discussion of speech sounds so far has an important omission. **Vowels** are far less central in our concept of speech sounds than consonants. This may be because vowels are thought to be rather less useful in distinguishing words than consonants are. You can test this assertion for yourself by reading aloud the first sentence of this paragraph, replacing every vowel sound with the very first (vowel) sound in the first word *alert*. You should find that the sentence is still understandable. A similar effect can be demonstrated with orthography: t s stll pssbl t dstngsh wrds evn f ll th vwls r rmvd frm th sntnc. The language of text messaging (➣ Unit 7) works on a similar principle.

Throughout the bulk of the phonetics literature, the centrality afforded to **consonants** is manifest. It seems that consonants really provide the ‘colour’ of speech, while the more featureless vowels merely hold it all together. In fact, vowels have a crucial role in speech which is not immediately apparent. Acoustic examination of speech using an instrument known as a spectrograph, reveals that vowels give us all sorts of important information about what is coming next in the speech stream. Often consonants are articulated so quickly that in noisy real life environments they can be missed. Speech occurs at an approximate rate of 3–5 syllables or approximately 10 individual speech sounds per second. At this speed it is impossible to make every speech sound separate and distinct. As vowels bind the consonants together, they exhibit important co-articulation effects. That is, features of the upcoming sounds appear in the preceding sounds as the speaker prepares their articulators to make them. Listeners use these co-articulation effects to enable them to predict the sounds which are coming up next. A similar phenomenon was discussed above in relation to the voiceless glottal fricative. Some of these co-articulation effects are discussed further below in the section on assimilation.

Vowels are also the main carriers of extralinguistic information such as that contained in the **intonation** contour of an **utterance**. Intonation refers to the way in which pitch is varied in speech and can be crucial in determining meaning.

Describing vowels is a rather more challenging task than describing consonants. Vowels do not involve contact articulations, but instead rely on a relatively unimpeded airflow shaped by movement and positioning of the vocal tract to make them distinct from other sounds. There are therefore no specific points within the vocal tract architecture (such as bilabial, velar, etc.) that we may make reference to in our descriptions of vowel sounds. Traditionally phoneticians use three features of a vowel’s articulation to make distinctions between them. These are: the highest position of the tongue during production; the degree to which the bulk of the tongue is located forward or back in the oral cavity; and the position of the lips, that is, rounded or unrounded. Vowels that are produced with the tongue relatively high in the oral cavity are described as ‘close’. Vowels that are produced with the tongue relatively low in the oral cavity are described as ‘open’. Vowels produced with the bulk of the tongue relatively forward in the oral cavity are described as ‘front’, while those produced with the tongue relatively retracted are described as ‘back’. Vowels produced with rounded lips are known as ‘rounded’ and those with spread or relaxed lip positions simply as ‘unrounded’. The terms ‘mid’, ‘open mid’ and ‘close mid’ are used to refer to vowels with intermediate tongue height positions, while the term ‘central’ is used to refer to vowels made in the central locations of the vowel space. Vowels are almost always produced with vocal fold vibration, although Japanese does make a systematic contrast between voiced and voiceless vowels.

The three English RP vowels which are easiest to distinguish, and, not entirely co-incidentally, the three vowels which tend to be acquired first by children (➤ Unit 10) are shown below.

> The vowel sound in *teeth*, *speed* and *freak* is front, close and unrounded.
> The vowel sound in *heart*, *dark* and *cask* is back, open and unrounded.
> The vowel sound in *pool*, *moon* and *stoop* is back, close and rounded.

In all, there are 20 vowel sounds in RP English. Twelve of these are monophthongs, that is, pure vowel sounds, and eight are diphthongs, that is, two vowel sounds run together so that the first glides into the second. Diphthongs, therefore, have a dynamic quality; a little like plosives, they are characterized by movement from one stage to another. Words like *coy*, *chime*, *choke* and *maid* contain diphthongs, while words like *heat*, *flute*, *spore* and *tarn* contain monophthongs.

The set of English monophthong vowels are shown in Table 8.2a along with their descriptive labels and phonetic symbols (see next section in this unit).

Table 8.2a English monophthong vowel sounds in RP

The vowel in …	described as …	is represented with this IPA symbol …
cheek	Front, close, unrounded	i
tip	Front, close mid, unrounded	ɪ
beg	Front, open mid, unrounded	ɛ
bag	Front, open, unrounded	a
curse	Mid, central, unrounded	ɜ
deli<u>ver</u>	Mid, central, unrounded, unstressed	ə
tuck	Open mid, central, unrounded	ʌ
hoop	Close, back, rounded	u
pull	Close mid, back, rounded	ʊ
force	Mid, back, rounded	ɔ
spot	Open, back, rounded	ɒ
march	Open, back, unrounded	ɑ

Table 8.2b   English diphthong vowel sounds in RP

The vowel sound in …	is represented with this IPA symbol …
fear	ɪə
hair	ɛə
lure	ʊə
may	eɪ
spy	aɪ
ploy	ɔɪ
dough	əʊ
now	aʊ

In addition the eight English diphthongs (see Table 8.2b) are exemplified by the following words: *fear*, *hair*, *lure*, *may*, *spy*, *ploy*, *dough*, *now*.

It should be noted that there is likely to be considerable variation between speakers in producing vowel sounds. Much of the difference that can be heard between regional varieties of a language derives from the articulatory features of vowels. Some London English speakers, for example, use a closer vowel in *bag* [a] than RP speakers, resulting in a pronunciation approximating the RP pronunciation of *beg* [ɛ]. Northern English speakers do not use the vowel in RP *tuck* at all, replacing it with the vowel in RP *pull*. Speakers of Midlands English tend to use a closer vowel in words like *tip* than RP speakers. The fluidity in vowel sounds is not due just to regional variation. For example, younger English speakers have moved the vowel sound in words such as *room* to a more fronted position than older speakers. Adults talking to babies or pets sometimes make their vowels closer, producing a 'cute' voice. It is for reasons such as these that those learning phonetics are encouraged to focus on a single variety of English, namely RP, and to avoid getting too bogged down in the detailed transcription of vowel sounds until the basics have been mastered.

THE INTERNATIONAL PHONETIC ALPHABET (IPA) AND TRANSCRIPTION

The IPA is a chart containing the full range of phonetic symbols of speech sounds. The latest version of the chart can be found on p. 492 of this volume. The chart is composed by the International Phonetic Association. This body maintains the international relevance of the chart and occasionally makes revisions to it to ensure that it continues to best serve its purpose. As its name suggests the IPA chart can be used to transcribe the speech sounds of the languages of the world. It is therefore critical that all who use it have the same understanding of the sounds and the system of their classification. The chart is only useful if the entire community of linguists and phoneticians understand and use it in the same way. It is important to note that the symbols on it are not specific to English. While some of the symbols may look familiar, you should be careful not to assume that the sounds they represent are the ones represented by the same symbols in English orthography.

The chart is broadly organized in the following way. The main grid, which is labelled 'consonants (pulmonic)', contains the majority of consonant symbols. The column headings of the consonant grid give us the place of articulation for the symbols while the row headings give us the manners of articulation. In many of the cells there are two symbols. Where this is the case, the symbol on the left denotes a voiceless sound, and the symbol on the right its voiced counterpart. Just below the main grid and on the left is a box headed 'consonants (non-pulmonic)'. These are consonants produced with an airstream mechanism which is either velaric or glottalic (see above for an explanation of what this means). Below the non-pulmonic consonants is a list of 'other symbols' (also consonants) whose labels do not permit them to fit easily into the main consonant grid. To the right of the non-pulmonic consonants box is the vowel quadrilateral which shows positions of the primary and secondary series of cardinal vowels (see below for an explanation). Below the vowel quadrilateral are the symbols used when transcribing 'suprasegmentals' and 'tones and word accents'. Finally, the bottom left corner contains a box headed 'diacritics'. This box contains symbols which may be added to speech sound symbols to add further detail to their pronunciation.

By means of the chart's main symbols in combination with the diacritics it is theoretically possible to transcribe any speech sound you may hear. As with any system of this sort however, contentions do arise. The International Phonetic Association works to resolve any such disagreements or grey areas, hence the various versions of the chart you may encounter in older texts. You should stick to using the symbols as shown in the most recent version of the chart for your own transcriptions.

After completing your study of this unit you should be able to make a broad phonetic transcription. However this will only be possible if your reading is supplemented by instruction from a suitably experienced tutor. There is unfortunately no substitute for real-life practice of the sounds that are described below and no realistic way to practise your transcription skills without the help and feedback of a tutor. Transcribing speech sounds is a skill which becomes easier with practice. There are passages for transcription throughout the following sections which are graded in terms of difficulty to enable you to build up your transcription skills gradually. It is recommended that you obtain assistance from a willing co-student or friend who reads the passages in short sections, slowly but not word by word, nor with any special emphasis. The delivery of the passages for transcription should be as natural sounding as possible. Once a section has been read it may be repeated, but it is important that the original delivery should be mimicked as closely as possible. Tape recordings may also be used to help you learn transcription skills. Do remember, however, that transcribers make use of visual information almost as much as auditory information. Important details such as lip rounding can be spotted far more easily visually than auditorally.

Transcribed speech should maintain word boundaries as far as possible. An exception may be made if small (usually function) words are run together by a speaker. No punctuation or capital letters should be used. Phonetic symbols are enclosed in square brackets, thus: [fɒnɛtɪks]. Where there is a pause in the speech (or a full stop or comma if you are working from a piece of orthography) you should use this symbol ‖ but note that in syntactic analysis (⇢ Unit 7), the same symbol is used to denote a clause boundary. In other texts you may see symbols enclosed in slash brackets like this /dɒg/. Slash brackets denote a phonemic transcription and are therefore not used here.

Classifying consonants

The layout of the IPA chart enables us to see clearly the descriptive characteristics of the sounds. Consonants are labelled by means of a three point term. First we must know the state of the vocal folds (that is, whether a sound is voiced or voiceless); secondly we need to know the place of articulation; finally we need to know the manner of articulation. [f] is therefore a voiceless labiodental fricative; [x] is a voiceless velar fricative. Using the three point term will enable us to describe the consonant in such a way that its distinction from other consonants is made clear. Conversely, such a descriptive labelling convention will allow us to note the similarities between speech sounds. The symbols [t] and [s] don't sound or look very similar but their three point terms (respectively, voiceless alveolar plosive and voiceless alveolar fricative) enable us to note that they differ only in manner of articulation.

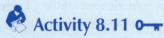

Activity 8.11 ⚬━

What are the three point terms for the following symbols?

β g ŋ h m ð ç χ ɾ f z ʒ

The English consonants for the RP accent are as shown below.

p	as in papa	ʃ	as in shamble
b	as in bravo	ʒ	as in measure
t	as in tango	h	as in hotel
d	as in delta	l	as in lima
k	as in kilo	ɹ	as in romeo
g	as in golf	j	as in yankee
f	as in foxtrot	w	as in whisky
v	as in victor	m	as in mike
θ	as in theatre	n	as in november
ð	as in that	ŋ	as in ring
s	as in sierra	tʃ	as in church
z	as in zulu	dʒ	as in judge

Classifying vowels

The IPA chart uses a graphic representation of the oral cavity in order to classify vowel sounds. The four-sided shape is known as a vowel quadrilateral. It is not intended to represent the entire oral cavity but rather the area within it which is used to make vowels, that is, the vowel space. Any speech sounds which are made close to or in contact with the upper (passive) articulators will result in stop or fricative articulations. The vowel space's upper boundary is therefore just below the region where fricative sounds are made. Longitudinally, only the region from the palatal to velar sections of the oral cavity are used during vowel production. A front vowel as in *cheat* [i] is therefore made with the bulk of the tongue bunched up below the palatal region while a back vowel as in *soup* [u] is made with the bulk of the tongue bunched up below the velar region.

In the earlier section on vowels we made use of the same **descriptive** terms that are used on the vowel quadrilateral: close, close mid, open mid and open for the vertical location of the tongue; front, central, back for the horizontal dimension; rounded and unrounded for lip positions. The vowel quadrilateral on the IPA chart has positions marked with a point and a symbol on either side of its outermost boundaries. These are the symbols for the cardinal vowels. Those to the left of the line are unrounded while those to the right are rounded. The cardinal vowels can be thought of as markers delineating the most extreme positions possible for vowels. [i] is therefore the closest, most front vowel possible, while [ɑ] is the most open back vowel possible. The vowel sounds on the IPA chart do not necessarily relate to the vowels used in particular languages. Rather they represent markers of the vowel space and enable phoneticians to locate specific vowels within that space.

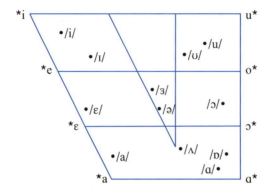

Figure 8.9   English monophthong vowels
* = cardinal vowels. English vowels are shown in slash brackets as phonemes

However, to simplify vowel transcription in English, it is often the case that cardinal vowel symbols are co-opted to represent English speech sounds. For example (and as discussed above) there are 12 English pure vowels represented by the middle sounds in the words *cheek, tip, beg, bag, curse, deliver, tuck, hoop, pull, force, spot, march.*

These should be transcribed by the following symbols:

cheek	i	tip	ɪ
beg	ɛ	bag	a
curse	ɜ	deliver	ə
tuck	ʌ	hoop	u
pull	ʊ	force	ɔ
spot	ɒ	march	ɑ

We can see how these vowels are actually located in the vowel space (and therefore how they relate to the cardinal vowels) by plotting their positions on the vowel quadrilateral as shown in Figure 8.9.

Anybody, regardless of their native language, looking at the location of the English vowels on the quadrilateral will be able to tell what they should sound like by relating them to the cardinal vowels.

We may use a similar strategy for transcribing diphthongs. The eight English diphthongs are shown below along with words which exemplify their production.

fear	ɪə	hair	ɛə
lure	ʊə	may	eɪ
spy	aɪ	ploy	ɔɪ
dough	əʊ	now	aʊ

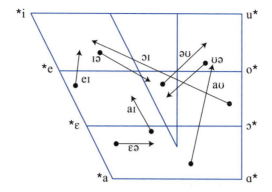

Figure 8.10   English RP diphthong vowels

Their positions on the vowel quadrilateral are indicated by arrows in Figure 8.10, since their dynamic nature makes pinpoint location unhelpful.

Those diphthongs whose movement is from open to close such as [aɪ] are called rising diphthongs. Those whose movement approaches [ə] such as [ɪə] are called centring diphthongs.

 Activity 8.12 ⚬━ㅜ

Transcription: practising monophthongs
Transcribe the following words using the IPA vowel and consonant symbols described above.

1 boxer	5 cheap	9 grant	13 thief	17 cart	21 women
2 shone	6 gnat	10 cease	14 exit	18 plastic	22 thirst
3 loot	7 caught	11 jig	15 trough	19 view	23 doom
4 book	8 church	12 deaf	16 shawl	20 shopping	24 grunge

 Activity 8.13 ⚬━ㅜ

Transcription: practising diphthongs
Transcribe the following words using the IPA consonant and vowel symbols described above.

1 exploit	5 Viking	9 vague	13 purist	17 hair	21 mighty
2 denote	6 plate	10 roll	14 tier	18 spice	22 ground
3 mayor	7 know	11 rowdy	15 expire	19 area	23 tower
4 moor	8 retire	12 bear	16 space	20 loiter	24 violin

Schwa

One of the most common mistakes in students' early attempts at transcription is the use of schwa [ə]. This is by far the most commonly occurring vowel in spoken English and, in an extended transcription of naturally spoken English, should therefore be the most frequently occurring symbol. The reason for schwa's prevalence is related to the use of stress in spoken language. Schwa also appears somewhat less frequently as part of a diphthong in words like *hair* [hɛə]. When used in this way it may appear in either stressed or unstressed syllables. However, when schwa is the main vowel in a syllable, as in the second syllable of the word *boxer* [bɒksə], the syllable in which it occurs is always weak or unstressed. Stress and its transcription are described in greater detail below. Students really need at least a basic understanding of stress before they will be able to make accurate transcriptions and so are advised to read through the sections on lexical and sentence stress now and then perhaps revisit activities 8.12 and 8.13 above.

On the IPA chart, schwa is represented as being a central mid vowel. In reality however, the articulatory position of schwa changes depending on what precedes and/or follows it. This is another example of a co-articulation effect, albeit one that occurs very frequently in speech. Schwa changes its location in this way because speakers try to be as economical as possible in the movements that they make between individual speech sounds. Speakers speaking at a moderate rate may produce as many as ten different sounds in a single second. Since an unstressed syllable is typically much briefer than a stressed syllable and since listeners tend to listen more closely to stressed than unstressed syllables to identify words, the articulatory location of schwa can vary considerably without any detrimental effect to clarity of speech.

Transcribing schwa accurately and correctly is therefore partly a matter of experience and partly a matter of having a clear understanding of its role in speech. As a general rule, when starting to transcribe, you should double check the transcription of any vowel in an unstressed syllable that has not been transcribed as schwa to make absolutely certain that you are using the symbol correctly.

Stress

Stress is best described as extra prominence given to a syllable relative to its environmental context. Syllable prominence derives from an increased amount of effort put into a syllable's production by the speaker. Typically this extra effort will manifest in increased volume, a slight rise in pitch and a slight lengthening of the vowel in the stressed syllable. It is very important to remember that stress is a property of syllables and not words.

There are two types of stress which are of interest in transcription: lexical stress and sentence stress. Here we will talk about lexical stress and leave the issue of sentence stress until later. Lexical stress refers to the idea that one syllable in every word is bound to be more prominent than the others. This characteristic is as important a feature of the word as the sounds which make it up. We show stress by the diacritic < ' > placed in front of the stressed syllable. Where lexical stress is placed in a word may vary between varieties of the same language (for example between British and Caribbean English ➤➤ Unit 9). The words below are shown marked with the stress associated with British English.

'elephant	ba'lloon	pho'tography
'ketchup	co'llapse	re'lease
'photograph	di'saster	ta'rantula
'spider	es'cape	to'mato

 Activity 8.14

One by one, pronounce the words above out loud, taking each syllable in turn and artificially add stress to it. You can do this simply by making the syllable louder and slightly slower than the others in the word. Notice how odd the word sounds when the stress is misplaced in it. If you are ever unsure where the lexical stress in a word should go, use this method to discover it. Remember, it is only by comparing stress on *every* syllable of the word that you will be able to tell which pronunciation of the word sounds right. In time, and by practising, you should find that your ability to identify stressed syllables in a word improves.

Stress can sometimes move around morphological variants of a word. Notice that in the list above, the stress in *photograph* and *photography* is on a different syllable. The same happens in *explain* and *explanation*, *exhibit* and *exhibition*. Sometimes the same word form receives different lexical stress depending on the grammatical function of the word. For example, *re'search* (**verb**) and *'research* (**noun**).

Activity 8.15

Place the lexical stress in the following words:

cinema	cinematic	discover	discovery	realize	realization
telephone	telephonist	variety	variation	mountain	mountainous
ignore	ignorance	extra	extraneous	neutral	neutrality
fantasy	fantastic	machine	machination	vital	vitality

When they occur in normal spoken conversation, the syllables in some words receive more stress than others. This pattern of stress is what is called *sentence stress*. The syllables that receive stress within a sentence tend to be mainly in the **content words** rather than in the **function words** (➞ Unit 7). Only for particular reasons and in relatively unusual speech contexts do function words receive stress, such as to impart emphasis or to express contrastive meaning. So for example, *with* in sentence (1) and *your* in (2) are likely to be produced without stress, but *with* and *at* in (3) and *your* and *hers* in (4) are more likely to be produced *with* stress.

(1)   Alice is the girl with kaleidoscope eyes.
(2)   Your head is filled with strange ideas and distorted facts.
(3)   No officer, we were laughing <u>with</u> you, not <u>at</u> you.
(4)   I said <u>your</u> head was funny not <u>hers</u>.

Activity 8.16

Read the sentences below out loud (or get a sympathetic friend to assist) in as neutral a tone as possible. Note which words are stressed.

1   Sue could not decide why she felt left out until she noticed everyone except her was wearing a hat.
2   When Stuart heard about the cat's missing tail he judged it wiser to say nothing.
3   Kitty's pride in finding the bus soon disappeared when she realized the driver had no intention of stopping to let her get off in Dogfield.

 **Activity 8.17**

Say the sentences below aloud, putting the stress on different words each time. What is the effect of adding stress to any of the function words?

1   I really like that dress but it may be a little bit too revealing for your grandmother's birthday.
2   As soon as they found themselves in Toronto, Jo and Alex checked under their seats and immediately found their passports.
3   Kate became confused although not upset after she had spoken to the man.

CONNECTED SPEECH

From the foregoing section on lexical and sentence stress it should become apparent that word forms in isolation behave differently from word forms spoken in the context of longer utterances. Since very little speech occurs as individual words with pauses before and after, it is necessary to become familiar with some of the phenomena that occur during connected speech. As mentioned above, the speed at which natural speech is produced means that speech sounds blend into one another, producing what are known as *co-articulation effects* or *assimilation*. Speakers may also miss sounds out. This is not done at random but systematically and in specific contexts. This phenomenon is known as elision.

In order to make pronunciation easier, speakers also sometimes insert a sound. For example, [ɹ] is inserted between vowels in particular contexts. This is known as *intrusive r* or *linking r* depending on the context, and is discussed in more detail later in this unit.

Both speakers and listeners are subconsciously tuned into connected speech phenomena and are rarely actually aware that a sound has changed to become more like the sounds around it, or that a sound has been missed out or added to an utterance. We are able to overcome any potential confusion because spoken language has a high level of redundancy. Listeners use the context of the situation, both linguistic and extralinguistic, their knowledge of the world and their knowledge of their conversational co-participant to help them interpret, and even to a certain extent predict, what is said (➻ Unit 3). In addition, the speech itself contains many cues as to what is coming next and listeners are sensitive to these. For example, vowels before voiceless sounds are shorter than those before voiced sounds. A listener can therefore predict a speaker's intention to say *bead* rather than *beat* before they have heard the final consonant sound. Visual cues such as lip rounding let a listener know that an upcoming sound is likely to belong to that class of speech sounds. Audible cues such as nasalization of a vowel tell a listener a nasal consonant is coming up next. Many of these features can be transcribed using the IPA chart.

A transcription which uses symbols to capture detail to this extent is called a *narrow transcription*. Unfortunately it is not possible to explore narrow transcription here but interested readers should refer to the further reading section at the end of the unit. Redundancy in speech is built in as a design feature of spoken language. It means that if an individual speech sound is muffled or inaudible due to a noisy or ambiguous context the message does not suffer.

The beginner transcriber needs to develop an awareness of connected speech phenomena. Since we are so used to reconstructing a message and seldom notice the fine details of spoken language output, it is sensible to read the sections on connected speech first and then listen to the language that takes place around you to see whether you are able to spot assimilations, elisions and linking r. Most lay people tend to believe that it is only lazy people who make these adjustments to their spoken language. Careful listening (and watching) of newsreaders and other professional language users should quickly enable you to become aware that no one is impervious to the use of connected speech phenomena.

Weak forms

Often function words when produced in the context of a sentence not only lack stress, but have a pronunciation different from that when produced in isolation. The unstressed pronunciation is known as the **weak form** of the function word and the stressed pronunciation is the **strong form**.

The typical weak forms of some common function words are shown in Table 8.3. There are many others and speakers may use other weak forms depending on context of use and their own linguistic background.

Pronunciation of weak forms can vary according to the immediate speech context. Note that in Table 8.3, the weak form of *the* differs according to whether the next word begins with a vowel or not. Similarly, [h] is dropped from the beginning of the weak form for *he* and *her* etc. unless following a pause, while *and* preserves final [d] in its weak form only as long as the first sound of the following word is a vowel. Weak forms are a result of speakers making their pronunciation of words as efficient as possible without compromising effective delivery of their message. Vowels are shortened, for example from [i] to [ɪ] or from [u] to [ʊ], or become [ə]. Consonants which occur in the middle of a string of consonants, or consonant cluster, may be dropped as is the case with the utterance 'stju ən 'tɪm 'lɛft where *and* loses the final [d]. This phenomenon is called elision and the alveolar plosives [t] and [d] are particularly vulnerable to it (elision is dealt with

Table 8.3 English weak forms

Function Word	Strong form	Weak form	Examples
have	ˈhav	əv	aɪ əv ˈlɛft ðə ˈmʌni wɪð ˈmʌm
can	ˈkan	kən	kən jʊ ˈpleɪ ˈtɛnɪs
you	ˈju	jə, jʊ	əv jʊ ˈsin ˈpitə
he	ˈhi	hɪ, ɪ	əz ɪ ɡɒt ˈskaɪ
she	ˈʃi	ʃɪ	ʃɪ ɪz ˈbjutɪfəl
to	ˈtu	tʊ, tə	ðeɪ ˈwɛnt tə ˈbɛd
but	ˈbʌt	bət	bət ɪ dɪdṇt ˈslip
and	ˈand	ənd, ən	ˈstju ən ˈtɪm ˈlɛft ˈkeɪti ənd ˈalɪs ˈlaft
the	ˈði	ðə, ðɪ	ðə ˈdɒɡ ɪz ˈdɛd ðɪ ˈapəl ɪz ˈɹaɪp
would	ˈwʊd	wəd	hɪ wəd ˈhɛlp ɪf ɪ kʊd
her	ˈhɜ	hə, ə	ɡɪv ˈsam ə ˈbɒl ˈbak

further later in this unit). The voiceless glottal fricative [h] may also be missed out in weak forms. Since it is a sound with low audibility its omission is unlikely to compromise understanding in the majority of contexts.

Assimilation

As the speaker pronounces one sound they prepare their articulators to produce later sounds. This means that for speakers speaking at a normal rate, features from later sounds spill backwards and affect the production of earlier sounds. Assimilation therefore relates to earlier sounds changing to become more like later sounds. In practice, assimilation is only usually clearly audible when particular speech sounds are involved. Assimilation effects can be clearly heard when a bilabial [p] [b] [m] or velar stop [k] [g] [ŋ] follows an alveolar stop [t] [d] [n] making the alveolar stops bilabial or velar respectively. For example, the following phrases if produced at normal speaking rate will result in the assimilated pronunciations shown.

hot potato	ˈhɒp pəˈteɪtəu	cute baby	ˈkjup ˈbeɪbi
white gold	ˈwaɪk ˈɡəuld	mad cat	ˈmaɡ ˈkat
red gold	ˈɹɛɡ ˈɡəuld	ten cooks	ˈteŋ ˈkʊks

Notice that the alveolars only assimilate the place feature of the following bilabials and velars. They do not change their voicing or manner features. This kind of assimilation which works so that a later sound affects an earlier sound is called *regressive assimilation*. Less often, assimilation can work the other way so that earlier occurring sounds affect later sounds. This is called *progressive assimilation*.

 Activity 8.18 o—

Transcribe the following sentences, showing all the places where assimilation might possibly occur.

1   Brad got Martha and Karl a great big plate of hot cakes, which was a wicked ploy.
2   The angry men chased poor Batman until the outboard motor died.
3   The American plane arrived in Mexico just before the fat pilot collapsed.

Elision

As well as making sounds share features in this way, speakers maintain speed and fluency during connected speech by dropping sounds. Typically these will be sounds which are relatively unimportant for listeners as they work to extract meaning from the speech stream. Listeners' focus is primarily on the stressed content words since these words carry most of the meaning of the utterance. Elision therefore tends mainly to affect function words and unstressed syllables. Elision also occurs during consonant clusters. These are places where two, three or more consonants occur in sequence, regardless of word boundaries. The clusters most susceptible to elision are those whose medial consonant is an alveolar plosive [t] or [d], and it is this consonant that will be dropped from the cluster. The points where elision occurs is marked with * in the sentences below.

(5)   Having crashed Karl's car, Samantha and Terry left Portugal in her old banger.
      havɪŋ 'kɹaʃ* kɑlz 'kɑ sə'manθə ən 'teɹɪ 'lɛf* 'pɔtjʊgəl ɪn əɹ 'əʊl* 'baŋgə

(6)   The stopped clock ground to its final halt during the war.
      ðə 'stɒp* 'klɒk 'gɹaʊn* tʊ ɪts 'faɪnəl 'hɔl* 'djuɹɪŋ ðə 'wɔ

(7)   Separate beds and different houses suggest the process of growing apart is almost complete.
      'sɛpɹəp 'bɛdz ən 'dɪfɹən* 'haʊzɪz sə'dʒɛs* ðə 'pɹəʊses əv 'gɹəʊɪŋ ə'pɑt ɪz 'ɔlməʊs* kəm'plɪt

Activity 8.19 0━━

Transcribe the following sentences paying particular attention to elision. Try to incorporate assimilation and weak forms as well.

1 In past times trucks and cars crawled through packed towns giving scant notice to pollution and fumes.
2 Last night they watched television and sipped cold coffee from chipped cups.
3 Grandma wiped down her old pantry for a second time.

Occasionally elision from a consonant cluster will result in an alveolar stop occurring before a bilabial or velar sound. In these cases, assimilation will take place just as if the consonant cluster had not existed. The phrases below show examples of this.

band manager	ˈbam ˈmanədʒə
grand prize	ˈgɹam ˈpɹaɪz
bent copper	ˈbɛŋ ˈkɒpə

Elision also often occurs when [h] is the first sound of an unstressed syllable. Since [h] begins words such as *he*, *her*, *him*, *his* and *hers* which are often pronounced as weak forms, [h] elision (or **h dropping** as it is often called) is a relatively common phenomenon. Many British English speakers also drop [h] at the beginning of stressed syllables as a feature of their accent, although h dropping does not usually occur in RP.

Linking r and intrusive r

When vowel sounds occur sequentially and in particular contexts a linking [ɹ] sound is inserted between them. The following phrases all contain examples of this.

soar away	ˈsɔɹ əˈweɪ
hearing aid	ˈhɪəɹɪŋ ˈeɪd
bear attack	ˈbɛəɹ əˈtak

Notice that despite the spelling, the words 'soar', 'hear' and 'bear' do not have an [ɹ] sound in their pronunciation ([ˈsɔ], [ˈhɪə], [ˈbɛə]). The <r> is present in the spelling because at one time these words were pronounced with an audible [ɹ] and the spelling reflected this. The context in which linking r occurs is between two vowels when the first vowel is either [ɑ], [ɜ], [ɔ] or [ə] and there is an <r> in the word's spelling.

Similar to linking r is intrusive r. This works in the same contexts but occurs when there is no <r> in the spelling. Thus in the following phrases [ɹ] is regarded as intrusive.

sawing logs   'sɔɹɪŋ 'lɒgz
Maria in my class   mə'ɹɪəɹ ɪm maɪ 'klɑs
paw at the door   'pɔɹ ət ðə 'dɔ

 ## Activity 8.20 ⚊

Transcribe the following passage taking into account weak forms, assimilation, elision, linking and intrusive r.

The real problem with living in a new town is boredom. You have to start all over again, learning the names of streets and places. You probably can't locate simple things like supermarkets, postboxes, banks and cashpoints. It is therefore extremely likely that you will begin to associate leaving the house with large amounts of effort and stress as you struggle to navigate your way round a mad maze of one way systems, no through roads, by-passes and interchanges, trying to remember which way you came so you can find the route back again. All this leads to a desire to stay home. Outside is unfriendly. Outside is difficult. Outside you fear for your wing mirrors. It's hard to believe that the pleasure of going to the cinema or a pub could outweigh the stress of getting there.

SUMMARY

This unit has shown how the architecture of the vocal tract determines the sounds that occur in human language. The individual phonemes of English have been classified according to the articulation of each sound. The links between pronunciation and the writing system of English have been considered as have the ways in which a sound can affect the pronunciation of a neighbouring one in connected speech. Phonetic transcription of isolated words and of connected speech has been demonstrated using the IPA system.

FURTHER READING

For students wishing to take their studies of phonetics further the following two books are recommended: *Introducing Phonetics and Phonology* (Davenport and Hannahs 1998) and *A Course in Phonetics* (Ladefoged 2001). Davenport and Hannahs' (1998) text is perhaps simpler and also includes an introduction to phonology. Ladefoged's (2001) book is an excellent and comprehensive text on the subject of phonetics and will be useful to the student who intends to undertake more advanced study of the subject. *Phonetics: The Science of Speech* (Ball and Rahilly 1999) provides a clear account of the articulation of speech. *A Practical Introduction to Phonetics* (Catford 1988) gives useful practical exercises to help with both production and recognition of speech sounds.

For students wishing to study English phonology the classic volume on the subject is Cruttenden (2001) *Gimson's Pronunciation of English*. *English Phonetics and Phonology* (Roach 2000) is perhaps a gentler introduction.

For students interested in the study of phonetics in relation to regional and social variation, *English Accents and Dialects* (Hughes and Trudgill 1996) and *Urban Voices* (Foulkes and Docherty 1999) are both clear and accessible. A sound working knowledge of phonetics is necessary if the subject matter is to be exploited to its full extent.

FURTHER ACTIVITY

 Activity 8.21

Transcribe the following passage taking into account weak forms, assimilation, elision, linking and intrusive r.

Kit stood moodily at the water's edge. Wellington was a little further back in the shade of the pines. The sun was getting low now; the day had baked them without mercy but now the heat relented. Little furrows ruffled the surface of the water and mosquitoes rose in busy clouds wherever a possibility of snacking attracted them. Kit brushed off a dozen or so of the parasites and headed into the lake, clearing her nose and pulling her mask on without so much as a backward glance at Wellington. He watched her neoprene backside lift briefly out of the water and the bright green flippers make a tidy little splash and then she was gone. Wellington pushed his toe into the shingle. The surface of his suit was beginning to dry and he felt it tighten around him. Nothing but him and the beach now. Kit might believe she had no flaw or fault but then Kit seemed incapable of believing anything else. Wellington made up his mind. In an instant the shame of failure had evaporated and he was ratcheting tight his flippers, moving quickly towards the water.

Activity 8.22

Take any other chunk of text from this book and transcribe it, noting as many phonetic features which have been discussed in this unit as possible.

COMMENTARY ON ACTIVITIES

Activity 8.1

Examples for each letter are given below:

<i>   pick; fight; Lima; first

<u>   puddle; cushion; student (speakers of northern English varieties may pronounce *puddle* with the same vowel as in *cushion*)

<e>   bed; dancer; me; perm; few; related

(<e> can also 'disappear' when words are read aloud, as in *prance* and the second <e> in *general*).

The irregularity in English spelling is in part a result of the invention of the printing press in the fifteenth century pre-dating one of the biggest sound changes in the English language: the Great Vowel Shift. Once printing took off, spelling became more conventionalized, meaning that any changes in pronunciation could not be incorporated into the written form of the language. This, together with the influence of other languages on English, makes the English writing system inconsistent and difficult to learn for both children and non-native speakers. On the other hand, English orthography offers fascinating clues as to the history of English pronunciation (➔ Unit 13). Inefficient as it seems, the English have so far resisted pressures to make their writing system more reflective of real pronunciation, unlike the Dutch who update their writing system regularly.

Activity 8.2

The [s] sound at the beginning of the word *speak* can also be represented in orthography by <c> in <cymbal>, <ps> in <psychology>, <ss> in <moss>.

The [n] sound at the beginning of the word *noose* can also be represented in orthography by <kn> in <knee>, <gn> in <gnome>, <pn> in <pneumonia>, <mn> in <mnemonic>, <nn> in <sunny>.

Activity 8.3

O'Brien is using eye dialect, a technique sometimes used by authors to convey to their audience that the characters are using non-standard pronunciations. Often the effect is humorous, as with the extract shown here, but eye dialect can be difficult to read and is limited in what it can convey effectively because it is difficult to accurately capture pronunciation with orthographic symbols. Only phonetic transcription can perform this task, hence its importance for so many people.

Activity 8.7

The sounds underlined in the following words are all made with tongue tip (or apical) articulatory movements of the tongue:

chew	booze	shaft	tissue	throw	doodle
nifty	sugar	cistern	junction	traitor	gaiter
loiter	mission	bubble	juice	tuna	lisp

In addition, the tongue sides are lifted for the sounds in the following words:

chew	booze	shaft	tissue	sugar	cistern
junction	mission	juice	tuna (for some speakers)		

The tongue sides are down for the sounds in the following words:

loiter   lisp

The sounds underlined in the following words are all made with dorsal (tongue body) articulations against the hard palate:

yesterday   youth

The sounds underlined in the following words are all made with dorsal (tongue body) articulations against the soft palate:

frock   google   microphone   bucket   aqua   haggle

In addition to reflecting on the tongue's role in the sounds in the above words, don't forget that letters and sounds do not necessarily map onto one another in a straight forward way. The middle sound in *mission* and the first sound in *shaft* are the same but are represented differently by the orthography.

Activity 8.8

The initial sounds in *bumble* and *pixie* are made with both lips and hence are known as *bilabial* plosives.

The initial sounds in *delicate* and *tuxedo* are made with the tongue tip articulating against the alveolar ridge and hence are known as the *alveolar* plosives.

The initial sounds in *galley* and *cavern* are made with the back of the tongue articulating against the soft palate or velum and hence are known as the *velar* plosives.

The first member of each pair is voiced and the second member voiceless. Languages often organize speech sounds into voiced/voiceless pairs in this way. This type of systematicity is the subject matter of **phonology**.

Activity 8.9

The initial sounds in *Viking* and *faint* are articulated with the upper teeth and the lower lip and hence are called *labiodental* fricatives.

The initial sounds in *those* and *thorn* are articulated with the tongue blade and the upper teeth and hence are called *dental* fricatives.

The initial sounds in *zone* and *sash* are articulated with the tongue tip or blade against the alveolar ridge and hence are known as *alveolar* fricatives.

The middle sound in *treasure* and the initial sound in *shifty* are made with the blade of the tongue against the area between the alveolar ridge and the hard palate and hence are known as *postalveolar* fricatives.

Just as the plosive sounds in Activity 8.8 are arranged in voiced/voiceless pairs, so the fricatives here are arranged so that for each place of articulation (for example, labiodental) there is a voiced and voiceless sound.

Activity 8.10

For most speakers:

- the initial sounds in *house* and *heart* are produced with a relaxed lip position and a fairly open jaw
- the initial sound in *hoof* is produced with a fairly closely rounded, almost pouting lip position
- the initial sound in *heat* is produced with spread lips and fairly closed jaw position
- the initial sound in *hug* is produced with a relaxed lip position and a moderately open jaw
- the initial sound in *horse* is produced with rounded lips, although their position is not as extreme as it is for *hoof*.

Activity 8.11

β is a voiced bilabial fricative

g is a voiced velar plosive

ŋ is a voiced velar nasal

h is a voiceless glottal fricative

m is a voiced bilabial nasal

ð is a voiced dental fricative

ç is a voiceless palatal fricative

χ is a voiceless uvular fricative

ɾ is an alveolar tap

f is a voiceless labiodental fricative

z is a voiced alveolar fricative

ʒ is a voiced postalveolar fricative

Activity 8.12
This transcription represents the pronunciation in RP. Your accent may be different.

1 bɒksə	5 tʃip	9 gɹɑnt	13 θif	17 kɑːt	21 wɪmɪn
2 ʃɒn	6 nat	10 sis	14 ɛksɪt	18 plastɪk	22 θɜst
3 lut	7 kɔt	11 dʒɪg	15 tɹɪf	19 vju	23 dum
4 bʊk	8 tʃɜtʃ	12 dɛf	16 ʃɔl	20 ʃɒpɪŋ	24 gɹʌndʒ

Activity 8.13
This transcription represents the pronunciation in RP. Your accent may be different.

1 ɛksplɔɪt OR ɪksplɔɪt	5 vaɪkɪŋ	9 veɪg	13 pjʊəɹɪst	17 hɛə	21 maɪti
2 dɪnəʊt	6 pleɪt	10 ɹəʊl	14 tɪə	18 spaɪs	22 gɹaʊnd
3 mɛə	7 nəʊ	11 ɹaʊdi	15 ɛkspaɪə or ɪkspaɪə	19 ɛəɹɪə	23 taʊə
4 mʊə	8 ɹɪtaɪə	12 bɛə	16 speɪs	20 lɔɪtə	24 vaɪəlɪn

Activity 8.15

'cinema	cine'matic	dis'cover	dis'covery	'realize	realiz'ation
'telephone	tel'ephonist	va'riety	vari'ation	'mountain	'mountainous
ig'nore	'ignorance	'extra	ex'traneous	'neutral	neu'trality
'fantasy	fan'tastic	ma'chine	machin'ation	'vital	vi'tality

Activity 8.16
If you read the sentences out loud, they are likely to have sounded something like this. The stressed syllables are nearly all on syllables in content words.

1   'Sue could not de'cide why she 'felt 'left 'out until she 'noticed 'everyone ex'cept her was 'wearing a 'hat.

2   When 'Stuart 'heard about the 'cat's 'missing 'tail he 'judged it 'wiser to say 'nothing.

3   'Kitty's 'pride in 'finding the 'bus 'soon disa'ppeared when she 'realized the 'driver had no in'tention of 'stopping to 'let her 'get 'off in 'Dogfield.

Activity 8.17
Some possible stress patterns for the sentences are shown together with their likely interpretation.

1a   I 'really 'like that 'dress but it 'may be a 'little 'bit 'too re'vealing for your 'grandmother's 'birthday.

Stress on the modal *may* as well as on *little bit too revealing* suggests the speaker is trying to qualify the critical tone of the utterance.

1b   'I 'really 'like that 'dress but it may be a 'little 'bit too re'vealing for your 'grandmother's 'birthday.

Stress on *I* suggests that the speaker is emphasizing their own opinion of the dress, possibly in contrast to the opinion of someone else.

1c I ˈreally ˈlike that ˈdress but it may be a ˈlittle ˈbit too reˈvealing for ˈyour ˈgrandmotherˈs ˈbirthday.

Stress on *your* suggests that the problem about wearing the dress may be related to the fact that it is the birthday of the listener's grandmother; a different grandmother may react more positively to the dress.

2a As ˈsoon as they ˈfound themselves in Toˈronto, ˈJo and ˈAlex ˈchecked under their ˈseats and imˈmediately ˈfound ˈtheir ˈpassports.

Stress on the second *their* suggests that the passports were those of Jo and Alex rather than of anybody else.

2b As ˈsoon as they ˈfound themselves in Toˈronto, ˈJo and ˈAlex ˈchecked ˈunder their ˈseats and imˈmediately ˈfound their ˈpassports.

Stress on *under* suggests that perhaps earlier Jo and Alex had checked on top of or even inside their seats and had not found their passports.

3a ˈKate became conˈfused although not upˈset after ˈshe had ˈspoken to the ˈman.

Stress on *she* suggests that previously someone other than Kate had spoken to the man.

3b ˈKate became conˈfused although not upˈset after she ˈhad ˈspoken to the ˈman.

Stress on *had* suggests a contrast with an earlier situation in which Kate had not spoken to the man.

Activity 8.18

1 ˈbɹag ˈgɒp ˈmaθə ən ˈkal ə ˈgɹeɪp ˈbɪb ˈpleɪt əv ˈhɒk ˈkeɪks wɪtʃ wəz ə ˈwɪkɪb ˈplɔɪ

2 ðɪ ˈaŋgɹi ˈmen ˈtʃeɪs ˈpɔ ˈbapman ʌntɪl ðɪ ˈaʊpbɒb ˈməʊtə ˈdaɪd

3 ðɪ əˈmeɹɪkəm ˈpleɪn əˈɹaɪvd ɪm ˈmɛksɪkəʊ dʒəs bɪfɔ ðə ˈʃap ˈpaɪlək kəˈlapst

Activity 8.19

1 ɪm ˈpɑs* ˈtaɪmz ˈtɹʌks əŋ ˈkɑz ˈkɹɔl* θɹu ˈpak* ˈtaʊnz ˈgɪvɪŋ ˈskan* ˈnəʊtɪs tə pəˈluʃən ən ˈfjumz

2 ˈlas* ˈnaɪt ðeɪ ˈwɒtʃ* tɛlɪˈvɪʒən ən ˈsɪp* ˈkəʊl* ˈkɒfi fɹəm ˈtʃɪp* ˈkʌps

3 ˈgɹamɑ ˈwaɪp* daʊn əɹ ˈəʊl* ˈpantɹɪ fəɹ ə ˈsɛkən* ˈtaɪm

Activity 8.20

ðə ˈɹɪəl ˈpɹɒbləm wɪð ˈlɪvɪŋ ɪn ə ˈnju ˈtaʊn ɪz ˈbɔdəm ‖ ju haf tə ˈstat ɔl ˈəʊvəɹ əˈgen ‖ ˈlɜnɪŋ ðə ˈneɪmz əv ˈstɹits əm ˈpleɪsɪz ‖ ju ˈpɹɒbəbli kan ləʊˈkeɪt ˈsɪmpl̩ ˈθɪŋz laɪk ˈsupəmakɪts ˈpəʊsbɒksɪz ˈbaŋks əŋ ˈkaʃpɔɪnts ‖ ɪt ɪz ðɛəfɔɹ ɪkˈstɹimli ˈlaɪkli ðət ju wɪl bɪˈgɪn tu əˈsəʊʃɪeɪt ˈlɪvɪŋ ðə ˈhaʊs wɪð ˈladʒ əˈmaʊns əv ˈɛfət ən ˈstɹɛs əz ju ˈstɹʌgl̩ tə ˈnavɪgeɪt jə ˈweɪ əˈɹaʊnd ə ˈmab ˈmeɪz əv ˈwʌn ˈweɪ ˈsɪstəmz ˈnəʊ ˈθɹu ˈɹəʊdz ‖ ˈbaɪ ˈpasɪz ənd ˈɪntətʃeɪndʒɪz ‖ ˈtɹaɪɪŋ tə ɹɪˈmɛmbə wɪtʃ ˈweɪ ju ˈkeɪm səʊ ju kən ˈfaɪn ðə ˈɹup ˈbak əˈgen ‖ ˈɔl ðɪs ˈlidz tu ə dɪˈzaɪə tə ˈsteɪ ˈhəʊm ‖ aʊtˈsaɪd ɪz ʌnˈfɹɛnli ‖ aʊtˈsaɪd ɪz ˈdɪfɪkəlt ‖ aʊtˈsaɪd ju ˈfɪə fə jə ˈwɪŋ ˈmɪɹəz ‖ ɪts ˈhad tə bɪˈlɪv ðət ðə ˈplɛʒə əv ˈgəʊɪn tə ðə ˈsɪnəmə ɔ ˈpʌb kəd aʊtˈweɪ ðə ˈstɹɛs əv ˈgɛtɪŋ ðɛə

REFERENCES

Ball, M.J. and Rahilly, J. (1999) *Phonetics: The Science of Speech*, London: Arnold.

Catford, J.C. (1988) *A Practical Introduction to Phonetics*, Oxford: Oxford University Press.

Cruttenden, A. (2001) *Gimson's Pronunciation of English*, 6th edn, London: Arnold.

Davenport, M. and Hannahs, S.J. (1998) *Introducing Phonetics and Phonology*, London: Arnold.

Foulkes, P. and Docherty, G. (eds) (1999) *Urban Voices: Accent Studies in the British Isles*, London: Arnold.

Hughes, A. and Trudgill, P. (1996) *English Accents and Dialects: An Introduction to Social and Regional Varieties of English in the British Isles*, 3rd edn, London: Arnold.

Ladefoged, P. (2001) *A Course in Phonetics*, 4th edn, Orlando, FL: Harcourt.

O'Brien, F. (1988) *The Poor Mouth*, London: Paladin.

Roach, P. (2000) *English Phonetics and Phonology: A Practical Course*, 3rd edn, Cambridge: Cambridge University Press.

9 VARIETY IN LANGUAGE

UNIT CONTENTS

- Introduction
- Key terms
- Dialect, accent, standard and language: a blurring of the edges!
- Links with branches of linguistics
- What factors cause language to vary?
- Variety – vive la différence!
- Prescriptive/descriptive approaches
- Putting all this into practice
- Summary
- Further reading
- Further activity
- Commentary on activities
- References
- Notes

INTRODUCTION

Do you speak the same way that you write? Would you write a love letter the same way as a note to the milkman? Do you use language the same way as your grandparents, or even as your parents? Do you address your teachers the same way as you do your friends? Do you use language now the same way that you did when you were three years old? We could keep asking this sort of question for pages. We might wager you answered 'No' to them all and we would also hope that some of you may even have thought 'Of course not – don't be so stupid!!'. Why? Because appropriately different ways of using language are absolutely everywhere – and that is what this unit is about: *variety in language*.

Material from all of the other units has the potential of being reasonably incorporated into a discussion of the concept of **variety** in language. In the next few pages it will not be possible to cover anything like all that material and so our ultimate aim is much more modest. The purpose of this unit is to show that language in use is (in)credibly diverse. As indicated by the brackets, this involves two aspects: (a) we will uncover just the very tip of the language variety iceberg to give some idea of how incredible the vast possibilities are and (b) at the same time, we will address how and why there is such diversity with the intention of making the incredible credible.

 ## Activity 9.1

It is probably unlikely that you would talk to an eight-year-old, eighteen-year-old or eighty-year-old in exactly the same way. This is but one example of how language is used in different ways. For this activity, list as many different ways as you can in one minute. If possible, compare your list with someone else.

There is no commentary at the end of the unit as the whole of this unit is effectively the commentary to this activity.

While Activity 9.1 should have been relatively simple enough to do, it could actually have taken you rather longer than a minute because (as you may have realized) almost anything can affect how language is used.

What the unit can do for you and what it can't

Having attempted Activity 9.1, you should have begun to realize that language in use is certainly dynamic and that in any living language, variety (difference) is everywhere – both linguistically as well as socially. The role of this unit is primarily to provide an introduction to some of the terms and concepts relevant to the study of regional and social varieties of language. While it includes examples from selected language varieties, this unit isn't designed to be a **descriptive** guide to any specific language variety in particular and, as a colleague used to say, I'm afraid it can't do your ironing, either!

An initial illustration

We can't encounter language without instantly being confronted with variety of some sort. A walk down the high street in Sheffield, UK (the setting for the film *The Full Monty*) revealed the wealth of greeting types between people from the same community, in theory sharing the same native language shown in Data Extract 9.1.

Data Extract 9.1

Nah den
Ah reet
Hi
Hiya
Morning
Mornin'
'ello luv
Geoff! (accompanied by a hand wave)

So why is there so much variety in the ways these few people chose to express themselves? Well, at the most microscopic level, every speaker's language use is unique in often subtle but complex ways. In other words, every person has their own idiolect. Yet every speaker shares some characteristics of the way they use language with other speakers – at a personal, local, regional, national and even global level. The variation we see in the way people use language generally falls into some more or less ordered and sophisticated pattern – how else would we be able to understand speakers of the same language but from different regions, walks of life, age groups, and so on? And how would we be able to tell that they belong to these various categories? Activity 9.2 illustrates that we do indeed have (though admittedly to varying extents) an ability to make judgements about people based on the type of language that they use.

Activity 9.2 0—┳

Try making some predictions about each of the speakers in the data from Data Extract 9.1. For example, what might you guess to be their age, gender, geographical origin and social status?

How accurately you feel you can make these types of social judgements will clearly depend upon your knowledge of the communities that the speakers belong to. For example non-UK residents might have found Activity 9.2 harder than speakers from London, who in turn might have found it harder than speakers from the north of England, who in turn might have found it harder than speakers from Sheffield. In short, the more familiar we are with a particular variety of language use, the more likely we are to be able to recognize and identify it accurately. Just in case you think Activity 9.2 was simply a contrived exercise and you really don't believe that people pay that much attention to such matters, consider internet chatrooms where quite often one of the very first questions asked is 'age/sex/location?'. If social attributes didn't matter to people, surely they wouldn't bother asking such questions.

But why is it useful to be able to categorize people in this way? Using Data Extract 9.1 as an example, considering who produced which greeting (old or young, male or female, approximate social status, geographical origin, etc.) could give linguists information (very impressionistic in this case) to feed into data banks about which people are likely to speak in which ways. This information could then, in future, help linguists suggest likely attributes of other speakers from samples of their language. Knowledge like this can also have applications beyond the purely academic; for example, it is the kind of information that forensic linguists focus on in helping the police to solve crimes, it affects how well novelists manage to write convincing regional dialogue and it is also how advertisers can attempt to target their advertisements to particular markets.

Initial impressions

Before we start on some key definitions, stop to consider your views on the questions in Activity 9.3.

 Activity 9.3 o—┰

Note down your responses to the following questions:
1   Why are there so many varieties of language?
2   How do varieties come about?
3   Why do they persist?
4   Is variety in language declining in an age of mass media and social mobility?
5   Why are varieties unequally valued?
6   Are new varieties coming into existence now and if so can you identify any?
7   How can knowledge of varieties be useful in 'real life'?

To help you to develop your answers to these questions, this unit will now provide an insight into the concepts, scope and importance of social and regional language variation. Even at an introductory level, there are many facets to this very broad field so the approach here is to focus on some of the key terms and ideas with brief examples which it is hoped will spark ideas for work on your own varieties data.

KEY TERMS

Variety

In linguistics the term *variety* is commonly used simply to refer to any way of using language which is somehow systematically different from other ways. That, however, just shifts the issue to the problem of defining language.

Language

It might feel like 'language' is a completely unproblematical concept. That is not actually the case (➻ Unit 1). Nevertheless, although it is something of a simplification, for current purposes we will assume that **language** refers to 'the [abstract] systems assumed to be inherent in the linguistic behaviour of a community and in their literature' (Le Page and Tabouret-Keller 1985: 190ff.). Of course, by this definition, Language X becomes the system underlying the linguistic behaviour of Community X and that just shifts the problem from defining language to the equally problematic task of defining community and although many people speak 'English' in England, the Channel Islands, Australia, the USA, the Caribbean, South Africa and so on (➤ Unit 14), it often makes little sense to say that inhabitants of these countries belong to the same community. For example, while English is spoken in both York (in the north of England) and Jersey (in the Channel Islands) and while both locations are governed by the British monarch, people from Jersey probably have much more in common with their Norman French heritage (and it certainly makes much less sense to say that the inhabitants of York and Jersey belong to the same community as folks from New York and New Jersey).

Standard language

As we have seen (and shall continue to see), even speakers of the same language persist in using both spoken and written language in systematically different ways. However, some people argue that all speakers of a language should strive to use just one form of that language in a set way. That form of the language will often be held to be the **standard** – a subset of whatever it is that is covered by the term 'language'. It tends to be the type of language which is used in academic, government and religious settings, and which is often associated with written and published material. Because of its use in these rather important-seeming contexts, and in written material, a standard often carries prestige. It is easy to see how this can give rise to situations where the standard starts to be seen as 'the' language, and differing ways of speaking or writing – often ones linked to particular locales or less powerful social groups – are somehow deemed 'deviant' or 'substandard' and these negative associations can quickly carry over into judgements on non-linguistic characteristics of speakers. A slightly more neutral alternative to the loaded term substandard (below standard) is 'non-standard'.

Code

To get around some of the difficulties associated with the term 'language', linguists often prefer to use the term **code** (➤ Units 1 and 3) to mean a set of arbitrary conventions for converting one system of signals into another – just as in Morse code where ··· − − − ··· represents <SOS>, or when at the end of a date 'Would you like to come in for coffee?' often signals an invitation to pleasures beyond those offered by a caffeinated beverage!

Accent

One way in which speakers can differ in the way they use language is in their pronunciation or **accent**. This includes the choice of sounds used as segments (**phonemes** ➤➤ Unit 8) in particular words as well as prosodic **suprasegmentals** such as **stress** and **intonation**. Often a spoken standard will be associated with a particular accent. In England it is often referred to as **Received Pronunciation** (abbreviated as **RP** and sometimes also referred to as the Queen's English or BBC English – though it should be noted that these two types of pronunciation have changed over the decades: BBC presenters no longer talk in the clipped tones of the early television broadcasts from Alexandra Palace in the 1930s and even the Queen has shifted her accent over the years of her reign). In the USA, the standard accent used in much media broadcasting is called *General American*.

Orthographic representations of different pronunciations appeared in Activity 9.2. The back rounded vowel [ʊ] is used in many northern accents in Britain where RP would use the vowel [ʌ] (➤➤ Unit 8). So, for example, in such accents there is no **phonetic** distinction between the words *put* and *putt*, both being pronounced [pʊt], whereas in RP the pronunciations would be [pʊt] and [pʌt] respectively. Other very common pronunciation variations would include the following:

- [ɑ]/[a] for the vowel in words such as *grass*, *glass*, *bath*
- [ɪŋ]/[ɪn]/[ɪŋg] in the final consonant of words ending in the morpheme {*-ing*}
- [h]/ø – i.e. [h] or nothing at all – in syllable-initial positions in words such as *hungry horses hate horrible hay*
- [ɹ]/ø in English words with an <r> after a vowel (known as post-vocalic r) as in *fourth* and *floor* (cf. Labov 1972b)
- [ð]/[v]/[d] in words such as *this*, *that*, *these*, *mother*, *father* and *brother*
- [θ]/[f]/[t] in words such as *think*, *thing* and *three*
- [ju:]/[u:] in words such as *new* and *tune*
- and many more.

While the above are examples of variety in segments (**vowels** or **consonants**), accent can also include suprasegmental variation (though this is less diverse). Perhaps the most recognizable intonational feature in an accent is the occurrence of high-rising terminals (HRTs) associated with Australian English. Put simply, a high-rising terminal means that there is a noticeably high rise in pitch at the end (terminal) of an utterance. Such an intonation is typical of **interrogative** syntax (questions) in many English accents, but in Australian, these HRTs also occur on **declarative** sentences (statements). This is why Australians (and others who have taken up this way of talking) can sound (at least to non-HRT speakers) like they are either always asking questions or are in constant need of confirmation from their

interlocutors. This phenomenon is sometimes also known as *Australian Question Intonation* (or AQI).

Another form of suprasegmental variation involves the placement of the main (or primary) stress (➦ Unit 8). In English, the placement of primary stress (marked by a < ' > before the stressed syllable) habitually moves when differentiating between nouns and verbs:

Verb	Noun
'irrigate	irri'gation
'promulgate	promul'gation
e'lucidate	eluci'dation

Of course, here, there is additional morphological (and hence phonetic) material to distinguish the two forms over and above the stress placement. However, in a few cases, stress bears the majority of the responsibility for marking the distinction:

Verb	Noun
con'tract	'contract
dis'pute	'dispute
ex'port	'export
ex'tract	'extract
im'port	'import

Now these examples of variable stress location affect the meaning of the words so in terms of just accent, they are not very interesting (yet interesting enough to note in passing). However some accents seem to employ different stress patterns on words with the *same* semantic meanings. The following lists show how stress is employed differently by two speakers – one from Cambridgeshire, in the south of England, the other from West Yorkshire, in the north of England:[1]

Southerner	Northerner
ad'vertisement	adver'tisement
dis'tributed	'distributed
'caravan	cara'van
'tinfoil	tin'foil
'chocolate cake	'chocolate 'cake
pork 'pie	'pork 'pie

Another particularly fine source of alternative stress patterns from those used in RP can be found in speakers from the West Indies – for example West Indian: Ca'ribbean *versus* RP: Cari'bbean.

Activity 9.4 o––r

1   Think about the sorts of accent variations we have just encountered. Can you ascribe any of the variants listed to any particular groups (geographical or social)?
2   If you are familiar with, or even speak any other notable accent, think about the ways it differs phonetically from whatever you consider to be the standard form of your language. (Hint: you are likely to find most variation in the use of vowels.)

As a final point in this section, it should be noted that 'accent' is concerned with the phonetics of an utterance – the way it sounds. It is therefore impossible not to speak with an accent of some kind – even when speaking a standard language: when a spoken standard is associated with a particular accent it is still an accent – RP and General American are both accents of English. Once differences extend beyond phonetics, however, we have to use a different term: *dialect*.

Dialect

Dialect is the term used when a variety of language is distinct in matters of **morphology**, **lexis**, **semantics** or **syntax** (➻ Units 5, 6 and 7). It is often assumed that a dialect must be different from the standard. Technically, this is not so: any standard is but a particular (admittedly privileged) dialect of the language concerned. The most common dialectal differences involve the existence of entirely different words. Because dialects are usually associated with *regional* types of language they also tend to involve a non-standard accent. Activity 9.5 deals with some examples of English dialect words.

Activity 9.5 ⚲⊸

1 Do you recognize any of the following dialect words?
2 Do you use any of them? If so, when?
3 What do they mean?
4 Where (for example, geographically) might they be used?

Note
- In this activity we are assuming British English to be the standard.
- Some words might have other meanings in Standard English.
- For some of these words (such as *ute*) the spelling is indicative only.

01	agait	14	dunny	27	lark	40	spogs
02	baguette	15	eagle	28	like	41	strides
03	banner	16	feast	29	manchester	42	titfer
04	bar	17	gannin	30	muggle	43	togs
05	bizzies	18	gate	31	netty	44	trews
06	bog	19	goodies	32	pants	45	trunks
07	charlie	20	greeting	33	pigs	46	tucker
08	chow	21	grub	34	pukka	47	twat
09	crack	22	huggy	35	rozzers	48	ute
10	docky	23	illocution	36	scran	49	while
11	dods	24	john	37	snap	50	yankee
12	driv	25	keks	38	sneeped		
13	dumpy	26	lake	39	spice		

A commentary is provided for questions 3 and 4 at the end of the unit.

DIALECT, ACCENT, STANDARD AND LANGUAGE: A BLURRING OF THE EDGES!

Activity 9.5 reveals several issues that, sadly, are far too complex to do any real justice to here, but yet important enough to at least raise. For example, was that list really a list of non-standard dialect terms or simply a list of more or less universally recognized colloquial words? Might some words, in fact, be standard English words but just so unusual or obscure that they *seem* to be dialect terms? Are some words, in fact, simply pronunciation variants on other words, in which case it is a matter not of dialect but rather of accent? And at what stage does one word change so much that speakers say that it has mutated into a different word, in which case it is a question of dialect? Data Extract 9.2 provides an example which illustrates this problem:

Data Extract 9.2

```
01   Andrew:  Do you want a coffee Sally?

02   Sally:   What sort are you making?

03   Andrew:  I'm making real coffee.

04   Sally:   Oh: (.) no thanks. (2.0)

05            Oh alright then I'll have a rail coffee

06   Andrew:  No you won't (.) that's what you get on trains!

07   Sally:   Huh?

08   Andrew:  Rail coffee.

09   Sally:   Ha ha!

10   Andrew:  I'm going to use that in my unit on language varieties.

11   Sally:   Piss off!
```

Admittedly, Andrew was making a linguistic joke on Sally's West Yorkshire pronunciation of *real* in L05, which sounds like (and hence is transcribed as) *rail*. Nevertheless, the fact that she didn't understand the (albeit poor) pun (cf. L07) and her condescension in L09 indicate that for her the issue was a matter of accent while for him it was a matter of dialect. Sally's angered retort in L11 is also worth mentioning in that it illustrates how use of language can be a personal and therefore potentially sensitive issue.

Jargon

Another point to be drawn from Activity 9.5 is the fact that dialect words do not necessarily have to be regional in origin. The (alternative) meanings for *baguette*, *eagle*, *illocution*, *muggle* and *yankee* are examples. They all 'belong' to Standard English (*muggle* will surely eventually make it into the dictionary) but the meanings used here all have a very restricted sense. They are words which clearly pertain to particular groups (architects, golfers, linguists, Harry Potter fans and gamblers) – in other words they count as jargon or **technical words** (⇒ Unit 5).

Register

It can also be possible to recognize certain *social* (i.e. non-regional) varieties of language use even in cases where specialized terminology is not employed. The technical term used for such a variety is **register**. Register is sometimes further sub-divided into **field of discourse** (subject matter, e.g. chemistry/linguistics/music),

tenor of discourse (sometimes referred to as *style*, e.g. formal/informal) and **mode of discourse** (medium of the language activity, e.g. written/spoken).

So far this unit has mainly been concerned with variation in phonetics and lexis (both in terms of morphology and semantics), but regular variation in the syntax and the structure (including layout) of the discourse can also be found in registers. Activity 9.8 at the end of the unit provides several examples of various registers.

LINKS WITH BRANCHES OF LINGUISTICS

Any consideration of regional varieties (based on geographical locality) and social varieties (based on other criteria such as age, gender, class, profession, mode of discourse and so on) requires some reflection on ideas and approaches from several linked disciplines within linguistics. The study of dialects became popular in the nineteenth century, though many involved were self-trained enthusiasts rather than academics. The study of dialect gained academic respectability in the twentieth century and major surveys of regional variation were undertaken in England (for example, the Survey of English Dialects – see Orton 1962), the United States and Canada, and elsewhere. In this traditional dialectology, the focus was largely on very specific types of informant who were anticipated to speak strong and old fashioned forms of local varieties (the so-called *NORMs*: non-mobile, older, rural males), and the approach was geared at producing dialect maps (not dissimilar in type to (but very different in detail from) those to be found in Figures 13.3 and 13.4) and showing links with older forms of language (hence its alternative name of *dialect geography*).

In the 1960s, several new approaches gained huge popularity. Largely following the lead of William Labov (1963 in Martha's Vineyard, USA; 1966 and 1972 in New York City, USA – see Labov 1972b for a summary) and later Peter Trudgill (1972; 1974 in Norwich, UK), the field of urban dialectology broadened the focus and aims of dialect work. Urban dialectologists are interested in the varieties of language spoken in particular locales (specifically towns, thought by traditional dialectologists to be unsuitable for their purposes). They are also interested in why there is variation even within those locales in terms of 'who speaks what way'. Furthermore, why do some people change the way they speak from one situation to the next? How and why do new varieties develop and change over time and what is their relationship to the standard language of that area? In order to answer these questions, and more, urban dialectologists developed new methodologies including new indirect oral interview techniques and ways of classifying informants according to social background. Their approaches also require a more inclusive cross-section of informants, incorporating women, who had tended to be very poorly represented in traditional dialectology work. (For a fuller background on the development of traditional and urban dialectology, see Chambers and Trudgill 1980; for a selection of recent detailed studies of urban dialects, see Foulkes and Docherty 1999; for a critique on gender representation, see Coates 1993: Chapter 3.)

From this base, the broader field of **sociolinguistics** has developed. Though originally more or less synonymous with urban dialectology, sociolinguistics has grown into a multi-faceted beast, linking many now virtually autonomous branches of linguistics, including (in addition to dialectologists) those studying language and gender, language and power (➻ Unit 4) and discourse and conversation (➻ Unit 2). While sociolinguistics studies the relationship between language and society, the balance between these two foci in researchers' approaches can vary. Some are most interested in what language can tell them about society and this approach is usually heavily linked to the social sciences. Others focus on what society can tell them about language, and this is more allied to a firmly linguistic approach.

WHAT FACTORS CAUSE LANGUAGE TO VARY?

There are many factors which can cause language to vary. One way of classifying factors which can cause language variation is to divide them into two broad groupings: the first comprises characteristics of the language users themselves, (which can be called *user factors*); the second is made up of features of the situation in which language is used and what it is being used for (*situational factors*).

User factors: WHO?

The WHO factors focus on the characteristics of the individuals involved – they include aspects such as the users' age, gender, profession, class, level of education, nation/region of origin, ethnicity, religion, disability, personality. These things matter for *all* the individuals involved – we cannot simplify it to just speaker (or writer) issues. For example, consider a white, Anglo-Saxon, protestant, middle-class, university-educated male, in his late thirties. Let's say he's an enthusiastic, friendly linguistics lecturer from the county of Cambridgeshire in England. Now here's the point: although we have accounted for many of his personal attributes (and so we can probably predict some of the ways in which he might use language differently from, say, a twenty-something, lower-class, uneducated, violent gangster rapper from New Jersey), unless we take into account who else is involved in the interaction, we will have only part of the story. For example, it is almost certain that he would use language differently when addressing one of his PhD students compared to how he would interact with his 18-month-old son. Indeed, the age difference needn't be so extreme – he would probably even speak differently, in some respects, to first year students compared to second years! So hearer (or reader) characteristics can matter just as much as those of speaker (or writer). Indeed it is also possible that language can be affected by a non-addressed (and even non-present) third party (see Bell 1997; Clark and Schaefer 1987; Schober and Clark 1989).

Over 40 years of sociolinguistic research has suggested that various user factors can help generate distinctive patterns in the way language is used. For example, in many cultures women have been found to be more cooperative and mutually supportive language users than their male counterparts. Nonetheless, there are differences in the way, and the extent to which, this is realized cross-culturally – comparing Japanese women and North American women, for example. And of course, there is variety amongst both American women and Japanese women!

What is important to stress is that simply being a woman, a child, someone from Singapore, someone from a lower socio-economic background and so on does not guarantee that a person will use language in a particular way. Each person represents a unique cocktail of influences and this is reflected in their personally-distinctive language use, or idiolect, as outlined above.

Some of the longer-established potential causes of language variation are not without controversy or difficulty. For example, how should social background be determined? The early work of Labov and Trudgill (mentioned above) established classifications largely based on status, occupation and income and they were quite closely tied to the social situations at the time of study in their respective nations (the USA and UK respectively). Even at the time, their 'class'-based categories and methods were questioned – for example, they excluded consideration of important social background influences such as education – and they have been revised or abandoned by later researchers in favour of other approaches, including social networks, described below.

So, the use of particular language patterns can identify us not just as individuals through our idiolects but as members of groups or communities. For each of us, there is a conscious or unconscious choice of how far we conform to the norms of language use in our speech community regarding issues like gender, age, social background, etc. It's worth noting that as individuals we may belong to several speech communities, each exerting different types of influence upon us and which may intersect with each other. For example, a teenage boy of Chinese ethnic origin, born and raised in Sydney, Australia, may mark membership of several groups in his use of language:

- local Sydney teenage culture and specific male peer groups to which he belongs and in which he uses particular rather non-standard forms of Australian English
- the broader standard English-speaking community in Australia
- the Chinese-speaking community in his area, including his family and family friends.

These considerations have suggested that there is an alternative way of reflecting an individual's language use and the influences on him or her to that offered by the potentially crude pigeonholing of *social class* and that is one based on social networks. This approach can also explain how the shared norms of group language behaviour are developed and perpetuated, as well as explaining individual behaviour.

A social network approach looks at the frequency and the types of contact between individuals in groups. These groups might be based around friendship, family or neighbourhood ties or on the place of work or education; they might even be very large-scale groups such as ones based on a particular religion. The basic principle is that the more we interact with other people in our various groups or networks (including virtual cyber communities), the more likely we are to identify with them and show this by adopting the language patterns of those groups. If we feel peripheral to a group, we are likely to show weaker linguistic ties with it. Labov (1972a) was one of the first sociolinguists to demonstrate this in his study of teenage gangs in Harlem, New York City (USA): central gang members showed the most distinctive language traits of the group and those on the fringes, dubbed *lames*, showed the weakest links linguistically.

Situational factors: WHEN? and WHY?

The WHEN and WHY factors are potentially infinite. They relate to the situation that the language is used in and what it is used for. For example, irrespective of who is using it, language is likely to be used differently when:

- in a courtroom, a classroom, a bedroom, a market, a therapy session, a playground, a job interview, a political speech, a poem, a horoscope, an obituary, a love letter, a suicide note, a football commentary, a horse racing commentary, an advice (agony aunt) column in a women's magazine, an advice (agony aunt/uncle?) column in a men's magazine, a personal ad., a movie trailer, a plane, a sitcom, an opera, a soap opera, a will, a delicatessen, a lecture, a tutorial, a textbook, a diary, a dairy, a children's story, a child's story, an undergraduate essay, a PhD, a proposal (business or marriage), a synagogue, a mosque, a chapel, a church, a temple, a chatroom, a pool hall, a different country

- on a basketball court, a deathbed, a bus, a train, a driving lesson, a shopping list, a breakfast cereal packet, a wedding invitation
- at a bank robbery, a marriage ceremony, a grocery checkout, a shrine, a bowling alley, a nursery (plant or child) or at a funeral.

It is also likely to be used differently depending on what we use it *for*, for example when it is used to:

- accuse, amuse, apologize, assert, boast, congratulate, console, demand, excuse, free, gloat, greet, hail, insult, jibe, kid, leer, mock, name, offer, persuade, please, promise, query, recommend, recriminate, scare, suggest, thank, urge, value, warn or to yearn (if you've already read Unit 3, this final list should look familiar).

All these issues (WHO/WHEN/WHY) show that how language is used is intimately dependent on a variety of social contexts and as such, they could reasonably be investigated by a sociologist. This book, however, has been written by and for linguists, and what makes us different from sociologists is that any linguist interested in different ways of using language (for that is essentially what variety is about) must also be interested in *linguistic* matters – which might be called the WHAT factors. In other words, when linguists are interested in variety they are also concerned with what it is in the language that varies. Again, the answer to the WHAT question can be anything – *accent*: phonetics, **phonology**, prosody (intonation and stress); *dialect*: morphology, lexis, syntax, choice of language; and *style* including issues such as the formality and overall structure of the discourse. Activity 9.8 at the end of the unit provides opportunities to analyse several varieties. But if you just can't wait, try Activity 9.6.

 ## Activity 9.6

Choose three user factors (WHO) and three situational factors (WHEN/WHY) and think about exactly how they might make a difference to language in use (WHAT). If possible, discuss your ideas with other students (who may well have chosen other factors).

VARIETY – VIVE LA DIFFÉRENCE!

Whichever way you look at it, the kinds of variation (or *différence*) in language that have so far only been hinted at here (though rest assured that Activity 9.8 will come) are vital for any language which is alive and kicking (hence *vive*) and wants to remain so! The existence of systematic variation within a language means that speakers are really using that language on a regular basis as part of a range of aspects of their lives and that they have made it their own by favouring particular forms of it. In other words, the language varieties people use will express a key part of their personal, regional and social identity. Since all sorts of people make up communities, there will be variation in the language they use, even if they are all technically speaking 'the same language'.

Unless communities are using language this way, languages will tend to fossilize and then die out when they are no longer able to express the concepts, needs and feelings of a range of different types of user, or when they start to seem remote or alien to their users. In a sense, this is the position with the so-called 'dead' languages like Latin. Welsh (spoken in Wales in the UK) was on the road to that fate (so-called *language loss* or *language death*) before a resurgence of linguistic and national interest, plus some language planning on behalf of government bodies, began to restore the dwindling numbers of speakers. (➻ Unit 12 for multilingual considerations and ➻ Unit 15 for issues relating to governmental intervention in education.)

PRESCRIPTIVE/DESCRIPTIVE APPROACHES

This section returns to the notion of standard for it may be thought that if variety is equivalent to difference, then it must inherently be not standard. Not so; variety and standard are not **complementary** terms (➻ Unit 6) because any standard language is but a particular variety of that language – admittedly a powerful and prestigious variety, but nonetheless a variety and often an accidental variety at that (➻ Unit 13). This is a very important point which should not be forgotten. If it *is* forgotten, then differing ways of speaking or writing (non-standard ones often linked to particular locales or less powerful social groups) might be deemed somehow 'deviant' or 'substandard' and these prejudiced, negative associations could quickly carry over into prejudiced, negative judgements on non-linguistic characteristics of speakers.

Within linguistics, a **descriptive** approach to the study of language is usually favoured. This is the approach set out in this book. Linguists strive to describe and study languages and the systematic ways in which any particular language is used, including the range of varieties of that language, standard or non-standard. This approach is based on the view that all varieties of a language which are systematically and successfully used by communities of speakers are linguistically valid and worthy of study. The term 'variety' is therefore adopted as a non-loaded term; it supposedly carries no judgements. Descriptive linguists will, of course, acknowledge that *socially*, the standard form may have more prestige but most would point out that it is wrong to assume it will be any 'better' as a *linguistic system*. In many cases, prestige or standard forms of languages are raised to their elevated positions purely by chance – by being 'in the right place at the right time' and spoken by the right people, as it were, and the rise of standard English in Britain is a wonderful case in point here (➡ Unit 13 for more details).

There is another, alternative stance on standard language which we are all probably quite familiar with. A **prescriptive** approach to the study of language literally 'prescribes' how language *should* be used, rather than trying to chart objectively how it *is* used, as a descriptive linguist would. This usually boils down to prescribing that all speakers of a language should use the standard form. Prescriptive arguments are usually tied to a rather nostalgic (often personal) view whereby whatever language is under discussion is seen to be in peril from current trends in usage, and effectively the so-called standard of yesteryear is held up as the 'true', 'pure', 'correct', 'beautiful' and 'complex' language. So a prescriptive approach would condemn the first sentence in this paragraph because it ends with a **preposition** – a use of language up with which prescriptivists just will not put! Regional and social varieties of a language tend to be viewed as inferior to the standard – both socially and linguistically. Extreme prescriptivists have difficulty seeing that anything other than the standard form of a language has any linguistic system, complexity, logic or ability to express a range of concepts and emotions. This view can apply not only to non-standard social and regional varieties but also to any new trends in language use adopted by otherwise standard language users (➡ see, for example, the Further Activity in Unit 7). Hopefully it is clear, from earlier discussion, that we feel there are some fundamental problems with a prescriptivist approach: variety and variation simply show that a language is alive – and they also keep it alive. Whatever the prescriptivists claim, languages do continue to change and change is now viewed by most linguists as both natural and inevitable.

However, there are thorny issues linked to the descriptive–prescriptive debate, not least of which are ones like those in Activity 9.7.

Activity 9.7 o—┳

Using the terminology introduced so far as much as possible, and identifying descriptive and prescriptive viewpoints in relation to each question, consider your responses to the following:

1 If all varieties of a language are linguistically valid, should we (and who would be meant by *we*?) still choose a single variety (for example, the existing standard) as a medium of education, government, religion, etc.?
2 Is there consensus on what the standard variety of any language actually is?
3 How do we (and who might that be?) decide where standard language ends and non-standard language begins?

To round off this section, it is worth returning to what was said earlier in this unit: even speakers of the same language persist in using both spoken and written language in systematically different ways. Descriptive linguists argue that variation in language use is a key way of keeping it alive. Variation in language is inevitable: it is part of human nature to mark our identity by the way we speak (or write) and that means showing how we are like those around us whom we admire as well as showing how we are different from those outwith that group.

PUTTING ALL THIS INTO PRACTICE

 Activity 9.8 o—┳

This is the final activity of this unit and it is designed to offer you more detailed practice in using the terms and concepts introduced thus far.

Consider the following **texts**[2] and analyse each in terms of field, tenor and mode and hence overall register of the discourse. Pay attention to as many WHO/WHEN/WHY/WHAT aspects as possible. This type of analysis that you are about to do is sometimes known as 'genre analysis' or 'stylistics'.

Text 9.1   Snowee and Multee (Teah Bennett)[3, 4]

Taytu
Snowee and myltee.
Ouns opon a time

Some Gunea pigs came
to stey at Teah's huos
and She colled them
Snowee and Multee.
Won day Snowee and
multee disd that
they wud aceyp
andthen snowee
Sead what wud
We eat huuu
Sead Multee
I dunt no.

I no Sead multee
What Sead Snowee
the fres grass
but what wud
We drink
huuu Sead
multee
I dunt no.

I no Sead multee

We WILL   Stay
Hary.

End of Snowee and
multee.

Text 9.2   Loan Agreement (AJM/SAF/SEH)

We the undersigned, <FULL NAME> and <FULL NAME>, hereinafter referred
to as 'the borrowers', both residing at <FULL ADDRESS> … Edinburgh in the
region of Lothian Scotland hereby acknowledge that we have received a loan
of twelve thousand pounds sterling from Sheila Ena <SURNAME> of <FULL
ADDRESS> … Peterborough in the county of Cambridge England, hereinafter
referred to as 'the lender'.

(DOCUMENT CONTINUES)

Text 9.3   Signature and Stamp (AJM/SPECS)

Hi

SORRY, SORRY, SORRY, SORRY
I'M SO EMBARREST AND SORRY THAT
I'VE BEEN SO SLOPPY (MAYBE NOT THE RIGHT WORD?)
I HOPE THIS CARD AND MY SIGNATURE
+ THE STAMP WILL HELP TO GET SOME
MONEY BACK.
 I'VE BEEN SO BUSY —
GOING ON HOLIDAYS ! FIRST A WEEK
AT MALLORCA TO PLAY GOLF AND NEXT
THE YEARLY HOLIDAY IN SKAGEN WITH
PER, KARSTEN AND MY FATHER. AND
NOW I'M WAITING FOR THE GOLFSENSON
TO BEGIN HERE IN DENMARK

ALL THE BEST
LOVE TO YOU ALL

Text 9.4   Barrier Reef (AJM/MUM)

Mon. 3 Nov.
Had a wonderful day on the Barrier Reef.
Huge Catamaran, 4 Decks, travelled 70 miles
out to a huge pontoon moored at the reef. We
Could step back & forth ship/pontoon- Top left
picture Shows the inside of semi submersible,
Passengers were under the water, but deck of sub
was still above water. It was so enjoyable
we went down twice, each trip lasting 30 min
Weather was Very hot, calm seas, blue sky.
Perfect. Lunch provided.
It was a whole day - 8·30 am
& returned at 4.

Love
Mum.
x
x

Is the Great Barrier Reef

Marina Mirage, Port Douglas, Qld. 4871 Australia.

Text 9.5   Good boy (M&M/M1/SA)

```
01   A:   Right can you see the church?=

     C:   =Yes.= ((simultaneously nods))

     A:   =Near it.=Yes. ((simultaneously nods)) OK go down to that church.
          ((pause)) From the traffic lights to the church.

05        ((pause))

     C:   °Done it°

     A:   Done it good boy, OK.=Turn off and go over the bridge.
          ((pause))

     C:   °Bridge°

10        ((pause))

     C:   Found it! ((simultaneously points to map))

     A:   Good boy.
          ((pause))

     C:   .hh There.

15   A:   Good boy. .hh Keep going until you get to the roundabout.
          ((pause))
          ((C points to the roundabout))

     C:   Found it.

     A:   Good boy then

20   C:   (°X round°)
          ((pause while C completes drawing then sits))

     A:   [[(°°X°°)    ]

     C:   [[°Done it.°]

     A:   You've done it so you're ready. Good boy.
```

Text 9.6   Extract from Jaworski *et al.* (2004) (AJ/MK/SL/VYM/SS15/EX2 (modified))[5]

01	V	you need the bowl? (.) I give for cheap price (.) you can go in (.) I have
02		(unclear) go inside don't mind no problem (.) ooh (.) you see I'm
03		mister cheap (.) I work with myself (.) anything you like I give
04		something for secret price anything (.) you have three wise monkeys (.)
05		thinking man and the (mother? unclear) (.) half faces (.) man who play
06		the kora (.) Africa kora
07	T1	is that an instrument (.)
08	T2	[yeah
09	Tchr	[yeah
10	T1	what's the instrument called
11	V	kora (.) kora kora (.) the man who play the kora
12	T	hmm mm
13	V	just feel it
14		((feeling))
15	V	this this Black and white
16	T1	hmm hmm
17	V	you know no problem I just offer [( ) you something for
18	T2	[( ) OK just looking
19	V	listen <u>listen</u> I just offer you something for hundred seventy-five (.) its
20		secret (.)
21	T1	hmm mm
22	V	anything you like you just tell you just tell and we can discu [ss
23	T1	[OK
24	V	because you are my first customer (.) anything you like hundred and
25		seventy-five (.) fifty (.) I give to you lower (.) you don't like this small
26		(mother) [yes?
27	T	[hmm
28		((laugh [ter))
29	V	[yes feel it (.) just feel it (.) don't mind (.)
30		yes no problem (.) ((sound of clackers)) it's my role

Text 9.7   Extract from Harris (1995: 127) (modified)

01	P:	how do you think he went down those stairs then
02	S:	well I don't know – (I just) I I I think he must have fell down them
03	P:	were you there when he fell down
04	S:	no I was not – I was in bed – all right – I must have been in bed
05	P:	you're sure of that
06	S:	I'm sure of it – I must have been in bed – yeh I was in bed anyhow (2) (yeh)
07	P:	you weren't at the top of the stairs
08	S:	no (2) I was not
09	P:	you had an argument in the morning didn't you
10	S:	in the morning [aye – but that wouldn't be nothin[g ( )
11	P:	[hmmm [what d'you
12		mean it'd be nothing
13	S:	that would be nothin' – an anyway that would only be a bit of – crack – that's
14		what I'd (think) – that it was the crack you know
15	P:	when you've had a few to drink and you had a few that morning
16	S:	yeh
17		(2)
18	P:	you're a bit argumentative aren't you
19	S:	(be Jesus) I wouldn't think so
20	P:	you don't think so

Text 9.8   'Shitwork' (AJM/LC/3LS050 (modified))[6]

01	F1	Right, can I get on with this now?
	L	She does as well, oh I see
	F	She's put it on…
	F1	It's quarter to eleven, come on, pay attention. I can do that now can't I
05		((louder)) It's a quarter to eleven
	L	And I'm gonna do Sacks' bit first
	F1	Eh? No you're not. Three before break, three after break come on, don't be rotten
		((general hubbub))
	F1	Right. So, basically, er the definition of appropriate versus inappropriate
10		conversation she says, is the male's choice therefore he decides what their reality is but the women work harder at the interactions therefore they erm…basically, they do all the routine work but they don't reap the benefits. And on page four-two-six we have just the biggest giveaway that she went in there with an agenda, it's 'women are the "shit" workers of routine interactions'.
15	F4	Yes
	F1	Now the lexical choice of 'shit' oh how emotively written is that! You know, I erm, I do think…anyway

SUMMARY

This unit has shown that language in use is incredibly diverse and yet that this diversity – that this difference – is not random, but systematic. This unit also provided an introduction to terms and concepts relevant to the study of regional and social varieties of language – in other words, it has provided an introduction to sociolinguistics.

What has not been covered

Sociolinguistics is a vast field and a truly comprehensive coverage would have to be encyclopaedic in magnitude. There is therefore so very much that has had to be left out. However, you may like to extend your studies in areas such as: accommodation; acts of identity; advertising; attitudes to language; audience design; code-mixing and **code-switching**; communicative competence; communities of practice; **diglossia**; forensic linguistics; guise experiments (matched or otherwise); institutional language; interactional linguistics; language and culture; language and gender; language and the internet; language change; language disorder; motherese; pidgins and creoles; politeness; power; stereotypes; taboo language and many more.

Some of these sociolinguistic issues are addressed in the other units. Others are not. Clearly it is not possible to go into details about what these concepts are about (this is a 'what has *not* been covered' section after all), but suffice to say that all these many different varieties of sociolinguistics are fascinating. And the variety in sociolinguistics exists because there is variety in language use.

Throughout this unit, quoting from many sources has been resisted, however it seems appropriate to close with the thoughts of some very eminent sociolinguists, starting with Hudson (1996: 18) who comments: 'as soon as we start to consider language as an object of research, social considerations are hard to ignore'. Next, Labov (1997: 23, original italics) has admitted that he has 'resisted the term *sociolinguistics* for many years, since it implies that there can be a successful linguistic theory or practice which is not social'. Finally, Le Page and Tabouret-Keller (1985: 188) note: 'We should constantly remind ourselves that languages do not do things; people do things, languages are abstractions from what people do'.

So as long as human beings gather together in a variety of identifiable social and regional communities for a variety of different social and regional purposes – in short, to do a variety of different things – then there will always be differences in the way they use their linguistic resources. Even if you have learnt nothing else from this unit, we hope you now realize that *variety in language is everywhere* because *everything is some variety*. Consequently, *any* linguistic data can be analysed in terms of regional and social variation. There are therefore many examples in all the units throughout this book.

If variety really is the spice of life, let's keep it spicy and *vive la différence* – or should that be *vive les différences*?!

FURTHER READING

There are very many textbooks on sociolinguistics. Recommendations for ones which focus particularly on accent and/or dialect would include *Dialectology* (Chambers and Trudgill 1980), *English Accents and Dialects* (Hughes and Trudgill 1996) and *Accents of English* (Wells 1982). More general introductions can be found in *Varieties of English* (Freeborn *et al.* 1993), *An Introduction to Sociolinguistics* (Holmes 2001), *Sociolinguistics* (Hudson 1996), *An Introduction to Language and Society* (Montgomery 1995), *Language, Society and Power* (Thomas and Wareing 1999), *Sociolinguistics: A Resourcebook for Students* (Stockwell 2002), and *An Introduction to Sociolinguistics* (Wardhaugh 2001).

In addition, *Sociolinguistics: A Reader and Coursebook* (Coupland and Jaworski 1997) and *Sociolinguistics: The Essential Readings* (Paulston and Tucker 2003) are excellent edited collections of original readings spanning a range of sociolinguistic topics. *Urban Voices* (Foulkes and Docherty 1999) is, as its subtitle promises, an excellent collection of accent studies in the British Isles. These three are, however, more advanced texts.

FURTHER ACTIVITY

 Activity 9.9

As per Activity 9.5:

1   Do you recognize any of the following dialect words?
2   Do you use any of them? If so, when?
3   What do they mean?
4   Where (for example, geographically) might they be used?

As before, there are some small clusters of terms (including ones relating to alleyways, being pleased, drinking receptacles, stickiness, talking and truancy).

01	aye	14	claggy	27	made up	40	snog
02	bairn	15	clarty	28	minging	41	stubby
03	barnet	16	crook	29	nick off	42	suited
04	blethering	17	divn't	30	nowt	43	summat
05	blower	18	dram	31	oldies	44	this avo
06	bonce	19	fag	32	owt	45	tinny
07	bonny	20	gigs	33	pinkie	46	tubular
08	booger	21	ginnel	34	play hooky	47	twag
09	brae	22	gobsmacked	35	ranchslider	48	wag
10	brass	23	happen	36	rellies	49	wee
11	bunk off	24	heffalump	37	skive	50	yammering
12	char	25	hood	38	snicket		
13	chuntering	26	low-set	39	snickleway		

COMMENTARY ON ACTIVITIES

Activity 9.2

Nah den! / Ah reet!

For both, the spelling provides an impressionistic rendering of the Sheffield accent.

Nah den! [naːdɛn]

Literally the greeting means 'Now then!'. In Sheffield, the <ow> or [aʊ] sound found in <now> commonly becomes <ah> or [aː] and <th> or [ð] in <the> commonly becomes <d> or [d]. The example is interesting both regionally and socially since it is characteristic of the Sheffield area and may not be recognized as a greeting even by other native British English speakers. It would tend to be used more between male friends and informal acquaintances at the lower end of the social hierarchy.

Ah reet! [aːɹiːt]

This greeting literally means 'Alright'. Though it is possible to imagine this simply as a regionally-accented and shortened version of the question 'Are you alright?', it is usually used without **utterance**-final rising intonation, typical of many question types in (British) English. Falling intonation is far more common with this Sheffield greeting. As with the last example, the form is characteristic of the Sheffield area and may not be easily decoded even by other native British English speakers. The rendition of [i] for the vowel in 'right' is a common Sheffield accent feature, though one which is increasingly identified with older speakers (see Stoddart *et al.* 1999: 75) and, impressionistically, with male speakers. Like many British English accents, Sheffield is being influenced by the spread of the **glottal stop**, a non-standard accent feature which many British English speakers are aware of and often associate with London accents. Many younger, male Sheffield speakers would be likely to replace the final [t] in 'right' with [ʔ]. Whichever of these features appear, they would tend to be used more between male friends and informal acquaintances at the lower end of the social hierarchy.

Hi

This greeting is far less easy to localize regionally since it is recognized in much of the English speaking world. It is usually seen as informal, especially amongst older speakers; younger speakers may feel it can be used in more formal situations. Some speakers would argue that it is not standard English; others that it is simply colloquial standard English. It is not easy to pinpoint a particular social class or gender of speaker who would use this as it has a fairly wide distribution.

Hiya

This greeting is currently a popular one amongst younger British speakers and possibly amongst more females than males. It is informal but not overtly associated with specific social backgrounds. If the initial [h] were dropped, this could be an accent indicator that the speaker, if British, originates from a mid to lower range social background. However, though many regional or non-standard British English accents do drop initial [h], not all do so. Exceptions include Scotland and Ireland.

Morning and mornin'

The use of these as a truncated form of 'Good morning' is quite common in the English speaking world. In many communities, they would be seen as less formal than 'Good morning' but considerably more formal than any others in this list. In the second example, the fact that the second syllable ends in [n] rather than [ŋ] suggests that this is a regional variety and thus that the speaker is not likely to be from the uppermost social hierarchy, since speakers of regional varieties tend not to be so (though, oddly, some old fashioned upper class British accents would use [n] in this **context**). The use of [n] for [ŋ] in such contexts is quite widespread in a number of British regional accents so on this feature alone it is not possible to localize precisely. All we can say is that the speaker is likely to be from a middle to lower range social background unless, perhaps, they are an older speaker of Received Pronunciation (defined later in this unit).

'ello luv

Literally 'Hello, love'. In Sheffield, this could be used as an informal greeting between people of assumed equal status, though not necessarily between people who know each other well! Interestingly, in Sheffield, 'luv' is often used by women or men with either gender of addressee. A colleague once told of a visiting Australian professor's look of alarm when he was addressed as 'luv' by a particularly hard-looking male Sheffield bus driver! The initial **h dropping** from 'hello' and the rounded vowel in 'luv' serve to confirm this as a northern British English variety. Linguistic research suggests that speakers from lower social backgrounds tend to use more of these accent features and that men are more likely to use them than women.

Geoff! (accompanied by a hand wave)

There is little to go on here in terms of speaker profile except to say that the speaker probably knows their addressee quite well, as is immediately suggested by the use of the addressee's first name. The use of the hand wave is common in many English-speaking areas, though the precise form of this wave may show regional variations. There could perhaps be differences in terms of gender: would as many men be prepared to wave as women; what would their waves be like?!

Activity 9.3
Here (very briefly) are some suggestions:
1   There are many varieties of language because there are so many people from so many different communities using language for so many different functions.
2   Varieties come about by a community needing (and hence evolving) specific ways for expressing the concepts, needs and feelings of their specific community. They spread when communities find themselves in social and linguistic contact with one another.
3   Varieties exist (and persist) to serve the purposes that they evolved for – to meet the expressive needs of the community. They also act as important linguistic badges of identity for the members of the communities involved. These can be used to express solidarity within the group as well as to express differentiation outwith the group (by distinguishing community X from community Y – just as sports fans wear the shirts of their favourite team and music fans wear T-shirts from the gigs they have been to).
4   Probably yes and no. Yes because through mass media we all have increased access to standard forms. No because our greater mobility brings us into contact with many more various communities.

5   Prejudice! Varieties are associated with the communities that use them. As some will necessarily be more powerful or more 'cool' than others they will carry more social prestige and hence a higher social value.

6   One relates to teenage intonational patterns in the UK (and elsewhere) where statements are uttered with a rise in pitch at the end: this is an alleged impact of Australian soaps. Others relate to the development (and popularity) of relatively new media such as NETSPEAK and SMS-speak (text-messaging – or should that be 'txt-msging'?): so fyi, imho, a/s/l? and lol r *gr8* ☺ (➤ Unit 7).

7   There are a range of uses from avoiding prejudice and helping people feel at ease to specific applications such as forensic linguistics, advertising, speech and language therapy, and acting. At a much more fundamental level, if we didn't have a reasonable knowledge of how to use varieties we could end up using language inappropriately in many situations (➤ cf. the 'Give me an extension, bitch!' example from Unit 4).

Activity 9.4

[ɑ]/[a]

Like the [ʌ]/[ʊ] distinction, in Britain this pair differentiates many southern speakers from northern ones.

[ɪŋ]/[ɪn]/[ɪŋg]

In British English, using [ɪn] rather than [ɪŋ] in these contexts suggests that the speaker is likely to be from a middle to lower range social background (unless perhaps, they are an older RP speaker – cf. Activity 9.2). It also suggests a regional variety, however the use of [ɪn] rather than [ɪŋ] is quite widespread in a number of British regional accents so on this feature alone it is not possible to localize precisely. The [ɪŋg] variant, however, is often associated with areas around Birmingham in the West Midlands of England.

[h]/ø

Many British accents use the ø variant. Linguistic research suggests that speakers from lower social backgrounds tend to use this accent feature and that men are more likely to use it than women. Note, however, that h dropping (not using [h]) may also occur for reasons other than social class (➤ for example the discussions on weak forms and connected speech in Unit 8).

[ɹ]/ø

Varieties that use the [ɹ] are called rhotic. Most British accents are not rhotic (with the main exceptions being Scotland, Ireland and the south-west of England). The same is true of Australia and New Zealand. In Britain, rhoticity tends not to be linked to any particular social varieties (such as class or gender) – either the accent is rhotic or it is not. Rhoticity is much more common in American English, and communities can attach social prestige to the use of [ɹ] (see Labov 1972b for his famous study of New York City).

[ð]/[v]/[d] and [θ]/[f]/[t]

In Britain, [ð]/[θ] are the standard pronunciations; [v]/[f] are associated with London and areas of the south-east (and particularly so in lower social classes); and [d]/[t] are often associated with Black English (both in Britain and the USA) as well as the Irish English of Eire (for example in Dublin).

[ju:]/[u:] (in words such as *new* and *tune*)

This distinction can differentiate most British speakers from many American ones. [u:] is also notably used in Norfolk and the Fenland area of the east of England (see Trudgill 1974).

Activity 9.5 (3 and 4)

Rather than deal with each word in a strict alphabetical order, this commentary is organized around clusters of words using the following abbreviations: Aus (Australian English), Br (British English), NZ (New Zealand English), Sc (Scots English), SE (Standard British English), US (American English).

Words for toilets

bog	Br-colloquial, non-specific geography
dunny	Aus and NZ: specifically for an outside toilet; Sc: *cellar* or *underground passage*
john	US-colloquial
netty	Br: specific to the north-east

Words for clothing

togs	NZ: *swimwear* (gender non-specific); colloquial Br: *clothes*
trunks	SE: *male swimwear*; US: the plural of the luggage space in a car
keks	Br-Yorkshire and Br-Liverpool: *trousers*
pants	US: *trousers*
strides	Aus: *trousers*
trews	SE: *trousers* (usually tartan material)

Words for sweets

dods	Br-Peterborough, Cambridgeshire
goodies	Br-Hull, East Yorkshire
spice	Br-West Yorkshire
spogs	Br-West Yorkshire

Words for police

bizzies	Br: mainly Liverpool and Merseyside
pigs	Br-colloquial (and derogatory), non-specific geography
rozzers	Br: mainly London and the south-east

Words for food

chow	Br-colloquial: *food*; Br-Hull, East Yorkshire: to berate/chide/rebuke – 'to chow at someone'
docky	Br-Peterborough, Cambridgeshire (Fenland): specifically food taken to eat at work
grub	Br-colloquial: *food*
scran	Br-Peterborough, Cambridgeshire (Fenland): *food*; Br-Liverpool and Merseyside: *food*
snap	Br-Yorkshire: specifically food taken to eat at work
tucker	Aus: *food*
feast	Despite appearances, this is a Br-West Yorkshire term for a funfair
pukka	Br: although now made famous in Britain by the London chef, Jamie Oliver, who uses *pukka* to mean 'superior' or 'first class', it can also mean 'genuine'. Interestingly for the chef (whether or not he realizes it), *pukka* comes from Hindi meaning 'cooked', 'firm' or 'ripe'.

Specialist jargon

baguette	Architecture: a narrow, convex moulding
eagle	Golf: a score of two shots under *par* (*par* is the expected number of shots for a particular hole)
illocution	Linguistics: see glossary
muggle	Wizardry and Witchcraft (or at least Harry Potter fans): a non-magic person
yankee	Gambling: a complex bet covering multiple combinations of four horses (or dogs) in four separate races

And then some …

agait (Br-West Yorkshire) and *like* (Br- and US-colloquial though probably becoming global) have meanings relating to 'say', as in: *She was like 'Oh my God!'* or *I wa' agait 'How much?!!'*.

   lake (Br-West Yorkshire) and *lark* (Br-Hull, East Yorkshire) mean 'to play', as in: *Are you lakin' out?* (= are you coming out to play?) or *He likes to lark with his toy soldiers*.

   gannin (Br-north-east) and *banner* (Br-West Yorkshire) have meanings related to 'going' – *gannin* = 'going', *banner* = 'going to', as in: *I'm gannin doon toon* (I'm going down [to] town) and *I'm banner twat you* (I'm going to hit you).

   bar and *gate* in York, UK, have non-standard meanings. For non-regional speakers fond of an alcoholic beverage it is sometimes shocking to learn that there are just four bars in York. But that is because a *bar* is not a public drinking establishment. A *bar* is a gate in the city walls. *Gates*, on the other hand, are abundant in York (and indeed elsewhere in the UK) for they are a name for a street/road, such as Micklegate, Monkgate, Walmgate, Whip-ma-whop-ma-Gate and so on. (In Old Norse, 'gata' is a path or passage.) In Britain, many pubs are owned by breweries and Theakston's is a popular Yorkshire one. This therefore leads to the witty quip: 'In York, the streets are gates, the gates are bars and the bars are Theakston's!'.

charlie and *crack* are our last pair of related terms. For those au fait with drug culture they are widely used names for the narcotic, cocaine. For those more wordly-wise than worldly-wise, they have yet other non-standard meanings. In British English, *Charlie* is a colloquial term for a fool, as in: *He's a right Charlie.*This meaning is probably more likely to be used by older speakers. *Crack* (also spelled <craic>) is also an Irish English word which has meanings related to fun, good times and good atmosphere, as in: *We just wrote this book for the crack* (we just did it for the fun of it).[7]

The rest of the words are unrelated. In parts of the Fens in the east of England, *driv* is used instead of *drove* (the past-tense of *drive*), as in: *He driv to town in his new car. Greeting* is a Sc word for crying. *Manchester* is a New Zealand word for cotton goods such as sheets and towels. *Sneeped* comes from the Stoke area of the Midlands in the UK. It means something like 'miffed' ('offended' or 'annoyed'). *Titfer* is a Cockney rhyming slang term for 'hat'. Complex slang terms work as rhymes for the standard term but they are often reduced in form. Here, *titfer* is a reduction of *tit for tat* ('hat'). In the same way, *butcher's* is short for *butcher's hook* ('look' – as a **noun**), *apples* is short for *apples and pears* ('stairs') and *whistle* is short for *whistle and flute* ('suit').

Apart from its vulgar meaning, *twat* is a Br-Yorkshire term for 'hit'. Pronounced [juːt], *ute* is an Aus term for a pick-up truck (a shortened version of *utility vehicle*). *While* is a Br-Yorkshire term which means 'until' and not 'for the duration of' as it does in standard English. This has led to the (almost certainly apocryphal) story of ill-fated Yorkshire folk who misinterpreted the signage at railway crossings: *wait while lights flash.* Whether apocryphal or not, these words are no longer used. Instead signs now read: *stop when lights flash* and, in addition, *keep crossing clear*.

Finally – *dumpy* and *huggy*. Dumpy means 'butter' and huggy means 'sugar': these words formed part of the idiolect of one of the authors when they were about three years old. It would be utterly amazing if anybody had linked these words to these meanings.

Activity 9.7

The questions raised in this activity are extremely complex. Commentary is therefore necessarily superficial.

1 There are arguments that doing so excludes people who don't speak the standard variety much, if at all, in their daily lives. It is therefore inevitable that elitism develops. But then again, isn't a standard needed as a reference point in education so that all children are exposed to the same variety and so that there will be a sort of **lingua franca** for all speakers of a language? A similar argument can be made for those learning English, for example, as a second or further language – which English should they learn? Is it not useful to have an agreed variety for this purpose?
2 Surely if language varies so much and is constantly changing, then 'the standard' is going to be a moving target; compare standard English from different historical periods: to modern eyes and ears they can look like barely related varieties (➳ the versions of the Lord's Prayer in Units 13 and 16). On a smaller scale, think how much standard language changes within a couple of generations: compare the language of

standard English speakers such as Queen Elizabeth II with that of her son, Prince Charles and her grandson Prince William. All of these versions of the standard exist at the same point in time. The very term 'standard' encourages us to think there is one version but in fact there are even varieties of whatever is considered to be standard.

3   This is hard to do and there won't be complete agreement between native language users or even standard language users. What often happens in language communities is that varieties are arranged on a continuum, with some closer to the standard end and others further away.

Activity 9.8

Text 9.1

This is an excellent piece of data to begin with as it is abundantly rich with clues about the variety (indeed, varieties) involved. So let's start with the bigger picture. This is a story. It follows a clear narrative structure displaying five of the six possible elements as set out by Labov (1999) (➨ Unit 7) even though four of these elements are optional in story-telling (only the complicating action is necessary).

Abstract: What is this about? We are told in the (explicit) title: Title – Snowee and Multee.

Orientation: When, where, who/what are involved in the story? Once upon a time, at Teah's house and guinea pigs called Snowee and Multee.

Complicating action: Then what happened? Snowee and Multee discuss the possibility of escape but realize there are issues of what they would eat and drink.

Resolution: What finally happened? Although the food issue is resolvable (eating fresh grass), their drink problem seems insurmountable. They therefore decide to stay 'here' (at Teah's house).

Evaluation: So what? Why is this story worth telling and hearing? This can appear at any point in story and is completely optional. While there is no explicit evaluation in Snowee and Multee, it does carry overtones of fable stories where there is a clear and often moral message which is implicitly the point of the telling. Here the moral might well be something like 'While the (fresh) grass on the other side might be inviting, it's often best to be content with what you've got'.

Coda: All done! End of Snowee and Multee.

So it is clearly narrative. But what else can we glean from this particular example of language in use?

Mode: Written language (and, more specifically, hand-written).

Field: Everyday life – though admittedly the everyday life of talking guinea pigs!

Tenor: In some respects this is a formal piece of writing. For example, it has an explicit 'title' and an 'end'. It was, in fact, also produced in a handmade hardback book entitled *The Book Of Snowee and Multee and Other Stories*; it had a contents page and an index; it was written in gold lettering evidencing the importance of the document; yet it was produced for the craic rather than any other purpose. In other respects, it is not formal – spellings are often non-standard for example. Also there are informal conversational-style musings ('Hmmm') of the guinea pigs. Of course, this mix of styles, this **code-mixing** (➟ Unit 12) is often normal in narrative discourse.

Register: Overall, the register has more than a certain written fairytale flavour about it – cf. 'Once upon a time…'.

There is also plenty of evidence that the author was a child (and, as it happens, only six years old) from the Midlands of the UK. This is mainly evidenced in the non-standard spellings throughout. For example, <Taytu> hints that this child might be an l-vocalizer (turning some occurrences of consonantal /l/ into a vowel, /u/) as is common in the West Midlands. Likewise, <opon> for *upon* and <won> for *one*, hint at the common realization of /ʌ/ as [ɒ] in this area (see Mathisen 1999). These spellings, while non-standard are therefore not random, but seem to be motivated by a sophisticated recognition of phonetic features. They also indicate that this child may have been schooled to read and write using a phonic method.

Finally, knowing that Text 9.1 is annotated as having Teah Bennett as source, and also 'Teah' featuring in the story, we can surmise that these individuals are the same person (Teah is not a very common name, after all) and that is in fact so. Interestingly, the uniqueness of the name *Teah* might give relatively few clues as to the gender of the author: is Teah male (like Lee or Taylor) or female (like Leah or Taylor)? Here the forensic linguist in us needs to appeal to social stereotypes: which gender is stereotypically likely to write stories for fun at the age of six in gold lettering about talking guinea pigs? Yes. Teah Bennett is a girl, and a very skilled linguist, already showing a fine command of varieties of English – and she lives near Stoke-on-Trent which is indeed in the Midlands, UK.

Text 9.2

This is an example of formal written legal language about a loan agreement. Evidence includes words such as *undersigned, hereinafter, hereby* (➟ Unit 3), *loan* and the explicit definition of terms 'the borrowers' and 'the lender', as well as stipulating that *pounds* refers to UK pounds (*sterling*). What can we ascertain about the backgrounds of the participants? Given the prescribed nature of legal language, we cannot really make any claims about regionality. Although we have the addresses of their residences (Edinburgh and Peterborough), that is not necessarily their region of origin – anyone can live anywhere. What we can claim, however, is that the forenames *Sheila Ena* might give some clue as to age and gender as they are currently more commonly associated with older female individuals. Finally, it is unlikely that Sheila is from a lower social class as she clearly has £12,000 at her disposal to lend.

Text 9.3

This is an informal spontaneously hand-written personal note from a friend. It starts with *Hi* and finishes with *Love to you all*. Informality can also be seen in the multiple (emphatically sincere) instances of *SORRY* and the lack of a name (instead a stylized pair of spectacles are drawn). The crossing out of the word NOT and the condensed font size of (MAYBE ~~NOT~~ THE

RIGHT WORD?) indicate the spontaneous nature of the text. What can we guess about the background of this author? Well he writes from and clearly is a resident of Denmark (he is awaiting the golf season there) and he has friends called Per and Karsten so he is possibly Danish (though remember anyone is allowed to live anywhere). The only hard linguistic clues to his non-native Englishness are his spelling of *embarrassed* (though even native speakers can make spelling errors) and his uncertainty of the appropriacy of the word *sloppy* (but again, native speakers may sometimes be uncertain). What of his social background? Well, he is a golfer. That has certain class associations in England, though of course these may not be the same in Denmark (as indeed they are not in Scotland where golf is just as much a sport of the working classes). He is unlikely to be of lower social status though, as he has been busy going on (what appear to be regular and multiple) holidays. He must therefore have a reasonably large disposable income. He also has some authority, as he hopes that his signature will carry some weight in the recipient reclaiming some money. He also mentions a 'stamp', implying that he may represent some official institution. As it happens, this author is an optician. But that is not the reason for the odd signature – his nickname is 'Brille' (Danish for *spectacles*) partly because he wears spectacles and partly because his father was also an optician. In English, his nickname is 'Specs'. This note relates to an official form and business stamp sent so that the recipient could claim money back from his UK employers for new eyewear that he had bought on a recent visit to Denmark.

Text 9.4

This is a hand-written, very informal account of an expedition to the Great Barrier Reef in Australia. Syntax is non-sentential throughout. Instead much of the structure is built out of **phrases** ($\rightarrow$ Unit 7). This type of register is typical of postcards and the **reference** to a 'top left picture' confirms these suspicions. It is written by someone's mother (*Love Mum XX*). There are very few regional clues here (except that she is unlikely to be from the USA as she signs herself 'Mum' not 'Mom'). Socially, on the other hand, this author is unlikely to be from a lower social class as not only does she have disposable income to holiday at the Barrier Reef, but she also has sufficient funds to take what must have been a fairly expensive excursion out 70 miles on a huge catamaran. OK, that's a bit of an assumption – it *is* possible that she could be working there, but stereotypically postcards are sent by people on holiday, and also, if it *had* been a work trip, then the fact that lunch was provided would not have been particularly noteworthy!

Text 9.5

This has been formatted according to conventions of conversation analysis (CA) ($\rightarrow$ Unit 2). It is therefore a text (transcription) of spoken data. It involves two speakers (C and A). There is very little evidence of regionality in this data. The interaction appears rather formal and entirely task-oriented (there is no social chat for example). Socially, however, A appears to have some authority or power over C ($\rightarrow$ Unit 4) because A is giving **imperative** instructions on record and baldly – i.e. explicitly and without redressive action – (e.g. L03: 'go down to that church'; L07 'Turn off and go over the bridge') and C appears to be following these instructions (e.g. L06: 'Done it'; L11 'Found it!'). A repeatedly calls C a 'good boy'. This indicates two things: (a) that C is a juvenile, and (b) that this is probably some form of adult-child talk as A is constantly providing supportive feedback to C. The pattern of sequences involved throughout this data (giving instructions, following instructions and giving supportive praise) is often categorized in Discourse Analysis as a three-part Initiation–Response–Feedback (IRF) sequence. Such IRFs are typical of institutional interactions such as those of Teacher–Pupil (for example, see Stubbs 1983: 29). A is therefore possibly a teacher, but almost certainly some kind of professional. As it happens, this data is from a speech and language therapy session (though the nature of C's speech and language problems is not overt in this extract) and A is the therapist.

Text 9.6

Again we have CA-formatted text. We are therefore dealing with talk. There are four participants: V, T1, T2 and Tchr. The talk is quite informal and spontaneous (cf. pauses, **overlaps**, repetitions, **backchannel** acknowledgements, etc. ➟ Unit 2). It revolves around the lexical field of buying, selling and bartering (L01: 'I give for cheap price'; L19: 'I just offer you something for hundred seventy-five; L22: 'we can discuss'; and lines 24–25 'anything you like hundred and seventy-five (.) fifty (.) I give to you lower'). V appears to be the vendor as he is explaining about the items (e.g. lines 04–06) and is the one authorized to 'give for cheap price' (L01) as he works by himself (L03). The others seem to be the potential customers (L24: 'you are my first customer'), though T2 is resisting that categorization (L18: 'OK just looking'). The goods involved seem to be African (L06: 'Africa kora'). This, together with V's apparent non-native English (lines 05–06 and 11: 'man who play the kora'), suggests that the source of this data may be an African (possibly souvenir) shop. The denotation of one participant as 'Tchr' suggests that they may be a teacher, and thus we might infer that T1 and T2 are students – but students who have funds to holiday in Africa (with the same caveats as for the Barrier Reef text). On these assumptions, we might feel that T1, T2 and Tchr have 'the power of the dollar' (the currency later turns out to be 'dalasi', the currency of the Gambia, thereby confirming this as African-based data), however in linguistic terms, it is V who demonstrates an authoritative position by using bald, on record imperatives (lines 13 and 29: 'just feel it'; L19: 'listen listen'; and L22: 'you just tell'). The notion of power is therefore far from a simplistic 'either you have power or you don't' concept (➟ Unit 4).

Text 9.7

Again talk data. Two participants, P and S. Talk is spontaneous (cf. pauses, overlaps, false starts, etc. ➟ Unit 2) but not especially informal. Turns are relatively short. There is a repeated pattern throughout of P asking S questions and S responding. This type of **adjacency pair** is never initiated by S. P therefore seems to wield more social power in this exchange. The talk seems to involve P establishing facts relating to an incident where a man 'went down those stairs' (L01). P does this through the use of questions, which might even be classed as accusations (lines 15 and 18: 'when you've had a few to drink and you had a few that morning … you're a bit argumentative aren't you') or at least challenges (lines 05 and 07: 'you're sure of that … you weren't at the top of the stairs'; and L20: 'you don't think so'). This type of questioning is typical of the register of interrogations (police, military, courtroom, teacher–pupil etc.) and there is a suggestion in S's repeated accounts about being in bed in lines 04 and 06 that S might be feeling intimidated by P. Other social clues point to S being an Irish English speaker (L10: 'aye'; lines 13 and 14: 'crack' (see commentary to Activity 9.5); and L19: 'be Jesus') and possibly one from a less desirable social background associated with excessive morning drinking (L15). Because of his drink habit, S is unlikely to be a very young speaker. S is also stereotypically more likely to be male.

As it happens, this data (gratefully taken from Harris 1995: 127) involves a policeman (P) 'interviewing an elderly Irish resident [(S)] of a local hostel regarding the "suspicious death" of another resident of the same hostel, who has been found at the bottom of the stairs'.

Text 9.8
The final text is also talk-in-interaction. It is spontaneous (lines 09, 11, 16: hesitations) and somewhat informal (L06: 'gonna'). There are two main participants, F1 and L with supporting roles played by F and F4. The lexical field seems to be about interaction (lines 09–10: 'appropriate versus inappropriate conversation'; lines 11 and 14: 'interactions'). While spontaneous, this interaction appears to be scheduled as time is an issue (L04: 'It's quarter to eleven, come on, pay attention'; and L07: 'Three before break, three after break'). So where might we have a scheduled interaction about interaction? Indeed so: in a class on linguistics and there is evidence that this is the case. There is talk of definitions (L09), references to a book (L12 – it's Coupland and Jaworski 1997, by the way), use of technical linguistic terminology (L06: 'Sacks'; L16: 'the lexical choice'; and lines 14 and 18–19: 'shit worker' – see Fishman 1997). What of the background of F1 and L? Given the specifics of the topic, they are likely to be university-educated linguists. Although regionality is not apparent, power is. F1 has to ask permission to take the floor using the deontic (= permission-seeking) **modal auxiliary** *can* (L01: 'Right, can I get on with this now?'; and L04: 'I can do that now can't I'). F1 also hedges their opinion (lines 16–17: 'You know, I erm, I do think…anyway'), which might indicate she is female. Conversely, L simply asserts their will (L06). F1 challenges L's self-imposed authority (L07: 'Eh? No you're not. Three before break, three after break') but eventually orients to L's apparent right to be so imposing as in L07, F1 exclaims 'don't be rotten' (arguably 'don't be rotten' can be interpreted as 'please do not abuse your right to impose your will'). While it is entirely possible that F1 and L are of equal rank, it is more likely that L is a lecturer and F1 a (female) student. This is indeed the case and L's turn in lines 18–19 functions not only as a personal challenge of F1's assumptions, but also as a way of making a pedagogic point about unbiased data collection.

REFERENCES

Bell, A. (1997) 'Language style as audience design', in A. Jaworski and N. Coupland (eds) *The Discourse Reader*, London: Routledge.

Chambers, J.K. and Trudgill, P. (1980) *Dialectology*, Cambridge: Cambridge University Press.

Clark, H.H. (1992) *Arenas of Language Use*, Chicago: University of Chicago Press and Stanford, CA: Center for the Study of Language and Information.

Clark, H.H. and Schaefer, E.F. (1987) 'Concealing one's meaning from overhearers', *Journal of Memory and Language*, 26: 209–225; and also in H.H. Clark (1992) *Arenas of Language Use*, Chicago: University of Chicago Press and Stanford, CA: Center for the Study of Language and Information.

Coates, J. (1993) *Women, Men and Language*, 2nd edn, Harlow: Longman.

Coupland, N. and Jaworski, A. (eds) (1997) *Sociolinguistics: A Reader and Coursebook*, Basingstoke: Palgrave.

Fishman, P.M. (1997) 'Interaction: the work women do', in N. Coupland and A. Jaworski (eds) *Sociolinguistics: A Reader and Coursebook*, Basingstoke: Palgrave.

Foulkes, P. and Docherty, G. (eds) (1999) *Urban Voices: Accent Studies in the British Isles*, London: Arnold.

Freeborn, D. with French, P. and Langford, D. (1993) *Varieties of English: An Introduction to the Study of Language*, 2nd edn, Basingstoke: Macmillan.

Harris, S. (1995) 'Pragmatics and power', *Journal of Pragmatics*, 23: 117–135.

Holmes, J. (2001) *An Introduction to Sociolinguistics*, 2nd edn, London: Longman.

Hudson, R.A. (1996) *Sociolinguistics*, 2nd edn, Cambridge: Cambridge University Press.

Hughes, A. and Trudgill, P. (1996) *English Accents and Dialects: An Introduction to Social and Regional Varieties of English in the British Isles*, 3rd edn, London: Arnold.

Jaworksi, A., Lawson, S. and Ylänne-McEwan, V. (2004) ' "Hei hello ... lovely Finnish wooden souveniers kivoja lahjaideoita": negotiating communication rights in tourist–host interaction', paper presented at Sociolinguistics Symposium 15, Newcastle, 3 April 2004.

Labov, W. (1972a) *Language in the Inner City*, Philadelphia, PA: University of Pennsylvania Press.

Labov, W. (1972b) *Sociolinguistic Patterns*, Philadelphia, PA: University of Pennsylvania Press.

Labov, W. (1997) 'Linguistics and sociolinguistics', in N. Coupland and A. Jaworski (eds) *Sociolinguistics: A Reader and Coursebook*, Basingstoke: Palgrave.

Labov, W. (1999) 'The transformation of experience in narrative', in A. Jaworski and N. Coupland (eds) *The Discourse Reader*, London: Routledge.

Le Page, R.B. and Tabouret-Keller, A. (1985) *Acts of Identity: Creole-Based Approaches to Language and Ethnicity*, Cambridge: Cambridge University Press.

Mathisen, A.G. (1999) 'Sandwell, West Midlands: ambiguous perspectives on gender patterns and models of change', in P. Foulkes and G. Docherty (eds) *Urban Voices: Accent Studies in the British Isles*, London: Arnold.

Montgomery, M. (1995) *An Introduction to Language and Society*, 2nd edn, London: Routledge.

Orton, H. (1962) *Survey of English Dialects: Introduction*, Leeds: E.J. Arnold.

Paulston, C.B. and Tucker, G.R. (eds) (2003) *Sociolinguistics: The Essential Readings*, Oxford: Blackwell.

Schober, M.F. and Clark, H.H. (1989) 'Understanding by addressees and overhearers', *Cognitive Psychology*, 21: 211–232; and also in H.H. Clark (1992) *Arenas of Language Use*, Chicago: University of Chicago Press and Stanford, CA: Center for the Study of Language and Information.

Stockwell, P. (2002) *Sociolinguistics: A Resource Book for Students*, London: Routledge.

Stoddart, J., Upton, C. and Widdowson, J.D.A. (1999) 'Sheffield dialect in the 1990s: revisiting the concept of NORMs', in P. Foulkes and G. Docherty (eds) (1999) *Urban Voices: Accent Studies in the British Isles*, London: Arnold.

Stubbs, M. (1983) *Discourse Analysis: The Sociolinguistic Analysis of Natural Language*, Oxford: Blackwell.

Thomas, L. and Wareing, S. (1999) *Language, Society and Power: An Introduction*, London: Routledge.

Trudgill, P. (1972) 'Sex, covert prestige and linguistic change in the urban British English of Norwich', *Language in Society*, 1: 179–195.

Trudgill, P. (1974) *The Social Differentiation of English in Norwich*, Cambridge: Cambridge University Press.

Trudgill, P. (1995) *Sociolinguistics*, revised edn, Harmondsworth: Penguin.

Wardhaugh, R. (2001) *An Introduction to Sociolinguistics*, 4th edn, Oxford: Blackwell.

Wells, J.C. (1982) *Accents of English*, 3 vols, Cambridge: Cambridge University Press.

NOTES

1 In the final three examples, the variant pronunciations are arguably using stress location to make a very subtle semantic distinction between whether or not the lexical items in question are **compound words** (➤ Unit 5), and therefore perhaps even these examples are not truly indicative of accent alone.

2 'Text' is a cover term for representations of both written and spoken language data (➤ Unit 7).

3 It is usual to employ some coding system in extracts to index the source of the data.

4 Thanks to Teah Bennett for allowing the use of this data.

5 Adam Jaworski has kindly allowed the use of this data. It comes from a paper jointly authored by Adam Jaworski, Sarah Lawson and Virpi Ylänne-McEwan presented at Sociolinguistics Symposium 15, Newcastle, 3 April 2004.

6 The source of this data is Andrew Merrison's, but it was transcribed by Lucy Carey as part of her final year sociolinguistics project.

7 None of the authors was ever under any illusion that it would make them rich!

10 CHILD LANGUAGE ACQUISITION

UNIT CONTENTS

INTRODUCTION

Closed doors can be frustrating for toddlers. An adult might offer help by saying 'Shall I open the door?' or '(Do you) want me to open the door?'. A young child, registering mainly the final word *door*, could think that *door* means something like 'do it'. This is a guess to try to explain how a girl aged 22½ months came to use the word *door* to ask an adult to unscrew the nuts on a construction toy, as in Example (1); R identifies the child, Ad the adult.

(1)   Ad: Those go on there. (Ad is screwing on two big nuts.)
      R: Please. (R's gestures indicate that she wants the nuts off.)
      R: Door, door.
      Ad: Now just wait and see a minute and I think you'll like it.
            (Ad persists in screwing the nuts on.)
      R: Door, door.
      R: Door, door please.

(Griffiths and Atkinson 1978: 313)

R was one of seven young children being recorded by researchers in weekly visits to their separate homes. Three of the children fairly often used *door* in comparable ways: to ask for the removal of lids, for help with extricating a pencil from a shirt sleeve, trying to persuade the research team to disconnect the cable from a microphone, requesting that a doll's shoe and its dress be taken off, to get assistance in pressing a bung into a hole in the base of a toy telephone, etc.

Children acquire their first **language** by intuitive analysis of instances of the language that they have heard being used in **context**. *Door* must have come from hearing people say it. The parents of each of the three children had earlier reported that their child was saying the word *door* in connection with doors. The parents perhaps thought, when their child said *door* to ask for help with opening a door, that the child was referring to the door that should be opened. But it seems probable that, around the age of two years, these children treated *door* as a general-purpose request for action.

The other four children studied on the same project used different words (*out*, *open* and *shut*, also adopted from people they had heard talking) to make a similar range of requests for action. We could say that *door* was being used as a **verb**, instead of the **noun** that it is in adult English. However, the label *verb* belongs to **syntax** (➤ Unit 7) – a verb is a part of a sentence – and, at this phase in the children's development, *door* and the other words being discussed here were usually used by themselves, not as parts of sentences. The conveyed meaning '(You) do it' is more like the meaning of a simple sentence than of a word. *Holophrase* is the technical term for an **utterance** that packs in the meaning of a whole sentence, but has as its spoken form only one word. That the children had actively used their brains to arrive at holophrase uses of *door, out, shut,* etc. is indicated by these words not simply having been taken over with the meanings that they have in the adult language. Language acquisition involves more than mimicry.

There are intellectual challenges for children in making sense of the organization of their first language and complicated skills have to be learnt to achieve fluency. First language acquisition is not a matter, however, of assembling all the separate items and skills and only then utilizing them. Instead, children launch themselves into **communication** very early and put together the vessel (language) as they go.

Infants show signs of understanding language in rudimentary ways from as young as six months old. Leopold (1939: 20) noted in a very detailed diary report that his daughter, shortly before the age of seven months, would usually turn expectantly towards anyone speaking her name, *Hildegard*. Starting at age nine months, another expression, *peek-a-boo*, was a cue for Hildegard to hide behind a blanket (1939: 118). In descriptions of child language there are many other accounts of children reacting similarly, i.e. showing basic recognition of particular words and phrases during the second half of the first year.

When children produce their first recognizable words, at around one year old, these are employed communicatively. For example, a precocious nine-month-old boy was reported as using [bø][1] to convey 'I want my ball' (Halliday 1975). The pronunciation is only approximately like *ball*, and it is a holophrase rather than a sentence.

Communication is possible from early on, with infants starting to use utterances to convey their wants and emotions and beginning to understand what other people say. One circumstance making this possible is that first language learning takes place in social interaction, with child and adult generally sharing the same focus of attention at the time of utterance, thanks to being sensitive to each other's gaze and pointing (Clark 2003: 138–9). Also, children use gestures communicatively before they communicate verbally, for instance requesting things with an open handed reach, or indicating refusal by a turning away of the head (Zinober and Martlew 1985). Some early language learning thus involves discovering how to translate into speech what can already be signalled with gesture.

Written language is generally learnt during the school years and **vocabulary** learning goes on throughout life, but children's preschool years are ones where a great deal of knowledge of language is acquired, as they develop their own language comprehension and production systems, then extend and refine them in use. What children have to acquire to become language users includes the following:

- lots of words, with their meanings (**semantics** ➻ Unit 6)
- patterns for putting **morphemes** together to make complex words (➻ Unit 5)
- the pronunciation system (**phonology** ➻ **Unit 8)**
- **grammar**, for linking words into **phrases**, **clauses** and sentences (syntax ➻ Unit 7) – for the purpose of encoding meanings (semantics again ➻ Unit 6)
- strategies and conventions on how to use language, e.g. how to be polite, how to be rude, how to get your own way, how to speak indirectly (and understand other people's indirectness), what it is appropriate to talk about in a range of different settings (**pragmatics** ➻ Units 3 and 4)
- the skills needed for rapid decoding and fluency in the assembly of utterances (➻ Unit 11).

Young children do not develop these separately. The different kinds of knowledge and skill have to be used together in conversations that they participate in from some point in their first year onwards. But, for clarity of presentation, the overview of children's first language development that makes up the rest of this unit is divided into sections dealing successively with semantics, phonology, syntax and pragmatics.

There isn't room for a comprehensive description, so an upper age limit of about two and a half years has been set on the period to be discussed. Arguably it is in this period that children become users of language in the characteristically human sense defined in Unit 1, with much of later development consisting of adding more items and structures to the framework rather than altering the overall scheme.

The sheer size and complexity of any language makes it interesting to investigate how children gain control of one. Because language is a human speciality, studying its acquisition also offers clues to human nature. Child language research is relevant to the work of speech and language therapists too, and has been a major source of ideas for language teaching.

This unit does not aim to cover theories of first language acquisition. See the book's website (www.routledge.com/textbooks/0415291798) for an overview of theoretical approaches to explaining first language acquisition. Here a broad sample of the ideas and findings that make the investigation of young children's language acquisition a fascinating subject is going to be introduced.

WORDS AND THEIR MEANINGS

 ## Activity 10.1 o—π

Recordings of children talking can suggest ideas about their developing competence. Here is a single child's turn from a conversation and a note about one aspect of the child's vocabulary.

> J aged 2;1.18[2] said as he looked at and handled a toy plastic elephant that had been passed to him:

> A cow, sheep, another cow.

> Weekly recordings over the preceding three months and weekly vocabulary questionnaire responses by his mother indicated that J had produced some 19 different animal terms by the time he was 2;1.18 (*cow* and *sheep* were two of them), but it would be a few more weeks before he spontaneously said *elephant*.

> (data from Griffiths 1986)

1 How would you describe J's utterance, above? What does he seem to be trying to do?
2 Does his utterance suggest anything about his mental filing system for English word meanings?
3 Any guesses about the features of the toy that influenced his choice of label for it?
4 Consider the grammatical words, *a* and *another*. J didn't just say 'Cow, sheep, cow'. Comment briefly on what the utterance perhaps indicates about his knowledge of grammar and pragmatics.

How many words?

Figure 10.1 summarizes the start that young children make on the task of learning the thousands of words they will have by adulthood. It is based on vocabulary research done for the MacArthur Communicative Development Inventory (or CDI; see Fenson *et al.* 1993, Dale and Fenson 1996). This large North American sample comprised substantial numbers of children representing each month over the age range 8–30 months. Their carers were asked to study lists of words that young children might know and to mark each word that their child had been heard to say. On the 'Infant' form of the CDI, used for the age range 8–16 months, carers were

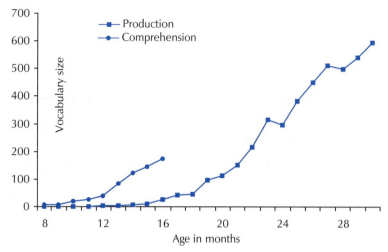

Figure 10.1   CDI median numbers of words reported in the production and comprehension vocabularies of children aged 8–30 months, a different group of children for each month (based on Dale and Fenson, 1996 CDI website data)

also asked to indicate the words their child understood. The CDI does not tap information about comprehension in children older than 16 months.

The graphs in Figure 10.1 reflect the numbers of words that at least half of the children at each age were reported as knowing (their median vocabulary scores).

The graph lines for production and comprehension over the age range 8–16 months reflect figures from the Infant form of the CDI. The part of the graph covering production from 16–30 months is based on the Toddler CDI, a separate questionnaire for the older age range. An average value for age 16 months has been used to join the two sets of production results into a single line here.

It looks as if vocabulary declines at 24 months and 28 months, but these falls in the graph line are probably just accidents of sampling, not developmental trends. Remember that results for each month are based on data from different groups of children.

An adult who is there for most of a young child's waking hours is a good source of information about which words the child knows. Another strength of the CDI vocabulary figures is that they are based on hundreds of children. Large samples are feasible because the CDI is an indirect method of estimating children's vocabulary: the information is collected by asking an adult to work through a checklist of words, which can even be sent out by mail.

It takes much longer to gather the information directly by making hours of recordings of individual children and then extracting lists of words known from transcripts of the recordings; so direct methods are generally applied to only small samples of children. Comprehension testing takes even longer, though it can be done. For instance, Harris *et al.* (1995) systematically tested comprehension of words by six children up to the age of two years, as well as cataloguing the words that they produced. Getting vocabulary information from working directly with children provides details that checklists might not (for example, the surprising uses of *door* mentioned earlier). But of course, recordings at intervals can miss words that the child happens not to say while the microphone is on.

Two potential problems with checklist data should be noted:

1   Though checklists offer spaces for writing in words not listed, there is a strong chance of such words not being reported, leading to underestimates of children's vocabularies.

2   Some parents might have a tendency – an unconscious one, perhaps – to over-report what their child can do.

If these tendencies are equally strong, then they will cancel out, but there is no certainty that one of them does not outweigh the other, and imbalances could easily be different for different children and at different points in a given child's development.

Recognizing that the numbers could be over- or under-estimates, Figure 10.1 nonetheless illustrates some important general points about vocabulary growth:

- comprehension begins earlier than production
- comprehension vocabulary increases faster than production vocabulary, up to age 16 months at least
- the age for speaking the first recognizable 'word' or two is about 12 months
- there is an acceleration, somewhere between 15 and 20 months, in the rate at which new words are acquired in production: an almost flat slope to 15 months turns into one that rises more steeply.

The last-mentioned of these features is called the word spurt: within a few months of age 1;6[3] a noticeable increase occurs in the rate of acquisition of new words. It is also around age 1;6 that many children produce their first sentences, initially only two words in length.

There are competing suggestions as to why there should be a word spurt. Goldfield and Reznick (1996) propose that a spurt occurs because children who have accumulated a 'critical mass' of words – possibly around 50 words – will have enough data to find patterns in word meanings, to mentally connect words known in production with ones comprehended and to become more efficient word learners.

Anisfeld *et al.* (1998) offer a different interpretation. Citing a tendency in their data for initial steps towards sentence-making to appear a short time before each child's vocabulary spurt, they argue that starting to put words together for the more explicit expression of meaning – i.e. the onset of syntax – generates a demand for more words and this might prompt the spurt. They also suggest that increasing knowledge of grammar facilitates the spurt by guiding children in the learning of word meanings.

There are enough similarities among children acquiring a given language – and even across the acquisition of different first languages – for child language acquisition to be a coherent field of study where general principles can be found. But it is important to be aware that there are also differences between children as to how rapidly their language develops, and perhaps even about the paths they follow to proficiency.

A notable instance of a difference in rate of acquisition is reported by Anisfeld *et al.* (1998): Debbie, one of the five children whose vocabulary growth they logged, was exceptional in her acquisition of new words. The number of different words recorded from her in weekly observation sessions between 1;2.0 and 1;9.11 was 849. If additional words noted in a diary kept by her mother are included, then Debbie's vocabulary total by age 1;9.11 was a staggering 1,382 words. This would be well off the scale in Figure 10.1. Have a look at where it would have to be plotted.

Working out word meanings

 Activity 10.2 o—т

Child R's parents reported that she had learnt the word *shoe* for her own shoes. In a one-hour recording session when she was 1;7.4, R spontaneously said 'shoe' in each of the following circumstances:
1   as she pointed at the shoes being worn by a doll
2   as she picked up one of the doll's shoes
3   as she handed one of the doll's shoes to an adult
4   when an adult was putting a shoe on the doll (3 different times)
5   as she put a sock on the doll
6   as she passed the doll's second arm to an adult who had just refitted the first (the arms having become detached)
7   as she handled her teddy bear's shoeless feet

(data first presented in Griffiths 1986)

In what ways did R's word *shoe* have a similar meaning to the adult English word *shoe* and in what ways did it apparently differ in meaning? In (7) was R using the word *shoe* to label the bear's feet, or can you suggest anything different that she might have been trying to communicate?

Grammar is going to be discussed later, but note that part of the difficulty over deciding what R meant when she felt her teddy bear's feet and said *shoe* is that a holophrase lacks the grammatical pointers needed to signal **reference** with more precision.

Shape might have been a relevant link across some items in R's *shoe* category. Similarity in shape perhaps led Child J (Activity 10.1) to consider classifying an elephant either with the animals that he called *cow* or into his *sheep* category. Landau *et al.* (1988) drew attention to a bias – a tendency – that young children seem to have for using shape as the link holding together items in the categories denoted by their words. Bloom (2001: 172–3) points out that the shape of an object is often a good clue to the object's function, i.e. what it can do.

Various other biases have been proposed as explanations for the rapid success of young children's word learning. For instance, from the beginning of vocabulary learning, infants seem to have a whole-object bias: a strong – and evidently useful – inclination, when adults use a new word in connection with a physical object, to understand the word as denoting the whole object rather than one of its parts or its size, colour, etc. (Bloom 2002: 97–105).

Markman and Wachtel (1988) suggested that young children operate with a mutual exclusivity bias: a tendency to avoid having more than one label for anything. If word meanings were rigorously constrained by mutual exclusivity, then *puppies* could not also be *dogs*. Of course they are: puppies are a subset of dogs. There is also obviously overlap between the categories denoted by the words *pet*, *dogs* and *puppies*. Nonetheless, it could be a helpful simplification for children in their earliest years if all pairs of words were treated like *cat* and *dog*, with no shared members. An experiment by Merriman and Stevenson (1997) showed that two-year-olds, at least some of the time, appear to have a mutual exclusivity bias. However, as they grow older, children have to relax the constraint and allow overlap in some cases. Au and Glusman (1990) found that four-year-olds were prepared to accept more than one label for a given thing.

There are three possibilities about the source of such biases, if they indeed exist to steer children towards humanly reasonable meanings for their words. They might be:

■ part of the general intelligence of infants (Bloom 2001)
■ built up during the laborious learning of the child's first batch of words, i.e. a matter of learning how to learn (probably the position of Goldfield and Reznick 1996)
■ part of the potential for language that humans are born with.

At present there is no conclusive evidence for choosing between the three positions, and it may be that two or all three of them operate together to produce the biases.

Gentner and Boroditsky (2001) accept that for some kinds of words (especially nouns denoting people, animals and separable objects) infants already have the meanings and merely need to discover the associated labels. This would offer a cognitive explanation for the whole-object bias. The idea is that having a human brain and intact sense receptors simply makes it obvious that domestic cats, for instance, are in a class of their own, not to be confused with mats that they might sit on, nor with anything else. Children who have domestic experience of cats will form a category of them at an early age and later discover the label provided by their language: *cat* in English, *neko* if they are growing up as speakers of Japanese, etc. But Gentner and Boroditsky argue that other kinds of words are more language-dependent, making it necessary for children to be guided by the language itself into an understanding of the meanings. A case of this kind is discussed next.

Bowerman and Choi (2001) analysed differences between Korean and English ways of talking about spatial relations and how children's understanding of these develops between one and three years. The contrast between *on* and *in* seems obvious and important to speakers of English, but the Korean language prioritizes different distinctions, notably between 'interlocking, tight-fitting' (*kkita*) relationships and ones where the things are only loosely together (*nehta*, *nohta*). Table 10.1 illustrates these differences.

Instances that English encodes with *on* are split between two different expressions in Korean: *kkita* for the tight fit of a pen's top, but *nohta* when a surface supports something. The bottom row in the table shows how English 'in' relationships are similarly split across two Korean expressions.

Table 10.1   Different spatial distinctions in English and Korean (Bowerman and Choi 2001)

	Korean		
	kkita[a]	*nehta*[b]	*nohta*[c]
English			
put on	the top on to a pen		a cup on to a table
put in	a cassette into its case	an apple into a bowl	

a *kkita* encodes interlocking, tight-fitting relationships between objects

b, c *nehta* and *nohta* encode loose-fitting relationships

Bowerman and Choi tested 30 children, aged 18–23 months, acquiring Korean or English, for comprehension of *kkita* and *put in*, respectively. While listening to a tape-recorded voice uttering one of the expressions, the children viewed two video displays, presented side-by-side. This arrangement allows comprehension testing of children as young as 18 months old: they tend to gaze more at the video clip that is a better match for what the voice is saying. Sometimes one of the videos showed an object going into tight-fitting containment, equally well described by either *kkita* or *put in*. In other trials, one clip illustrated loose containment (e.g. an apple being put into a bowl, which matches *put in* but not *kkita*), while the competing clip showed tight-fitting attachment (e.g. the cap being put on to a pen, matching *kkita* but not *put in*); i.e. different video screens displayed the 'right answers' for English and Korean.

In their spontaneous speech the majority of the children were not yet using the tested words, but their gaze preferences indicated comprehension in accord with the language being learnt: 'English learners know that "containment" is relevant for *in* but "tight fit" is not, while Korean learners know that "tight fit" is relevant for *kkita* but "containment" is not' (Bowerman and Choi 2001: 496). Already at this early age, the children's understanding of spatial words was apparently being influenced by the particular language they were growing up with.

PHONOLOGY

Young children's pronunciations can be unintelligible, as when a child aged 1;0 said [ᵐbõ] *pen* (an example to be discussed later). Are childish pronunciations attributable to articulation difficulties or to mishearing of the targets?

Hearing the important contrasts

Languages differ over which pronunciation differences matter for distinguishing words and which can be ignored (➻ Unit 1). For instance, Japanese, Fijian and English all require listeners to distinguish between short and long vowels; so a *ship* is something different from a *sheep*, and *pull* must be distinguished from *pool*.[4] But, among these three languages, only in Japanese is there a significant distinction between short and long **consonants**, in many pairs such as [saka] 'slope' and [sakːa] 'writer', [oto] 'noise' and [otːo] 'husband' (the colons after [k] and [t] mark them as long).[5] Consonant length is distinctive in Italian too.

Another example is that English, but not Fijian, contrasts voiceless [θ] with voiced [ð], e.g. in the words *thigh* and *thy*. Yet another illustration is the Hindi distinction between dental and retroflex stops, which sound pretty much the same to most speakers of English. Many more examples could be given.

There are two possibilities regarding how children home in on the phonological contrasts relevant in their language:

- they might start out generally incapable of hearing differences between speech sounds, then learn the ones that their speech community requires
- they might be able to hear all the differences used in any language, then learn to be less sensitive to ones not needed for their language.

A survey of experiments done over the past 30 years indicates that the second possibility is very likely correct:

> These studies showed that up to the age of 8 months, infants can discriminate any consonant contrast including those which have no phonological status [that is including ones that have no distinctive signalling value] in their L1 [= first language]. Between the ages of 10–12 months, however, infants attune to the contrasts of their ambient language so that only those contrasts which are phonologically relevant in their L1 remain highly discriminable.
>
> (Bohn 2000: 7)

According to Bohn's survey, infant perception of **vowel** distinctions narrows down to those of their own language even earlier than this age.

Pronouncing words

Infant pronunciations show that learning to articulate words is a substantial task. In a single half-hour recording, a one-year-old girl said the word *pen* in ten different ways (Ferguson and Farwell 1975), including the three which are shown in (2).

(2)   i. [pʰɪn]   ii. [tʰn̩tʰn̩tʰn̩]   iii. [ᵐbõ]

The target is an adult pronunciation like [pʰɛ̃n] and in (i) the child obviously comes close. Versions (ii) and especially (iii) seem unrecognizable for *pen*, but they both contain a fair number of the necessary ingredients, just somewhat out of sequence (see Table 10.2). That there should be sequencing problems is not surprising, given that we articulate speech at 3–5 syllables per second (➻ Unit 8).

To understand Table 10.2, first read the whole of the left-hand column for a description of the sounds that make up the target word *pen*. Then start again at the top and, following rows across, see in the columns to the right how each target sound was changed in the child's attempts to say the word. The point to notice is that quite a number of **phonetic** features of the target pronunciations are carried across into (ii) and (iii). In both (ii) and (iii), the child has compressed the vowel and final consonant into the same slot, making it a consonant with vowel-like

Table 10.2   The phonetics of *pen* and a one-year-old's attempt to say it (Ferguson and Farwell 1975)

	Target [pʰɛ̃n]	Child's version (ii) [tʰn̩] repeated	Child's version (iii) [ᵐbõ]
1st consonant	voiceless bilabial [pʰ] (raised [ʰ] marks aspiration)	[tʰ] voiceless and aspirated, but anticipates alveolar position of the [n̩]	not voiceless, but [ᵐb] is bilabial; pre-nasalization [ᵐ] anticipates nasalized vowel
Vowel	front, mid-open unrounded vowel (swung dash on [ɛ] marks nasality, anticipating the [n])	no vowel, but little mark under [n] indicates that n has syllabic force, like a vowel	mid-open, but back rounded; has the expected nasality
End consonant	alveolar nasal [n]	present, but in the vowel slot	missing, but the 1st consonant and vowel show nasal traces

syllabic force in (ii), but a vowel with an overlay of the consonant's nasality in (iii). All speech shows anticipations of following sounds (➻ Unit 8), as when a vowel is **nasalized** (to varying degrees) ahead of an upcoming nasal consonant. This child's anticipations are just a little different from some that adults would make, for example when, at the beginning of the word in (ii), she uses the alveolar place of articulation required for the [n] at the end, and when nasality (and voicing) are there from the start of the syllable in (iii).

Adults employ relatively small sets of vowels and consonants to produce all of their speech – not many more than 40 distinctive sounds (**phonemes**) for most varieties of English. But infants' first 'words' are produced as wholes, instead of being assembled from a limited number of vowels and consonants. Near the beginning of this unit a nine-month-old's holophrase [bø] 'I want my ball' was cited. Two other holophrases in the repertoire of this child at the same age were [nã] 'Give me that!' and [gʷɤi] 'I'm sleepy' (Halliday 1975). The child's expression meaning 'Give me that!' consists of the consonant [n] followed by a nasalized vowel, but neither of these sounds occurs in his ways of communicating 'I want my ball' or 'I'm sleepy'. None of the expressions shares sounds with the others. The pronunciation system of a child a few months older will be outlined next to illustrate a different phase in development.

Around 1;3 a child described by Cruttenden (1981) had words that each used only one of just five consonants /b, d, g, m, n/ and a vowel chosen from a small set.[6]

The words consisted either of a consonant followed by a vowel, for example [da], [ga], [dɛ], or of such a consonant-vowel sequence repeated (in technical terms *reduplicated*), e.g. [baba], [dada], [gaga], [mama] and [nunu]. By contrast with this, [bø], [nã] and [gʷɣi] – see previous paragraph – do not appear to be *constructed* according to a pattern. It seems that soon after the age of one year a child has a phonological system for *assembling* pronunciations, rather than just a collection of unanalysed whole pronunciations.

Possible explanations were discussed earlier in this unit for a word spurt around 15–18 months. Another candidate explanation is that the spurt perhaps occurs because it is much easier to store and produce words once a child has an elementary phonological system.

From 15 months, children's phonological systems take at least another two and a half years to develop. It is interesting to see how adult words are modified to fit the developing systems. Three kinds of adaptation have been noted:

- Consonant harmony makes it possible to squeeze words with more than one different consonant into a pattern that is closer to reduplication. The different consonants are produced with the same place of articulation, e.g. *doggy* might be pronounced [gɒgɪ]. Anticipation of velar articulation, as in this case, is very common (➤ Unit 8 on **assimilation**).
- Cluster reduction simply drops some consonants to fit words such as *stripes* [stɹaɪps] into child patterns that do not allow consonants to occur next to each other, e.g. *stripes* is pronounced as [daɪp]. Or a vowel can be inserted between two consonants to break up a cluster, turning *stripes* into [daɪpɪs]. Applying both consonant harmony and cluster reduction, some children pronounce *stripes* as [baɪp], where the bilabial articulation of [p] is anticipated in the first consonant of the word.
- Substitutions by sounds already in the child's system for ones not yet included are common, e.g. [dat] for *that* when the system lacks the fricative consonant needed for the beginning of this word.

Figure 10.2   Stripes

SYNTAX

Syntax – the construction of sentences (➤➤ Unit 7) – enables language users to express meanings with greater precision than can be done with holophrases. Unit 3 explains the difference between sentence types (differentiated from each other grammatically: **declaratives**, **interrogatives** and **imperatives**) and **speech acts** (the conventional uses of utterances: as assertions, questions, requests, orders, promises, etc.). Holophrases are used to perform speech acts (such as requesting and rejecting) but they lack syntax. As well as acquiring syntax, children have to learn the partial correspondences that there are between sentence type and different kinds of speech act.

What do people generally use interrogative sentences (like the one you are reading now) for? Answer: interrogative sentences are normally used for asking questions. However, Halliday (1975: 31–2) reports that around age 1;10 his son used interrogative sentences not as questions (to ask for information), but to *give* information that would be news to the listener (i.e. he was using interrogatives for telling rather than asking):

> for example, if he was building a tower and the tower fell down, he would say to someone who was present and who was taking part with him *The tower fell down*. But to someone who had not been in the room at the time, and for whom the information was new, he would say *Did the tower fall down?*

Halliday's child had learnt a pattern for the construction of interrogatives, but his speech act use of them as assertions was creatively different from what is conventional in English. The point having been made that appropriate uses of sentence structures have to be learnt, the rest of what is said about syntax here will focus more narrowly on how children begin to assemble sentences from parts.

A two-and-a-half-year-old says '*Where's my mummy gone?*'. Being able to put together a sentence like this, requires syntactic knowledge (➤➤ Unit 7) of the following different kinds:

- The 'building blocks' of sentences are syntactic classes of words, such as **nouns** (e.g. *mummy*) and **verbs** (e.g. *gone*).
- Sequences of words are grouped into **phrases** (such as the **noun phrase** *my mummy*).
- Phrases act as units and fulfil various roles in sentences (*my mummy* is **Subject** of the example sentence).
- Some words are inflectionally marked, e.g. *my* (not *I* or *me*) has to be used when the word is a determiner, as in *my mummy*; and the main (**lexical**) **verb**

must be *gone* (not *go* or *went*), because that is the form needed with *has*. (The *'s* on *Where's* is short for the **auxiliary verb** *has*.)

The following is a selection of theoretically interesting milestones in the acquisition of syntax. In practice it can be hard to be sure when an individual child reaches a particular milestone, so the list is an idealization and the bracketed ages are approximate. Milestones 1, 2 and 3 establish the **hierarchy of rank** (words make phrases, or groups, which make clauses, and clauses make sentences ➛ Figure 7.1).

1   (1;6) The first sentences are produced, just two words long.
2   (1;10) Three-word sentences appear and, from now on, grouping of words into phrases can be significant, e.g. *Want my ball* or *My tower fall*, where the underlined words are phrases.
3   (2;0) One clause is now sometimes put into another clause, e.g. *I don't know where's a boat* (from J, the child in Activities 10.1 and 10.3, at age 2;6.20). The clause *where's a boat* is a **Complement** of the verb *know*.
4   (2;3) Two clauses can now be coordinated with *and*, e.g. (from a child aged 3;0.4, Fletcher 1985: 96): 'one is big and one is small'. As much as six months earlier two related clauses may be spoken as a single utterance without a linking conjunction *and*.

Language gains its tremendous communicative power – the possibility of making a sentence to suit any occasion – from features picked out for this list: hierarchical structure (Milestone 2), recursion (Milestone 3; also called **rankshifting** ➛ Unit 7) and coordination (Milestone 4 ➛ Unit 7).

Here are two quotations about early instances of two-word sentences (Milestone 1). They are from a chapter on children's language development in a book by a professor of education. (In the first the child is his son B. The second was spoken by EW, daughter of one of his students.)

> We find B's first two-word sentences, 'Dada gone,' at 1;8½ preceded by the use of 'go' (gone) alone at 1;5¾, spoken when something had disappeared.
>
> (Valentine 1942: 422)

> E.W. at 1;9 (who had often heard herself called a 'good girl'), apparently wishing to express her approbation of something that her father had done, said 'Daddy good girl.' But here 'good girl' is evidently not the expression of two ideas …
>
> (Valentine 1942: 421)

It is reasonable to treat B's sentence as the product of putting two items together because *Dada* had already been used for a year as a holophrase, described by Valentine as a 'father-joy-play cry' (1942: 406) and *gone* for nearly three months. On the other hand EW's *good girl* seems, at 1;9, to have been a single item meaning 'good', making it reasonable to regard her example as also a two-word sentence.

These are typical of children's first sentences. Open-class **content words** (➤➤ Units 5 and 7) are given priority, while closed-class **grammatical words** (➤➤ Unit 7) tend to be absent: B did not use an auxiliary verb *has* (or *is*) ahead of *gone*; EW's sentence omitted *is*. (If *good girl* is thought of as a noun, like *goody-goody* or *saint* – neither quite what is needed for a single noun that simply means 'good person' – then a fully grammatical adult version would need the indefinite article *a* as well as *is*.)

Closed class words and inflections

Instead of the first of the two-word sentences quoted above, a rather older child might have said *Daddy has gone* or *My father has gone*. If Valentine's son aged 1;8½ had said 'My father has gone', then (without more evidence) we would not be able to tell whether it was an imitation of what he had heard someone else say or a rather precocious construction of his own. His omission from 'Dada gone' of words that a proficient speaker would have included, *has* (and perhaps also *my*), strongly suggests that this utterance was constructed out of parts, not memorized as a whole. Young children often do pick up unanalysed wholes from other people, and sometimes things that adults would rather they didn't repeat! Some of their utterances are constructed and some are imitated. Fully grammatical utterances might have been constructed or might have been imitated; ungrammatical utterances are most probably constructed by the child.

Tending to keep the content words while omitting closed-class words and inflections does not necessarily indicate ignorance of grammar. Infants might learn much about grammar through comprehension before they first produce sentences. Perhaps the sheer difficulty of organizing speech output causes them to leave out the grammatical markers (compare this with Broca's **aphasia** ➤➤ Unit 11).

Hyams (1998) argues that it cannot be lack of grammatical knowledge that accounts for the dearth of verb inflections, subject **pronouns** and **determiners** in children's early utterances. She notes that, as well as omitting grammatical items, children also often do produce these in their utterances from the earliest ages. She has evidence too that important grammatical distinctions are honoured in the utterances of young children. For instance, she reports studies showing young French children matching adult French grammar by placing the negation *pas* after

finite verbs (as in *Veux pas lolo* 'I don't want water'), but before infinitive verb forms (as in *Pas manger la poupée* 'The doll doesn't eat').

Against this, however, are results that point to lack of grammatical sophistication in young children. For instance Theakston *et al.* (2002) investigated the learning of *go, going, goes, gone* and *went* by 11 children, over the whole of their third year. In adult English these are a word family (➤ Unit 5), five different inflectional forms (➤ Unit 7) of one verb *go*, but Theakston *et al.* found that they were initially unconnected in the children's systems, tending to be restricted to different meanings, e.g. *goes* was predominantly used to say where something belonged, but the main meaning of *gone* was 'disappeared' and *went* was most often used to talk about movement; *going* was used about equally for movement and future intent. Tomasello (1992) introduced the term *islands* for potentially relatable verb forms that have not yet been linked by the child. The issue of children's early knowledge of grammar is still open.

Some children, for a while, use a general-purpose substitute syllable in place of a range of adult grammatical words. Such syllables, which seem to recognize the need for things in various slots, without the child knowing quite what is required there, have been called *fillers* (Peters 2001). Activity 10.3 focuses on a child who used a schwa vowel [ə] as a filler. Schwa is the usual vowel sound in the first syllable of *about* or the last syllable of *deliver* (➤ Unit 8).

 ## Activity 10.3 ⊙▬ᵀ

Child J, aged 2;6.20, is interacting with an adult (Adt). In brackets to the right of the utterances are numbers identifying eight occurrences of the vowel [ə]. Make the best guesses you can about English words that would fit in place of each of J's schwas. The first schwa appears where an indefinite article *a* could be used, and an adult would most likely pronounce it [ə] too. What about (2–8)?

J: There's ə tooth. (1)
        (referring to a picture of toothpaste in a book)
J: 'S takes ə more. (2)
Adt: Yes. What's this white stuff here?
        (referring to toothpaste in picture)
J: I don't know.
Adt: Oh go on. What is it?
J: This is ə stuff. (3)
J: (J closes book.) That story end.

Adt: Shall we take up a constructional toy now?
(J rummages in the toy box.)
J: (J takes out Chairoplane.) Want ə play this. (4)
Want ə play this. (5) Want ə play this. (6)
Adt: Mm? Alright.
J: (J pushes away brick box offered by Adt.)
I don't want ə play ə this. (7, 8)

(from the project described in Griffiths, Atkinson and Huxley 1974)

The word *some* would fit where schwa (2) occurs. Notice that the previous word, *takes*, ends with [s] and the next one, *more*, begins with [m]. The sequence [səm] is a reasonable pronunciation for the word *some* that could be used here. Perhaps the transcribers who put down on paper what they heard on the tape should have transcribed this utterance as *'S takes some more*, making the utterance look more mature (though what J was getting at with the bit transcribed as *'S* is anybody's guess). When J heard other people say *some more* after a verb that ended in [s] – e.g. *takes*, *gets*, *eats*, *sips* – he would have faced a similar difficulty to that of the transcribers: does [teɪksəmɔ:] split into *take some more*, *takes some more*, *takes a more*, or what? (➔ Unit 8, on connected speech.)

If schwa number (3) also stands for *some*, then it is an immature pronunciation. There is another possibility, however: at this age J might not control the difference between count and non-count nouns (➔ Unit 7). In his system it might be acceptable to use the indefinite article *a* with non-count nouns. In that case, (3) would be an error of syntax – use of *a* when the adult language requires *some* or no article at all. But if this is true, it could be that he was making the same syntactic error in (2), aiming at *a more*, rather than *some more*. It is important for analysts to be open to alternative possibilities. They must also resist the assumption that there is just one 'correct' answer and this goes for *whatever* aspect of language is being analysed.

Why do young children use fillers? Part of the reason is that proficient speakers of English normally pronounce grammatical words without much **stress** (➔ Unit 8). The brief and insubstantial signal must make it harder for children to discern what has been said. Second, recognition of these grammatical words has to be guided by knowledge of syntax. It is from knowing English sentence structure that we can work out that [ə] at the beginning of a noun phrase probably represents the indefinite article *a*, but [ə] after the verb *want* probably represents the marker *to*.

COMMUNICATIVE STYLES

Ervin-Tripp *et al.* (1984) recorded children in family interactions. The researchers themselves often participated in the conversations. One of their findings was that two- and three-year-olds used polite expressions much more often to the researchers than to their parents or to other children.

Platt (1986) reports data from four children between 2;1 and 3;9 growing up as speakers of Samoan. These children generally used the request form *sau* 'come' only to children younger than themselves. This is in accord with a Samoan view that a summons to come should be issued only to persons lower in status than the speaker.

The two observations above are about conventions for using language (➤➤ Unit 4) – something beyond vocabulary, grammar and pronunciation. Such conventions differ between speech communities. In Fiji one is expected to use a specific apology, *Tilou*, when encroaching on other people's space, including passing behind them when they are seated. In Japan, no one at a meal should start eating until the Japanese expression *Itadakimasu* has been said. See Berko Gleason *et al.* (1984) for an interesting account of the acquisition of *please* and *thank you* by English-speaking children.

Speech communities are not uniform and children are not exact replicas of one another. One difference that has been noted, between the ages of one year and about 2;6, is probably the product of both the child's individuality and the style of interaction favoured by the people from whom the child most immediately learns language. The two poles of the distinction have been labelled *expressive* and *referential* (Nelson 1973).

Children with an expressive style operate as if their motto was 'Conversation first!' (Boysson-Bardies 1999: 167). They seem to enjoy interacting with others. Their holophrases can be several syllables long and the **intonation** pattern is more likely to be reliably reproduced than the vowels and consonants. Conversationally versatile expressions seem to be the ones they use most, for example a French child at 16 months had in her repertoire *C'est beau ça* ('That's nice'). This was a holophrase for her, not a sentence constructed out of parts and it was pronounced as [ebotsa] (Boysson-Bardies 1999: 163). Children with an expressive predilection also acquire greetings and the names of quite a range of people from early on.

Children exhibiting a referential preference concentrate first on noun learning. They interact less readily than expressive children and build up a vocabulary of labels for things in the environment. These children's utterances tend to be shorter and less varied than those of expressive children. They apparently pattern their utterances according to a phonological system from a younger age.

No child uses either of these styles exclusively and by the age of two and a half or three years obvious differences, such as the proportion of nouns in the child's vocabulary, have usually disappeared. Nonetheless, they may represent nursery forerunners of later style differences (➥ Unit 9), such as those between conversation and academic discourse, or between speech and writing.

Social and pragmatic development continues well into the school years. Two other important topics belong here, but cannot be surveyed now. One is gender differences in children's ways of talking. Coates (1993) gives a good overview. The other is children's learning of the many speech acts needed for practical communication. See Griffiths (1985) for a start on the description of speech act development.

SUMMARY

Child language acquisition is one of the most impressive achievements of humans, made possible through a combination of the human capacity for language, our general intellectual abilities and interactive practice. Children usually show understanding of language before age one year, which is roughly when they produce their first word. Initial vocabulary growth is slow, but it accelerates and they soon have hundreds of words. There is much that children have to learn about word meanings, and some of this learning is guided by the child's developing grasp of the language itself. Infants under one year old can hear more sound distinctions than they need, but producing speech is a complicated skill. The earliest sentences are made around the age of one and a half years. By age two and a half years many children are producing sentences that exhibit hierarchical structure, recursion (of clauses within clauses) and coordination. Conventions for the use of language are another substantial learning task.

FURTHER READING

Clark's *First Language Acquisition* (2003) is an up-to-date, wide-ranging and readable book. Pinker's (1994) *The Language Instinct* is a lively account of language acquisition from an innatist perspective. The linguist Noam Chomsky provided great impetus to first language acquisition studies. His (1986) *Knowledge of Language* is a reasonably accessible statement of his ideas. Bloom (2002) *How Children Learn the Meanings of Words* is a comprehensive treatment of its topic. Karmiloff and Karmiloff-Smith's (2001) *Pathways to Language: From Fetus to Adolescent* is easy to read and strong on research methods. Johnson's contribution to a book called *Methods for Studying Language Production* (edited by Menn and Ratner 2000) is an interesting discussion of issues in the transcription of child language data. A selection of research articles is reprinted with guidance for newcomers in *The Child Language Reader* (Trott *et al.* 2004).

FURTHER ACTIVITY

 ## Activity 10.4

If possible, find a video- or audiotape or written diary account illustrating your own preschool language development. Talk to people who knew you before you turned five. Look through the data carefully trying to see the ways in which it fits with or contradicts what has been said in this unit and other sources. If you cannot locate records about yourself, ask people currently bringing up a preschooler for permission to use some taped or diary material. Of course, if you are yourself caring for an infant or toddler you should be able to make observations directly. If two or more students can get together to discuss each other's data, so much the better.

COMMENTARY ON ACTIVITIES

Activity 10.1

1 J seems to be mulling over what to call the toy elephant.
2 Apparently his vocabulary includes an 'animals section' (of words that belong under the **superordinate** word *animal* ➻ Unit 6).
3 The example perhaps suggests that, when trying to decide how to label something, J gives priority to its shape because – ignoring trunk, tusks and horns as details – there is a general similarity in shape between cows, sheep and elephants. Shape seems more important to him than size, given that he is holding the cow/sheep candidate in his hand. His hesitation between *cow* and *sheep* suggests that an elephant is not a good example, for him, of either of these.
4 As for grammar, the phrase *a cow* is some evidence that J tacitly knows that an indefinite article *a* can be used in front of a singular count noun. In terms of pragmatics, using *a* instead of *the* is appropriate because *a* signals something that has not already been identified and spoken about (➻ Unit 7). His use, in the same turn, of a different phrase also containing the word *cow*, namely *another cow*, suggests that these phrases were constructed rather than retrieved 'prefabricated' from storage: *a cow* was probably not a memorized whole that we could print as *acow*. Many more examples of J's utterances would have to be studied to adequately justify conclusions like these. (The point of this commentary is not to stipulate correct answers that you should have given, but to show how much food for thought there is in even a small sample of child language data.)

Activity 10.2

The meaning of R's word *shoe* matched adult English when she used it to label her own shoes and the shoes of a doll (1–4). As in 10.1, shape seems more important than size. If she was calling the doll's sock *shoe* too, as she seems to have done in (5), then that is a difference from the adult meaning, but understandable: shoes are 'footwear with a sole' and socks are 'footwear without a sole'; a child who has not yet realized what the distinguishing feature is, might treat both simply as 'footwear'. Observation (6) seems much stranger. The connection is perhaps that a 'shoe' (including the kind that adults call *sock*!) can be put on to and taken off a person, or doll. If so, then R's 'shoe' category was possibly based on function (what we do with the thing) rather than shape. The teddy bear's feet (7) do not fit with this suggestion about function, but perhaps R wasn't trying to label the bear's feet. She might have been requesting shoes for the bear. Comprehension testing sometimes helps, but tests have to be devised and applied before the child's meanings for the words have changed. Careful examination of available transcripts can provide relevant evidence too. In the present case we could compare observation (7) with all other instances on record of R making requests, to see whether the utterance on which (7) is based was like her other requests. Adults and children in conversation often check understanding with each other, and examining the details of these 'negotiations over meaning' can be enlightening.

Activity 10.3

Where J's fillers occur, an adult would probably have: (1) indefinite article *a*, (2) *some*, (3) *some*, (4–7) *to* in the sequence *want to* (but the spelling *wanna* is used to represent casual speech precisely because *to* can be reduced to just schwa), (8) *with*.

REFERENCES

Anisfeld, M., Rosenberg, E.S., Hoberman, M.J. and Gasparini, D. (1998) 'Lexical acceleration coincides with the onset of combinatorial speech', *First Language*, 18: 165–84.

Au, T.K. and Glusman, M. (1990) 'The principle of mutual exclusivity in word learning: to honor or not to honor?', *Child Development*, 61: 1474–90.

Berko Gleason, J., Perlmann, R.Y. and Greif, E.B. (1984) 'What's the magic word?', *Discourse Processes*, 7: 493–502.

Bloom, P. (2001) 'Roots of word learning', in M. Bowerman and S.C. Levinson (eds) *Language Acquisition and Conceptual Development*, Cambridge: Cambridge University Press.

Bloom, P. (2002) *How Children Learn the Meanings of Words*, Cambridge, MA: MIT Press.

Bohn, O-S. (2000) 'Linguistic relativity in speech perception: an overview of the influence of language experience on the perception of speech sounds from infancy to adulthood', in S. Niemeyer and R. Dirven (eds) *Evidence for Linguistic Relativity*, Amsterdam: Benjamins.

Bowerman, M. and Choi, S. (2001) 'Shaping meanings for language: universal and language specific in the acquisition of spatial semantic categories', in M. Bowerman and S.C. Levinson (eds) *Language Acquisition and Conceptual Development*, Cambridge: Cambridge University Press.

Boysson-Bardies, B. de (1999) *How Language Comes to Children*, trans. M.B. DeBevoise, Cambridge, MA: MIT Press.

Chomsky, N. (1986) *Knowledge of Language: Its Nature, Origin and Use*, New York: Praeger.

Clark, E.V. (2003) *First Language Acquisition*, Cambridge: Cambridge University Press.

Coates, J. (1993) *Women, Men and Language*, 2nd edn, London: Longman.

Cruttenden, A. (1981) 'Item-learning and system-learning', *Journal of Psycholinguistic Research*, 10: 79–88.

Dale, P.S., and Fenson, L. (1996) 'Lexical development norms for young children', *Behavioral Research Methods, Instruments, and Computers*, 28: 125–7. Online. Available HTTP: <http://www.sci.sdsu.edu/cdi/> (accessed 28 March 2003).

Ervin-Tripp, S., O'Connor, M. and Rosenberg, J. (1984) 'Language and power in the family', in C. Kramarae, M. Schulz and W. O'Barr (eds) *Language and Power*, Beverly Hills, CA: Sage.

Fenson, L., Dale, P.S., Reznick, J.S., Thal, D., Bates, E., Hartung, J.P., Pethick, S. and Reilly, J.S. (1993) *The MacArthur Communicative Development Inventories: User's Guide and Technical Manual*, San Diego, CA: Singular Publishing Group.

Ferguson, C.A. and Farwell, C.B. (1975) 'Words and sounds in early language acquisition', *Language*, 51: 419–39.

Fletcher, P. (1985) *A Child's Learning of English*, Oxford: Blackwell.

Gentner, D. and Boroditsky, L. (2001) 'Individuation, relativity, and early word learning', in M. Bowerman and S.C. Levinson (eds) *Language Acquisition and Conceptual Development*, Cambridge: Cambridge University Press.

Goldfield, B.A. and Reznick, J.S. (1996) 'Why does vocabulary spurt?', in A. Stringfellow, D. Cahana-Amitay, E. Hughes and A. Zukowski (eds) *Proceedings of the 20th Annual Boston University Conference on Language Development*, Somerville, MA: Cascadilla Press.

Griffiths, P. (1985) 'The communicative functions of children's single-word speech', in M. Barrett (ed.) *Children's Single Word Speech*, Chichester: Wiley.

Griffiths, P. (1986) 'Early vocabulary', in P. Fletcher and M. Garman (eds) *Language Acquisition*, 2nd edn, Cambridge: Cambridge University Press.

Griffiths, P. and Atkinson, M. (1978) 'A "door" to verbs', in N. Waterson and C. Snow (eds) *The Development of Communication*, Chichester: Wiley.

Griffiths, P., Atkinson, M. and Huxley, R. (1974) 'Project report', *Journal of Child Language*, 1: 157–8.

Halliday, M.A.K. (1975) *Learning How to Mean: Explanations in the Development of Language*, London: Edward Arnold.

Harris, M., Yeeles, C., Chasin, J. and Oakley, Y. (1995) 'Symmetries and asymmetries in early lexical comprehension and production', *Journal of Child Language*, 22: 1–18.

Hyams, N. (1998) 'Underspecification and modularity in early syntax: a formalist perspective on language acquisition', in M. Darnell, E. Moravcsik, F. Newmeyer, M. Noonan and K. Wheatley (eds) *Functionalism and Formalism in Linguistics, Volume 1 General Papers*, Amsterdam: John Benjamins.

Johnson, C.E. (2000) 'What you see is what you get: the importance of transcription for interpreting children's morphosyntactic development', in L. Menn and N.B. Ratner (eds) *Methods for Studying Language Production*, Mahwah, NJ: Lawrence Erlbaum Associates.

Karmiloff, K. and Karmiloff-Smith, A. (2001) *Pathways to Language: From Fetus to Adolescent*, Cambridge, MA: Harvard University Press.

Ladefoged, P. and Maddieson, I. (1996) *The Sounds of the World's Languages*, Oxford: Blackwell.

Landau, B., Smith, L.B. and Jones, S. (1988) 'The importance of shape in early lexical learning', *Cognitive Development*, 3: 299–321.

Leopold, W.F. (1939) *Speech Development of a Bilingual Child: A Linguist's Record, Volume 1*, Evanston, Il.: Northwestern University Press.

Markman, E.M. and Wachtel, G.F. (1988) 'Children's use of mutual exclusivity to constrain the meanings of words', *Cognitive Psychology*, 20: 121–57.

Merriman, W. and Stevenson, C. (1997) 'Restricting a familiar name in response to learning a new one: evidence for the mutual exclusivity bias in young two-year-olds', *Child Development*, 68: 211–28.

Nelson, K. (1973) *Structure and Strategy in Learning to Talk*, Monographs of the Society for Research in Child Development, 38 (Serial No. 149).

Peters, A.M. (2001) 'Filler syllables: what is their status in emerging grammar?', *Journal of Child Language*, 28: 229–42.

Pinker, S. (1994) *The Language Instinct: The New Science of Language and Mind*, New York: HarperCollins.

Platt, M. (1986) 'Social norms and lexical acquisition: a study of deictic verbs in Samoan child language', in B.B. Schieffelin and E. Ochs (eds) *Language Socialization across Cultures*, Cambridge: Cambridge University Press.

Theakston, A.L., Lieven, E.V.M., Pine, J.M. and Rowland, C.F. (2002) 'Going, going, gone: the acquisition of the verb "go"', *Journal of Child Language*, 29: 783–811.

Tomasello, M. (1992) *First Verbs: A Case Study of Early Grammatical Development*, Cambridge: Cambridge University Press.

Trott, K., Dobbinson, S. and Griffiths, P. (2004) *The Child Language Reader*, London: Routledge.

Valentine, C.W. (1942) *The Psychology of Early Childhood: A Study of Mental Development in the First Years of Life*, London: Methuen.

Zinober, B. and Martlew, M. (1985) 'The development of communicative gestures', in M. Barrett (ed.) *Children's Single-Word Speech*, Chichester: Wiley.

NOTES

1 For help with the phonetic symbols given in square brackets ➻ Unit 8 and p. 492 for the International Phonetic Alphabet chart.

2 In child language studies, young children's ages are conventionally given in the format *years;months.days* (e.g. 2;1.18 stands for 2 years 1 month and 18 days) or just *years;months* (e.g. 1;6 represents the age 1 year 6 months).

3 See Note 2.

4 Length is not the only difference between 'short' and 'long' vowels in English.

5 When Japanese is written in the Western alphabet, long consonants are represented by writing two of them together, e.g. *sakka* 'writer' and *otto* 'husband'. But *kk* or *tt* is spoken with a single long closure, not as a sequence of two consonants (see Ladefoged and Maddieson 1996: 92). In phonetic transcription, a colon (:) is used as a length marker.

6 The child's system was less tidy than stated in the text. A small number of words that do not quite fit the pattern have been ignored, simply because it would take too long to deal with them.

11 PSYCHOLINGUISTICS

UNIT CONTENTS

- Introduction
- Brain and language
- Lexical knowledge
- Memory and language
- Language processing: receptive skills
- Language processing: building meaning
- Language processing: productive skills
- Language disability
- Summary
- Further reading
- Further activity
- Commentary on activities
- References

INTRODUCTION

You are sitting in an airport lounge when a string of sounds reaches your ear. You automatically distinguish them from musak, from the air conditioning, from the sound of a plane landing. They are in an entirely different category, one which human beings label speech. You respond to the string of sounds by getting up and walking towards Gate number 6, where your flight to Cairo is waiting. Looking around you, you see that other passengers are behaving likewise.

An extremely complex operation has occurred, but one that we take for granted. Physically speaking, what reached your ear was simply a series of sounds, differentiated in terms of frequency and intensity but not of themselves meaningful. (Consider what would happen if you did not know the language of the announcement.) It is *your mind* which matches the sounds with those of the ambient language, breaks the string into **words** (➜ Unit 5), retrieves meanings for those words (➜ Unit 6), unravels the **syntax** that holds them together (➜ Unit 7) and relates the whole to a stored knowledge of what to expect of a flight announcement (➜ Unit 3). What is more, the same process is going on in the minds of your fellow passengers who interpret the string of sounds in similar ways.

Psycholinguistics is the study of this relationship between language and the mind. It tackles at least six huge areas of vital importance to an understanding of what language is.

- *Language acquisition*: How do children come to acquire their first language? How do adults acquire a second language?
- *Brain and language*: Where is language stored in the brain and how does the brain handle it? Associated with this is discussion of how language evolved and whether it is peculiar to the human race.
- *Lexical knowledge*: How are words stored in the brain and how do we find them when we need them?
- *Memory and language*: What part does memory play in the handling of linguistic input?
- *Language processing*: How do language users apply their knowledge of language when speaking, listening, reading and writing? How do listeners and readers manage to build complex meanings from the strings of words that they encounter?
- *Language difficulties*: What insights can psycholinguists obtain that might assist speech and language therapists (speech and language pathologists) and clinicians? What can we learn about normal processing from cases where language has been disrupted by illness, accident or disability? What are the effects on language development of unusual circumstances in childhood?

This unit aims to dip into all these areas with the exception of the first (➻ Unit 10).

BRAIN AND LANGUAGE

Using a **language** is an extraordinarily complex operation. It is complex in the enormous amount of linguistic information that has to be stored in our minds; and it is complex in the way that a speaker retrieves this information and assembles it into **utterances**. Neuroscientists have studied the human brain closely for evidence of how these processes occur. Today, thanks to sophisticated brain imaging equipment, they can track the electrical currents and blood flow which occur when the brain is engaged in linguistic processes.

The upper part of the human brain consists of two hemispheres, one on the left and one on the right, joined by a dense web of interconnecting nerves. In the late nineteenth century, the neurosurgeon Paul Broca reported that a number of his patients exhibited severe speech problems (**aphasia**) after damage to a small area in the frontal part of the left hemisphere. A few years later, another neurosurgeon, Carl Wernicke, associated aphasia with a rather different area, a little further back (see Figure 11.1).

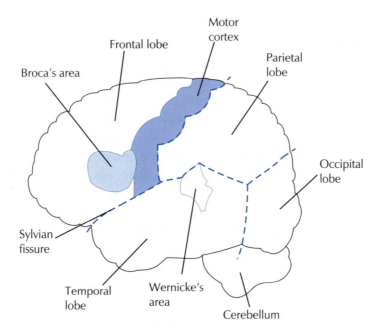

Figure 11.1   The left hemisphere of the human brain

Activity 11.1 ⚊

Here are examples of Broca's aphasia (A) and Wernicke's aphasia (B) (Gardner 1977: 61, 68). What differences do you notice?

A   'Could you tell me, Mr Ford, what you've been doing in the hospital?'
      'Yes, sure. Me go, er, uh, P.T. nine o'cot, speech … two times … read … wr … ripe, er, rike, er, write … practice … get-ting better.'
      'And have you been going home on weekends?'
      'Why, yes … Thursday, er, er, er, no, er Friday … Bar-ba-ra … wife … and, oh, car … drive … purnpike … you know … rest and … TV.'

B   'What brings you to the hospital?' I asked the 72-year-old retired butcher four weeks after his admission to the hospital.
      'Boy, I'm sweating, I'm awful nervous, you know, once in a while I get caught up, I can't mention the tarripoi, a month ago, quite a little, I've done a lot well, I impose a lot, while, on the other hand, you know what I mean, I have to run around, look it over, trebbin and all that sort of stuff.'

Though the two cases above seem quite different linguistically, it is not always so easy to distinguish between types of aphasia. Many aphasic patients show a mixture of symptoms. Furthermore, language is not as localized in the brain as the reports of Broca and Wernicke suggested. Brain imaging technology has shown us that the areas which contribute to language are very widely distributed. What enables us to handle language with such ease is a massive system of interconnections between neurons, which enables information to be transmitted very rapidly across the brain. It may be that the areas identified by Broca and Wernicke are important to speech because they are crossroads for these interconnections.

Broca and Wernicke established that the left hemisphere plays a crucial role in the processing of language; but there is increasing evidence that the right plays a part as well. It would appear that the left hemisphere specializes in rapid small-scale operations (e.g. recognizing **phonemes**) while the right hemisphere handles large-scale units of language (e.g. **intonation** patterns, and discourse structure).

In the 1950s and 1960s, researchers studied patients who had suffered brain damage to the left hemisphere when they were very young (under about five years old). A number of cases were found where the child's language functions appeared to have recovered as a result of relocating to the right hemisphere. It was suggested that there might be a flexible stage early in life during which language had yet to establish itself in either hemisphere. If one were damaged, it would transfer to the other.

The idea that the brain was 'plastic' in early life became associated with a theory that there was a critical period (most commentators suggested up to adolescence) for a human being to acquire a first language. If, for any reason, a child was not exposed to language during this period of its development, it would never achieve complete competence. Evidence for a critical period was sought in cases of wolf children who had grown up in the wild and of attic children who had been neglected by carers and deprived of language.

Activity 11.2 ⚬━┳

Here is an example of the speech of Genie, an American attic child who was rescued at the age of 13 from a life of complete isolation. What do you notice about it?

> Father hit arm. Big wood. Genie cry ... Not spit. Father. ... Father hit big stick. Father is angry. ... Father take piece wood hit. Father make me cry. Father is dead.

(Curtiss 1977: 35)

The limitations of Genie's language appear to support the critical period hypothesis. On the other hand, Genie's language deficit may simply result from the fact that she was badly traumatized by her early experiences or had suffered brain damage. It may be misleading to use these tragic cases in order to make generalizations about normal development.

LEXICAL KNOWLEDGE

Words are the bearers of meaning; and it is by organizing them systematically into larger structures that we convey our messages (➤➤ Units 6 and 7). Small wonder, then, that psycholinguists have shown great interest in how language users store words in their mental dictionary (or **lexicon**), and how they find them when they have need of them.

Lexical storage

It is assumed that we have a separate lexical entry in our lexicon for each word that falls within our vocabulary. But are these entries connected in ways that assist us when we need to find them? One of the longest-established methods used by cognitive psychologists is word association, where the researcher reads a word aloud and the subject reports the first word that comes to mind. Today, this has been replaced by a more sophisticated method based upon an effect known as priming. The principle behind priming is quite simple: it has been demonstrated many times that, if you have recently heard a word such as WINTER you will go on to identify associated words such as *summer* or *snow* more quickly than you would do normally. This is more scientific than word association because it enables experimenters to time the extent by which recognition has speeded up.

 Activity 11.3 o––

The first word in each of the pairs below primes the second. Describe the relationship between them (➔ Unit 6).

   (a) APPLE – orange   (b) BIG – little   (c) FAST – quick
   (d) BIRD – parrot   (e) FISH – chips   (f) TULIP – flower

Another method for establishing how words are stored is to examine what happens when speakers make mistakes. If a speaker produces the word *absolute* when they really want to say *obsolete*, it may tell us something about the information they are using in order to find the word. What do the two words have in common?

 Activity 11.4 o––

Here are examples of some slips of the tongue (Sources: Fromkin 1973; Aitchison 2003). Compare the word that was chosen with the target word. What kinds of cue do the speakers seem to be using when trying to find the word?

   1   He got hot under the belt (= collar)
   2   It's at the bottom – I mean top – of the stack of books
   3   I don't expose anyone will eat that (= expect/suppose)
   4   You can hear the clarinets clicking (= castanets)
   5   white Anglo-Saxon prostitute (= Protestant)
   6   The emperor had several porcupines (= concubines)

So what does this tell us? Importantly, it indicates that we do not seek out words just by the meaning that we want to express but that we also call upon clues as to *form*. The extension of this is that words which share these characteristics must be quite closely linked in some way in the mental store – which is why one gets substituted for another.

We can conclude that, within an individual's lexicon, words are associated with each other both by meaning and by form. But how do these associations operate? Current models of the lexicon represent words as linked by a massive set of *connections*. Sometimes the connections are strong (as they would be between, say, TREE and BRANCH); sometimes they are weaker (TREE and FLOWER). The strength of the connection is shown by the amount of priming (i.e. the extent to which recognition of one word is speeded up by the previous sight or sound of another).

Lexical access

A second issue is how we recognize words when we encounter them. A process known as lexical access involves matching a string of sounds or letters to an entry in the lexicon, and then drawing upon stored information about the word (including its meaning). It may be that several lexical entries somehow fit what we have heard or read; they are said to compete with each other to be selected. So when we hear the sequence *resp-* [ɹɪsp], the result is to trigger competition between RESPONSIBLE, RESPOND, RESPONSE and RESPECT.

Competition is often described in terms of activation. Think of activation as a kind of electric current that is capable of lighting up lexical entries. Where a word is strongly favoured by the incoming evidence, it is brightly lit; where the evidence is less clear, it is only dimly lit. So RESPECT would be strongly activated by hearing the syllable *resp-* while RESIDE or DESPITE would be more weakly activated.

Activity 11.5

You hear the sequence [sɛn]. If the only criterion were how well a lexical entry matches this string of sounds, the words below would all be equally activated as competitors. But are they actually equal? Are some of them more likely to be the target word than others? If so, which ones? Can we explain this in terms of activation?

CENOTAPH – CENSOR – CENSURE – CENSUS – CENTURY – CENTIGRADE – CENTRE – CENTRAL – CENTRIFUGAL – SEND – SENATE – SENNA – SENSE – SENSELESS – SENSIBLE – SENSITIVE – SENSITIZE – SENSOR – SENTENCE – SENTIMENT – SENTRY

MEMORY AND LANGUAGE

In order to process what somebody is saying, we need to hold it in our minds for a brief period. We also need to retain a recollection of what has been said in the conversation so far. So memory clearly plays an important part in language.

But it is important to distinguish between two kinds of memory:

■ working memory, which handles current operations (including incoming messages)
■ long-term memory, a permanent store for world knowledge and also language knowledge.

The present discussion will focus on the first.

Activity 11.6a

Read the words below. Spend about a second on each one, with a view to remembering as many as possible. Do not look back to revise. Close your book and try to write down as many of the words as you can.

| ground | dropped | clothes | through | choose | flower |
| breathe | twelve | scratch | please | friend | string |

1   Make a note of how many words you remembered.
2   Were you aware of using any particular techniques to help you to remember these words?

As long ago as 1956, in the early days of Cognitive Psychology, George Miller published an article entitled 'The magical number seven, plus or minus two'. In it, he used evidence from auditory and visual discrimination to suggest that our working memory is very limited in capacity and may only be able to hold around seven pieces of similar information at a time. We can only conserve information by rehearsing it in our minds and by transferring it to long-term memory.

The idea that working memory is limited in its capacity has been very influential, especially in theories of how readers and listeners handle the input they receive. Some tasks (including some language tasks) stretch working memory beyond its limits. We might find it impossible, for example, to hold a conversation and type a letter at the same time.

Processes that are automatic (done without conscious attention) make minimal demands on working memory. We thus have a vested interest in making many of our everyday mental operations (including those that involve language) as automatic as possible. Consider this in relation to learning and using a foreign language. At first, you might find that you can only assemble grammatically correct sentences by means of a series of slow and painful steps. But, if you make progress in using the language, the different steps gradually become combined into procedures which demand less and less of your attention. You may even get to the point where your use of the language is so automatic that you can no longer remember the original **grammar** rules that you started out with.

 Activity 11.6b o––

Now read the words below. Spend about a second on each one, with a view to remembering as many as possible. Do not look back to revise. Close your book and try to write down as many of the words as you can.

| family | occupy | visible | another | educate | cinema |
| uneasy | holiday | potato | terrify | animal | inhabit |

1   Compare your results with those from Activity 11.6a.
2   What methods did you use to try to remember the words?
3   In written form, these words are similar in length to those in Activity 11.6a. In what way are they different?

It would seem that working memory holds and recycles language in some kind of phonological form – even when the language was originally in written form. This may be one way of preserving the material before transferring it into long-term memory.

LANGUAGE PROCESSING: RECEPTIVE SKILLS

Let us consider reading first. One way of investigating reading has been to study dyslexia. By working out what deficits a dyslexic individual suffers from, psycholinguists can gain insights into the components of the normal reading process.

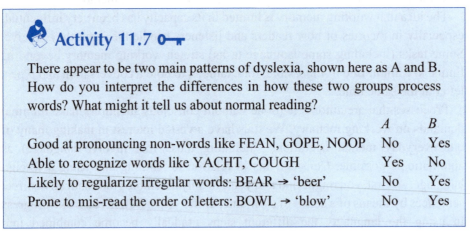

Activity 11.7

There appear to be two main patterns of dyslexia, shown here as A and B. How do you interpret the differences in how these two groups process words? What might it tell us about normal reading?

	A	B
Good at pronouncing non-words like FEAN, GOPE, NOOP	No	Yes
Able to recognize words like YACHT, COUGH	Yes	No
Likely to regularize irregular words: BEAR → 'beer'	No	Yes
Prone to mis-read the order of letters: BOWL → 'blow'	No	Yes

Not everybody agrees with this two-way classification, and indeed many dyslexic people show signs of both types of deficit. But the finding has given rise to a theory that an efficient reader needs two routes when reading. One, the lexical route, enables the reader to recognize whole words. The other, the sub-lexical route, enables the reader to work out how to pronounce unfamiliar names and words that he/she has never before seen in print by applying rules (grapheme–phoneme correspondence rules) which match letters to sounds in a systematic way. The value of the lexical route will be obvious for readers of a language like English with an opaque spelling system (one where there are many inconsistencies in the sound–spelling relationships). But it appears that readers also make use of the lexical route with more regular alphabets, as it is faster.

Let us now consider how we read words when they occur within a text.

Activity 11.8

The text below has been adapted from an Agatha Christie novel, *The Body in the Library*. Read it as quickly as you can.

> Miss Marble's telephone rang when she was dressing. The sound of it faddied her a little. It was an unusual hour for her telephone to ring. So well ordered was her life that that unforeseen telephone calls were a source of vivid conjecture.
>
> 'Dear me', said Miss Marble, surveying the ringing instrument with perplexity. 'I wander who that can be?'
>
> Nine o'clock to nine-thirty was the recognized time for the village to make friendly calls to nieghbours. Plans for the day, invitations and so on were always issued then. The butcher had been known to ring up just before nine if some crisis in in the meat trade had occurred. At intervals during the day, spasmodic calls might occur, though it was considered tarvish to ring up after nine-thrity at night.
>
> (Christie 1959: 9)

1   What do the words *faddied* and *tarvish* mean?
2   Did you notice anything odd about the text? Did it prevent you from understanding the text? If not, why not?

We have seen that readers seem to process at letter level as well as at word level. They seem to look at almost every word, but occasionally skip short words (especially very frequent function words). It is mistakes involving these words that you are most likely to overlook when proofreading an essay.

We have also seen that in reading (and indeed in listening too), two different processes enable us to extract meaning from a text:

- bottom-up processes, based upon what is actually present on the page or in the ear of the hearer. They are called 'bottom-up' because they go from smaller units to bigger – for example, from letters to words to grammatical patterns to meaning.
- top-down processes, where the reader or listener brings in knowledge from outside the text. It is important to distinguish four types of top-down knowledge:
  1 *knowledge of words*, which might enable us to overlook misspellings or unusual pronunciations

2 *knowledge of syntax*, which enables us to impose a pattern on what we read
3 an understanding of the *context in which the words occur*, which might enable us to work out the meaning of unknown words
4 *world knowledge*, which might enrich our overall understanding.

Now let us turn to listening. It is a more difficult process to study than reading, as Activity 11.9 shows.

 Activity 11.9 o━☖

Here is a sentence in written form:

The police have arrested a man.

Look at the same sentence in its spoken form. It is shown in broad **phonetic** transcription (➻➻ Unit 8 and/or IPA chart on p. 492).

[ðə'pliːsəvə'rɛstidə'man]

In what way is processing different for the listener when compared to the reader?

Any theory of the listening process also has to account for the fact that the sounds (or phonemes ➻➻ Unit 8) in a given language take many different forms. You can test this by saying the words KILL and CUT. Notice the different positions adopted by your tongue when you make the /k/ sound at the beginning of each of these words. This is because the place of articulation of the /k/ anticipates the vowel that comes next. If both of these sounds are recognized as 'k', it is *thanks to the mind of the listener*, which classifies them as variants of the same phoneme.

In point of fact, phonemes vary so much that some psycholinguists have suggested that we may not actually divide speech into sounds like /k/ or /ɪ/. Some have suggested a smaller unit of analysis, based upon the acoustic features that go to make up a particular sound. Others have suggested that perhaps we process language in syllables because syllables are much more constant in form than phonemes.

Activity 11.10 ⚬━┳

In a well-known experiment, Morais *et al.* (1986) studied two groups of Portuguese subjects. One group was illiterate, and the other had acquired literacy as adults. The researchers read aloud non-words to the two groups and asked them to repeat what they heard, omitting either the first **consonant** or the first syllable. The illiterate group found the task much more difficult than the literate one; they were especially bad at the consonant task. What conclusions do you draw?

LANGUAGE PROCESSING: BUILDING MEANING

The ultimate goal of the listener or reader is to build words into larger meanings. We have already seen how readers can use world knowledge in order to support inadequate understanding or to compensate for mistakes in a **text**. But world knowledge also enables them to add to the raw meaning that the text provides (➻ Unit 3).

 Activity 11.11 ⚬━┳

This extract comes from the novel, *Regeneration* (Barker 1991). Read it carefully and suggest how adding world knowledge to word meaning helped you to understand what was going on.

> Rivers folded the paper and ran his fingertips along the edge. 'So they're sending him here?' Bryce smiled. 'Oh, I think it's rather more specific than that. They're sending him to *you*.' Rivers got up and walked across to the window. It was a fine day, and many of the patients were in the grounds, watching a game of tennis. He heard the *pok-pok* of rackets, and a cry of frustration as a ball smashed into the net. 'I suppose he is – "shell-shocked"?' 'According to the Board, yes.'

Our knowledge about the world is said to be stored in knowledge structures called *schemas*. A schema for a hospital would include factors such as: beds, doctors, nurses, smell of disinfectant, operating theatre, etc. A special kind of schema called a *script* stores our knowledge of what happens in the kind of ritualistic encounters that make up much of everyday life. A script for getting a taxi might be: stand on kerb, look for a taxi that is free, put out hand, shout 'Taxi!'.

Schemas enable writers and speakers to use a kind of shorthand. They do not need to explain that 'the phone rang – John walked across to it – John picked up the receiver – John spoke'. It is enough for them to say *John answered the phone*. They know that they share with the reader/listener a knowledge of what happens in this particular situation.

Sometimes, the only way we can make full sense of a text is by drawing **inferences** – a process in which schemas and scripts assist us.

 Activity 11.12 ⚬━

Read the following sentences:

The hated employer lay on the floor. A knife lay beside the body.

What do the sentences tell us literally? What are you likely to assume?

 Activity 11.13 ⚬━

Do not look back at Activity 11.11. But try to decide which of these sentences occurred in the text you read.
1   Rivers folded the paper and ran his fingertips along the fold.
2   Rivers got up from his chair and walked across to the window.
3   He looked out at the grounds.
4   It was a fine day, and many of the patients were sitting in the grounds, watching a game of tennis.
5   He heard the *pok-pok* as the balls hit the rackets …
6   and a cry of frustration as a ball smashed into the net.

So readers and listeners extract two kinds of meaning from a piece of language:

■ literal (or propositional) meaning
■ inferred meaning.

They use both of them to build a mental representation of what they have read or heard. They may later find it difficult to say exactly how much information they gained from a text and what they then added to that basic meaning.

LANGUAGE PROCESSING: PRODUCTIVE SKILLS

We now turn to the productive skills of speaking and writing. Spoken and written language differ in form. Here, we are especially concerned with the *circumstances* which give rise to those differences of form:

(a) Speaking is almost always spontaneous, whereas writers have time to plan and polish what they produce.

(b) Speakers can rely on feedback from their listeners, whereas writers have to anticipate problems and revise pieces of text that their readers may not understand.

One way of representing how a piece of speech or writing is assembled is to assume that the speaker/writer takes the relevant language through a number of distinct stages. Let us consider writing first. The writer has to:

- form a set of ideas
- organize the ideas
    - (a) into a logical sequence
    - (b) taking account of what the goal is and who the reader is
- find words to express a particular idea
- store the words in his/her mind
- physically produce the words with a pen or computer.

That might seem like the end of the process, but what is important about writing, as we have seen, is that the writer has time to rethink what has been written. Writing involves constant editing of the text. The editing can take place while writing or after a draft has been written. It may involve changes at any of the levels that we have identified so far – anything from changes in overall planning to changes that correct spelling mistakes.

 Activity 11.14

Below there are two versions of a paragraph on writing systems, written for a non-specialist reader. Version A is the first draft and Version B is the final one. Decide what changes the writer made and why they were made.

Version A

There are three major systems of writing. An alphabetic system is phonological, with letters representing the phonemes of the language. But some alphabetic systems (e.g. the Spanish one) are more transparent than others (e.g. the English). A syllabary is also phonological, though here the unit represented is a syllable rather than a phoneme. The Japanese *kana* script is a syllabary. A logographic system has a character fro each word of the language. An example of such a system is the system used fro writing Chinese.

Version B

The world's languages make use of three major systems of writing. One is logographic, with each character representing a whole word. An example is the system used for writing Chinese. A second system, known as a syllabary, uses a character for each syllable – as, for example, in the Japanese *kana* script. The third system is an alphabetic one in which (in principle at least) there is a letter for each sound of the language. In fact, alphabetic systems vary widely. Some are transparent, with a one-to-one match between a letter and a sound. But in more opaque systems, like the English one, a letter may represent more than one sound or several letters may represent the same sound.

It might appear that speakers have no time to plan ahead like writers. But, given the many choices that are involved in assembling an **utterance**, it is clear that planning must take place – even if it is so rapid and highly automatic that, under normal circumstances, we are virtually unaware of it. It is when we are tired and searching for words that we get some idea of the complexity of what a speaker does.

Here are the planning stages involved in constructing a spoken utterance:

- finding a key word for the utterance – often a verb, say, LIKE
- constructing a syntactic pattern that fits the verb — LIKE — {-*ING*}
- inserting words into the pattern   MY SISTER + LIKE + SWIM + {-*ING*}
- giving the words phonological form [mai+ sɪstə + laɪk + swɪmɪŋ]
- inflecting the verb [laɪk] → [laɪks]
- sending instructions to the articulators (tongue, jaw, lips, etc.).

 Activity 11.15 o—┰

Describe how a speaker might plan the sentence:

John is writing his mother a letter.

So when exactly does planning take place? And how much is planned at a time?

Activity 11.16 ⚿

Examine this piece of connected speech. It is perhaps more regular than some speech because the speaker is a politician and the **context** is a radio interview. Suggest the points at which the speaker's planning is taking place and what the normal unit of planning is. Note that + represents an untimed pause and that capital letters indicate **stress**.

> well there are probably about a million CARS unregistered at the moment + we need to have + far better enFORCEment + we need to take unlicensed cars + SERious because the rest of us er + who pay our licence are basically SUBsidising + people who are not complying with the legal reQUIREments + and [ænd] we effectively need to have a rolling REGister + so we have a registered KEEPer + of each car on the road + and they have to take responsiBILity + for that car
>
> (Field 2003: 34)

Some researchers suggest that there are two types of pause – planning pauses which occur at predictable syntactic boundaries and hesitation pauses which often occur *within* syntactic units. Our politician has few hesitation pauses, which is why he comes across as fluent.

LANGUAGE DISABILITY

The final area for discussion concerns what happens when language goes wrong. There can be developmental language impairment, when a child fails to develop a normal command of spoken or written language, or acquired language impairment, when injury, illness or surgery incapacitates a formerly fluent language user.

Psycholinguists are interested in language impairment for three reasons. First, their insights can assist clinicians and therapists in treating some of these disorders more effectively. Second, as we have already seen with dyslexia and aphasia, when language malfunctions, it can sometimes provide insights into the skills and cognitive processes that are essential to normal operations. Third, the study of developmental impairment may shed light on the extent to which the language faculty is or is not innate in human beings.

Since developmental studies are very much associated with work on first language acquisition (➦ Unit 10), we will examine an example of acquired impairment. One sadly frequent type is the language loss which occurs in old age, and which may be heightened by dementia or by a condition such as Alzheimer's Disease.

 Activity 11.17 ⚬━

In the two extracts below (source: Maxim and Bryan 1994: 190–1), the speakers are describing a picture of a kitchen scene. Extract B is from a man of 74 with Alzheimer's Disease, Extract A from a woman of 76 who does not have Alzheimer's Disease. What differences do you notice? Consider: vocabulary access, syntax and the way the sentences are linked.

A   well the woman is washing up / but the sink is overflowing / and the boy is on the stool / which is collapsing / he's getting cookies out of the jar / and he's going to fall because the stool's collapsing.

B   there's a boy boy there standing on a stool / a lady here / she looks / she's got a / bowl in her hand / (unintelligible) / look like some dishes there or bowls / I don't know which / there / there's a window there / curtains and a window again / I don't know what this is / …oh that's a sink unit with taps on.

Sufferers from Alzheimer's and other types of dementia often find it difficult to locate words (see *I don't know what this is* in B in Activity 11.17). A regression theory hypothesized that the order in which words were lost was the reverse of the order in which those words had originally been acquired but evidence has not supported this view.

A major problem with dementia lies in establishing whether the language impairment is *linguistic* (reflecting damage to the stored systems of grammar and lexis) or *cognitive* (reflecting damage to areas such as memory, attention and problem-solving which support the use of the grammar and the lexicon). It may be that sufferers lose some of their working memory capacity, which means that they can no longer hold as much language in their minds or monitor their own speech.

SUMMARY

This unit has covered the brain and memory, how words are stored and how they are accessed, the productive and receptive skills, the processing of meaning and language loss. Some complex topics such as the processing of grammar have, sadly, had to be omitted.

It is said that studying mathematics is more than mastering formulae; the important thing is to start thinking like a mathematician. By studying the data in this unit and by reflecting on the issues that have been raised, you have, however briefly, thought like a linguist – and, in particular, a psycholinguist.

FURTHER READING

Regrettably few titles offer introductions to psycholinguistics for those with a linguistics background. Altmann's *The Ascent of Babel* (1997) provides an easy-to-read overview of some central issues. Field's *Psycholinguistics: A Resource Book for Students* (2003) covers the essential topics accessibly, and includes exercises and important readings.

On specific topics, Jean Aitchison's books are lively and readable: particularly *The Articulate Mammal* (1998) on the nature of language and language processing and *Words in the Mind* (2003) on lexical storage and access. Obler and Gjerlow's *Language and the Brain* (1999) provides a refreshingly clear introduction.

A comprehensive reference guide to the subject is *Psycholinguistics: The Key Concepts* (Field 2004), which gives non-technical explanations of 350 core issues and ideas.

FURTHER ACTIVITY

 Activity 11.18

Many of us will know the nursery rhyme 'The House that Jack Built'. To remind you, here it is (Enchanted Learning 2004):

> This is the farmer sowing the corn,
> That kept the cock that crowed in the morn,
> That waked the priest all shaven and shorn,
> That married the man all tattered and torn,
> That kissed the maiden all forlorn,
> That milked the cow with the crumpled horn,
> That tossed the dog, that worried the cat,
> That chased the rat, that ate the malt,
> That lay in the house that Jack built.

This verse consists of just one sentence. It should, therefore, not be difficult to understand. However, it does contain many clauses (➤ Unit 7 on **relative clauses**). Nevertheless, comprehensibility is not impaired.

Why then, does comprehensibility become problematic (and at what stage?) when the same information from the last four lines is structured with a different (yet still theoretically possible way of using) English syntax as shown here?

1 The rat the cat chased ate the malt that lay in the house that Jack built.
2 The rat the cat the dog worried chased ate the malt that lay in the house that Jack built.
3 The rat the cat the dog the cow with the crumpled horn tossed bit chased ate the malt that lay in the house that Jack built.

Now consider the following, less familiar examples which exhibit the same syntactic patterning. At what stage do these become difficult to understand? Why?

4 The students the examiners praised wrote an essay.
5 The students the examiners the lecturers appointed praised wrote an essay.
6 The students the examiners the lecturers the parents applauded appointed praised wrote an essay.

 ## Activity 11.19

Read the following sentences. When you are reading, try to be aware of any difficulties that you might encounter in understanding the sentences, and then think about what caused your problems (data from Barker 2004):

1 The horse raced past the barn fell.
2 I convinced her children are noisy.
3 Until the police arrest the drug dealers control the street.
4 The man who whistles tunes pianos.
5 The old man the boat.
6 The cotton clothing is made of grows in Mississippi.
7 Have the students who failed the exam take the supplementary.
8 Every woman that admires a man that paints likes Monet.
9 The raft floated down the river sank.
10 We painted the wall with cracks.

COMMENTARY ON ACTIVITIES

Activity 11.1

Speaker A (with Broca's or non-fluent aphasia) cannot use syntax to construct sentences. Inflections (past tense forms) and **function words** are missing. His speech is not very fluent, and he hesitates a lot. He seems to be able to find the **content words** he needs, but sometimes retrieves the wrong word (*read* and *ripe* for *write*). He sometimes has trouble forming words (*o'cot, ripe*). Speaker B (with Wernicke's or fluent aphasia) speaks in long, fluent sentences, but does not seem to be able to find the correct words. He even makes up words. His syntax seems to be intact, but it may be that he is relying very much on well-established chunks of language (*I get caught up*, *on the other hand*, *you know what I mean*, *look it over*, *all that sort of stuff*). He does not link his ideas coherently (➤➤ Unit 7), and often seems to be talking nonsense (*tarripoi, trebbin*).

Activity 11.2

Genie uses few function words, omitting the **determiners** and the **preposition** *with*. She does not use inflections such as past tense forms. She has a limited **vocabulary**. Just occasionally (*Father make me cry*), she shows signs of being able to form more complex syntactic patterns.

Activity 11.3

(a)   **Co-hyponyms**, both **hyponyms** of FRUIT.
(b)   **Antonyms**.
(c)   Partial **synonyms**.
(d)   BIRD is the **superordinate** of *parrot*.
(e)   Collocates (or coordinates, as they are often joined by *and*).
(f)   TULIP is a hyponym of *flower*.

Activity 11.4

Evidence from slips of the tongue shows that we search through lexical sets when looking for a word (example 1); and that, within these sets, words are linked to their opposites (example 2). Sometimes we blend two words from the same set (example 3: *expect* + *suppose* = *expose*). There are often similarities of form between the target and the erroneous word; this suggests that when we search for a word, we have some idea about what it sounds like. The wrong word may resemble the target one in several ways:

- the first syllable is often the same (example 5)
- the last syllable is often the same (example 4)
- the number of syllables is often the same (examples 3, 4, 5 and 6)
- the stress pattern is often the same (examples 3, 4, 5 and 6).

   Sometimes (example 4) the wrong word is similar to the target one in both form and meaning.

Activity 11.5
Some of the words are more frequent than others: CENTURY – CENTRE – CENTRAL – SEND – SENSIBLE – SENSITIVE – SENTENCE. We must assume that these words are more easily activated than the others because they are more frequent (and therefore more likely to be the correct match). So here we have two criteria for activation: goodness of fit and frequency.

Activity 11.6a
1   You probably remembered around seven of them.
2   You probably:
   (a)   tried to chunk two or more words by bringing them together in some kind of meaningful pattern
   (b)   'said' the words in your head to help you to remember them.

Activity 11.6b
1   You almost certainly remembered fewer words.
2   You probably again 'said' the words in your head. By turning words over in our minds, we conserve them and make it more likely that we will be able to transfer them to long-term memory. This is known as *rehearsal*. Notice that rehearsal appears to take place in phonological form, although you were studying written words.
3   The words are similar in number of letters to those in Activity 11.6a. But they have three syllables instead of one. This means that they take longer to 'say' in your head. As a result, you probably conserved fewer of them. Activities 11.6a and 11.6b show that we encode words in our memory in phonological form – *even when we originally met them in writing*.

Activity 11.7
Group A cannot work out how to say words from their spellings or from analogies with other words. But they can recognize whole words. They are said to have phonological dyslexia. Group B can use sound–spelling rules to work out how to pronounce non-words. But they cannot recognize whole words with irregular spellings. They use analogies with parts of other words (EAR, FEAR, DEAR, etc.) – so they mispronounce words which have an unusual pronunciation (BEAR, TEAR (verb)). They are said to have surface dyslexia.

Activity 11.8
1   *faddied* = 'disturbed'; *tarvish* = 'bad mannered'. These two words were invented. You were probably able to work out their meanings from the context in which they occurred.
2   There are a number of mistakes in the text.
   (a)   You may not have noticed the repeated words *that* and *in*. When we are reading, our eyes fixate almost every word – but occasionally we see that a short and familiar function word lies ahead, and our eyes skip over it.
   (b)   You may have noticed the following: *neighbours* → *nieghbours*; *nine-thirty* → *nine-thrity*. If you did, it indicates that you were reading at letter level as well as

at word level. Current theories believe that readers process (at one and the same time) letters, letter order and complete words.

(c)   You were perhaps less likely to have noticed *wonder* → *wander*. The reason is that the word occurs in a familiar chunk of language. You may have allowed your lexical knowledge of the sequence *I wonder who...* to overrule the evidence of your eyes.

(d)   You may have noticed that Miss Marple has become *Miss Marble*. But you could only have noticed this error if you had top-down world knowledge of the name of Agatha Christie's detective.

Activity 11.9

(a)   Sounds, not letters. Many of the sounds are reduced to the weak form schwa (➤ Unit 8).

(b)   Sounds are suppressed (have → [əv], and unstressed syllables may be missed out in the spoken forms of words such as POLICE.

(c)   No punctuation.

(d)   No gaps between words to show where one ends and the next begins.

(e)   Some syllables are stressed and more prominent than others. Where they carry sentence stress, it may help to highlight important words.

Activity 11.10

The experiment suggests that we only become aware of the different phonemes of our language as a result of learning to read and matching letters to those sounds.

Activity 11.11

Fold creates an *edge*. *Sending* suggests that somebody could not come of their own free will. A *window* is something that we can look through. *Fine* weather allows people to play sports outdoors. *Patients* suggests that this is a hospital. *Rackets* and a *net* are used in tennis. *Shell-shocked* suggests that the person being discussed is a soldier with special associations with the First World War.

Activity 11.12

The sentences simply say that somebody was prone on a floor, and that there was a body with a knife beside it. You are likely to assume, however, that the body in question is a dead one and moreover the body of the employer. You might also assume that the knife was the murder weapon.

Activity 11.13

Only sentence 6. If you thought that some of the other sentences were from the text, it is because you blended what the text says literally with your own inferences.

Activity 11.14

(a)   There is a change to the *content*: the words *in principle at least* have made the information more accurate.

(b) There are changes in *organization*. The writer has decided to mention the less familiar systems first. The terms *One*, *A second system*, *The third system* are used to knit the paragraph together (➤➤ Unit 7).

(c) There are changes reflecting *who the reader is*. Extra definitions and examples have been added; *phoneme* has been replaced by *sound*.

(d) There are changes to emphasize the *topic of the paragraph*. The first sentence links writing systems to the languages of the world.

(e) There are changes to correct errors of *execution*: *fro* instead of *for*.

Activity 11.15

(a) Finding a key word: WRITE.

(b) Constructing a syntactic pattern that fits the verb: writer + WRITE + recipient + written material.

(c) Inserting words into the pattern: JOHN + WRITE + HIS MOTHER + A LETTER.

(d) Giving the words phonological form: [dʒɒn + ɹaɪt + hɪz mʌðə + ə lɛtə]

(e) Inflecting the verb: [ɹaɪt] → [ɪz ɹaɪtɪŋ]

(f) Sending instructions to the articulators.

Activity 11.16

The speaker often pauses after a complete syntactic unit in order to plan the next unit. The unit is usually a **clause**. The end of the clause is often marked by a word that carries sentence stress. One odd exception is *we need to take unlicensed cars* + *SERious*, where the speaker pauses unexpectedly immediately before the end of the clause.

Activity 11.17

The man in extract B has difficulty in retrieving words and in distinguishing between words with similar meanings. He uses short sentences, often incomplete and without a clear grammatical structure. But he still manages to produce common chunks of language: *I don't know what this is*. He does not make clear connecting links between his sentences, and does not manage to express the kind of conceptual relationship (*but*, *which*, *because*) seen in Extract A.

REFERENCES

Aitchison, J. (1998) *The Articulate Mammal*, 4th edn, London: Routledge.

Aitchison, J. (2003) *Words in the Mind: An Introduction to the Mental Lexicon*, 3rd edn, Oxford: Blackwell.

Altmann, G. (1997) *The Ascent of Babel: An Exploration of Language, Mind, and Understanding*, Oxford: Oxford University Press.

Barker, K. (2004) Online. Available HTTP: <http://www.site.uottawa.ca/~kbarker/garden-path.html> (accessed 29 November 2004).

Barker, P. (1991) *Regeneration*, London: Penguin.

Christie, A. (1959) *The Body in the Library*, London: Pan.

Curtiss, S. (1977) *Genie: A Psycholinguistic Study of a Modern-Day 'Wild Child'*, London: Academic Press.

Enchanted Learning (2004) Online. Available HTTP: <http://www.enchantedlearning.com/Jackshouse.html> (accessed 29 November 2004).

Field, J. (2003) *Psycholinguistics: A Resource Book for Students*, London: Routledge.

Field, J. (2004) *Psycholinguistics: The Key Concepts*, London: Routledge.

Fromkin, V. (ed.) (1973) *Speech Errors as Linguistic Evidence*, The Hague: Mouton.

Gardner, H. (1977) *The Shattered Mind: The Person After Brain Damage*, Hove: Psychology Press.

Maxim, J. and Bryan, K. (1994) *Language in the Elderly: A Clinical Perspective*, London: Whurr.

Miller, G.A. (1956) 'The magical number seven, plus or minus two', *Psychological Review*, 63: 81–93.

Morais, J., Bertelson, P., Cary, L. and Alegria, J. (1986) 'Literacy training and speech segmentation', *Cognition*, 7: 323–31.

Obler, L.K. and Gjerlow, K. (1999) *Language and the Brain*, Cambridge: Cambridge University Press.

12 MULTILINGUALISM

UNIT CONTENTS

INTRODUCTION

Figure 12.1   Gracias

The term *mother tongue* (sometimes called the user's first language or L1) refers to the language that an individual uses from birth and use of the term suggests that each individual has one single mother tongue. However, multilingualism is far more prevalent world-wide than monolingualism is. A greater number of people use more than one language to manage their everyday lives than the number of people who manage their lives through the medium of just one language. The multilingual individual has very often acquired more than one language from birth and this leads to the question of which language is the mother tongue, and, indeed, whether a multilingual individual has more than one mother tongue.

Bilingualism really means two languages (from *bi* = 2 + *lingua* = languages) but the term is often used when the individual speaks more than two languages though the term *multilingualism* (*multi* = many) is increasingly being used in linguistic discussions. In non-technical arenas, the term *bilingual* tends to be used, irrespective of the number of languages that the individual speaks. Despite theoretical discussions about the differences (Wei 2000), these terms are often used interchangeably. The terms can be applied both to individual people and to communities or societies. In this unit we address both situations, beginning with the individual.

INDIVIDUAL MULTILINGUALISM

 Activity 12.1

Read the following linguistic biography. Would you describe Alex as multilingual (or bilingual) or not, and why? Ask other people what they think.

Alex was brought up with English as mother tongue (L1). After a degree course in French taken at a British University where the focus of the course was on reading and writing French, oral fluency in French was acquired while working in Sweden in a situation where there were many French colleagues. At the same time, some Swedish was learnt but the need for Swedish itself was minimal as so many Swedes spoke excellent English. Even so, Alex learnt enough Swedish to shop for everyday necessities in the unusual situation that a Swedish **interlocutor** could not speak English. Two years teaching in Germany improved Alex's skills in German (learnt earlier at school to a minimal level of competence), especially orally. Working for a year in North Vietnam resulted in Alex being able to count to 100 (useful for shopping in the local markets) but as there were many Swedish colleagues, the Swedish improved as well. At the end of a year spent teaching English in China and studying the language with a teacher, Alex felt able to shop in the local markets (with lots of pointing), count to 100, ask for directions and buy railway tickets.

Responses to this biography show that there are many opinions on what actually counts as being multilingual and any definition is likely to be controversial. Bloomfield's (1933: 56) classic definition of bilinguals as having 'native-like control of two languages' has always been problematic in that it begged the question of what he meant by this. Do all native speakers of any given language have the same abilities with and in that language? Recent research (Harley and Wang, cited in Harley 2001: 132) leads to the conclusion that 'monolingual-like attainment in each of a bilingual's two languages is probably a myth (at any age)'. Baker (1993: 17) uses Diebold's term of 'incipient bilingualism' which is explained as 'the early stages of bilingualism where one language is not strongly developed'. This is almost at the other extreme from Bloomfield's definition and begins to conflict with the more widespread understanding and use of the term.

There are many detailed labels (see Baker 1993) that can be used to describe the different levels of individual multilingualism. Harley (2001: 132, bold script has been removed from original) suggests that a 'better distinction is to be made between *simultaneous* bilingualism (L1 and L2 learned about the same time), *early sequential* bilingualism (L1 learned first but L2 learned relatively early, in childhood) and *late* bilingualism (L2 learned later, in adolescence onwards)'. He adds that 'Early sequential bilinguals form the largest group world-wide and the number is increasing, particularly in countries with large immigration rates'.

Multilingualism is not a static concept as any (monolingual or multilingual) individual's command of any language or languages is continually developing and that development is very individual. Whatever **descriptive** labels are used, the problem remains of deciding at what stage in language development and use one might begin to describe any individual as multilingual. The following activity helps to demonstrate the issues.

 ## Activity 12.2 o—т

Consider each of the following and decide whether you think the individual being described is monolingual or bi-/multilingual. Do you need any other information about any individual to help you form a judgement?

1   Anne is a British citizen who studied for and was awarded a degree in French Studies at a university in England.

2   Bien is a Vietnamese refugee who arrived in the UK 25 years ago who can use Vietnamese, Mandarin Chinese and English equally fluently in any situation.

3   Carla is a child just learning to talk using English with her British mother and Spanish with her Chilean father.

4   Dunja is a refugee who speaks Croatian as mother tongue and who in English and in French can greet an official but achieve nothing more through the medium of either language.

5   Elise is a Belgian citizen who has an English language degree from a British University.

6   Fakir is a nine-year-old child living in London who regularly uses Gujarati at home with the family and as the language of play with some friends, who uses Hindi as the language of play with other friends and who occasionally uses English as the language of play at school where English is the medium of instruction.

7   Geraldine is an elderly French lady who lived in Britain throughout her adult life, who was in hospital in Aylesbury (England) after suffering a stroke, after which she could apparently only use French despite having used English fluently for many years.

8   Hu is a technical translator translating scientific papers from English to Chinese which is her mother tongue.

9   Ingmar is a Swedish businessman using English to talk to Japanese counterparts at an international conference in Brazil.

10 Juan is a Chilean who chose to come to the UK to study for a Master's Degree, met and married an English person and stayed in the UK for the next 20 years before returning to Chile on the English spouse's retirement.

11 Yourself with your own knowledge of language(s).

Of the languages that any individual uses, there is likely to be one language that can be classified as that individual's dominant language. This may be the language that is used most frequently which may well also be the language that the individual feels most comfortable using. On the other hand, there are situations (such as living in another country for an extended period of time) when L2 becomes the dominant language. A fluent Spanish/English Chilean (Juan in the list above), on returning to his home country of Chile after an absence of about 20 years living in England, commented that he sometimes found it more of an effort to speak Spanish (his mother tongue) than English in some situations.

 Activity 12.3 ⊶

Denise is American and has lived in Switzerland for 35 years. She says of her family:

I am not bilingual – that would be stretching it a good deal … because I am not fluent. I can get by very well on the everyday things but if it comes to a complicated conversation I'm not that good and I don't feel that good expressing myself in German. [My husband] is Swedish and his English is perfect. He speaks German and Danish and Norwegian all fluently and he would probably have to say that his English and German are probably the best. [My daughters] were born here and they heard English for their first year. Then they started playing with other children, they picked up Swiss German very rapidly and then all their schooling was in Swiss German. I must say their best language is Swiss German. We all speak English together but when just the two girls are together, they speak Swiss German because for them it is their most natural language, it is their stronger language.

From what she says, how is Denise defining 'being bilingual'? What are the implications of what she says about her daughters in relation to the concept of mother tongue?

In the middle of the twentieth century the term *semilingual* was coined to label people who displayed some proficiency in a language but not a proficiency that could be compared with a monolingual. Baker (1993: 9) characterizes the semilingual as someone who 'displays a small vocabulary and incorrect grammar, consciously thinks about language production, is stilted and uncreative with each language, and finds it difficult to express emotions in either language'.

The concept and the term *semilingual* were used by some in educational circles to explain poor examination results by pupils attending schools conducted in a language that is not much used in their homes, for example, children from ethnic minorities in Europe and North America (➻ Unit 15), without regard to the wider **context** of the individual student's learning. However, the overriding negativity of this approach (towards both/all languages that the multilingual is using) ignored the currently recognized important cognitive benefits of facility in and knowledge of more than one language and culture. Hoffmann (1991: 126) argues much more positively in favour of bilingualism that:

> bilinguals have a wider and more varied range of experience than monolinguals, as they have access to two cultures and operate in two different systems … Their need to switch from one code to another has also been seen as beneficial to flexible thinking, as each language may provide the speaker with distinct perspectives.

Some of the recent research in this area is summarized by Harley (2001: 132–3) who recognizes that there are benefits to be gained by being multilingual. However, he also accepts that there are costs in certain linguistic situations where the effort of using a second language can impinge detrimentally on other cognitive processes. Wei (2000: 23–25) details communicative, cultural and cognitive advantages to being a bilingual in a discussion on the dimensions of bilingualism.

CODE-SWITCHING

Whether the languages are stored separately or not, there is evidence that multilingual individuals may use different languages within the same conversation/interaction and that this process can show a variety of patterns. **Code-switching** means that the languages are used together in the same conversation but they are kept separate. An English teacher working in Germany found himself saying 'You have to anmelden, don't you?', using the German word in the English **utterance** when no easy translation could quickly be found.

Code-switching is often confused with **code-mixing** which occurs when the languages are almost fused together. An English traveller recalls being surprised during a car journey from Germany to France when a garage attendant did not understand her question. Later she realized that she had put French verb inflections onto German verb stems. A German/English bilingual recalls talking in her childhood about 'butterlings' – a fusion of the English word *butterfly* and the German word *Schmetterling* and reported confusion in a business meeting when she said 'Das habe ich schon gementioned'. A very excited three-year-old English/French bilingual child showed her 'new shoes blue' to her English father. She then ran to tell her French mother in French that 'Papa aime mes nouveaux bleus souliers' – but she used the English syntactic order of **adjective** + **noun** when speaking French in which language colour adjectives usually come after the noun. She knew all the right words but she sequenced the English words in the English **noun phrase** according to the syntactic structure of French and vice versa. Whether such data as this can help us learn anything about how people produce speech is a question addressed by psycholinguists (➻ Unit 11). Individuals also use different languages depending on, for example, who they are talking to or where the conversation is taking place or what the conversation is about. It may depend on custom and practice throughout the duration of a friendship or patterns set in childhood where one language is used in the home and another for all interactions outside the home. It may simply depend on how fluent the interlocutors are in the relevant languages. It may be that there is a subconscious choice to talk in the language that will allow for the best interaction – in whatever terms one defines 'best'.

Activity 12.4 ⚬━

Marta, a Greek Cypriot teacher of English, was asked which language she used with different members of her family. In her response, what different reasons does she identify for choosing which language to use?

> It depends who I am talking to. I mean with my sisters, if I ring them up I speak in English. If I ring my mother up, I speak Cypriot … Because I've just got used to speaking English with my sisters … If we are all together, I think we just hop from one language to the other. Maybe with my older sisters I tend to speak more Greek because their Greek is better whereas with my younger sister who hardly speaks any Greek it is more natural to speak in English. With my parents … sometimes we might say something in English but it sounds unnatural. … If we talk about the home for example, kitchen language, then I am much more comfortable with Greek language because obviously we've been exchanging comments with my mother and we've always spoken Greek so it's easier and maybe if I discuss education or teaching English then maybe I feel more comfortable speaking English.

DIGLOSSIA

The term **diglossia** (meaning 'two tongues') was originally coined by Ferguson (1959) and relates to the situation where two or more language varieties are used systematically within a community where the choice is socially constrained. Ferguson's work was extended by Fishman to 'include different dialects, vernaculars or classical varieties, as well as distinct languages – so long as they are functionally differentiated' (Hoffmann 1991: 167). Crystal (1997: 43) defines diglossia as 'a language situation in which markedly divergent varieties, each with its own set of social functions, coexist as standards throughout a community'. In a diglossic situation, one language or **variety** is seen as a High (H) or prestigious form and is used in formal contexts such as business, the courts and education whereas a Low (L) or non-prestigious form is used in more informal circumstances and is the language of the family and friendship. Examples often quoted (Ferguson 1959; Hoffman 1991; Romaine 1989; Holmes 2001) as illustrations include: Swiss German where H is Standard German and L the various dialects of Swiss German; Arabic where H is classical Arabic and L the local varieties of the different Arab countries; or the situation in Paraguay where Spanish is used as H and Guaraní (an American Indian language) as L. In this unit we will consider the situation in

Cyprus (in Activity 12.5), Wales and Canada. Case studies on Cameroon, Fiji and Switzerland will show how the history of each country has led to its current multilingual position.

 Activity 12.5 o—┳

Consider Marta's account (from later in the same conversation as in Activity 12.4) of the use of different varieties in Cyprus. To what extent might this be seen as a diglossic situation? You will find it helpful to identify which language is used in which situations.

> If a Cypriot speaks to a Greek in the dialect, the Greeks won't understand a thing. However, a Cypriot can communicate with a Greek through the standard language because the language of education is standard Greek. All our literature is written in the standard Greek language. We've got some Cypriot dialect written down but it's difficult to read because the writers have had to make a sort of letter combination in order to represent the Cypriot sounds which are not usually Greek combinations. And there is some literature in the dialect. The dialect is usually used in the family and it would sound very strange should we use the mainland language among the family or friends. Sometimes people try to use the mainland language among a circle of friends – they are usually laughed at because they sound very pompous. … With colleagues we usually speak the dialect. However, if I go, for example, to a government office I will start off speaking the mainland language or something that resembles the mainland language and then maybe revert back to the Cypriot dialect.

The country of Wales operates with two official languages – English and Welsh – and official documents are produced in both languages. An online commentary on the 2001 UK census headlines a 'significant increase in use of Welsh language' and adds as supporting detail that:

> In Wales as a whole 28.4 per cent say they have one or more skills in the Welsh language, in north west and west Wales it is much higher – 76 per cent in Gwynedd, 70 per cent in the Isle of Anglesey, 64 per cent in Carmarthenshire and 61 per cent in Ceredigion. 16.3 per cent of Wales as a whole can speak, read and write Welsh.

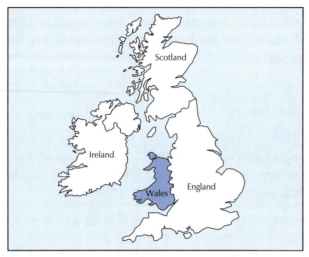

Figure 12.2 Wales

Even in the local authority with the lowest proportion, Monmouthshire, nearly 13 per cent of people say they have one or more skills in the Welsh language.

(National Statistics Online)

Whilst the variation in language use across Wales is clearly noted, it is immediately obvious as you cross the border between Wales and England that Welsh appears on all the road signs as well as English. Despite the increase noted in the use of Welsh, there are still fears about the possible demise of the Welsh language (Crystal 2000: 22).

In Canada, most individuals are English-speaking monolinguals but many of the residents in Quebec have at least some command of French. To progress to the higher posts in the Federal Government, an individual needs to be fluent in French as well as English. The official status of English and French is enshrined in the constitution and the preamble to the Official Languages Act (1988) of Canada recognizes that:

> the Constitution of Canada provides that English and French are the official languages of Canada and have equality of status and equal rights and privileges as to their use in all institutions in the Parliament and government of Canada.

The Act prescribes that all parliamentary records shall be maintained in both official languages. Judicial cases can be brought in either language and the federal court has:

the duty to ensure that any person giving evidence before it may be heard in the official language of his choice, and that in being so heard the person will not be placed at a disadvantage by not being heard in the other official language.

Fair as this might seem initially, concern is often expressed in Canada about whether the two languages do, in reality, share equal status.

The Canadian government chose and legislated to have two official languages for the nation but neither language has been designated as the national language. Other countries have followed more closely the argument that 'one language = one nation' and that the chosen language is part of the definition and identity of the nation. This could be seen to be the case in Kenya where Swahili was deliberately chosen as the national language because it is the language of none of the indigenous tribes but was linguistically related to the vast majority of those languages. It was also a language of trade through large parts of East Africa. However, whilst Swahili is the national (and, arguably, unifying) language, Swahili and English are both official languages with the result that a Kenyan can carry out official business in either.

Clearly, whether or not any one individual agrees with the final outcomes, most decisions about language use have been taken after a great deal of discussion and probably heated argument. It cannot be surprising that such discussions become very emotional for the obvious reason that issues relating to individual and community identity matter to us all at a subjective as well as at an objective level and therefore lead to emotional as well as rational debate. What must be recognized, however, is that the content of these discussions will have ranged over matters way beyond the narrowly linguistic. Any and all relevant social, philosophical, political and economic considerations must be considered by those empowered to decide and there can be no guarantee that legislation about language and language use will in any way guarantee language (or any other) equality (➻ Unit 15).

CASE STUDIES

Case studies can serve various purposes: they can act as models for your own research (see the activities later in this unit) and they can provide interesting information. As you read the case studies presented in this section, notice how the historical context informs and, in many ways, explains the current situation and also how different the situation in one country can be from that in another country and yet both are considered to be multilingual. Whilst each case study is far from exhaustive, they do collectively indicate the kind of information that you need to dig out to carry out any of the activities which follow. Such information can be gleaned from any good encyclopaedia or from official websites for the relevant country. To find relevant detail for the following case studies, typing 'official languages in xxx' (where xxx is the name of the country being researched) into a search engine immediately led to sites with interesting and relevant information for that country.

Cameroon

The historical context

Before any Europeans arrived in Cameroon, the country was inhabited by many different groups, each with their own language and customs. Islam had spread from the northern countries of Africa into the northern parts of Cameroon and there is still a significant number of Muslims in the northern areas.

The Portuguese were the first of the European powers to arrive in the late fifteenth century and there is a story (Lonely Planet Online) that the name of the country derives from the arriving sailors' shouts of 'camarões' (their name for shrimp) in their amazement at the size of the giant shrimp widely available. For the next 400 years, Cameroon's history, like that of most of the countries of West Africa, was intimately bound up with the slave trade and its aftermath. Missionaries also played a significant role in the development of the country. The Germans

Figure 12.3   Cameroon

established a protectorate over the area in 1884 and were instrumental in developing a railway system and an education system. After the First World War, the country was divided between the French and the British in an arrangement subsequently confirmed by the United Nations after the Second World War. The French had control of the larger eastern part of the country and the British of two smaller parts in the west. After a plebiscite in 1961, the northern part of West Cameroon chose to join Nigeria and the southern part of West Cameroon opted to join East Cameroon. French Cameroon and British Cameroon gained independence from their colonial powers at about the same time and united as a single country.

The current language situation

Each of the groups in Cameroon has their own language and there are now about 240 languages in use throughout the country, of which about 100 have a written form. One way of forging nationhood is through the use of a common language. In Cameroon, however, to choose one of the languages was not going to be practical and neither of the colonial powers was willing to allow their language not to be used in official situations. To forge one language from French and English was simply not possible. So there are two official languages: English and French. Wolf (2001: 152) claims that to the best of his knowledge 'Cameroon is the only African state with two official languages which are geographically distributed and, beside Rwanda, the only one with English and French as joint official languages'. He also argues (2001: 217) that 'to speak of bilingualism may be an understatement ... and *multilingualism* may characterise the situation better'. It is clear that the part of the country that was formerly French Cameroon still tends to use French (to be Francophone) rather than English and the former British Cameroon tends to use English (to be Anglophone). Wolf quotes at length (2001: 219), from Spreda's then unpublished thesis, a description of a typical day of language use for an Anglophone Cameroonian, an account which demonstrates the number of languages involved for any individual. In this account, quoted below, *PE* is used as an abbreviation for Pidgin English, widely spoken throughout Cameroon and West Africa as a **lingua franca**.

> The educated urban West Cameroonian is multilingual, usually speaking at least three languages in the course of a day. As marriages are generally intra-ethnic, the language of the home is usually the language of the ethnic background. With other Cameroonians of the same background and education he will speak the common indigenous language, often with some code switching. With anglophone Cameroonians of another ethnic

background he will speak either Educated Cameroonian English or Cameroonian Pidgin English, depending on the situation. PE will be used with someone with little education but also as a language of intimacy with those of a similar educational background, for example in the teachers' common room in a school. Should he be resident in the francophone area of Cameroon, he will usually speak French with those of comparable educational background, and in every day business in shops and in public transport, French is also necessary.

From this account, it appears that the choice of language remains with the individual based on his/her perception of their interlocutor. Social issues such as intimacy, respect, educational background and language purpose will all inform the decision about which language to use. Wolf comments (2001: 221) that 'bilingualism does not exist in an all-or-nothing manner' and he quotes research from others to show that, in Cameroon, English–French bilingualism can 'range from near perfect bilingualism to near-zero bilingualism'. It is important to note that the English part of the English–French bilingualism is itself a continuum from Pidgin English through to Standard Cameroonian English, which has many features of American English. The presence of American English features may well stem from a period of history when many of the teachers in Anglophone Cameroon secondary schools were Peace Corps volunteers.

Within Cameroon, both French and English have equal status in law but whether this equality extends to actual language use is debatable: do all Francophone Cameroonians use English to the same extent as Anglophone Cameroonians use French? Kouega (2002: 112) doubts this and wonders whether 'what has been going on in the country since Reunification some forty years ago has not been a one-way expansion of bilingualism, with speakers of English operating increasingly or fully in French, but their French-speaking counterparts remaining largely monolingual'. If this is the case, then Cameroon provides another example (remember the fears expressed in Canada, reported above) that shows that it is not enough simply to legislate that two (or more) languages should be treated as equal for that equality to happen. The situation in Cameroon is also interesting because, if Kouega is right, the use of English does not seem to be increasing within the country and that is in sharp contrast to the position of English in many other parts of the world (⇢ Unit 14).

Fiji

The historical context

Archaeological evidence shows that Fiji was first inhabited about 3,500 years ago but we need not go so far back in history for developments relevant to the current bilingual situation.

Tent (2001: 210–211) relates the history of the area in detail and a summary of his account is presented here. In the early nineteenth century, the first non-indigenous inhabitants who introduced English to the islands were 'deserters, marooned sailors and runaway convicts' who 'settled and became beachcombers'. Commercial interest in the islands was increased by the bêche-de-mer and sandalwood traders and then in 1835 the first missionaries arrived. With the establishment of churches and schools with Fijian as the medium of instruction there was, as yet, no imposition of English on the indigenous population. In the 1870s the earlier stability of the islands and their peoples was threatened by imperialist interests of France and the USA which inevitably led to internal political pressures. In 1874 Fiji became a Crown colony of Great Britain until 1970 when it achieved independence.

The linguistic situation is complex and Tent (2001: 210–211) is the central source of information in what follows. In the early 1930s, English became 'the official language of instruction after class three' but 'Fijian was generally the medium of communication in the colonial administration' and 'was mandatory for

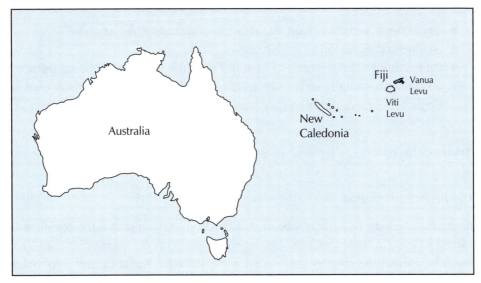

Figure 12.4   Fiji

British civil servants'. When some 60,000 Indian labourers were indentured between 1879–1917 Hindi arrived on the Fijian linguistic scene. British civil servants were 'encouraged to learn Hindi' and by 1928 all were allowed to 'meet their language requirements in either Fijian or Hindi' (Siegel 1989 cited in Tent 2001: 211). At this time 'the use of English to communicate with Fijians and Indians was strongly discouraged by the authorities' but then a 'sudden influx of teachers from New Zealand' in the 1930s who 'did not know the local languages, were not keen to learn them or inclined to use any language other than English' led to English becoming the medium of instruction in the school system. At this stage, English started to gain a prestige in the islands at the expense of the Fijian language and was 'promoted by the colonial authorities in the belief that it would serve as a "neutral" lingua franca allowing Fijians and Indo-Fijians to live together harmoniously'.

The current language situation

Currently, the situation in Fiji (data from the Summer Institute of Linguists and the Ethnologue websites) is that there are three official languages: Fijian, Fiji Hindi and English. The 1997 Constitution makes clear that these three languages 'have equal status in the State' though a total of ten currently spoken living languages are listed for Fiji. Tent (2000) notes that 'up to 36% of inter-ethnic conversations in the workplace are conducted in the vernacular. In rural areas the percentage is considerably higher'. He summarizes the domains where English is used as follows:

- government, administration, the judiciary, business and education
- commercial signs and advertisements
- media, though 'interviews in Fijian or Fiji Hindi have started being featured on the news. Initially such interviews were either voiced-over or subtitled in English, but more recently, they have been left in without any translation'.

Switzerland

The historical context

In the first century BC, Julius Caesar and the Romans conquered the region and named it Helvetia, a name which Napoleon Bonaparte revived many centuries later when he unified the country and called it the Helvetic Republic and imposed a written constitution, an imposition that most Swiss bitterly resented. Given the country's geographical location, it is not surprising that after the Roman invasion

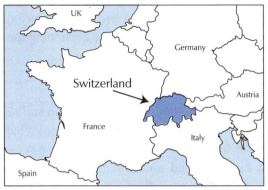

Figure 12.5   Switzerland

the area was invaded by other groups before becoming part of the Holy Roman Empire. At that time, it consisted of 'a collection of petty states, ruled by dukes, counts, bishops and abbots, and of a number of small city-states, independent by imperial charter, which later became cantonal commonwealths' (Encarta Online). The cantons now constitute an important and significant level of regional government within Switzerland which has maintained a national policy of neutrality in global affairs.

The frequent invasions from all points of the compass explain the arrival of the different languages into the area. French and Italian are both derived from Latin, brought by the Romans and later invasions. The Alemanni who invaded from the north brought German and Rhaeto-romanic, a dialect used in some of the isolated valleys in the Alps which developed into Romansch.

The current language situation

There are four national languages in Switzerland – German, French, Italian and Romansch – but only three have official language status– German, French and Italian. Swiss German is spoken by about 65 per cent of the population, Swiss French by about 18 per cent, Swiss Italian by about 10 per cent and Romansch by about 1 per cent (statistics from Encarta Online). It is unlikely that any individual Swiss citizen is quadrilingual. The languages are largely divided regionally and the history of the country explains the geographical distribution of the language use across the country. Swiss German is spoken in 17 of the 26 cantons, French in four, Italian in four and Romansch in one.

Language rights and statuses are written into the Swiss constitution together with provisions to ensure support in the relevant cantons for Romansch and Italian. However, despite the officially recognized and supported multilingualism, there are those who would argue that the country is no longer quadrilingual and that use of the official languages is fading with a preference developing for the use of English. In particular, there is concern about the continuing use of Romansch.

SUMMARY

This unit has considered how the terms *bilingualism* and *multilingualism* might be defined and then applied to a very wide range of situations relating to individual or societal language which occur in the world. In the discussion of individual bilingualism, code-switching and code-mixing have been exemplified. In the consideration of societal multilingualism, case studies were used to show how widely such situations can vary.

FURTHER READING

The Bilingualism Reader (Wei 2000) discusses both individual and societal bilingualism in a selection of important papers on topics both theoretical and applied. *Sociolinguistics: A Reader and Coursebook* (Coupland and Jaworski 1997) has one section (Part VI) devoted to multilingualism. *An Introduction to Sociolinguistics* (Holmes 2001) contains a wealth of useful information relevant to many aspects of multilingualism in Section 1 of a very readable volume. Loreto Todd's *Modern Englishes: Pidgins and Creoles* provides more detail about Cameroon and also information about Papua New Guinea in a very readable volume which also addresses some of the educational implications (➛➛ Unit 15). The journal *English World-Wide* will provide information on many issues relative to material in this unit and is available online as well as in print.

FURTHER ACTIVITY

 ## Activity 12.6

One of the most complex linguistic situations is currently to be found in South Africa where language planning policies post-apartheid have had a clear political dimension. Use the official websites for the government of South Africa to discover what languages are accorded official and/or national language status, how many other languages there are in use in the country and why some languages were chosen for wider use and others not.

Other countries are also worth researching. Finland, Hong Kong, Israel, New Zealand, Papua New Guinea and the USA will all provide illuminating information about language policies and language situations.

 ## Activity 12.7

Even within apparently monolingual countries there are multilingual communities, such as Bradford, Sheffield or Leeds in the United Kingdom, New York and Los Angeles in the United States, Paris and Marseilles in France. Explore what languages are used in each city within normal interactions and try to explain how and why the language choices are made by those living in the city.

This activity is not only possible in relation to large cities. One casual conversation with one of the authors' friends who live in a village in North Yorkshire in the UK revealed many multilingual families living in village communities in the more rural areas of that apparently monolingual county. Choose a community (e.g. school, village, town, friendship group) and by interviewing community members, find out:

1 how many languages are known and used in the community and by whom
2 how frequently or regularly each language is used
3 what percentage of the community uses which language(s)
4 for what purpose individuals choose to use any one language of their repertoire.

You might like to link this activity with Activity 15.6.

COMMENTARY ON ACTIVITIES

Activity 12.2

You might wish to consider the following points:

Anne and Elise are both late bilinguals, if bilingual at all. The major difference between them is that Elise studied English in an English speaking country whereas Anne studied French in a non-French speaking country. Juan is similarly a late bilingual but by staying in England for the following 20 years, fluency in English may well equal fluency in Spanish. That equal fluency after 20 years might lead many to decide that Juan is bilingual whereas the other two may not be.

Most would describe Bien as bilingual or multilingual.

Carla is learning English and Spanish at the same time in childhood. Each parent speaks his/her/their own language to Carla and only later in life will Carla choose which language she prefers to use. Fakir is in a more or less similar position to Carla but with a greater repertoire of languages for use at an earlier age.

Dunja and Ingmar use English only in certain situations. Whether they are considered to be bilingual depends on whether the definition of bilingualism requires that the individual must be equally proficient in more than one language. Hu only uses English for work as a technical translator and should perhaps be considered in this group as well. If Hu's competence as a technical translator only involved understanding English and not producing it, would it affect your conclusions and if so, how?

Geraldine's situation suggests that bilingualism can be lost as well as gained. Prior to her stroke, she was regarded by all who knew her as equally fluent in English and French. After the stroke, all competence in English seemed to have disappeared.

As for your own situation, only you can know what you think about your own language position. Share the information with others and see if they agree with your assessment.

Activity 12.3

If Denise's daughters heard English in their first year from both parents, then English is arguably their mother tongue. But Denise is quite clear that their stronger language in adulthood is Swiss German. In the light of this not-unusual situation, what importance should be given to the idea of mother tongue? In the light of the two activities in this unit and before you read any further, you should take some time to consider how *you* would define 'being bilingual' or 'being multilingual'.

Activity 12.4

Family patterns of custom and practice have largely determined which language is used with whom. However, when thinking about talking to her sisters, she does talk about ability in the language as being part of the reasoning – they use the language in which they can have the easier conversation and that relates to individual ability.

Activity 12.5

In that she states that formal interviews tend to start in the standard Greek language, this situation does have some of the characteristics of a diglossic situation. However, given that the **dialect** (➻ Unit 9) form is a variety of the **standard language**, the situation here does not comply with the strict definition of diglossia where there are 'two markedly divergent categories' (Crystal 1997: 43). It is notable, however, that there can be some incomprehension between speakers of the standard variety and of the dialect variety.

Compare what Marta says with language use in your own country. Are there any parallels that you can draw?

REFERENCES

Baker, C. (1993) *Foundations of Bilingual Education and Bilingualism*, Clevedon: Multilingual Matters.

Bloomfield, L. (1933) *Language*, New York: Holt Rinehart and Winston.

Coupland, N. and Jaworski, A. (eds) (1997) *Sociolinguistics: A Reader and Coursebook*, Basingstoke: Palgrave.

Crystal, D. (1997) *The Cambridge Encyclopedia of Language*, 2nd edn, Cambridge: Cambridge University Press.

Crystal, D. (2000) *Language Death*, Cambridge: Cambridge University Press.

Encarta Online. Available HTTP: <http//:encarta.msn.com> (accessed 18 September 2004).

English World-Wide Online. Available HTTP: <http://www.benjamins.nl/cgi-bin/t_seriesview.cgi?series=EWW> (accessed 2 December 2004).

Ethnologue. Online. Available HTTP: <http://www.ethnologue.com> (accessed 2 December 2004).

Ferguson, C.A. (1959) 'Diglossia', *Word*, 15: 325–40.

Harley, T. (2001) *The Psychology of Language: From Data to Theory*, 2nd edn, Hove: Psychology Press.

Hoffmann, C. (1991) *An Introduction to Bilingualism*, London: Longman.

Holmes, J. (2001) *An Introduction to Sociolinguistics*, 2nd edn, Harlow: Pearson Education.

Kouega, J-P. (2002) 'Uses of English in Southern British Cameroons', *English World-Wide*, 23: 93–113.

Lonely Planet Online. Available HTTP: <www.lonelyplanet.com/destinations/africa/cameroon/history.htm> (accessed 18 September 2004).

National Statistics Online. Available HTTP: <http://www.statistics.gov.uk/census> (accessed 18 September 2004).

Official Languages Act Canada. Online. Available HTTP: <http://laws.justice.gc.ca/en/O-3.01/> (accessed 18 September 2004).

Romaine, S. (1989) *Bilingualism*, Oxford: Blackwell.

Summer Institute of Linguists (SIL). Online. Available HTTP: <http://sil.org> (accessed 18 September 2004).

Tent, J. (2000) Online. Available HTTP: <http://www.abc.net.au/m/arts/ling/stories/s173503.html> (accessed 30 November 2004).

Tent, J. (2001) 'A profile of the Fiji English lexis', *English World-Wide*, 22: 209–45.

Todd, L. (1984) *Modern Englishes: Pidgins and Creoles*, Oxford: Blackwell.

Wei, L. (ed.) (2000) *The Bilingualism Reader*, London: Routledge.

Wolf, H.-G. (2001) *English in Cameroon*, Berlin: Mouton de Gruyter.

13 HISTORY OF ENGLISH

UNIT CONTENTS

- Introduction
- Modern English
- Middle English
- Old English
- Before Old English
- Summary
- Further reading
- Further activity
- Commentary on activities
- References

Look at these pictures and then do Activity 13.1 before you start reading the unit.

Figure 13.1   Cool

Figure 13.2   Gay

 Activity 13.1

For each word illustrated at the beginning of this unit consider the following questions:

1   Do you use the word to mean the same thing every time you use it? Whether you use it to mean the same thing or not, what meanings do you express with each word?

2   Does the word mean the same thing for you and for your grandparents, your parents and your friends? How do their uses of each word differ from yours?

INTRODUCTION

For all its current pre-eminent position in the world (➤ Unit 14), the English language is only about 1,500 years old but it has changed enormously in that length of time. In this unit we will consider the historical changes in English and we will work backwards from Modern English, which you know and use, to Old English which looks very different from Modern.

Modern English (ModE) dates from about 1500. The period of Middle English (ME) is from 1100–1500 and the forms of the language used between 450–1100 are referred to as Old English (OE). All these dates are approximate, of course, and nobody would suggest that in a single given year the language changed radically but the dates serve as useful staging posts in the development of English. OE looks almost like a foreign language to anyone nowadays trying to read an OE text but there are still many words in use in the twenty-first century which date from that era. It is also true that many OE words have dropped out of regular use, such as *kith*, now obsolete other than in the complex **noun phrase** *kith and kin* (meaning one's friends and relations); *churl* used, if at all in ModE, only in its **adjective** form, *churlish*; or *shrive* now used almost exclusively in the name *Shrove Tuesday*, but many core words in ModE (e.g. *he, man, live*) do have OE roots. ME is more recognizable to the modern reader but there are still points where the meaning or the usage of a word has changed or where the **syntax** strikes the modern reader as non-standard. ModE is very familiar but it is still clear that the language has changed from the 1500s and the term Early Modern English is often given to the period from 1500–1700. In any text that you read, what proportion of the words do you think come from each of the major periods listed above? Just guess first of all and then check your estimate against what you find out in Activity 13.2.

 Activity 13.2 ⚬━┳

Look up the words in the following paragraph in a good dictionary to find when each word was first recorded in the written language. This is the beginning of the first paragraph of *Northanger Abbey* by Jane Austen (1775–1817):

No one who had ever seen Catherine Morland in her infancy, would have supposed her born to be an heroine. Her situation in life, the character of her father and mother; her own person and disposition, were all equally against her. Her father was a clergyman, without being neglected, or poor, and a very respectable man, though his name was

Richard – and he had never been handsome. He had a considerable independence, besides two good livings – and he was not in the least addicted to locking up his daughters. Her mother was a woman of useful plain sense, with a good temper, and, what is more remarkable, with a good constitution.

MODERN ENGLISH

Other units in this book provide a clear description of current Modern English. A reader of Jane Austen's or Charles Dickens' novels will not normally have problems in understanding their **variety** of English, other than where words have changed their meaning as was shown in the Austen text used in Activity 13.2. Readers may have difficulties where the authors are describing social customs that are no longer practised or may not understand a particular **reference** (to the name *Richard*, for example, in *Northanger Abbey* in Activity 13.2) but in such cases, the problem is not with the language but in our understanding of the cultural references.

In this unit, texts from the earlier period of Modern English will be considered, where the modern reader might have more difficulties with the language itself, not just with the ideas. In Act III, Scene 2 of *Hamlet* by William Shakespeare (1564–1616), the eponymous hero directs some visiting players (called actors in ModE) on how they are to deliver the speech that Hamlet has written for them to insert into their play:

Hamlet: Speak the speech, I pray you, as I pronounced it to you,
2   trippingly on the tongue. But if you mouth it as many of our
       players do, I had as lief the town crier spoke my lines. Nor do not
4   saw the air too much with your hand, thus. But use all gently. For in
       the very torrent, tempest, and, as I may say, whirlwind of your
6   passion, you must acquire and beget a temperance that may give it
       smoothness. O, it offends me to the soul to hear a robustious
8   periwig-pated fellow tear a passion to tatters, to very rags, to split
       the ears of the groundlings, who for the most part are capable of
10   nothing but inexplicable dumb shows and noise. I would have such
       a fellow whipped for o'erdoing Termagant. It out-Herods Herod.
12   Pray you avoid it.

Activity 13.3

Put Hamlet's speech into English appropriate for the twenty-first century before you read the next paragraph.

No matter how the speech has been rewritten or rephrased, some lexical changes are predictable. It is most unlikely that the word *lief* (L3 meaning 'rather' and used with *have* to express preference) was kept and it is described as obsolete in the Oxford English Dictionary (OED). Similarly described in the OED as obsolete are *periwig* (L8 from the French 'perruque' meaning a wig) and *pated* (L8) which meant the top of the head in ME but which, according to the OED, is 'not now in serious or dignified use'). Archaic according to the OED is the word *robustious* (L7), though the later coinage of *rumbustious* is still in use, if relatively rarely. *To split the ears* (L8–9) is perhaps less often used in this V + Cdo (➻ Unit 7) form but it is still heard, if indirectly, as a participial/adjective form, *ear-splitting*. *Groundlings* (L9), meaning those who frequented the pit of the theatre, has its first appearance in this text (OED) though the same form is used to talk of fish both before and after this theatrical meaning was attached to the word. The use of *beget* (L6) is now limited to a religious **register** and *temperance* (L6) was a dated word at the turn of the millennium – perhaps because in some Western societies the idea itself is now dated and out of fashion. It is also unlikely that any rewriting talked of having somebody whipped, unless they were using the word metaphorically, as in many societies that would now be considered socially unacceptable.

It is not only the lexis that has changed, however. The double negative of *Nor do not saw the air* (L3–4) is unlikely to have found its way into the rewriting of the speech if that rewriting was into Standard British English. The double negative has been a stigmatized form (though still frequently used in **dialects**) since Lowth's Grammar of 1762 (Crystal 2003b: 79). Shakespeare's use of the proper **noun** *Herod* (L11) as a verb (startlingly and creatively innovative at the time of writing) will pass most modern readers by completely and will almost certainly have been omitted from any rewriting as will the reference to Termagant, an imaginary deity from medieval times.

Looking at the original scripts of Shakespeare's plays, there are clearly different spellings of the same word – indeed Shakespeare is known to have spelt his own name in several different ways. Despite the earlier advent of the printing press, there was still some time to go before the spelling of English became fixed and settled, though it is noticeable that there are still variations in spelling and word forms. American English and British English have some systematic differences in spelling (⇢ Unit 14) such as *theatre/theater* or *colour/color* and there are some variations in spelling according to meaning e.g. *programme/program*. Samuel Johnson's Dictionary, first published in 1755, is generally regarded as the first authoritative dictionary of the English Language in that it provides examples of usage as well as definitions of meaning and the spelling of words.

MIDDLE ENGLISH

Whilst the language used by Shakespeare is different from that used in later centuries, it is much more familiar to modern ears than the language used by Chaucer (*c*.1343–1400) which will be considered shortly. In Shakespeare's language, as in many words in ModE, there are letters in the spelling that are not pronounced as in 'tongue' or 'knight'. We know they were not pronounced from evidence such as rhymes in verse. In ME, however, almost every letter in a word was pronounced. There have constantly been changes in the pronunciation of English and such changes still occur (as in the current rise of so-called Estuary English and the increasing use of the intervocalic glottal stop ⇢ Unit 8). During the ME and early ModE period, there was a systematic sound shift in the long vowels of English, a shift now referred to as the Great Vowel Shift. Freeborn (1992: 128) explains that that while there was 'variation between regional and social dialect speakers, ... in time all the long vowels were either raised or became diphthongs'. He links this to the ModE writing system when he comments that, in English, the 'spelling system has never been altered to fit the changed pronunciations. Consequently, the sound of the short vowels, represented by the letters <a> <e> <i> <o> <u>, has remained more or less the same, while the sounds of the long vowels no longer match the letters'.

Historically, this section on Middle English (1100–1500) must begin with the Norman invasion onto the south coast of England in 1066, in what is chronologically still the OE period. However, the effects of their arrival on the English language do not really manifest themselves until well into the twelfth century. Edward the Confessor had been on the English throne for 23 years, having retaken it from the Scandinavian kings and on his death, the throne passed to Harold II who reigned for only ten months before his death in 1066 at the Battle of Hastings. In his reign, he had been beset by invasions from Scandinavia to the north of his kingdom and earlier invasions from France to the south. The political outcomes were serious but more important for the concerns of this book are the effects on the English language of this last (Norman) invasion onto English soil.

The lexical explosion of vocabulary as a result of the incorporation of French words into English is one explanation for the number of near **synonyms** in Modern

English: *big* (ME unknown origin perhaps from Scandinavian), *large* (ME from Old French (OF)) and *great* (OE); or *king* (OE) and *monarch* (ME from OF); *kingly* (OE) and *regal* and *royal* (both OF). The pairs *guard/guardian* and *ward/warden* form near synonyms that ultimately derive from OE or Old French.

With the arrival of the Norman king William the Conqueror, it is hardly surprising that Norman French became the language of the English court and this continued for about two centuries. French therefore became the language of the aristocracy and the upper classes of the society of the time. Baugh and Cable assert that French 'was used in Parliament, in the law courts, in public negotiations generally' (2002: 135). However, they also argue that 'English was widely known among all classes of people, though not necessarily by everyone' (2002: 139). The writers of the fourteenth century, among whom Baugh and Cable name Chaucer, Langland and Wycliffe, 'constitute a striking proof of the secure position the English language had attained' (2002: 156) by the end of that century. They argue (2002: 151) that by 'the fifteenth century the ability to speak French fluently seems to have been looked upon as an accomplishment' rather than as a necessity.

A social distinction between the use of French and English still appears, if indirectly, in Modern English. We keep cows (OE) and pigs (OE) in the fields (OE) but we eat beef (ME from OF) and pork (ME from OF) at the dining table. Similarly, we grow potatoes in the fields, but rarely see potatoes by name on a menu: they are referred to in other ways often using French words to name the method of preparation e.g. *pommes de terre dauphinoises*. *Mansions* (ME from OF and originally Latin) and *houses* (OE) are lived in by people at different levels of society and such examples provide a clear indication of how words of French origin to some extent are still seen as privileged or preferred when compared with their OE near synonyms.

Mass production of written texts was unnecessary when the majority of the population could not read or write but the advent of the printing press (Caxton set up his first press in 1476) starts to settle the spelling of English. That the original spellings reflected the then current pronunciation of many words explains the apparently redundant letters in some modern spellings such as *right* or *knee* and also demonstrates how much the pronunciation of English has changed in the intervening centuries.

Wells-Cole (in Chaucer 1995: v) states that 'Chaucer is often regarded as the first English poet because he more or less turned the English language into an appropriate medium for poetry as his writing career progressed'. *The Canterbury Tales*, though incomplete at the time of Chaucer's death, is regarded as a masterpiece of English poetry largely because of the diversity of styles found in the tales which are told by a group of fellow travellers during their pilgrimage from London to Canterbury. There is no manuscript still extant that is known to have been hand-written by Chaucer himself and so, as is the case for many ME and OE texts, there are apparently various versions of the text. The Wife of Bath begins the *Prologue* of her tale thus (Chaucer 1995: 291):

1   ' Experience, though noon auctoritee
2   Were in this world, were right y-nough to me
3   To speke of wo that is in mariage ;
4   For, lordinges, sith I twelf yeer was of age,
5   Thonked be god that is eterne on lyve,
6   Housbondes at chirche-dore I have had fyve
7   For I so ofte have y-wedded be ;
8   And alle were worthy men in hir degree.

   Though most of this is comprehensible to the modern reader, there are still clear differences between this and later English writing. *The Canterbury Tales* is written in rhyming couplets, one feature that helps determine some of the pronunciation of ME. So, *mariage* and *age* (L3/L4), *lyve* and *fyve* (L5/L6) rhyme at the end of the lines as do the final vowel sounds in *auctoritee* and *me* (L1/L2). Noun plurals are mostly formed by adding the **suffix** {-s} and the irregular OE plural of *man* still remains in ModE (L8). *Yeer* when talking about age (L4) does not appear in the plural which may seem surprising until ModE phrases like *a five-year-old* are brought to mind. Verbs have a **prefix** (from OE) {y-/i-}on the past participle (L7) but what looks like the same **morpheme** in L2 is not prefixed to a verb – and is recognizable as an early spelling of *enough*. **Pronouns** are not the same as in ModE. *Hir* (L8) can only mean 'their'. *Alle* (L8) has a plural marker on it.

 Activity 13.4 ⊶

The Wife of Bath's tale continues thus. Find examples of differences between Modern English as you know it and the text as presented here.

   9   But me was told certeyn, nat longe agon is,
10   That sith that Crist ne wente never but onis
11   To wedding in the Cane of Galilee,
12   That by the same ensample taughte he me
13   That I ne sholde wedded be but ones.
14   Herke eek, lo ! which a sharp word for the nones
15   Besyde a welle Jesus, god and man,
16   Spak in repreve of the Samaritan :

17   ' Thou hast y-had fyve housbondes,' quod he,
18   ' And thilke man, the which that hath now thee,
19   Is noght thyn housbond ; ' thus seyde he certeyn ;
20   What that he mente ther-by, I can nat seyn ;
21   But that I axe, why that the fifthe man
22   Was noon housbond to the Samaritan ?
23   How manye myghte she have in mariage ?
24   Yet herde I never tellen in myn age
25   Upon this nombre diffinicioun ;
26   Men may devyne and glosen up and doun.
27   But wel I woot expres, with-oute lye,
28   God bad us for to wexe and multiplye ;
29   That gentil text kan I wel understonde.

The dialect boundaries for ME (Figure 13.3) look very similar to broad dialect boundaries widely accepted in Modern English. Within the East Midlands dialect area, the **accent** spoken in the so-called 'golden triangle' of London, Oxford and Cambridge provides the birthplace of Standard British English pronunciation, which has variously been labelled Queen's English, BBC English or **Received Pronunciation (RP)**. Given that the three points of the triangle mark the two oldest seats of learning in England and the place of national government, it is perhaps hardly surprising that this accent developed into the standard accent. Crystal

Figure 13.3   Middle English dialect boundaries (Crystal 2003b: 50)

(2003b: 365) claims that 'less than 3% of the British people speak pure RP. Most educated people have developed an accent which is a mixture of RP and various regional characteristics – "modified RP", some call it'.

OLD ENGLISH 450–1100

Historically this period begins with the arrival of Saxon invaders from Germany in 449 after the withdrawal of the Roman armies. The Jutes came with the aim of dispossessing the Celts from their lands and they gradually pushed them to the west, towards what is now Wales. In time, the Anglo-Saxon kingdoms were formed by means of alliances between the local aristocrats or *eorlas* (from which the still-used title *earl* is derived) to improve resistance to invaders. The seven kingdoms that were finally established were Northumbria, Mercia, East Anglia, Kent, Essex, Sussex and Wessex and supremacy passed between them as the years passed. The OE dialect boundaries (Figure 13.4) can be linked to the borders between the kingdoms.

In the second half of this period in the eighth century, the Vikings invaded from Scandinavia. According to the Anglo-Saxon Chronicle (cited in Baugh and Cable 2002: 93), they arrived in 787 on the north-east coast of England and plundered the abbeys and monasteries, such as Lindisfarne and Jarrow. Later attacks were made on the coast of East Anglia and even the south coast of England and by the late 800s they were in charge of most of Eastern England. They turned to the west and were

Figure 13.4   Old English dialect boundaries (Crystal 2003b: 28)

met by Alfred the Great and his armies and their incursions were halted. The Vikings were pushed back to a line roughly from Chester to London – and to the east of that line was known as the Danelaw as the people were subject to Danish law. Towards the end of the next century, there were further, more successful, incursions by the Danes onto the south east coast of England and in the early 1000s there was a Danish king, King Canute, on the throne for a period of about 25 years.

Such a summary does not indicate the number of Scandinavians who came and, even more importantly, who stayed, for whatever reasons, when their ships left to return home. The result of this is that there was also much peaceable interaction between the invaders and the indigenous population. They farmed neighbouring fields, they married each other and the incomers took part in local customs as well as introducing some traditions of their own. Inevitably, the two languages, which were not particularly dissimilar in the first place, started to influence each other and some of the features of OE which make it so distinctly different from any modern form of English came to be lost. The inflections that appeared on nouns in OE began to disappear and the fact that there are now two words in ModE, *shirt* and *skirt*, is due to the Viking influence: *shirt* coming from OE and *skirt* from Old Norse.

In that eastern part of England which was ruled by the Danelaw, place names are frequently Scandinavian in origin. Near to York, its own name from the OE *Eoforwic*, the villages of Tholthorpe and Bishopthorpe both contain the Scandinavian Old Norse *thorpe* (village), Whitby and Helperby contain *by* (Old Norse (ON) for town). Kirkbymoorside contains *kirk* (church) and *by* with the OE *moor* (wasteland, marsh or mountain) and OE *side* (extending lengthways), a name (the town by/with the church on the side of the moor) which is both descriptive of itself and its location at the southern edge of the North York Moors. One might wonder whether the name itself is indicative of peaceful coexistence of two groups of people speaking different languages that were fast becoming merged.

 Activity 13.5 o—π

Examine a map of the north-east part of England, the part of the country that was ruled by the Danelaw, and find examples of place-names with Scandinavian roots and of places with OE roots. Of particular interest will be those places where OE and Norse seem to have been merged in the name. A good dictionary will help you and Cameron (1996) will provide further information if needed.

Read the OE version of the Lord's Prayer (taken from Baugh and Cable 2002: 62) which is printed here and work out the meaning of the clauses (➡ Unit 7). There are more modern versions of the prayer (➡ Unit 16) which you could use if necessary to help you understand this OE version.

> Fæder ūre,
> þu þe eart on heofonum,
> sī þin nama gehālgod.
> Tōbecume þīn rīce.
> Gewurþe ðīn willa on eorðan swā swā on heofonum.
> Ūrne gedæghwāmlīcan hlāf syle ūs tō dæg.
> And forgyf ūs ūre gyltas, swā swā wē forgyfað ūrum gyltendum.
> And ne gelǣd þū ūs on costnunge,
> ac, ālȳs ūs of yfele. Sōþlīce.

If you would like to hear how this OE text sounds, the University of Georgetown website at <http://www.georgetown.edu/faculty/ballc/oe/paternoster-oe.html> is one possibility.

Graphology

The letters used in OE are not exactly the same as those used in ModE. The **consonant** letter forms that have now fallen out of non-phonetic use are <ð> (the letter was called *eth*; the form is now used as a **phonetic** symbol) and <þ> (called *thorn*) which represented both the sounds spelt in ModE with <th> (the OE letters were used interchangeably and did not represent pronunciation) and <ƿ> (called *wynn*) which represented the sound [w]. The letter <g> was sometimes written as <ᵹ>. The consonants <j>, <q>, <v>, and <z> do not appear in the OE alphabet. There were seven letters to represent **vowels** <a>, <e>, <i>, <o>, <u> and <y> which are still used but <æ> (called *ash*) no longer appears in ModE written text. The letter <y> is still used to represent vowel sounds in some ModE words such as *hymn* or *rhythm*.

Vocabulary

There were two words for the ModE *you*: *þū* (*thou*) for the second person singular (no longer used in ModE Standard English but still used in dialects) and *ᵹē* for the plural form. Many modern function words still in regular use in ModE are clearly evident. The OE forms for *our*, *on* and *and* are easily recognizable – though *on* might be translated in a modern version of the prayer in different ways. The OE word *rīce* (kingdom) is used as a bound morpheme in ModE in words like *bishopric* though it is no longer used as a free morpheme as here. The OE forms of many ModE words are easily found, for example, *heaven*, *guilt* (usually *sins* in the most recent versions of the prayer) and *today*. Other words are less closely related to any modern forms and have fallen out of use, though the meaning can still be discerned.

Morphology

OE verbs are conjugated to agree with person and number (⤳ Unit 7) in the singular with the endings {*-e*}/{*-(e)st*}/{*-(e)þ*} for first, second and third person singular respectively, though in the plural a single form <aþ> was used with no variation for number. Some ModE dialect forms still use these inflections (⤳ Unit 7).

OE nouns were masculine, feminine or neuter in syntactic gender. Nouns and pronouns were inflected for case (⤳ Unit 7) to show their function in the clause. Examples in this text include the second person singular pronoun, *þū* and *þin*, in nominative (as the Subject of a clause ⤳ Unit 7) and genitive (possessive) case, respectively. Nouns are inflected to indicate case, *heofonum* and *gyltendum* being in dative case (Cio in a clause) and *constnunge* in accusative case (Cdo in a clause ⤳ Unit 7). Such inflections appear most noticeably in ModE within the pronoun system where the choice about which form of, for example, *I/me*, *he/him*, *we/us* to use in a sentence is determined by the role of the pronoun within the clause/sentence. The possessive case is still regularly marked in ModE nouns, as in, for example, *John's car*.

BEFORE OLD ENGLISH

This unit has worked backwards through time to show how Modern English has emerged from its antecedent forms and it is quite possible for the quest to continue. Dictionary work for Activities 13.1 and 13.2 showed how the meaning of words in English have changed over the centuries and you will have noted as well how English words are derived from words in earlier languages as well as borrowing words from other contemporary languages. Latin and Greek as well as Old English have provided many words and morphemes now in use in Modern English as a quick scan of any dictionary page will show.

Activity 13.6 ○━ᴛ

1   Look at Table 1.2 on p. 29 for this activity. List words currently in use in Modern English which show that these ModE words could be seen as deriving from Latin or Greek. For example, the first morpheme in *hexagon*, a six-sided figure, comes from the Greek *hex*; the first morpheme in *sextuplets* from the Latin *sex*.

2   If Latin *novem* is number 9 and Latin *decem* number 10, why are they so clearly a morpheme in the months of November and December, respectively the eleventh and twelfth months of the calendar year?

Latin also provided many of the words in Spanish, Italian and French. Metaphorically speaking, therefore, Latin can be seen as an ancestor of these languages and, indeed, it is often described as a parent language to them. In the same way that Latin can be seen as a parent language for French, Spanish and Italian, West Germanic can be considered a parent language for English, Dutch and German. The Scandinavian languages are also quite closely related (the same metaphor being used) both to each other with a parent language called North Germanic and to the other descendants of Germanic. West Germanic and North Germanic are closely related and have a single parent, Germanic. The detail is complex but the principle of reconstructing the languages works and leads us to another question. If Latin or Germanic is the parent, what language is the grandparent and so the questioning can continue into the mists of the past (➻ Unit 1). Family trees of language abound in various sources such as Crystal (1997) or Fromkin and Rodman (1998).

Whilst it is known that Latin and Ancient Greek were used in everyday life, languages from earlier periods still are more difficult to research. In the nineteenth century, linguists such as Jones, Grimm and Rask were convinced that the similarities between Sanskrit, Latin, Ancient Greek and the Germanic languages (into which family fits English) were too many to be pure coincidence (➻ Unit 1). This is all very well and shows how a genealogy of the world's languages can be established but the question still remains of where language itself came from, a point that was considered briefly earlier (➻ Unit 1) when comparing human language to other forms of **communication** as well as to animal language and communication systems.

SUMMARY

The English language has developed over a period of about 1500 years from a highly inflected language with four cases and three grammatical genders to a superficially simpler language with virtually no marked grammatical gender, few inflections for agreement of case and number on nouns and relatively few verb conjugations. The spelling system seems relatively complicated. That can be explained by the earliest written forms of the language being set in relation to the pronunciation of the time, being maintained as originally devised and not changing in line with the changes in pronunciation. The **lexicon** of the language has developed continually throughout that period, as a result of invasions, contact with other languages, industrial and scientific inventions and it continues to expand in a process of language change that appears unstoppable.

FURTHER READING

McCrum *et al.* (1992) provide a useful overview and the BBC films *The Story of English* provide useful additional information to the book. *The Adventure of English* (Bragg 2003) was also written in conjunction with a television series and provides a 'biography' of the language from 500–2000. Bryson's *Mother Tongue* (1990) is an entertaining survey of the major developments in English. Freeborn (1992) provides activities to encourage active engagement with the many samples of ancient and not so ancient texts as does Leith (1997) in *A Social History of English*. Watts and Trudgill (2002) collect various papers which require a more thorough knowledge of the area but which are nonetheless useful for the student. These accounts also show clearly that the development is not as clear or as linear as an outline such as that presented in this unit might suggest. Cameron (1996) is an interesting book to read on the meaning and derivations of place names.

FURTHER ACTIVITY

 Activity 13.7

Consider how the meaning and use of the following words has changed over the centuries by looking up the relevant entries in a good dictionary:

chronic	commute
nature	nice
queer	sophisticated
touch	wan

 Activity 13.8

Look at the quotation from the Genesis at the beginning of Unit 14. How does the language in that version differ from the language in other versions of the Bible, whether those versions are older or more modern?

COMMENTARY ON ACTIVITIES

Activity 13.2

This commentary does not comment on every word in the text.

Words from Old English include: *daughter, father, good, had, her, in, least, life, locking, mother, no, one, seen, temper, the, was, who, without* (originally two words, and different in meaning from *outwith* which often is used to mean 'outside'), *woman*. Most of the **function words** (➞ Unit 5) in current use in English date from this period.

Words from Middle English include: *beside* (in this form – in OE it had been two words), *character, considerable, constitution, disposition, infancy, living, person, plain, poor, sense, situation, suppose, useful*.

Words from (early) Modern English include: *addicted, clergyman, handsome, heroine, independence, neglected, remarkable, respectable*.

Some words, like many others, have changed their meaning or referent over a period of time:

- *living* only acquired this meaning (an office or a job in the church that provides an income for the person holding the post) in the 1500s, having been used only as a **verb** in OE
- *addicted* in this **context** will surprise many modern readers
- *handsome* is now mainly used to describe men but was earlier used to describe all people.

Given that each period lasts about 500 years, it should not be expected that the divisions between the periods are watertight, nor that the English language is unchanging throughout the period. *An* clearly comes from OE but the entry in the Oxford English Dictionary (OED) continues with explanations of changes that occurred in both ME and early ModE. It should also be remembered that any word in the dictionary will probably have been used orally for some considerable time before it is listed. New editions of any dictionary, but particularly of the OED, can provoke outrage and dismay as new words (e.g. *muggle* in Unit 9) are included and newly-obsolete terms dropped.

Having read the commentary, compare the proportions of OE/ME/ModE words in the *Northanger Abbey* passage with your guess. Were you right? Are you surprised?

Activity 13.4

The spelling differences are obvious and for the most part it is clear to see how the ModE spelling develops from this ME form. The noun-forming morpheme {*-cioun*} (L25) becomes {*-tion*} in ModE and the use of <y> for ModE <i> in *besyde* (L15) and *lye* (L27) are but two examples. Other words, e.g. *never* (L10), *wedding* (L11), *sharp* (L14), and *word* (L14), have not changed in spelling. The spelling of *axe* (L21) for 'ask' suggests a pronunciation change has occurred.

Thilke (L18) does not appear in ModE in this form but the word *ilk* is still used in Scotland and some northern English dialects in the phrase *of that ilk* with the meaning 'of the same kind'. *Glosen* (L26) can be understood as 'to gloss' in the sense of 'to explain', a word that seems to be being increasingly used in ModE, especially in textbooks!

The third person singular masculine appears in nominative case as *he*. The second person singular forms *thou* (L17), *thee* (L18) and *thyn* (L19), have now dropped out of use other than in religious texts and in some ModE dialects. In modern Standard British English the form *you* is used for singular and plural, formal and informal. Pronouns in ModE are the clearest descendants of the case system of OE and ME though the case endings on nouns are beginning to be lost in ME.

Forms of the verb *have* appear throughout the text: *hast* (L17), *hath* (L18) are inflected to agree with the **Subject** of the **clause**; *have* is the base form of the verb (L23) and the past participle (➔ Unit 7) of the verb *y-had* appears in L17. Forms of the verb *be* include *was* (L9) and *is* (L9). The past tense alveolar plosive ending (➔ Unit 8) appears in *seyde* (L19), *herde* (L24) and *myghte* (L23). *Spak* (L16) is the past tense form from *speke*.

The word order (e.g. L12, L24) shows some of the flexibility that is possible when case endings on nouns indicate the function of the noun in the clause though it must be remembered that word order in verse is more flexible than in prose.

The double negative of L10 is maintained in many dialect forms of ModE but is no longer accepted (and is often stigmatized) in modern Standard British English.

Activity 13.5

Old Norse (ON) appears in place names through the use of forms such as *by*, *thorpe*, *booth*, *lathe*, *garth*, *thwaite*. OE appears in place names through the use of forms such as *borough*, *ton*, *ham*, *leigh*, *toft*. Roman place names are often indicated by {*-cester*}. Some place names indicate the merging of the two languages e.g. Askrigg (OE + ON). Crystal (2003b) and Cameron (1996) will provide more examples.

Activity 13.6 (2)

Early Latin calendars contained ten months and November and December were the names of the last two months in that calendar. Sometime in the period 800–400BC as calendars were adjusted to ensure that the calendar remained in synchrony with the natural rhythms of the rotation of the earth, two months, January and February, were added at the beginning of the year but the names of other months were not changed to allow for their 'numbering' in the new calendar. Go to www.en.wikipedia.org for more information.

REFERENCES

Austen, J. (2003) *Northanger Abbey*, London: Penguin Books.

Baugh, A. and Cable, T. (2002) *A History of the English Language*, 5th edn, London: Routledge.

Bragg, M. (2003) *The Adventure of English 500AD to 2000: The Biography of a Language*, London: Hodder and Stoughton.

Bryson, B. (1990) *Mother Tongue*, London: Penguin.

Cameron, K. (1996) *English Place Names*, 2nd edn, London: B.T. Batsford.

Chaucer, G. (1995) *The Canterbury Tales*, Ware: Wordsworth Editions.

Crystal, D. (1997) *The Cambridge Encyclopedia of Language*, 2nd edn, Cambridge: Cambridge University Press.

Crystal, D. (2003b) *The Cambridge Encyclopedia of the English Language*, 2nd edn, Cambridge: Cambridge University Press.

Freeborn, D. (1992) *From Old English to Standard English: A Course Book in Language Variation Across Time*, Basingstoke: Macmillan.

Fromkin, V. and Rodman, R. (1998) *An Introduction to Language*, 6th edn, Fort Worth, TX: Harcourt Brace College Publishers.

Leith, D. (1997) *A Social History of English*, 2nd edn, London: Routledge.

McCrum, R., Cran, W. and MacNeil, R. (1992) *The Story of English*, revised edn, London: Faber and Faber.

Oxford English Dictionary (1973) *The Shorter Oxford English Dictionary*, Oxford: Clarendon.

Shakespeare, W. (1996) *Hamlet*, London: Penguin.

University of Georgetown. Online. Available HTTP: <http://www.georgetown.edu/faculty/ballc/oe/paternoster-oe.html> (accessed 23 September 2004).

Watts, R.J. and Trudgill, P. (eds) (2002) *Alternative Histories of English*, London: Routledge.

Wikipedia Online. Available HTTP: <http://en.wikipedia.org/wiki/Calendars> (accessed 23 September 2004).

14 WORLD ENGLISHES

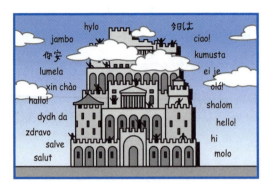

Figure 14.1   The Tower of Babel

And the whole earth was of one language and of one speech. ... And the Lord said, Behold, the people *is* one, and they have all one language; ... and now nothing will be restrained from them, which they have imagined to do. Go to, let us go down, and there confound their language, that they may not understand one another's speech.

(Genesis 11: 1, 6–7)

How would 'the whole earth ... of one language and of one speech' differ from the world as you experience it in your every day life? Is there any cause and effect relationship between the two statements 'the people *is* one' and 'they all have one language'? How many languages do you think that there are in the world today?[1] Were you anywhere near right? Why might (a Christian) God want 'that they may not understand one another's speech'? How limiting is it to human endeavour that they do not 'understand one another's speech'? Should 'they' try to find a common speech or not? Is 'a common speech' coming about without any explicit trying and might that 'common speech' be English? Leaving aside all the theology, so many questions about language emerge for consideration.

INTRODUCTION

There is little doubt that the English language has a role in the modern world quite unlike that of any other language. It is used as the **lingua franca** at international conferences in non-English speaking countries even when none of the participants speaks English as their mother tongue. Worldwide, aircraft are talked down to landing in English, whatever the nationalities and mother tongues of the pilot and the air-traffic controller. The World Wide Web is largely structured through the medium of English though it is increasingly possible to use other languages. Most pop music has lyrics in English.

These apparently obvious points hide various important questions for a linguist, especially a linguist considering language in use. What does the term 'English as a world/global language' mean and why do some people now prefer to talk about English as an *international* language? Is English used in the same way throughout the world (and, if so, why is this unit called 'World Englishes' and not 'World English'?) or are there different varieties of English or might one argue that there are different forms of English in use in the world that are so different from each other that they are almost like different languages? How has this international situation come about? How might this international role of English change? Should it? Why are linguists concerned about such issues? Such questions will be addressed in this unit.

ATTITUDES TO ENGLISH AND TO LANGUAGE

 Activity 14.1

What does the term *English* mean to you and to people about you? Is it a mother tongue? Is it a foreign language? Is it a language that you are comfortable using or that you like using? When and where do you use English – for work only, perhaps, or for socializing only? What is your emotional attachment to English? Do you feel that its use is imposed on you? How have you set the spellchecker for English on your computer (for US English or for UK English) and why? Think about these questions carefully both from your own position and from the position of others before you read further in this unit.

Some people find these questions far easier to answer than others: mother tongue speakers of English may never have even considered such matters. Any one group's or any one individual's view of English will be informed by their personal or group experiences. An individual's views about language and language use can be very personal, derived from their own personal experiences or experiences of those around them. A society's historical relation to Britain and to the British (colonization by whose Empire was not always seen everywhere as a good thing) or to the Americans (whose global economic and/or military might is not always and everywhere perceived as positive) might affect how that society views the language of the perceived 'oppressor'. Aborigine people in Australia or Maori in New Zealand, for example, could well see the English language as one form of oppression. The question is not always answered negatively, however. The Chinese are apparently learning English with enthusiasm, seeing competence in English as one of the prime drivers in their modernization programmes.

It could be argued that a society's proverbs give some indication of their underlying attitudes. Before doing Activity 14.2, try to find proverbs from your own culture and society which might indicate an attitude to language.

Activity 14.2 ⚭

The following translated proverbs have all been taken from Alladina and Edwards (1991) with the language communities indicated in brackets:

- Your language [English] on our shoulders like a burden (Welsh Gwenallt).
- A people without their own language is only half a people (British Romani).
- Speech is wealth (Hausa).
- Anyone who does not love their own native language is disgustingly worse than a smelly fish (Filipino).

Your task is to consider what you think each proverb says about the importance of language to the community and then to compare this with your own attitudes from the initial activity in this unit. You will also find it helpful to compare your own opinions with those of as wide a group of other people as possible.

INTERNATIONAL VARIETIES OF ENGLISH

 Activity 14.3 ⚭

What do you think these words mean: *jumper, lift, pavement, truck*? Make your definitions as precise as possible.

Reflect now on your own use of English. Would you say *flat* or *apartment*, *truck* or *lorry*, *pavement* or *sidewalk*, *tap* or *faucet*, *powdered sugar* or *icing sugar*, *Pyrex* or *corningware*? Your responses to these questions will help you to assess whether your use of English is British based or North American based, a distinction that is still maintained (e.g. Trudgill and Hannah 2002: 2). Crystal (2003a: 70) represents the way English has spread round the world using the image of a family tree, with British English (EngEng) and American English (AmEng) as the two main branches of the English language family (see Figure 14.2). The usefulness of this distinction is now being questioned but the map shows clearly the number of descendants of English and their wide distribution throughout the world.

You should also consider whether you ever use your non-preferred form? In what circumstances and why do you think you might use your non-preferred form? The prevalence of AmEng is becoming so widespread that many British English

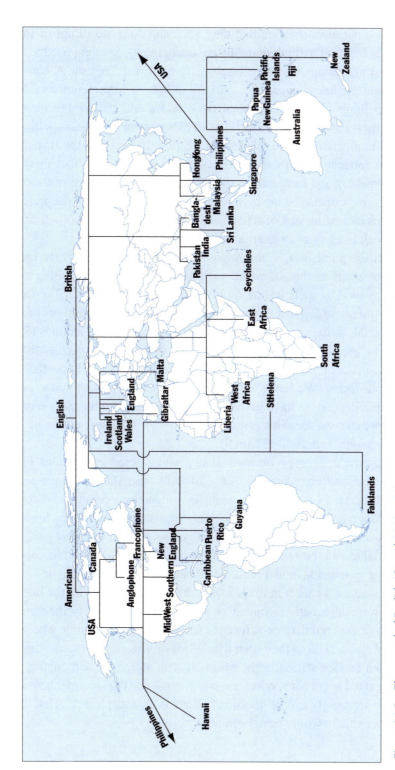

Figure 14.2   The spread of English (Crystal 2003a: 70)

speakers are not always aware that they are using American English forms (and some might be upset to think that they are using them). Spelling used to be a clear way of distinguishing American English from British English. A United States writer would use *labor, maneuvre, criticize* or *theater* in preference to the British English spellings of *labour, manoeuvre, criticise* and *theatre* but many British English writers have adopted some if not all of the North American spellings. North American English *aluminum* reflects the US pronunciation as the British spelling *aluminium* reflects the British pronunciation. However, the fact that 'you say tomato (tomahto), and I say tomato (tomeyto)' (as in the well-known song) shows that the reverse can also be the case: the spelling is the same but the pronunciation differs. This increasing lack of active awareness, however, is itself indicative of the way in which English as an international **variety** is developing.

The British publishers, Cambridge University Press, use what used to be regarded by many as the American spelling *encyclopedia* (a spelling marked as incorrect by the UK spellchecker on my computer) for Crystal's *The Cambridge Encyclopedia of the English Language* and at least two of the authors of this book admit to (mild) irritation on reading Routledge's editorial guidelines (Routledge 2001: 18) to 'use "ize" spellings as opposed to "ise" for words such as "organized" etc., for the benefit of the US market', even though the authors know that the OED accepts both forms. We have, however, staged a mini-protest and – aside from Crystal's publications – have actively chosen to consistently use *encyclopaedia* rather than *encyclopedia*. This is a clear example of language use being linked to issues of personal identity (➤ Unit 9).

The playwright, George Bernard Shaw, who offered suggestions on how to rationalize the spelling of English, is one of many who, it is said, have commented that the UK and the US were 'two countries divided by a common language'. It is true that there can be times when the choices of words are confusing for somebody trying to work in both varieties but the languages are, for the most part, mutually understandable and the misunderstandings can be used as the basis for many an entertaining discussion and broadcast. Anecdotes include that, on hearing an announcement on the train in the US that 'there was a jumper on the line', British travellers were apparently intrigued as to why this should delay the train unduly. They soon discovered that the **reference** was to a potential suicide who was being counselled against taking their own life. When driving across North America, and going into a service station in the Midwest with an overheated engine, a British traveller wanted to get some water and was surprised at the incomprehension which greeted the apparently simple question 'Where is the tap, please?'. Had they asked for the *faucet*, there would have been no problem.

Activity 14.4

From your experience do you think that such misunderstandings are likely to increase or to decrease? Explain your answer.

HOW ENGLISH BECAME A WORLD LANGUAGE

The English language is over a thousand years old (➤➤ Unit 13) and in the last 50 years, 'a mere eye-blink in the history of a language' (Crystal 2003a: 71), it has achieved a unique position in the world. How has this happened? In the fifteenth and sixteenth centuries, the European countries started to expand their horizons, both literally in terms of the discovery of lands new to the explorers at the time and metaphorically, in terms of knowledge. This Renaissance period was a time of great achievement in the arts, architecture and science. The use of English was largely confined to the British Isles but Britain was expanding its influence, as were many European countries, discovering countries new to them at the time and each taking their own language to those countries. So Portuguese arrived in South America, French and English in West Africa and English along with Dutch and German in the American continent.

Individuals and groups left England for many reasons, some willingly and some unwillingly. Sir Walter Raleigh was sent by Queen Elizabeth I to explore and to find further lands and territories. He took the English language with him and he brought back the potato (now a staple food in Britain) as well as information about the lands that he had discovered. The Pilgrim Fathers left with the intention of finding a land where they could practise their religion as they wished to without the trappings and heavy rituals that they found unacceptable in the Anglican Church. Traders went from Britain to the west coast of Africa to transport slaves from there to the southern states of North America and they completed the triangle by returning from America to Britain with spices, tobacco, sugar, molasses and treacle (amongst other goods) for trade. Convicts were sent from Britain to Australia in an attempt to ensure that they would never return to the scenes of their crimes and they were soon followed by free settlers who chose to move to another land to improve their lot in life.

PIDGINS AND CREOLES

Abhorrent and unacceptable as the slave trade is now unequivocally considered to be, linguists find some interest in the historical situation in relation to pidgin and creole languages. Slaves were taken from countries on the west coast of Africa.

Different tribes were mixed on the ships to reduce the chances of any attempt at insurrection on board. (Were the ships' masters 'playing god'?) Inevitably and naturally, there was going to be some attempt to communicate between the slaves and such a situation forms rich linguistic soil for the development of a pidgin. A pidgin language is a contact language, created for a particular purpose (for example, **communication** in the slave ships or for trade between peoples in South-East Asia) and it falls into disuse as soon as that specific need disappears. On the slave ships, pidgin languages allowed the slaves to communicate with each other in a language that would not be understood by the ships' masters. In Hong Kong, a profitable trading centre (originally based on opium, silk, silver, tea and spices) was established that still remains today. Though no longer using pidgin English for its multi-million dollar deals, it does use its own variety of international English and the development from pidgin to international variety of English is worth noting.

One of the widely-accepted etymologies for the word *pidgin* is that it was a reduced pronunciation form of the word *business* in South China pidgin. Mühlhäusler (1986: 1) offers other suggestions for the derivation of pidgin as coming from a Chinese corruption of the Portuguese word *ocupação* (business) or from the Hebrew word *pidjom* (exchange, trade, redemption), or from Yago (a South American Indian language spoken in an area colonized by Britain) in which language *pidian* means people, or from a South Seas pronunciation of the English word *beach* (pronounced as 'beachee') which is where the language was typically used. Whilst this list of possible derivations is not definitive (as Mühlhäusler himself accepts), what is interesting is the number of possible sources from so many different languages world wide.

Pidgin languages are contact languages which are created for a particular purpose and which die when they are no longer needed. Jenkins (2003: 10) explains that 'in theory, a creole arises when the children of pidgin speakers use their parents' pidgin language as the mother tongue. In other words, a creole has native speakers'. A pidgin does not have native speakers. However, it can be the case that the language which children acquire is still called a pidgin language and the West Coast of Africa provides a clear example still today (➔ Unit 12). Children are raised multilingually (➔ Unit 14) using the home language of their parents and a form of the West African Pidgin as a regional *lingua franca*.

ENGLISH IN THE WORLD

We have established that English is used world-wide and we have looked at how and why the language comes to be in this unique position. Different countries or groups of people, however, identify with the language in different ways and the

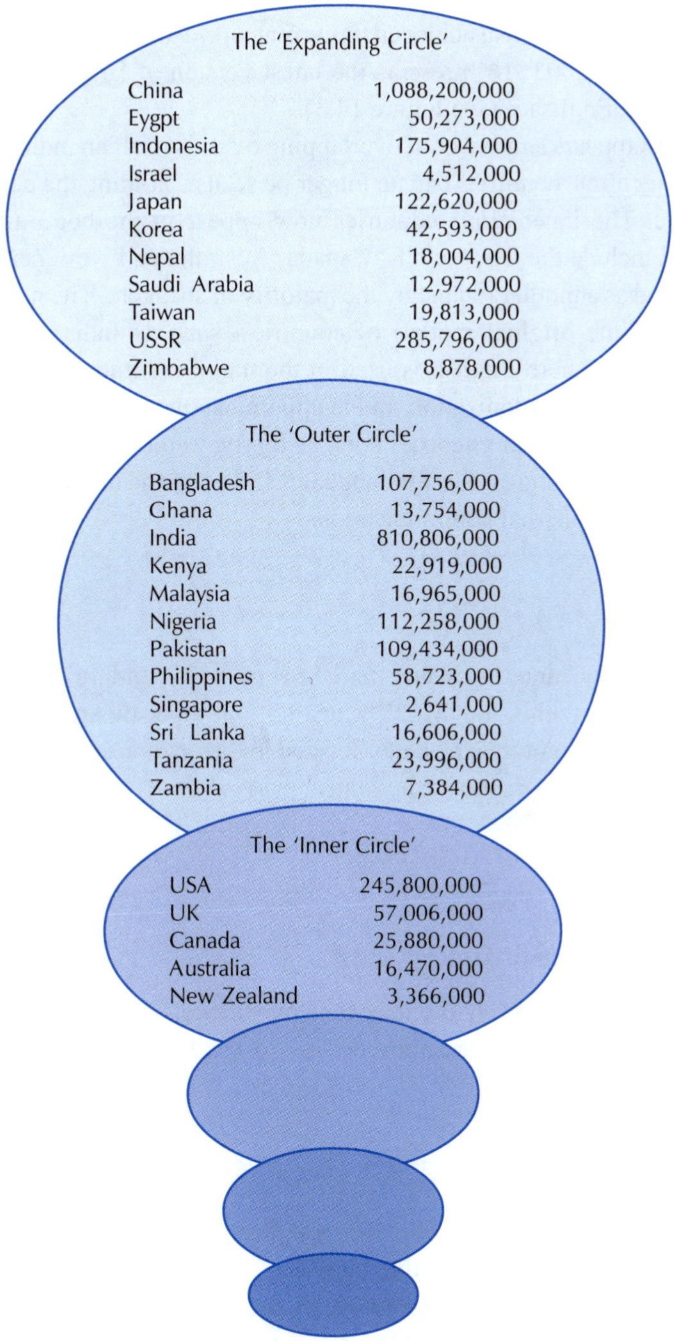

The 'Expanding Circle'

China	1,088,200,000
Eygpt	50,273,000
Indonesia	175,904,000
Israel	4,512,000
Japan	122,620,000
Korea	42,593,000
Nepal	18,004,000
Saudi Arabia	12,972,000
Taiwan	19,813,000
USSR	285,796,000
Zimbabwe	8,878,000

The 'Outer Circle'

Bangladesh	107,756,000
Ghana	13,754,000
India	810,806,000
Kenya	22,919,000
Malaysia	16,965,000
Nigeria	112,258,000
Pakistan	109,434,000
Philippines	58,723,000
Singapore	2,641,000
Sri Lanka	16,606,000
Tanzania	23,996,000
Zambia	7,384,000

The 'Inner Circle'

USA	245,800,000
UK	57,006,000
Canada	25,880,000
Australia	16,470,000
New Zealand	3,366,000

Note: In this, the most frequently cited version of the model, the circles are oval rather than circular, and presented vertically rather than concentrically, with the lowest circles representing earlier versions of English. Note also that the model was first published in 1988 and thus the figures (which are for whole populations rather than English speakers alone) are now out of date.

Figure 14.3   Kachru's three-circle model of World Englishes (Jenkins 2003: 16)

brief account of how English achieved its current world-wide role begins to explain that fact. Jenkins (2003: 16) presents the latest version of Braj Kachru's famous model of World Englishes (see Figure 14.3).

That it now appears as a tower of overlapping ovals is itself an indication that the so-called inner circle countries can no longer be seen as holding the central core of the language. The inner circle countries now appear in the bottom oval of the diagram and include the US, the UK, Canada, Australia and New Zealand, where English is used as a mother tongue by the majority of speakers. The next group (the outer circle of the original model) of countries, such as India, Singapore and Zambia are those where English is used in the major institutions of the country, often as a legacy from colonization. In the uppermost oval (the expanding circle of the original model) appear countries such as Egypt, Saudi Arabia and the USSR, where English is learnt as a foreign language and used for international business rather than for any internal communications.

Activity 14.5

Kachru places China, Japan and the USSR in the expanding circle. In the light of events within the last 20 years, do you think this placing is still appropriate or might they be better located in the outer circle? What about Nicaragua, Sweden or the Netherlands?

Activity 14.6 ⚬━┳

Now that you have had chance to consider the model in more detail, do you see any problems in representing the use of English in the world in this way?

HOW MANY PEOPLE SPEAK ENGLISH?

If English is a (the?) world language, does that mean that there are more speakers of English in the world than of any other language? That depends entirely on what is counted. Crystal lists some 75 territories in which he claims (2003b: 108) that 'English has held or continues to hold a special place' and explains that:

> to have a special place can mean various things. ... But in all cases, the population is living in an environment in which the English language is

routinely in evidence, publicly accessible in varying degrees, and part of the nation's recent or present identity.

In Australia and the UK, there are far more speakers of English as a first language (L1) than as a second language (L2), in Hong Kong and in Fiji there are far more speakers of English as L2 than as L1 and in Kenya and Bhutan there are only L2 speakers and no L1 speakers of English listed.

The use of English in many other countries could be considered but the question remains: who would be counted? Would speakers of English as the first language (L1) only be included? What about other users of English as a second language (L2) or as a foreign language? You might like to relate this question to Kachru's model. Would users of all the international varieties of English (and how many are there?) be included? If not, why not and on what grounds might such a variety be excluded?

These are but some of the issues raised in relation to asking the apparently simple question of how many speakers of English there are in the world. The final number itself is perhaps not particularly significant. More important are how the calculations are carried out, the debates about the role(s) that English currently has and the implications for other languages. Graddol (1997: 8) quotes statistics from 1996 which place English second behind Chinese in a list of major world languages counting first language speakers only. Alongside this, he lists the major domains in which English is used in world institutions (e.g. banking, science, tourism, tertiary education, film, TV, popular music) in which other languages used to hold greater sway, such as the use of French in diplomatic circles.

Even if the total number of speakers in itself is not particularly important, there is a question about how English is used in relation to the use of other languages. At the time of writing, some of the authors are supervising undergraduate and postgraduate studies by students from Norway and from Japan on the role of English in each country and the effects of English on the individual languages of Norwegian and Japanese. It is not that the effect of English loan words on languages such as Norwegian or Japanese is to be thought of as a pidginization of the languages. The contact is not between two speakers, each having their own language and no knowledge of the language of their **interlocutor**. The students' concern is that so many loan words from English are being incorporated into other languages at such speed that they question whether the boundaries between languages are now becoming more blurred. The students are also questioning whether their own languages are being 'overrun' by English, a view which is strikingly similar to Phillipson's concern about linguistic imperialism (Phillipson 1992).

Activity 14.7

By focusing on the words in the following text (and looking them up in a dictionary if you are unsure of their meaning), can you determine the country or the region the writer is writing about?

Our compound consisted of two houses facing each other with a small courtyard in between them. The walls were of bamboo and mud, and roofed with grass. Each house had a wide veranda all round it and the roof was tall, forming almost a second floor. But this was never lived in. It was used as a store for maize and groundnuts and millet. The door into the second floor was on the veranda and you climbed up to it using a portable bamboo ladder.

Papa's house was the bigger one. It had two rooms. In the centre of the main room was a hearth, and against the walls were bamboo beds, some for sleeping on, and some for storing things on. Mama's house had the same arrangement except that it had, in addition, bamboo shelves where pots and cooking utensils were kept. Calabashes and vessels for holding water stood on the floor against the wall.

All the land around the compound was farmed for fifty yards or more and planted with maize, plantains and other food crops. We kept chickens which lived on the veranda or in the trees around the compound. Everyone had his own chickens, one, two, or three, and we sold them whenever the need arose. Papa usually had most. He prepared a place for them to lay their eggs in, and Mama fed them every morning.

Activity 14.8

This data was found by a student who was trying to find samples of Caribbean English. Identify the specific features of this variety of English which mark it as different from the variety that you use.

HI <NAME>
I DON'T KNOW IF THIS IS WHAT U EXPECT BUT HERE GOES THE BEST MOMENT OF MY LIFE
   AS A YUTE GROWIN UP, MI ALWAYS HEAR DEM TALK 'BOUT GOD, 'BOUT HOW 'IM GOOD, AN HOW IM SEN' 'IM SON FI DEAD PON DI CROSS FI SAVE US FROM WI SIN. BUT MI

NEVA UNDASTAN UNTIL MI START GET BIG AN' CAN REASON OUT T'INGS FI MI'SELF.

MI WAS A TROUBLE MEKA IN SCHOOL SO EVRY BADY KNOW MI, MI FAMILY NEVA HAVE MUCH, BUT DAT NEVA REALLY BADDA MI CAUSE MI CUDA BEAR DI HUNGRY. ANYWAY, MI WASTE MOST A MY TIME A SCHOOL SO MI NEVA GET NUH SUBJEC' 'BOUT A YEAR AFTA MI LEF' SCHOOL MI GAA WAN CRUSADE DAT DI CHURCH DUNG DI ROAD DID A PUT ON, DI PASTA DID A TALK 'BOUT HELL AN FIRE AND ALLA DEM T'ING DEH. AT DI END A DI CRUSADE 'IM ASK IF NUH BADY WAAN GI DEM LIFE TO CHRIST AN' MI DID FEEL CONVICTED FI DWEET SO MI WALK UP AN' RIGHT DERE AND DEN MI AXEP' CHRIST AS MI PERSONAL LORD A SAVIOUR, DI ONLY REGRET I HAVE IS DAT I NEVA DWEET SOONA.

SO ... DAT IS DI BEST MOMENT OF MY LIFE.

I REALLY HOPE THAT THIS HELPED.

HAVE A GREAT DAY   <NAME>

 ## Activity 14.9 o━

Identify in each of the following texts lexical items and syntactic constructions which differ from your use of English and which might provide some clues to the international variety of English being used. The two passages have been written by different writers.

The commentary at the end of the unit includes bibliographical information.

(a)

In the year nineteen hundred and nineteen I was a young clerk in the Niger Company at Umuru. To be a clerk in those days is like to be a minister today. My salary was two pounds ten. You may laugh but two pounds ten in those days is like fifty pounds today. You could buy a big goat with four shillings. I could remember the most senior African in the company was one Saro man on ten-thirteen-four. He was like Governor-General in our eyes.

Like all progressive young men I joined the African Club. We played tennis and billiards. Every year we played a tournament with the

European Club. But I was less concerned with that. What I liked was the Saturday night dances. Women were surplus. Not all the waw-waw women you see in townships today but beautiful things like this.

(b)

mi know yu couldn tek it dada
di anguish an di pain
di suffaharin di prablems di strain
di strugglin in vain
fi mek two ens meet
soh dat dem pickney coulda get
a lickle something fi eat
fi put cloaz pan dem back
fi put shoes pan dem feet
wen a dallah cant buy
a lickle dinnah fi a fly

mi know yu try dada
yu fite a good fite
but di dice dem did loaded
an di card pack fix
yet still yu reach fifty-six
before yu lose yu leg wicket
'a noh yu bawn grung here'
soh wi bury yu a Stranger's Burying Groun
near to mhum an cousin Daris
nat far fram di quarry
doun a August Town.

THE FUTURE OF ENGLISH

Throughout this book, there is a fundamental belief that any comments on language should be based on evidence from authentic language use, analysed systematically and in detail. How then, can the future of English be considered? Surely, this is now crystal-ball gazing – an approach fundamentally opposed to the data-based approach which has so far underpinned the book? True – but the recent Millennium provoked much speculation about the future in relation to a whole range of topics and language was not immune from this Zeitgeist. This unit ends with a series of points made by experts in the field for you to consider in the light of what you have read here and elsewhere.

Activity 14.10

Much of the discussion at the turn of the Millennium focused on the question of whether there will develop a single world-wide standard spoken English (WSSE) or whether the language will fragment and the currently mutually intelligible varieties become mutually unintelligible. If you think that a world standard is likely to develop, then presumably you think that misunderstandings of the kind noted earlier in the unit are likely to decrease rather than to increase in number. If you think that such misunderstandings are likely to increase, then you must be more pessimistic about the possibility of a world standard English developing. From your experience, what do you think will happen?

 Activity 14.11

Graddol (1997: 56) wondered whether second-language countries (countries using English as L2) 'may bring new, non-native models of English ... into competition with the older standard varieties' and thereby questioned whether the current supremacy of AmEng and EngEng will continue. Crystal (2003a: 184) commented 'that some of the territories of the expanding circle ... may be bending English to suit their purposes' and that 'local usages are emerging, and achieving a standard status within a region'. He also notes (2003a: 188) that 'there is no reason for L2 features not to become part of WSSE'. What are the arguments in favour of this suggested state of affairs; what advantages might be derived from the emergence of a range of regional standards in spoken or in written English? Are there any disadvantages?

 Activity 14.12

Jenkins (2003: 142) recognizes the current supremacy of AmEng and EngEng in a position which she characterizes as:

> educated (but monolingual!) L1 English speakers, unaware of the superiority of the bilingual's linguistic repertoire and skills, assume the right to the senior position in the English language hierarchy. English

for international use thus has at its pinnacle and serving as global models the varieties of English used by a small number of (L1) English speakers

What points might you make to argue that this linguistic situation should be maintained and what opposing points might you use to argue that this situation is perverse and should be reversed? Make sure that your points can be supported with evidence and are related to language issues.

Activity 14.13

Melchers and Shaw (2003: 196) conclude that:

Wide use of English is a natural consequence of the way the world is now. It benefits inner circle countries in many ways. It helps them spread their conscious or unconscious ideologies, and offers opportunities for their education systems, publishers, entertainment industries, newspapers and magazines to exploit wider markets. This process may well be damaging to the survival and scope of other languages ... but it is probably not realistic to expect the USA, Britain, and Australia to act to hinder something which is so advantageous to them. The governments of other countries have to strive to manage language use in their own countries so as to maintain linguistic diversity and the vitality of their own languages. Some countries, even small ones like Iceland, are remarkably successful in this type of policy, but English is so popular and so much in demand worldwide, that many democratic systems do not seem to be able to do more than tinker at the margins. One effect of globalization is to weaken national governments and make it more difficult for them to carry out language policies that resist its trends. ... Concerted action to manage the spread of English is a long way off.

What do you think?

Activity 14.14

Jenkins (2003: 44–46) demonstrates that English is not the easiest language in the world to learn as L2, not least because of some aspects of its syntax and pronunciation as well as its confusing spelling system. As a result, she comments (2003: 46) that:

> it would not be surprising if there was eventually a move to abandon English in favour of an international language with fewer complicating linguistic factors along with less of a colonialist discourse attached to it. Spanish appears to be a major contender, with its simpler pronunciation, spelling and verb systems, and its increasing influence in both the EU [European Union] and America.

How might such a change affect you and your country directly? How would you (and others) react to such a change?

SUMMARY

The English language has expanded from being a language used in a small island off the north western coast of Europe to a language that is used throughout the world for an astonishingly wide range of social purposes (➤ Unit 9). Its spread has been swift and was not widely discussed until the extent of its incursion into other languages and communities was recognized. The distinctions between the major international varieties of English are becoming blurred. Predictions around the time of the Millennium ranged from anticipating that English would become the main language of the world to anticipating the death of English as a single language as the number of different international varieties increased and became perhaps mutually unintelligible. Time alone will tell what the outcomes of the changes might be but it is certain that the language will continue, as do all languages, to change in line with the ever-changing circumstances of its use.

FURTHER READING

World Englishes (Melchers and Shaw 2003) provides a very clear and a very readable account of many international varieties of English, organizing their material on the 'three circles' model together with a CD which provides good data for analysing the different accents. *International English* (Trudgill and Hannah 2002) covers similar material. *World Englishes* (Jenkins 2003) introduces key topics in the debate, the implications of which are developed and explored further before presenting a series of original papers from others who are working in the area. Graddol's (1997) *The Future of English* was commissioned by the British Council to 'facilitate informed debate about the future use and learning of the English language worldwide'. The British Council clearly had its own agenda in commissioning the work but Graddol covers a wide range of issues and provides some useful statistics.

FURTHER ACTIVITY

 Activity 14.15

Record (segments of) speeches in English from three world leaders, each from a different country. As this unit has focussed largely on AmEng and EngEng, use Figure 14.3 as an indication of other varieties you might consider. Identify the differences and the similarities in the way the different speakers use English.

 Activity 14.16

From your own circle of friends and acquaintances, record somebody who uses a different international variety of English from your own. Analyse the features which mark their use of English as different from yours.

COMMENTARY ON ACTIVITIES

Activity 14.2

The proverbs exemplify different attitudes to language. The Welsh proverb demonstrates how a language can be seen as an oppressive force and the oppression may be political or social. The Romani proverb, and to a certain extent the Filipino proverb, demonstrates the importance of language in an individual's sense of identity – to make this more concrete, consider how you might feel if, overnight, you were told that your education were to be through the medium of another language. Consider also how your lecturers might feel! The Hausa proverb is concerned with the importance of language in development (of the individual or the society) and how the imposition of one language on another can disempower one group of people in relation to another group.

Activity 14.3

For the authors who largely use British English (EngEng), the meanings of each lexical item are as follows. Definitions (adapted from Oxford English Dictionary) and alternative meanings for other international varieties of English are included for each word.

jumper: a knitted or crocheted garment worn to cover the upper part of the body. In American English (AmEng), this lexical item can be used to mean a pinafore dress or a person or animal that jumps.

lift:
(a)   as a **noun**, *lift* means
    (i)   a platform, compartment or cage raised or lowered in a vertical shaft to transport goods or people in a building (e.g. *They went up to the top floor in the lift*)
    (ii) a ride (e.g. *Can you give me a lift to the station, please?*)
(b)   as a **verb** *lift* means to raise something/someone from a horizontal surface (e.g. *She lifted the baby from its crib* (but *crib* in South Island New Zealand English is used to mean a weekend cottage).

In AmEng, *lift* is only used as a verb with meaning (b) from British English.

pavement: a hard-surfaced path alongside a roadway for pedestrians. In AmEng the term *sidewalk* would be used for this meaning and *pavement* might be used for the roadway itself. The potential for dangerous misunderstanding here is obvious and can be compared with the similar potentially dangerous misunderstanding of the word *while* (➤ Unit 9).

truck: a vehicle for carrying goods (or freight, a word some might argue is part of AmEng) on the railway which in AmEng is often used as a **synonym** (or near synonym) for *lorry*.

From just these four examples, the potential for inter-variety misunderstanding is obvious. To continue your research in this area, work from your own experience of English and identify other **lexical items** which are used differently in different international varieties. For starters, you might like to consider the following: *purse*, *bill*, *wallet*, *flat*, *apartment*, *pants*, *rubbish*, *push chair* and *motorway*.

Activity 14.6

You might have wondered how multilingual issues are accounted for (➤ Unit 12) or whether the same linguistic situation obtains in countries which appear in the same circle. You might have wondered about levels of speaker proficiency or competence in relation to the circles. Would you accept and agree with the implication that speakers of inner circle countries have a greater proficiency in English use than those in other circle countries? Jenkins (2003: 17) considers these and other issues in more detail.

Activity 14.7

Some of the lexical items might initially have made you think that you were reading a text by a North American author. However, items such as *calabash*, *millet*, *vessels for holding water* and *plantain* probably made you want to revise that view as might also the statement that the *walls were of bamboo and mud, and roofed with grass*. The design of the houses being described and the purpose to which different parts of the house are put might also have made you pause for thought. In fact, you have been reading the first paragraphs of *The White Man of God* by the Cameroonian author, Kenjo Jumbam.

Activity 14.8

This commentary is in comparison to standard British English. This text appeared in the message section of an e-mail.

- There are some inconsistencies in the spelling in that *me* is spelt 'mi' and 'me' and non-standard spelling is used e.g. *yute*, *dem*, *neva*, *sen'*, *u*, *subjec'*, *dweet* for 'do it'.
- The non-standard spelling is an attempt to represent pronunciation: <d> for [ð], <t> for [θ], <ə> for final schwa, the apostrophe in *sen'* and *subjec'* indicating the simplification of the final consonant cluster [nt] in *sent* and [kt] in *subject*.
- *U* for 'you' may represent pronunciation or may be an abbreviated spelling.
- The first person **pronoun** is used in the same form, whatever its syntactic function in the clause (*mi always hear, evry bady know mi*).
- The first person singular possessive **determiner** appears in standard form whereas for the first person plural, 'wi' is used where in Standard English *our* would be used.
- *Fi* is used for *to* in the infinitive of the verb in the **clause** of purpose 'to save us from our sins' and is reminiscent of the older form of Standard English 'He did this for to save us from our sins'. *Fi* is used elsewhere to mean 'for'.
- 'Dead' is used for the verb *die* on the cross to save us from our sins.
- The **adjective** *hungry* is used for the noun *hunger*.
- *A* is used to indicate a past participle in 'did a put on' and 'did a talk about hell an' fire'.

Activity 14.9

(a)   In this text, *Uncle Ben's choice* by the Nigerian writer, Chinua Achebe, you might have noticed amongst others the following points. Lexical issues include the use of *waw-waw* to describe women (referred to as 'things' later in the text) and *surplus* with the meaning of 'in great number'. The definite article is omitted where other varieties of English would require its use. Achebe's way of expressing the old form of money in terms of pounds shillings and pence is unusual in *ten-thirteen-four*.

(b)   This text comes from Linton Kwesi Johnson's *Reggae fi Dada*. Linton Kwesi Johnson was born in Jamaica but moved to London when he was nine years old. The non-standard spelling reflects a Caribbean English accent. The use of *fi* to indicate purpose and the use of uninflected *mi* for the first person singular pronoun in whatever position are regular features of the **syntax** of this variety (cf. Activity 14.8). **Auxiliary** *did* leads to a double marking of the past tense (e.g. did loaded). The lexical item *pickney* for 'child' is part of the **dialect** and the use of the cricket metaphor is not surprising in a text rooted in the West Indies (➔ also Unit 9).

REFERENCES

Achebe, C. (1988) 'Uncle Ben's choice', in R. Sharrock (ed.) *The Green Man Revisited*, Oxford: Oxford University Press.

Alladina, S. and Edwards, V. (1991) *Multilingualism in the British Isles*, 2 vols, Harlow: Longman.

Crystal, D. (1997) *The Cambridge Encyclopedia of Language*, 2nd edn, Cambridge: Cambridge University Press.

Crystal, D. (2003a) *English as a Global Language*, Cambridge: Cambridge University Press.

Crystal, D. (2003b) *The Cambridge Encyclopedia of the English Language*, 2nd edn, Cambridge: Cambridge University Press.

Genesis, in The Holy Bible, The King James Version.

Graddol, D. (1997) *The Future of English?*, London: British Council.

Jenkins, J. (2003) *World Englishes: A Resource Book for Students*, London: Routledge.

Johnson, L.K. (1986) 'Reggae fi Dada', in P. Burnett (ed.) *The Penguin Book of Caribbean Verse*, London: Penguin.

Jumbam, K. (1980) *The White Man of God*, London: Heinemann Educational Books.

Melchers, G. and Shaw, P. (2003) *World Englishes*, London: Arnold.

Mühlhäusler, P. (1986) *Pidgin and Creole Linguistics*, Oxford: Blackwell.

Oxford English Dictionary (1973) *The Shorter Oxford English Dictionary*, Oxford: Clarendon.

Phillipson, R.H.L. (1992) *Linguistic Imperialism*, Oxford: Oxford University Press.

Routledge (2001) *Taylor & Francis Books: Instructions for Authors*, London: Taylor & Francis.

Trudgill, P. and Hannah, J. (2002) *International English: A Guide to Varieties of Standard English*, 4th edn, London: Arnold.

NOTE

1 Crystal (1997: 286) states that 'Most reference books give a figure from 5,000 to 6,000, but estimates have varied from 3,000 to 10,000'. Why should there be such wide variation in these figures? Crystal (1997: 286–7) will provide further insights.

15 LANGUAGE IN EDUCATION

UNIT CONTENTS

INTRODUCTION

Within living memory, some schools for the Deaf made pupils sit on their hands and in other ways tried to prevent them from using Sign Language. Except in their own clubs and a few very small communities, Deaf people are a minority, and minority languages have often been sidelined in education. Perhaps you would say that the majority must have precedence. But think how speakers of a minority language feel when informed that their language is not going to be taught in schools, or when – as in the history of Deaf education – it is actively discouraged. Another example is that children in the Alsace border area of France used to be punished for speaking Alsatian – their local Germanic language – anywhere on school premises, including the playground.

As an introduction to this unit about language issues that impinge on education, it is worth seeing how the policy of discouraging sign languages in schools came about, and why the idea is nowadays rejected almost everywhere.

The Milan Congress

In 1880, educators of the Deaf discussed their work at an international conference in Italy. One of the decisions made at that meeting had consequences for what happened in schools for the Deaf around the world over the next 75 years, or longer:

> availability of a sign language hindered a Deaf child from learning how to speak … it was decided that signing should be discouraged and that Deaf children should be encouraged to develop lipreading and speaking skills.
>
> (Bettger 2000: 325)

It was felt that if signing was accepted in schools, pupils would lose the incentive to make the effort needed to learn to speak and understand an oral language accurately enough to communicate with hearing people. The resolution was motivated by good intentions, but many Deaf people and educators of the Deaf maintain that it had negative effects.

Firstly, the Milan Congress resolution is regarded as mistaken because it proposed a single solution for all, even though there are widely different communicative needs, preferences, signing skills and hearing abilities amongst people termed *Deaf* or *Hard of Hearing*.

> ### 🖋 Activity 15.1 ⚬━┳
>
> How successfully can speech be decoded from just seeing a talking face?
>
> Find a section in a video where a few sentences are spoken carefully and where the speaker's face, including the mouth, can be seen clearly. Write down what the speaker says. Then, with the sound turned off, play the chosen part a few times over to a friend who is not familiar with that particular video and see how well your friend can understand what is being said. (Of course, it must be in a language your friend knows and the original speech must not have been 'dubbed' over by another voice.)

In practice only a minority of pupils in schools for the Deaf became proficient at speaking and lip-reading. This is because speaking involves articulations made in parts of the mouth and throat that are hidden from view (➻ Unit 8). Furthermore, rather than discouraging the learning of another language, being able to use a sign language appears to facilitate literacy (learning to read and write). There will be more about this later in the unit.

Gallaudet University

Gallaudet University, Washington DC – famous as the world's only liberal arts university exclusively for Deaf and Hard of Hearing students – is a good example of current approaches to language in Deaf education. The university, which traces its degree-awarding powers back to a charter signed by Abraham Lincoln, emphasizes effective **communication**:

> Gallaudet University is a bilingual community in which both American Sign Language and English thrive. … our community will incorporate and respect ASL and recognize that students, faculty members, and staff members may each have different visual communication needs. We will respect the sign language style of each individual and use whatever is necessary to communicate in a given situation.
>
> (Gallaudet 2002)

Educational linguistics

This unit is about language issues in the context of schools. Teaching cannot be done without communication, and communication at school is overwhelmingly through language. (Direct demonstration, diagrams and encouraging smiles are important too, but education as we know it could hardly be restricted to these.) As well as learning *through* languages, there is, in schools, much learning *of* languages, as preparation for communication in life and work. There is often public debate – sometimes heated – over which languages should be available, at what levels, and how they should be taught. *Educational linguistics* is a label for the branch of linguistics that – in collaboration with educationists, psychologists and sociologists – attempts to provide well-informed guidance in this field.

A taste will be given here of the range and complexity of educational linguistics in terms of three recurring themes:

- global English
- the acquisition of literacy (= learning to read and write)
- minority languages.

The United States of America, the country with the world's largest number of first language speakers of English, provides the main case study of language policy discussed in this unit. For comparison, a telling piece of research which suggests that Sign Language skills facilitate the learning of English reading and writing is recounted first.

SIGN LANGUAGES AND ENGLISH

Sign languages, such as ASL (American Sign Language) used by the Deaf community in the USA, are real **languages**. Sign languages are articulated mainly with the hands and face. They are the natural languages of Deaf communities. They are not mime efforts struggling to help the receiver guess at a meaning, but are communicative systems of patterned signals as complex as spoken languages (➤ Unit 1). Sign languages are not signed variants of the local spoken language,

Figure 15.1   The word *college* being signed in BSL (British Sign Language)

even though finger-spelling conventions for translating from spoken languages form a subsidiary component of sign languages.

The geographical boundaries of spoken languages and signed languages often do not coincide. For instance, despite the fact that the dominant language in both the USA and the UK is English, the Deaf communities in these two countries have different sign languages, ASL and BSL (British Sign Language), respectively. And – another example – although Welsh is a very different language from English, in Wales the language of the Deaf is BSL. Furthermore, the BSL of Welsh signers from Welsh-speaking families is the same as the BSL of signers from English-speaking families in Wales (Woll 2002).

 Activity 15.2 🔑

Here are four BSL sentences (from Sutton-Spence and Woll 1999: 54, 68). Each of the **words** in capital letters represents a BSL sign. See Figure 15.1 for an example of a BSL sign.

BSL	Translation into English
TEDDY WHERE?	'Where's Teddy?'
KEYS WHERE?	'Where are the keys?'
LINGUISTICS WHAT?	'What is linguistics?'
TOM WHO?	'Who is Tom?'

What does this dataset suggest about differences between the **syntax** of BSL and English? (Of course, four sentences is too small a sample for confident statements.)

People labelled as *Deaf* do not constitute a homogeneous category. They vary in many ways, with the following dimensions being particularly significant:

- degree of deafness: profoundly deaf (i.e. having no functional hearing) through varying levels of hearing loss
- age of onset: from birth or soon afterwards through to old age
- initial language learning environment: ones where a sign language is dominant – the usual circumstances of the 10 per cent or so of Deaf children raised by Deaf parents – through to environments in which almost all communication is in a spoken language.

There are Deaf communities ranging in size from village clubs to national and international groupings. Their main defining feature is use of a sign language. The central members of a Deaf community tend to be profoundly deaf people, deaf from birth and raised in a signing environment. But many Deaf communities have some hearing members, who may be comfortable with a sign language because of having a Deaf parent, friend or spouse.

Sign facilitates English literacy

For many Deaf people, it is not feasible to learn to speak and lip-read an oral language. However, for participation in wider society most members of Deaf communities need to be literate in the main spoken language of their country or region.

The findings of a research study (Strong and Prinz 1997) on 155 Deaf children aged 8–15 years, all with severe or profound hearing loss, go against some common assumptions about Deaf education. Strong and Prinz made careful assessments of the children's ASL signing skills (comprehension and production), their English reading comprehension and, for writing in English, their vocabulary, grammatical and narrative proficiency. Thinking along Milan Congress lines would lead to the expectation that those with the best developed ASL skills and those who had a Deaf parent would be less capable of reading and writing English, on account of reduced incentive, given that they had ASL as a means of communication and that ASL was probably used in their homes. Conversely, children with two hearing parents might be expected to have more exposure at home to English and thus be better able to learn English literacy skills when they go to school.

In fact, Strong and Prinz (1997) found that those who were more skilled in ASL were significantly more likely to have higher levels of English literacy skills. You might think that this could just be because the more intelligent children and the older ones are better at everything, but in calculating the correlations Strong and Prinz partialled out the effects of intelligence and age, so the results cannot be explained away like that.

Strong and Prinz's data also showed that Deaf children whose parents were Deaf scored significantly higher, on average, in not only the ASL tests but also the English literacy tests. Very interestingly, this is apparently not because of some non-language factor such as children with Deaf family members having better adjustment to life. Strong and Prinz established this by making further comparisons between children from Deaf and Hearing homes in which the level of ASL was kept constant. In these comparisons across similar levels of ASL performance, the enhancement of English reading and writing for children with Deaf parents largely disappeared. Thus it seems that a Deaf home environment promoted the learning of ASL; and, in turn, ASL skills made it easier for children to learn to read English.

LANGUAGE POLICY ISSUES IN THE USA

Educational planners around the world cannot avoid consideration of US influences. For around 80 years, the United States has been a dominant influence on popular culture (think of Hollywood movies, for instance), through the medium of English. It is today at the centre of globalization. So, even if you have no particular interest in language policy issues in the USA, they could easily be relevant to you, and that is a reason for including the topic here.

Ebonics

In California, in December 1996, the board of Oakland Unified School District (OUSD) decided on a new school policy for African American students, then slightly more than half of the students in the district's schools. School board resolutions do not usually grab national attention, but this one created a stir in the US and was widely reported internationally. The OUSD board revised the resolution a month later, while maintaining its central proposals. Some of the changes made will be mentioned later.

In the following quotation from the resolution, the board accepted that African American students in its schools were not performing well in English and put forward what proved to be a very contentious proposal:

> the standardized tests and grade scores of African American students in reading and language art skills measuring their application of English skills are substantially below state and national norms and ... such deficiencies will be remedied by application of a program featuring African Language Systems principles in instructing African American children both in their primary language and in English.
>
> (OUSD 1996)

The original resolution stated that most African Americans 'are not native speakers of black dialect or any other dialect of English' and proposed that federal funds available for bilingual education should be amongst those tapped to help African American pupils. It also said that:

> All classroom teachers and aids who are bilingual in Nigritian Ebonics (African–American Language) and English shall be given the same salary differentials and merit increases that are provided to teachers of the non-African American LEP pupils [pupils with limited English proficiency]
>
> (OUSD 1996)

US teachers bilingual in, for example, Spanish and English and thus able to assist children whose home language is Spanish were eligible for certain incentives. (A home language is a language used at home, normally learnt in the earliest years of life.)

Reactions to the OUSD school board's proposals often focused on the matter of language versus **dialect**. Many people were surprised at the claim that African American ways of talking constituted a separate language. They thought it obvious that African American speech is a variety of English. However, concentrating on this misses an important point: the matters that the school board was grappling with are tied up with politics and self-esteem, and would not be solved by an expert's opinion on whether or not Ebonics is a distinct language.

Charles Fillmore, a respected linguist, memorably remarked that asking whether African American vernacular varieties are dialects of English or a different language is like worrying about whether Greenland is a small continent or a large island. Distinguishing between a dialect and a language is not a simple matter of science. It does relate to the extent of communication possible between people, but it also depends on people's feelings of friendship or disaffection (and, of course, intelligibility is influenced by willingness to understand one another – which, in turn, can be affected by feelings of attachment or remoteness). Linguists generally avoid disputes regarding the boundaries between languages and dialects. Their preferred term is **variety** (⇥ Unit 9), which includes both language and dialect.

Activity 15.3 ⚬━

There are certainly differences between the approved school variety of Standard American English (SAE) and characteristic African American speech. (As with any other group, there is variability among African Americans regarding which varieties they use and prefer in various situations.) One difference is a systematic distinction found in the progressive forms of African American varieties, but signalled differently in SAE. (Progressive forms consist of the **auxiliary verb**, *be*, followed by a main verb bearing the **suffix** {-*ing*} ⇥ Unit 7.) Here are some examples (from Fasold 1999: 2); the meanings in quotes are in SAE:

Present progressive	Present habitual
She eatin or *She is eatin*	*She be eatin* or *She do be eatin*
'She is eating'	'She is sometimes/usually/always eating'

SAE can express habituality with words such as *usually* or *always*, or by using simple present tense, e.g. *She eats chili peppers* meaning that she 'sometimes/usually/always eats them'.

Given that proficiency in Standard English is an agreed goal of the school system, which of the imaginary teacher responses listed below would you recommend, when students have written sentences such as *She be eatin*, intending in this case to express the meaning 'She is always eating'? Try to think about it in general terms, rather than as just about this particular sentence. Explain the reasons for your answer.

- That's not right. You should have written *She is eating*.
- If you mean 'she's eating right now' then the way to write that is *She is eating*. If you mean 'She usually eats or she always eats' then the way to write it is *She usually eats*.
- That's the way people talk, but we do it differently when we write English. Do you know how?
- *She be eatin*: I understand what you mean, but lots of people would say that you made a mistake. If you want me to tell you more about it, come and see me, after I have looked at the other students' work.
- This afternoon we'll have a class about different ways of talking and different ways that people use language. Remind me then about this sentence. It's a good example.

Quick and easy solutions are not available for language education issues. Education affects life chances and embodies people's views on what is right and just. Expert knowledge can make important contributions but there are ideological dimensions to language education policy.

The amended version of the Oakland Board's resolution, passed on 15 January 1997, proposed incentives for teachers certified as having expertise needed to enable speakers of the African American vernacular make the transition to Standard English (OUSD 1997). This requires more than Ebonics–English bilingualism to qualify for an enhanced salary. The assertion that Ebonics is not a dialect of English was modified to a claim that African American ways of talking 'are not merely dialects of English'. The directive that, as well as English, African American children should receive instruction 'in their primary language' was not in the amended resolution. The main points retained were a clear determination to improve students' command of Standard English, to do so by giving recognition and respect to their home language and requiring teachers to use knowledge of the latter in class.

Official English

In trying to understand the Ebonics argument, it is natural to wonder what US policy is on language. What does the American Constitution say about official use of languages? What is the basis for federal funding of bilingual education, mentioned in the original Oakland resolution? US power has, for about a century, ensured the global pre-eminence and continuing spread of English (Crystal 2003a), so its stance on language policies can affect the rest of the world.

It is obvious that English is the official language of the United States of America. Obvious it may be, but neither the Constitution nor the Bill of Rights lays that down (Schiffman 1996: 232). In an interesting chapter on language policy in the United States, Schiffman maintains that it has not needed to be made explicit, as 'its strength lies in the basic assumptions that American society has about language' (1996: 213). English is taken as incontestably necessary for the unity and character of the United States of America. (In England too, it is by tradition rather than law that English is the official language, Dickson and Cumming 1996: 25.)

Support for bilingual education might appear to be at odds with such assumptions, particularly in a country where massive immigration seldom left much of a trace in the form of bilingualism (Schiffman 1996: 227). According to Schiffman (1996: 240), the 1967/8 Bilingual Education Act was largely attributable to the arrival in South Florida of exiles from Cuba after Castro's revolution in 1959. Many of these people thought of themselves as only temporarily resident in the US. Many of them were middle class. In general, they had no wish to give up Spanish. They had considerable public sympathy and US Government support. Bilingual classes were set up for their children, to maintain the community's Spanish language while giving them competence in English. This provided the example to justify experimenting with federal support for bilingual education if it seemed likely to help school students from any minority language background to become competent in English.

A substantial body of opinion in the US is sceptical or even hostile towards such initiatives. Bilingual education is viewed as a waste of money and perhaps a threat to the status of English. People from monolingual majorities can feel very much excluded when they travel in countries where their own language is not the main one. For them it can be unnerving to think that areas of their own country might become similarly unintelligible through immigrant languages getting public recognition, or that a bilingual immigrant might one day be preferred for a job over an indigenous monolingual.

The most prominent organization pitted against bilingual education in the United States is *US English*, founded in 1983. It campaigns for legislation, preferably at the federal level, to affirm English as the official language of the United States:

> Declaring English the official language means that official government business at all levels must be conducted solely in English. This includes all public documents, records, legislation and regulations, as well as hearings, official ceremonies and public meetings.
>
> (*US English* 2002)

In 1996 the House of Representatives passed an Official English bill supported by *US English*, but time ran out before it reached the Senate. *US English* is now concentrating its lobbying on state governments and was able to claim in 2002 that 27 of the USA's 50 states 'have some form of official English law'.

US English is not against other languages. The type of law they support would not prohibit the teaching of foreign languages and would permit the use of languages other than English when necessary for public health and safety, in tourist publicity and so on.

Crystal (2003a) gives a balanced discussion of the arguments that have been used in the debates over Official English and Bilingual Education. A point emphasized by *US English* is that the shared English language unites the United States. They note that it costs money to provide official services in more than one language and it would probably be impossibly expensive to do so for all the minority languages in the US. English is essential for immigrants, so concentrating resources on the teaching of English, instead of on bilingual education, can be expected to help immigrants. Offering bilingual education and providing translations of official information and forms into languages other than English, it is suggested, might even be a disincentive for learning English; immigrants could wrongly gain the impression that they can manage without English.

Various groups in the US contest the need for Official English legislation, on grounds such as the following: English is not at risk in the US; immigrants – and especially their children – continue to learn English as a matter of choice and high priority; bilingual education facilitates the learning of English rather than subtracting from it; bilingual individuals are a resource for any country, e.g. in international trade and foreign relations; and knowing other people's languages promotes understanding across communities within the country.

Heritage languages

In 1990, the US Congress passed the Native American Languages Act, which aims to encourage these languages: 'It is the policy of the United States to preserve, protect, and promote the rights and freedom of Native Americans ... to use, practice and develop Native American languages' (Schiffman 1996: 246). The US Census 2000 indicates that over four million Americans (approximately 1.5 per cent) declared American Indian or Alaska Native ancestry. The Native American Languages Act did not face objections from lobbyists who are against bilingual education. This is largely because they come into the category of *heritage languages*, ones that are important to a nation or some section of it for historical and cultural reasons, such as Maori in New Zealand and Gaelic in Scotland.

A heritage language is usually spoken by a minority of a country's population and most of its users will be bilingual because there is a dominant language that they need to know for wider interaction. For instance, the proportion of Ireland's citizens who use Irish extensively is only around 5 per cent (Gardner *et al.* 2000: 315) and, although Catalan is not a minority language in its native areas – it is a minority language in Spain – all speakers of Catalan are bilingual (Gardner *et al.* 2000: 338). Government recognition of heritage languages tends to come only after long periods of neglect or suppression. For example, Catalan and Basque were fiercely suppressed in Franco's Spain, for decades after 1939; and though these two languages are also spoken in parts of France, they still receive no recognition there (Gardner *et al.* 2000: 331).

The reasons for giving official support to heritage languages are similar to those motivating the establishment of national parks, wildlife reserves and world heritage sites. The basis is moral (e.g. atonement), political, aesthetic and perhaps sentimental, rather than immediately practical (though their existence may attract tourists and thus bring in money). Government backing usually includes allocating the language some role in education. Acceptance into a national education system significantly enhances the prestige of a language. Welsh, the indigenous language of Wales, had no formal place in Welsh schools until 1947, when the first official Welsh-medium primary school was established. The status of Welsh has increased markedly and it is now a subject of study in all schools in Wales, and more than a quarter of Wales's schools are either Welsh-medium or Welsh–English bilingual (Baker and Prys Jones 2000: 129).

Some countries that have in recent years received many immigrants have made efforts to give the languages of origin of immigrants a role in education. Preserving cultural connections is generally the justification. A 1988 law in Canada, the Canadian Multiculturalism Act, is a case in point. One of its goals is that all federal institutions should 'facilitate the acquisition, retention and use of all languages that contribute to the multicultural heritage of Canada' (Canadian Government 1988: 5 (1) (f)). Australian encouragement for the learning of immigrant heritage languages by the descendants of immigrants enabled Australia to provide excellent translation and interpretation services for the Sydney Olympic Games, in 2000.

ESL LITERACY

Having considered language policy in the country that is the motor for the spread of English around the world, this section takes a brief look at one of the many countries where English is used as a second language (ESL). This is a continuation of the three themes promised at the end of the Introduction: global English, minority languages and the acquisition of literacy.

Papua New Guinea's pre-schools

Hundreds of different languages are spoken in Papua New Guinea (PNG). Because there are so many languages it might seem an unreachable goal to teach children how to read and write in their own language, whichever one it happens to be. However, Siegel (1997) documents the establishment of low-budget rural schools that successfully provided initial literacy instruction in many of PNG's languages. The schools were called 'pre-schools' (*Pri Skul*) because they were for six- to eight-year-old children and when the movement that set them up began, in the late 1970s, formal schooling in PNG commenced at age eight years. The language then used in PNG government schools was English.

Figure 15.2   Papua New Guinea

Villagers themselves made the decision to have a pre-school. A local person volunteered to be the teacher. The community erected a building and helped to prepare teaching materials, usually in the local language. The reading books were mostly funded by charities that supplied line drawings which could have stories written on to them in any language, for photocopying. By 1994, such pre-schools were providing education for 80,000 pupils in a total of 200 languages.

Siegel (1997: 210–11) reports that the pre-schools were assessed as generally successful. They linked education to village life, rather than generating alienation. Of particular interest was the widespread impression that children moving on from pre-schools into the national education system of PNG were doing better at school, even in the learning of English and how to read English, than those who had not been to pre-schools.

Some speculative explanations that might apply here are:

- Learning to read is not easy, and if children have to learn the language at the same time as they are trying to learn how to read, the task becomes very hard indeed.
- Several concepts are unavoidable in teaching literacy: *pronounce, meaning, sound, sentence, word, spell* and *letter*, for instance. (Language used to discuss and describe language itself is called **metalanguage**.) Having such notions explained in a familiar language must be helpful.
- Initial schooling is more intelligible when it is conducted in a language known to the pupils.
- A school system that affirms the worth of the pupils' home language is likely to be viewed more positively by pupils and their parents than a system making it just one subject among others.

The last three of these could also be relevant to an explanation of why the Deaf children with a better grasp of ASL were more advanced in English literacy, in the Strong and Prinz study (1997) that was mentioned earlier.

 Activity 15.4 ⚬━┓

Siegel's (1997) survey suggests that, even if there is a focus on learning a language of wider communication, such as English, it can be advantageous for pupils first to learn how to read and write in their own language. But could there be difficulties over deciding which language is the 'home language' for some children? Are any other problems likely to arise for attempts to provide early education for all children in their first language?

FOREIGN LANGUAGES AND LITERACY IN ENGLAND

Language education policies in Northern Ireland and Wales are closely similar to those of England. Scotland has a different education system, but analogous issues arise there.

The first topic to be considered here is the justification of foreign language learning for a school population that already has English, the world's most widespread foreign language. This puts the British in with the more than a billion people – a very large number – around the world who have a good command of English, but among English speakers it is a minority of around 400 million who have it as their first language (see Crystal 2003a).

English has a central place in UK primary and secondary education, and schools are often judged by their perceived successes or failures in the teaching of English. England's National Curriculum, in operation since 1988, specifies English communication as a key skill, practised in all subjects but a particular responsibility for language teachers (QCA 2002). The second half of this section looks at literacy learning as an example of English language policy and practice.

Foreign languages in the curriculum

When motives are practical they are called *instrumental*: as when a language is studied because it is seen as a useful tool (an 'instrument') for trade, training, migration, tourism etc. Instrumental goals are almost always part of the justification for foreign languages in national education systems. A perennial question in language planning is whether to offer foreign languages at primary level (versus arguing that the generally greater efficiency of adolescent learning offsets the benefits of more years spent studying a foreign language). Could enough qualified teachers be trained and persuaded to stay in elementary schools (Graddol 1997: 44)? And would early teaching of foreign languages be regarded as unpatriotic by supporters of a country's official language (Schiffman 1996: 238)? The Further Activity at the end of this unit invites you to explore issues like these.

Because of its global reach, English is the foreign language most often studied in schools around the world, and lack of qualifications in English can block entry to jobs or universities. In many countries English as a foreign language (EFL) classes are taken by nearly all pupils from the age of ten years, or even younger, until the end of their compulsory schooling (Dickson and Cumming 1996, Graddol 1997, Crystal 2003a).

> ### 🖋 Activity 15.5 o━┳
>
> Young people who happen to have English as their first language already
> know 'the global language'. Are there reasons for them, nonetheless, to
> study foreign languages at school, or is this just a waste of time for English
> speakers?

England's National Curriculum guidelines list the following as benefits to be
expected from foreign language learning in the age range 7–11 years (currently an
option in a minority of schools, Dickson and Cumming 1996):

> Pupils develop communication and literacy skills that lay the foundation for
> future language learning. They develop linguistic competence, extend their
> knowledge of how language works and explore differences and similarities
> between the foreign language and English. Learning another language raises
> awareness of the multi-lingual and multi-cultural world and introduces an
> international dimension to pupils' learning, giving them an insight into their
> own culture and those of others. The learning of a foreign language provides a
> medium for cross-curricular links and for the reinforcement of knowledge,
> skills and understanding developed in other subjects.
>
> (NC 2004)

A recent major statement of UK government strategy for foreign language study
at all ages sets similar goals, e.g. citing cultural as well as economic advantages
(DfES 2002: 12). However, Mitchell (2003: 120) points out that, so far, the
National Curriculum's specifications for the assessment of foreign language
achievement by school pupils:

> focus exclusively on the skills of listening, speaking, reading and writing. The
> practical effect, once assessment 'backwash' is taken into account, is that
> classroom procedures generally focus on the development of practical
> language skills. Thus, [Modern Foreign Languages] education as currently
> implemented in schools seems to be driven primarily by a quite narrowly
> instrumental rationale.

Backwash is the influence that examinations have on the teaching which leads up
to them: a tendency to tailor teaching to the tests. UK language planners are aware
of the benefits of foreign language study, even for students who already know the
world's most popular foreign language, but National Curriculum testing guidelines
seem likely to focus effort on the 'must have it for practical communication'

reasons that are not as generally relevant to first language users of English as to most of the rest of the world.

Literacy is a good bargain

In a long-term social investigation, called the British Cohort Study, detailed records have been kept over the years on a group of people who were born during a single week in 1970. Using information from this source, including how well each person could read when tested in 1980 and how much each was earning in 2000, Machin and McNally (2004) estimate that the extra income over one's working life attributable to being able to read competently at age ten years is £2,000–£5,500. This figure was calculated as a basis for evaluating the economics of the National Literacy Project, a sizeable attempt to improve reading and writing standards in primary schools.

The National Literacy Project (NLP) ran for two years, 1996–1998, in some 400 junior schools. Its central feature was a daily 'literacy hour'. Teachers were given support and detailed advice on how to use time already allocated to literacy instruction. It was not an extra hour added to the school day. Machin and McNally (2004) found that there were significant improvements, after one year, in the average reading scores and general English assessments (known as *Key Stage 2*) for the schools that had the literacy hour, compared to a control sample of schools.

Furthermore, around 5,000 of the NLP pupils, who were finishing primary school during the first year of the project, took the national (GCSE) examinations five years later, in 2002. The GCSE English grades for NLP schools were significantly up on the previous year's levels, in comparison to the non-NLP control sample. The improvements from one year of primary school 'literacy hour' tuition were thus effective at least through to age 16. The additional cost of providing the organized literacy hour for one year had been £25 per pupil. Comparing that with the estimate based on the British Cohort Study – that good literacy at the end of primary school can be worth as much as £5,500 on later earnings – justifies the title of Machin and McNally's (2004) report: 'Large benefits, low cost'. The literacy hour was subsequently extended, as the National Literacy Strategy (available online), to all primary schools in England.

The use of metalanguage to talk about language – as with words like *sound* and *spell* – not only makes literacy instruction possible, but its use gives children an early example of the abstract, reflective attitude that is characteristic of much of education.

Literacy opens the way to types of study that are hardly feasible without writing. This goes beyond the fact that we learn from books. Notes enable us to keep better records and extend the scope of generalizations and theories. Mapping out reasoning in written form facilitates the development and checking of lines of argument. Trying to formulate our ideas clearly enough to be able to write them down often brings real insight into what was only vaguely sensed.

SUMMARY

Language study is part of the curriculum in most school systems, usually a substantial part. Countries differ in their policies regarding which languages may, may not or must have which roles in education. Language policies – not always explicitly formulated – concern matters such as the amount of time given to the teaching of dominant languages, whether or not classes can be taught through other languages and which other languages are offered as subjects. This unit has illustrated some of the factors that drive language policies: national unity and harmony, international understanding, the preservation of ancestral links, a desire to ensure that students gain languages needed for employment and economic development, that they are trained in academic ways of thinking and explaining, and so on. English is a major foreign language studied in schools around the world, often justified on practical grounds. But there are cultural and mental development reasons for learning foreign languages too, even by those who have English as their first language. Educational linguists have to think about language, mind and society, but need to do so in an environment where money, votes and feelings count too.

FURTHER READING

Oliver Sacks's *Seeing Voices* (1989) is a committed and accessible account of ASL and the Deaf community in the US. In *Beyond Ebonics: Linguistic Pride and Racial Prejudice*, Baugh (2000) gives a lot more detail on the context and consequences of the Oakland Ebonics resolution. An interesting collection of articles on another of the topics in this unit appears in *Heritage Languages in America*, edited by Peyton *et al.* (2001). Crystal's book *English as a Global Language* (2003a) offers background for most of the unit. Siegel's (1996) report, *Vernacular Education in the South Pacific*, covers 12 Pacific Island countries and discusses development issues connected with language policies in education.

FURTHER ACTIVITY

 Activity 15.6

Use the internet or reference books, or both sources, to find out about a village, city or country where more than one dialect or language is used in the community. It could be that your home town is an example of such a place if you think about all the people who live there. Describe the situation and, giving reasons, outline what you feel would be a fair and workable language education policy to apply there. Foreign languages should be included in your scheme. Consider how many languages, which ones and at what ages they might be offered.

You might like to link this activity to Activity 12.7.

COMMENTARY ON ACTIVITIES

Activity 15.1

Unless your friend is one of the rare individuals who has succeeded in learning to lip-read, then not much success is likely to have been achieved. Of course, clever guesses are sometimes possible, based on the action, emotions and characters portrayed in the video. But when it comes to directly trying to 'read' speech off a talking face, the clues are minimal: some tongue movements near the front of the mouth, lip position (closed, rounded or spread), and the openness of a **vowel** (from the extent that the speaker's jaw drops). These indications can be enough for some skilled people with residual hearing to work out what is being said, but with no hearing at all (like video with the volume down at zero), too much has to be guessed.

Activity 15.2

BSL **interrogatives** apparently have the question words (*where*, *what*, *who*) at the end, whereas these go at the beginning of a sentence in English. At least in these examples, BSL does not seem to use a **verb** corresponding to English *is* and *are*. BSL also appears to do without a definite article, *the* in English. (In these respects, BSL syntax is not all that unusual. Russian, for example, does not have a definite article and makes much less use of copula verbs than English does. A reasonable Russian translation of *Olga is in the Post Office* would be – using English words in capitals to stand for the Russian words: OLGA IN POST OFFICE.)

An interesting observation not illustrated by the way the BSL examples were presented, is this: a signer's brow is generally furrowed when signing questions like those in Activity 15.2 (Sutton-Spence and Woll 1999: 68). In both Finnish and Japanese a small, uninflected word – technically called a *particle* – is added to the end of interrogative sentences. A furrowed brow is not the same thing as a particle, but considered rather abstractly, BSL is similar in this respect to Finnish and Japanese.

The point of this activity was to emphasize that, like other languages, BSL sentences have distinctive patterns that can be different from those of English.

Activity 15.3

The big question here is whether or not teachers of English in US schools need knowledge of the home varieties of their students. For instance, should the ways of talking that the OUSD board's proposal labelled *Ebonics* be brought into the classroom as a resource for the teaching of Standard American English? A teacher who ignores other varieties and just says that the student should have written *She is eating* could confuse the child into thinking that that is the way to express the habitual meaning (which it is not; see the pair of examples at the beginning of Activity 15.3).

Another issue is whether home varieties should actually be taught in schools. If children feel that the linguistic usage of their home is rejected by the school, that could make some of them resistant to what school can offer. Equating differences between varieties to the difference between the spoken and written medium 'we do it differently when we write English' sidesteps the matter of why the accepted written norms happen to be closer to other people's ways of talking. It allows the teacher to be clear about meaning differences, but might not help the student feel accepted by the school.

Teaching Ebonics as a language might help some pupils engage more positively with school and would be good for developing an understanding of variability across languages and how differences between varieties have social significance (➤ Unit 9), but – as the reception of the original OUSD proposals showed – it would be highly controversial. There are people who fear that recognition for anything other than the standard variety would be a disservice to students and might threaten the unity of the nation. The foundation for sentiments like these is looked at in the next subsection of the unit.

The response 'This afternoon we'll have a class about different ways of talking and different ways that people use language' could refer to the study of 'language awareness' (one of the language goals in England's National Curriculum; see the final section of this unit). Language awareness classes generalize the matter, instead of restricting it to the Ebonics–English interface, and a wider perspective could be useful in many twenty-first century city schools, which have students from lots of different language backgrounds.

Activity 15.4

Gupta (1997) argues that there are circumstances when it can be difficult to justify mother tongue education. Which of a bilingual child's languages should initial literacy be offered in? Choosing one rather than another might cause ill feeling. In **diglossic** situations (➤ Unit 12) the home variety of a child's first language might not be one that is ever used in education. Parents or community leaders might insist that only a traditional 'high' variety should be used. For instance, Siegel (1996: 117) points out that people of Indian descent in Fiji commonly speak Fiji Hindi, a language that differs very considerably from the two formal languages, Hindi and Urdu, which Indo-Fijians are usually offered as their 'mother tongue' in Fiji's schools. In linguistically diverse urban schools it could be that most of the languages are not represented by enough pupils to justify employing teachers competent to teach them.

Activity 15.5

There is less need for native English-speaking school goers to learn Mandarin, Spanish, French, Hindi, German or Vietnamese, etc. than for people with those as their first language to become proficient in English. As Mitchell (2003: 120) puts it: 'UK learners can switch off and drop out in ways that learners of EFL cannot, without obvious immediate penalties in terms of their life chances'. But, even so, countries like the US, the UK, Canada, Australia, and New Zealand do need some people with foreign language skills, e.g. for diplomacy. Furthermore, through learning another language English speakers stand to gain: friends; perspective on the world; sensitivity to diversity; a vantage point for reflection on their own language and culture; analytical, organizing and memory skills transferable to other learning; the confidence to set out unafraid on a foreign holiday; and the satisfaction of an impressive achievement.

REFERENCES

Baker, C. and Prys Jones, M. (2000) 'Welsh language and education: a strategy for revitalization', in C.H. Williams (ed.) *Language Revitalization: Policy and Planning in Wales*, Cardiff: University of Wales Press.

Baugh, J. (2000) *Beyond Ebonics: Linguistic Pride and Racial Prejudice*, New York: Oxford University Press.

Bettger, J.T. (2000) 'Viewing deaf children in a new way: implications of Bellugi and Klima's research for education', in K. Emmorey and H. Lane (eds) *The Signs of Language Revisited: An Anthology to Honor Ursula Bellugi and Edward Klima*, New York: Erlbaum.

Canadian Government (1988) Canadian Multiculturalism Act. Online. Available HTTP: <http://laws.justice.gc.ca/em/C-18.7/> (accessed 26 August 2003).

Crystal, D. (2003a) *English as a Global Language*, 2nd edn, Cambridge: Cambridge University Press.

DfES (2002) *Languages for All: Languages for Life*, Nottingham: Department for Education and Skills. Online. Available HTTP: <http://www.dfes.gov.uk/languagesstrategy> (accessed 28 February 2004).

Dickson, P. and Cumming, A. (1996) *Profiles of Language Education in 25 Countries: Overview of Phase 1 of the IEA Language Education Study*, Slough: NFER.

Fasold, R.W. (1999) 'Ebonic need not be English', *CAL Digest Issue Paper*, Centre for Applied Linguistics. Online. Available HTTP: <http://www.cal.org/resources/digest/ebonic-issue.html> (accessed 3 June 2004).

Gallaudet (2002) Website of Gallaudet University. Online. Available HTTP: <http://pr.gallaudet.edu/VisitorsCenter/> (accessed 2 November 2002).

Gardner, N., Puigdevall i Serralvo, M. and Williams, C.H. (2000) 'Language revitalization in comparative context: Ireland, the Basque Country and Catalonia', in C.H. Williams (ed.) *Language Revitalization: Policy and Planning in Wales*, Cardiff: University of Wales Press.

Graddol, D. (1997) *The Future of English?*, London: British Council.

Gupta, A.F. (1997) 'When mother-tongue education is *not* preferred', *Journal of Multilingual and Multicultural Development*, 18: 496–506.

Machin, S. and McNally, S. (2004) 'Large benefits, low cost: is the government's National Literacy Strategy effective?' *CentrePiece* (Centre for Economic Performance, London School of Economics. Online. Available HTTP: <http://cep.lse.ac.uk/centrepiece/v9i1/machin_mcnally.pdf> (accessed 1 March 2004).

Mitchell, R. (2003) 'Rationales for foreign language education in the 21st century', in S. Sarangi and T. van Leeuwen (eds) *Applied Linguistics and Communities of Practice*, London: Continuum (and British Association for Applied Linguistics).

National Literacy Strategy. Online. Available HTTP: <http://www.standards.dfes.gov.uk/literacy/publications> (accessed 27 October 2004).

NC (2004) 'Modern Foreign Languages: Key Stage 2 programme of study', National Curriculum Online. Available HTTP: <http://www.nc.uk.net/nc/contents/mflks2.htm> (accessed 2 March 2004).

OUSD (1996) Resolution $597–0063 of the Board of Education of Oakland Unified School District. Online. Available HTTP: <http://www.emich.edu/~linguist/topics/ebonics/> (accessed 16 October 2002).

OUSD (1997) Resolution 9697–0063 of the Board of Education of Oakland Unified School District. Online. Available HTTP: <http://www.emich.edu/~linguist/topics/ebonics/> (accessed 16 October 2002).

Peyton, J.K., Ranard, D.A. and McGinnis, S. (eds) (2001) *Heritage Languages in America: Preserving a National Resource*, Washington, DC: Center for Applied Linguistics.

QCA (2002) 'The National Curriculum', Qualifications and Curriculum Authority. Online. Available HTTP: <http://www.qca.org.uk/> (accessed 18 October 2002).

Sacks, O. (1989) *Seeing Voices: A Journey into the World of the Deaf*, Berkeley, CA: University of California Press.

Schiffman, H.F. (1996) *Linguistic Culture and Language Policy*, London: Routledge.

Siegel, J. (1996) *Vernacular Education in the South Pacific* (= International Development Issues, number 45), Canberra: AusAID.

Siegel, J. (1997) 'Formal vs. non-formal vernacular education: the education reform in Papua New Guinea', *Journal of Multilingual and Multicultural Development*, 18: 206–22.

Strong, M. and Prinz, P.M. (1997) 'A study of the relationship between American Sign Language and English literacy', *Journal of Deaf Studies and Deaf Education*, 2: 37–46.

Sutton-Spence, R. and Woll, B. (1999) *The Linguistics of British Sign Language*, Cambridge: Cambridge University Press.

US English (2002) Website of US English Inc. Online. Available HTTP: <http://www.us-english.org/inc/official/about/> (accessed 13 November 2002).

Woll, B. (2002) Personal communication. (Bencie Woll is Professor of Sign Language and Deaf Studies at City University, London.)

16 ANALYSING MORE LANGUAGE IN USE
Do me!

UNIT CONTENTS

INTRODUCTION

Most linguistic **texts** (written or spoken) can be analysed from many of the perspectives that have been offered throughout this book, though some analytical approaches will inevitably be more fruitful in relation to some texts than others. This unit provides more texts for you to consider and each of these can be analysed from a range of perspectives.

In all other units, we have indicated how an activity might be carried out in relation to the text(s) presented: in this unit, we indicate only one *possible* starting point while knowing that there are other possibilities. You might like to adopt this approach to other texts in *Introducing Language in Use* and so choose to analyse a text found in one unit using an analytical approach found in a different unit. Here, we ask simply that you apply (some of) the techniques offered earlier in the book to illuminate how each text is being used to achieve its intended purpose.

As in other units, where appropriate, we provide minimal contextual details for texts.

TEXT 16.1 AMBIGUITY AND LACK OF CLARITY

A starting point: Explain as precisely as possible the reason(s) for any uncertainty there might be in understanding these texts. Each text is separately numbered.

(1)   I didn't leave because I was scared.

(2)   I'd like another beer.

(3)   I'm looking for a beautiful young woman.

(4)   Lecture Theatre Notice:
        I might be a bit late today. While you are waiting, write down what you think will be the first thing I say.

(5)   Notice to the milkman:
        Please leave no milk today.
        When I say today, I mean tomorrow, for I wrote this note yesterday.

TEXT 16.2 GETTING CO-DEFENDANTS NOT TO COLLUDE

A starting point: Warnings can be given in various ways. Explain the differences in the way the Chair of Magistrates speaks to the two defendants. Each text is numbered separately.

Context: Tuesday. A Magistrates Court in the UK (the lowest level of court in the UK legal system). The prosecution has finished examining one of three co-defendants. (1) and (2) were used to different defendants in court.

(1) Chair of Magistrates: You mustn't speak to anyone else about what's gone on in court the case may go on past Friday, so I'm warning you!

(2) Chair of Magistrates: I must warn you, you must not speak to anyone about the case it may go on beyond Friday.

TEXT 16.3 APOLOGIZING

A starting point: How does this apology compare with other ways of making apologies?

Context: The West Indies cricket team had performed abysmally during the cricket test series against Australia in the West Indies in summer 2003. In spring 2004, they were being defeated by England.

14 March 2004 19:46

OFFICIAL APOLOGY FROM WEST INDIES TEAM

By windiescricket.com

KINGSTON, Jamaica – The West Indies Cricket team sincerely apologizes to the West Indies public for the shocking performance on the fourth day of the first Test match which resulted in defeat by England.

The team further apologizes for the inappropriate conduct of four members of the team who were seen in a party stand at Sabina Park following the loss.

According to team manager Ricky Skerritt this matter is being investigated and the players will be dealt with appropriately. 'I am disgusted at the thoughtlessness and shamelessness displayed by these players following such a horrific performance', Skerrit [*sic*] said.

The manager said that he wanted to reassure the public that the team has been working hard and is committed to winning this series.

Coach Gus Logie said, 'We will continue to ask the players for a higher level of discipline and a higher level of commitment to themselves and West Indies cricket.'

In commenting on the situation, captain Brian Lara said, 'The result of the first Test does not give a true reflection of our team's preparation for the match. We as a team will continue to work diligently towards the betterment of West Indies cricket.'

According to the West Indies captain, 'The team shares the pain caused by the defeat and will be doubling its efforts towards achieving success in this series.'

Source: Windiescricket (2004)[1]

TEXT 16.4 RADIO DRAMA: *UNDER MILK WOOD*

A starting point: Why is there so much sound patterning in this prose text and what patterns are there?

Context: These are the initial speeches from *Under Milk Wood: A Play for Voices* by Dylan Thomas (1954) which was first broadcast on BBC radio.[2]

[*Silence*]
FIRST VOICE [*Very softly*]
To begin at the beginning:

It is spring, moonless night in the small town, starless and bible-black, the cobble streets silent and the hunched, courters'-and-rabbits' wood limping invisibly down to the sloeblack, slow, black, crowblack, fishingboat-bobbing sea. The houses are blind as moles (though moles see fine tonight in the snouting, velvet dingles) or blind as Captain Cat there in the muffled middle by the pump and the town clock, the shops in mourning, the Welfare Hall in widows' weeds. And all the people of the lulled and dumbfound town are sleeping now.

Hush, the babies are sleeping, the farmers, the fishers, the tradesmen and pensioners, cobbler, schoolteacher, postman and publican, the undertaker and the fancy woman, drunkard, dressmaker, preacher, policeman, the webfoot cocklewomen and the tidy wives. Young girls lie bedded soft or glide in their dreams, with rings and trousseaux, bridesmaided by glow-worms down the aisles of the organplaying wood. The boys are dreaming wicked or of the bucking ranches of the night and the jolly, rodgered sea. And the anthracite statues of the horses asleep in the fields, and the cows in the byres, and the dogs in the wetnosed yards; and the cats nap in the slant corners or lope sly, streaking and needling, on the one cloud of the roofs.

You can hear the dew falling, and the hushed town breathing.

Only your eyes are unclosed to see the black and folded town fast, and slow, asleep.

And you alone can hear the invisible starfall, the darkest-before-dawn minutely dewgrazed stir of the black, dab-filled sea where the Arethusa, the Curlew and the Skylark, Zanzibar, Rhiannon, the Rover, the Cormorant, and the Star of Wales tilt and ride.

Listen. It is night moving in the streets, the processional salt slow musical wind in Coronation Street and Cockle Row, it is the grass growing on Llareggub Hill, dewfall, starfall, the sleep of birds in Milk Wood.

Listen. It is night in the chill, squat chapel, hymning, in bonnet and brooch and bombazine black, butterfly choker and bootlace bow, coughing like nannygoats, sucking mintoes, fortywinking hallelujah; night in the four-ale, quiet as a domino; in Ocky Milkman's lofts like a mouse with gloves; in Dai Bread's bakery flying like black flour. It is tonight in Donkey Street, trotting silent, with seaweed on its hooves, along the cockled cobbles, past curtained fernpot, text and trinket, harmonium, holy dresser, watercolours done by hand, china dog and rosy tin teacaddy. It is night neddying among the snuggeries of babies.

Look. It is night, dumbly, royally winding through the Coronation cherry trees; going through the graveyard of Bethesda with winds gloved and folded, and dew doffed; tumbling by the Sailors' Arms.

Time passes. Listen. Time passes.

TEXT 16.5 TEXT MESSAGES

A starting point: How is the language of text messaging developing differently from other forms of written English (and why)? All the spelling/punctuation in each text is authentic/accurate.

Context: These text messages[3] were collected in 2002–3. Each message should be treated as a separate text.

Message 1

Out   Holding party 4 St George Day on Sat. Wanna come? – Alone or with friend

In   Up 4 party! Time/location? Will be alone.

Out   Gr8, 2morrow @ my house. Theme red & white. C U then

Message 2

In   Thanks for the party!

Out   U R welcome. Our pleasure

Message 3

DO U STILL
FANCY GOING
OUT 2MORO
NITE? ME AND
EMMA R
DEFINATES ILL
RING DAN AND
ANY1 ELSE WHO
WANTS 2 JOIN US
IS MORE THAN
WELCOME!

Message 4

Hi,had a gud
wkend? im gona
spnd nx wkend
movin
rms&helping linz
move in. cum
ova4a coffee if u
can,how sounds
fri5for nite in
ncl? we can
celebr8 ur
bday! hugs em

Message 5

Okay darlin. Call
Me whenever u
Want. l.o.l. jxxx

Message 6

Cherie so
sorry2bother u i
cant remember
the door
code4the
office&the keys
r in their soif u
could give me a
call or text it
would to greatly
appreci8d.thx.x

TEXT 16.6   TELEPHONE CALLS

A starting point: Analyse the calls in terms of **field**, **mode** and **tenor**.

(a) In the bathroom (AJM/MUM/TAMM)

```
01   hello! just a quick call from peterborough!

02   er really it was two queries.

03   (.hh) i- i didn't know what sort of coffee to

04   buy for you for christ↑mas↑, and i didn't
```

```
05    know what sort of cereals to buy. (0.8)
06    (.hh) so: (.) well perhaps you can have tha-
07    you needn't ring back to tell me, but
08    whenever we next speak perhaps you can: (.h) tell me
09    the answer to those two.
10    hope you're okay!
11    (.hh) er i've had my new: carpet laid in
12    the kitchen and the (.) ↑bathroom↑, (.hh)
13    u:m new roller blinds for the kitchen coming
14    (.) one day next week.
15    (.hhhh) right. okay? cheerio!
```

(b) We're all students here (AJM/TC)

01   ((Telephone Rings))

Caller: ((multiple telephone conversations in background)) Mr. Firth?

AJM: No. Mr. Merrison. We're all students here.

          You can't sell us anything!

05   Caller: Okay, bye.

TEXT 16.7   GUINEA PIGS AND MOSES[4]

A starting point: look at the spelling in this text in relation to the meaning. Reading the text aloud should help you understand its meaning. What does this tell you about the author? Why was this text produced? You should note that the spelling/punctuation is authentic.

<u>Guinea pigs</u>
<u>Morning</u>
1.   Lift The blayn up.
2.   Theyc The food bole owt.
3.   Put oun hand ful in The bole
      That is ond er The ceydch.
4.   put cleen whot in The whot
      botl.
<u>afd nun</u>
1.   put sum vedbuls in
      ouw gras in.
2.   at nayt Tamie
      put The blayn dawn.

<u>Moses</u>
1.   put cleyn whote in The whote
      botle.
2.   Put som Cleyn food in
      The food bool

TEXT 16.8 A PRAYER

A starting point: How has the language of this prayer changed over the centuries?

Context: The OE version of the Lord's Prayer appears in Unit 13 on page 400. Later versions appear here.

Middle English c.1400
(Finnie 1972: 83)

Oure fadir
that art in heuenes,
halewid bẹ̄ thī nāme ;
thī kyngdọọm come tọ̄ ;
bẹ̄ thī wille dọ̄n in ẹ̄rthe as in heuene ;
ȝyue tọ̄ vs this dai oure brẹẹd ọ̄uer ọ̄thir substaunce ;
and forȝyue tọ̄ vs oure dettis, as wẹ̄ forȝyuen tọ̄ oure dettouris ;
and lẹ̄de vs not in tọ̄ temptācioun,
but dẹ̄lyuere vs frọ̄ ȳuel. Amẹ̄n.

Early Modern English c.1600
(Finnie 1972: 95)

Our father which art in heauen,
hallowed be thy name.
Thy kingdome come. Thy will
be done, in earth, as it is in heauen.
Giue us this day our daily bread.
And forgiue us our debts, as we
forgiue our debters.
And lead us not into temptation,
but deliuer us from euill : For thine is
the kingdome, and the power, and the
glory, for euer, Amen.

Contemporary English
(Pinker 1994: 248)

Our father who is in heaven,
May your name be kept holy.
May your kingdom come into being.
May your will be followed on earth, just as it is in heaven.
Give us this day our food for the day.
And forgive us our offenses, just as we forgive those who have offended us.
And do not bring us to the test.
But free us from evil.
For the kingdom, the power, and the glory are yours forever.
Amen.

REFERENCES

Finnie, W.B. (1972) *The Stages of English: Texts, Transcriptions, Exercises*, Boston, MA: Houghton Mifflin Company.

Pinker, S. (1994) *The Language Instinct: The New Science of Language and Mind*, New York: HarperCollins.

Thomas, D, (2000) *Under Milk Wood: A Play for Voices*, London: Phoenix.

Windiescricket (2004) Online. Available HTTP: <http://www.windiescricket.com/article. asp?ID=191369> (accessed 27 September 2004).

NOTES

1 The next two test matches were also won by England. The fourth and final test was a draw. England therefore won the series 3-0. This was a truly humiliating (and historic) defeat as England had not beaten the West Indies *in* the West Indies for over three decades. Fortunately, at least some West Indian **face** was saved in the final test by the West Indian captain, Brian Lara, who produced a world-record innings of an unbeaten 400 runs, thereby giving the home fans something to be proud of!

2 In the original version, this text is written in italics. We have used plain text for ease of reading.

3 Thanks to Dale Donley and to Bob Redwood for allowing Aileen Bloomer to use these texts.

4 Thanks to Teah Bennett for allowing Andrew Merrison to use this data.

EPILOGUE

What we call the beginning is often the end
And to make an end is to make a beginning.
The end is where we start from. And every phrase
And sentence that is right (where every word is at home,
Taking its place to support the others,
The word neither diffident nor ostentatious,
An easy commerce of the old and the new,
The common word exact without vulgarity,
The formal word precise but not pedantic,
The complete consort dancing together)
Every phrase and every sentence is an end and a beginning …

Eliot, *Four Quartets* (1944: 42f)

Glossary

accent   multi-faceted aspects of the pronunciation of a spoken linguistic form. It includes the choice of sounds used as segments (phonemes) as well as prosodic suprasegmentals.

active voice   see **voice** (ii).

adjacency pair   a sequential unit consisting of two communicative actions.

adjective   an open word class, whose members characteristically premodify nouns in a noun phrase or realize intensive complement in clause structure.

adjective phrase   a phrase with an adjective functioning as head word.

Adjunct   functions at clause level along with Subject, Finite, Predicator and Complement usually expressing a wide range of circumstantial meanings such as time, place, manner and reason.

adverb   an open word class, whose members characteristically premodify adjectives (_rather_ difficult) or realize the Adjunct slot in clause structure indicating a range of meanings such as time, place and manner, e.g. _They left later_.

affix   prefix or suffix.

ambiguous   having more than one interpretation.

antonym   see **antonymy**.

antonymy   one kind of oppositeness, a semantic relationship between pairs of words which, when substituted for each other in sentences that are otherwise the same, yield only an entailment from an affirmative to a negative sentence, but not in the reverse direction. See **complementarity**.

aphasia   loss of language as a result of damage, illness or surgery affecting a part of the brain.

articulator   the speech organs which move to produce speech sounds are the active articulators; the speech organs against which the active articulators move are the passive articulators.

aspect   a grammatical system indicating the duration of an action.

auxiliary verb   the primary auxiliary verbs (*do*, *be* and *have*) indicate aspect or voice. In *Felicity is starting a new job* and *Robert has been promoted*, the primary auxiliaries have been underlined. The modal auxiliary verbs (modal auxiliaries) are used to express a range of meanings relating to possibility, probability and obligation such as (modal auxiliary is underlined) *Kate can have three weeks leave.*

backchannel behaviour   short responses, such as 'mm' or 'aha', which provide feedback to the speaker.

cancel   to reasonably deny an inference.

clause   appears above phrase in the hierarchy of rank and is typically analysed in terms of Subject, Finite, Predicator, Complement and Adjunct.

code   a set of arbitrary conventions for converting one system of signals into another.

code-mixing   using the rules of one language while speaking another.

code model   a model of language whereby a speaker simply says the words and a hearer simply decodes them to get the intended message.

code-switching   moving from one language to another in the course of a conversation.

co-hyponyms   the hyponyms under a given superordinate word.

communication   the transmission and reception of messages between two or more participants using any mode of communication; may or may not include the use of language.

Complement   functions with Subject, Finite, Predicator and Adjunct at clause level. There are three main types of complement: complement direct object, complement indirect object and intensive complement.

complementarity (also called *binary antonymy*)   a non-gradable semantic relationship between pairs of words, e.g. *wrapped* and *unwrapped*; when the words are used in sentences, entailments go both from affirmative to the corresponding negative sentences and from negative sentences to affirmatives; in the vocabulary of the language, the members of a pair of complementaries are treated as having no middle ground between them. See **antonymy**.

compound word   a word made by joining two (or more) words together, e.g. *newspaper*.

conjunction   the linking of words, phrases or clauses. Coordinating conjunctions (a closed word class, e.g. *and*, *but*, *or*) link elements of equal weight, e.g.

coffee or tea? (where nouns are linked) or *the lion roared but the cat purred* (in which clauses are coordinated). Subordinating conjunctions (a closed word class, e.g. *after, although, because, whenever*) link elements of differing weight, e.g. *the lion roared while the cat purred* where a subordinate clause is inserted in the main clause, often but not always in the Adjunct slot.

consonant   a speech sound in which articulators typically come close together or form a complete closure. Consonants are typically peripheral in a syllable.

content words   nouns, verbs, adjectives and adverbs; they carry the content of communications by making connections to the world outside of language. See **function word**.

context   the complex totality of the situation in which an utterance is made, including aspects such as time, geographical location, cultural norms, social relationships between individuals, preceding linguistic material and so on.

Cooperative Principle   the assumption that interlocutors are cooperative in their utterances (including being informative, truthful, relevant and clear).

declarative   one of three elements in the mood system; typically used for making statements. In declaratives, the Subject usually precedes the Finite (e.g. *Nick brought us a vegetarian pizza*).

deixis   use of language which can only be understood in context, e.g. *I*, *here*, *yesterday* which can only be understood when the speaker or the time or place of utterance is known.

descriptive   an approach to the study of language which objectively describes how it is actually used. See **prescriptive**.

determiners   a closed word class whose members typically come at the beginning of the noun phrase and determine the scope of the noun as in *each individual*, *all the time*, *some potatoes*. The word class includes the definite article (*the*) and the indefinite article (*a/an*).

dialect   the term used when a form of language is distinct in matters of morphology, lexis, semantics or syntax.

diglossia   the situation where two or more language varieties are used in different social domains and for different social functions where one language is perceived as the High (H) variety and the other as the Low (L) variety. Use of L in an H context could be seen as comical at the least and offensive at the worst.

direct illocution   the illocution most directly indicated by the literal meaning of what is uttered. See **direct speech act**.

direct object   one of three Complements, typically realized by a noun phrase and expressing the goal of a material process. (Cdo is underlined in *The students read the whole book.*)

direct speech act   the speech act obtained when syntactic form and pragmatic function match.

entailment   the conclusions (inferences) which are *guaranteed* to be true given the truth of an initial proposition. Attempting to cancel an entailment leads to contradiction.

entities   people, things, places, events, times, tunes, ideas – indeed, whatever we can think and talk about.

face   'the positive social value a person effectively claims for himself' (Goffman 1967: 5 ↠ Unit 4).

field (of discourse)   subject matter, e.g. chemistry/linguistics/music.

finite   a verb form which is marked for tense (e.g. *saw*, *eats*). A verb form which is not marked for tense is non-finite (e.g. *taking*, *ridden*).

Finite   functions at the level of clause with Subject, Predicator, Complement and Adjunct and appears as the first verb in a finite verb group.

function word   a word which has little identifiable meaning and which is typically involved in grammatical work in the sentence. Auxiliary verbs, conjunctions, determiners, prepositions and pronouns are members of this class of words.

glottal stop   the plosive consonant articulated with the vocal folds, often associated with the regional variety of London English in words such as *letter* pronounced [lɛʔə].

grammar   the structure of a language. The term was traditionally used for sentence grammar (see **syntax**) and has more recently come to include text grammar.

grammatical words   not content words; they carry very general meanings and link words into sentence structures, e.g. *of, or, and*.

h dropping   omission of the consonant [h] particularly from initial position in a word.

hierarchy of rank   words in sentences are not usually all strung together on the same level; instead they are grouped into phrases which, in turn, are joined to make clauses, which may go together to make sentences and texts (cf. Figure 7.1).

homophone   words which sound the same even if spelt differently, e.g. *through* and *threw*.

hyponym   under a superordinate, a word with a more specific meaning, e.g. *chair* is a hyponym of the superordinate *seat*; the meaning of a hyponym is that of its superordinate plus some modifier(s), e.g. a *chair* is a 'seat with a back, for one person'.

illocutionary act (illocution) the act (defined by social convention) which is performed when making an utterance, e.g. accusing, apologizing, asserting, boasting, congratulating and so on.

imperative one of three elements in the mood system; typically used for giving instructions.

implicature an implied inference derived through applying the Cooperative Principle.

indirect illocution any illocution an utterance might have beyond the direct illocution.

indirect object one of three Complements, typically realized by a noun phrase and expressing the recipient or beneficiary of a material process. (Cio is underlined in *Richard bought Kate a new car*.)

indirect speech act see **indirect illocution**.

inference a conclusion worked out from information. See **entailment** and **implicature**.

intensive complement one of three Complements typically realized by a noun phrase or an adjective phrase and expressing the quality or attribute in a relational process. (Cint is underlined in *Edinburgh is the capital of Scotland*.)

interlocutor a participant taking part in the interaction.

interrogative one of three elements in the mood system; typically used for asking questions.

interruption an attempt to take the floor from the current speaker while they are still producing their turn constructional unit. Cf. **overlap**.

intonation the movement of pitch during speech.

language the abstract system underlying the linguistic behaviour of a community based on conventions for the use of sounds or signs; considered by many to be an important part of what defines humans as human.

lexical choice choosing a unit of vocabulary.

lexical item a unit of vocabulary.

lexical verb not an auxiliary verb, underlined in *She has spoken*.

lexicon an individual's mental store of words.

lingua franca a language used between two (or more) individuals who normally use different languages. English often fulfils this role in the modern world.

metalanguage language when it is being used to discuss and describe language itself, e.g. the terms *word*, *sound*, *sentence* are metalanguage words in English; includes all the technical linguistic terms used in this book.

minimal pair words which differ by a single phoneme such as *peat* [pit] and *pat* [pat].

modal auxiliary see **auxiliary verb**.

mode (of communication)   any one of the five senses (sight, sound, smell, touch or taste) through which communication can be effected. The main ones for language are visual (sign language and writing) and vocal-auditory (speech).

mode (of discourse)   medium of the language activity, e.g. written/spoken.

mood   a grammatical system including declarative, interrogative and imperative.

morpheme   the smallest meaningful unit that words are constructed from, e.g. the morphemes that make up *fire-eaters* are *fire*, *eat*, {*-er*} and {*-s*}.

morphology   the study of the structure of words. See **morphemes**.

nasalized   a feature of speech sounds which occurs when air is allowed to escape orally and nasally at the same time.

non-finite   see **finite**.

non-verbal communication   communication other than language, using any mode of communication.

noun   an open word class containing the subgroups count, non-count and proper noun.

noun phrase   a phrase with a noun or pronoun as head word.

overlap   simultaneous talk which does not violate the current speaker's turn often because it occurs near a possible transition relevance place. Cf. **interruption**.

passive voice   see **voice** (ii).

phoneme   a speech sound used distinctively in a language to make contrasts between words. See **minimal pairs**.

phonetics   the study of speech sounds.

phonology   the study of pronunciation systems, concentrating on those speech sound contrasts in each language that make a significant difference in communication.

phrase   directly above word in the hierarchy of rank. Phrases are labelled according to the headword in the phrase and they themselves combine to form clauses.

pragmatics   the study of how interlocutors use their knowledge of a language to convey and interpret meanings. See **semantics**.

Predicator   all words other than Finite in a verb group.

prefix   a morpheme that is less than a freestanding word and which goes on to the beginnings of words.

preposition   a closed word class, e.g. *on*, *in*, *through*, *underneath* which typically combines with a noun phrase to create a prepositional phrase, e.g. *at the corner of the street*.

pre-request   a type of pre-sequence used to check that a subsequent request is not inappropriate.

prescriptive   an approach to the study of language which prescribes how language *should* be used. See **descriptive**.

pre-sequence a sequence of turns built in orientation to a further upcoming sequence. Pre-sequences check that the necessary conditions for the subsequent sequence do in fact obtain. For example, if conditions are right, pre-announcements lead to announcements, pre-arrangements lead to arrangements, pre-closings lead to closings, pre-invitations lead to invitations, pre-requests lead to requests and so on.

pronoun a closed word class, e.g. *I, him, that, each*. A pronoun stands in place of a noun phrase.

propositional meaning the literal meaning of a piece of speech or writing, without involving context or outside knowledge.

rankshifted clause functions as the Subject or Complement of a main clause or as a postmodifier in a noun phrase.

Received Pronunciation the accent most often associated with standard British English; used as an index for describing other accents of English. It is sometimes also referred to as the Queen's English or BBC English.

reference referring to an entity involves providing enough detail for the hearer/reader to successfully pick out whatever the speaker/writer is talking about (the referent).

referent the entity in the real world to which a noun refers.

register a combination of field, tenor and mode of discourse (sometimes known as 'genre').

relative clause clause postmodifying head in noun phrase structure, e.g. *the house which Jack built*.

RP see **Received Pronunciation**.

semantics the study of meaning in language. In contrast to pragmatics, semantics focuses on the potential for meaning that comes from knowing a language, rather than how we interpret utterances in context.

Sign languages the natural languages of Deaf communities, articulated with the hands and face.

sociolinguistics the branch of linguistics interested in the links between language and society.

speech act when words perform some action beyond describing the world we say that they are performing a speech act.

standard language the (often prestigious) dialect of a language associated with academic, government and religious settings, and with written and published material.

stress extra prominence given to a syllable in terms of loudness, increase in pitch or increase in length.

strong form the pronunciation of a word when produced with stress. See **weak form**.

Subject   functions at clause level with Finite, Predicator, Complement and Adjunct. The Subject agrees with the finite verb in terms of number, e.g. _Ann speaks Italian fluently_.

substitution   (i) in syntax: a pro-form used for a previously mentioned element (substitution can be clausal, verbal or nominal); (ii) in child language: the use by young children of sounds that they already control in place of ones not yet mastered (e.g. [d] in place of the consonant [ð] needed for the beginning of the word _this_).

suffix   a morpheme that is less than a freestanding word and which goes on to the ends of words.

superordinate   a more general word, a cover term. See **hyponym**.

suprasegmentals   phonetic features which apply to more than one phonemic segment (such as pitch, stress and voice quality).

synonym   see **synonymy**.

synonymy   sameness of meaning of words; based on paraphrase between paired sentences differing only by the replacement of one word, e.g. _begin_ and _commence_ are synonyms.

syntax   the study of sentence making according to grammatical principles. Cf. **grammar**.

technical words   occur with relatively high frequency in texts on particular subjects and often have special meanings in the subject, e.g. _syntax_ and _tenor_ are technical words in language study.

tenor (of discourse)   sometimes referred to as style, e.g. formal/informal.

text   a term for representations of both written and spoken language data.

transcript/transcription   a written representation of speech sounds using symbols.

transition relevance place   a place where it is relevant for there to be a transition (change) of speaker.

turn constructional unit   a unit of talk.

utterance   the physical production of linguistic behaviour.

variety   a term that covers both language and dialect, but is intended to be neutral between them.

verb   an open word class. English lexical verbs characteristically have five forms, most clearly seen in irregular verbs, e.g. _drive, drives, drove, driving, driven_.

verb group   a label for a group of words which consists only of auxiliary and lexical verbs (cf. second meaning given for verb phrase), e.g. _She might have been thinking about it_.

verb phrase   used in different ways in different approaches to grammar. It can be used to label (i) everything in the clause other than the grammatical subject of the clause or (ii) only the verb group.

vocabulary   the set of words that a language or variety has, or the set of all the words in a given language known to an individual person.

vocal folds   the two folds of tissue mainly composed of muscle which lie horizontally across the glottis and which vibrate to produce voice. Sometimes called vocal cords.

voice   (i) in phonetics: the product of vocal fold vibration; (ii) in syntax: the system which allows choice about which participants in any process will be named and in what order. In active voice, the actor in the material process is named in the Subject slot, e.g. *Joyce played the piano*. When using the passive voice (auxiliary *be* + past participle) the speaker chooses as grammatical Subject of the clause a semantic role other than that of actor/doer of the process, e.g. *The piano was played by Joyce*.

voice quality   the characteristics defining an individual's speech as belonging to that individual. Can include qualities such as breathiness, speed of utterance, loudness etc.

voiced   sounds produced with vocal fold vibration.

voiceless   sounds produced without vocal fold vibration.

vowel   a speech sound during which articulators are not sufficiently close together to create friction. Vowels are typically central in a syllable.

weak form   the pronunciation of a word when produced without stress. See **strong form**.

word   a meaning, a pronunciation (optionally a spelling too) and a syntactic word class conventionally linked; e.g. learning the word *sandal* amounts to learning the linkage between 'ventilated shoe', [sændl̩], noun position in sentences and, optionally, the spelling <sandal> (instead of, for instance, <sandle>).

Index

THE INTERNATIONAL PHONETIC ALPHABET (revised to 1993, updated 1996)

CONSONANTS (PULMONIC)

	Bilabial	Labiodental	Dental	Alveolar	Postalveolar	Retroflex	Palatal	Velar	Uvular	Pharyngeal	Glottal
Plosive	p b			t d		ʈ ɖ	c ɟ	k g	q ɢ		ʔ
Nasal	m	ɱ		n		ɳ	ɲ	ŋ	N		
Trill	ʙ			r					ʀ		
Tap or Flap				ɾ		ɽ					
Fricative	ɸ β	f v	θ ð	s z	ʃ ʒ	ʂ ʐ	ç ʝ	x ɣ	χ ʁ	ħ ʕ	h ɦ
Lateral fricative				ɬ ɮ							
Approximant		ʋ		ɹ		ɻ	j	ɰ			
Lateral approximant				l		ɭ	ʎ	ʟ			

Where symbols appear in pairs, the one to the right represents a voiced consonant. Shaded areas denote articulations judged impossible.

CONSONANTS (NON-PULMONIC)

Clicks		Voiced implosives		Ejectives	
ʘ	Bilabial	ɓ	Bilabial	ʼ	Examples:
ǀ	Dental	ɗ	Dental/alveolar	pʼ	Bilabial
ǃ	(Post)alveolar	ʄ	Palatal	tʼ	Dental/alveolar
ǂ	Palatoalveolar	ɠ	Velar	kʼ	Velar
ǁ	Alveolar lateral	ʛ	Uvular	sʼ	Alveolar fricative

OTHER SYMBOLS

ʍ	Voiceless labial-velar fricative	ɕ ʑ	Alveolo-palatal fricatives
w	Voiced labial-velar approximant	ɺ	Alveolar lateral flap
ɥ	Voiced labial-palatal approximant	ɧ	Simultaneous ʃ and x
ʜ	Voiceless epiglottal fricative		
ʢ	Voiced epiglottal fricative		
ʡ	Epiglottal plosive		

Affricates and double articulations can be represented by two symbols joined by a tie bar if necessary.

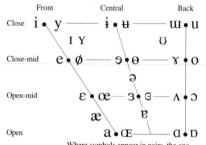

VOWELS

Where symbols appear in pairs, the one to the right represents a rounded vowel.

SUPRASEGMENTALS

ˈ	Primary stress	ˌfoʊnəˈtɪʃən
ˌ	Secondary stress	
ː	Long	eː
ˑ	Half-long	eˑ
˘	Extra-short	ĕ
ǀ	Minor (foot) group	
‖	Major (intonation) group	
.	Syllable break	ɹi.ækt
‿	Linking (absence of a break)	

DIACRITICS

Diacritics may be placed above a symbol with a descender, e.g. ŋ̊

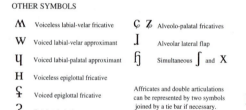

̥	Voiceless	n̥ d̥	̤	Breathy voiced	b̤ a̤	̪	Dental t̪ d̪
̬	Voiced	s̬ t̬	̰	Creaky voiced	b̰ a̰	̺	Apical t̺ d̺
ʰ	Aspirated	tʰ dʰ	̼	Linguolabial	t̼ d̼	̻	Laminal t̻ d̻
̹	More rounded	ɔ̹	ʷ	Labialized	tʷ dʷ	̃	Nasalized ẽ
̜	Less rounded	ɔ̜	ʲ	Palatalized	tʲ dʲ	ⁿ	Nasal release dⁿ
̟	Advanced	u̟	ˠ	Velarized	tˠ dˠ	ˡ	Lateral release dˡ
̠	Retracted	e̠	ˤ	Pharyngealized	tˤ dˤ	̚	No audible release d̚
̈	Centralized	ë	̴	Velarized or pharyngealized ɫ			
̽	Mid-centralized	e̽	̝	Raised	e̝	(ɹ̝ = voiced alveolar fricative)	
̩	Syllabic	n̩	̞	Lowered	e̞	(β̞ = voiced bilabial approximant)	
̯	Non-syllabic	e̯	̘	Advanced Tongue Root	e̘		
˞	Rhoticity	ɚ a˞	̙	Retracted Tongue Root	e̙		

TONES AND WORD ACCENTS

LEVEL			CONTOUR		
e̋ or ˥	Extra high		ě or ˩˥	Rising	
é ˦	High		ê ˥˩	Falling	
ē ˧	Mid		e᷄ ˦˥	High rising	
è ˨	Low		e᷅ ˩˨	Low rising	
ȅ ˩	Extra low		e᷈ ˧˦˧	Rising-falling	
↓	Downstep		↗	Global rise	
↑	Upstep		↘	Global fall	